Order from Transfer

STUDIES IN COMPARATIVE LAW AND LEGAL CULTURE

Series Editor: Vernon Valentine Palmer, *Tulane University, USA*

In today's shrinking world it's important to extend our horizons and increase our knowledge of other people's laws. This series publishes in-depth volumes covering various aspects of private and public law in diverse legal traditions. Additionally, it seeks to encourage improved techniques and methods of comparative legal research, including the use of interdisciplinary studies. Individual volumes may deal with the law and culture not merely of well-known and frequently studied countries, but also with lesser-known, mixed, religious, and plural systems of the world. The focus ranges from important aspects of legal history, culture, and institutions to local experience and evolving legal trends.

Order from Transfer

Comparative Constitutional Design and Legal Culture

Edited by

Günter Frankenberg

Professor of Public Law, Legal Philosophy and Comparative Law, Goethe University, Germany

STUDIES IN COMPARATIVE LAW AND LEGAL CULTURE

Edward Elgar

Cheltenham, UK • Northampton, MA, USA

Published by
Edward Elgar Publishing Limited
The Lypiatts
15 Lansdown Road
Cheltenham
Glos GL50 2JA
UK

Edward Elgar Publishing, Inc.
William Pratt House
9 Dewey Court
Northampton
Massachusetts 01060
USA

A catalogue record for this book
is available from the British Library

Library of Congress Control Number: 2013932984

This book is available electronically in the ElgarOnline.com Law Subject Collection, E-ISBN 978 1 78195 211 5

FSC www.fsc.org MIX Paper from responsible sources FSC® C013056

ISBN 978 1 78195 210 8

Typeset by Columns Design XML Ltd, Reading
Printed and bound in Great Britain by T.J. International Ltd, Padstow

Contents

Contributors

Helena Alviar García is Dean and Professor for Constitutional Law and Public Policy, Law and Development, Latin American Law and Institutions, Feminist Theory and Critical Theory at the Universidad de los Andes in Bogotá (Colombia). She is the author of numerous publications in these areas, most recently: *Feminismo y Crítica Jurídica: El análisis distributivo como alternativa crítica al legalismo liberal* (Siglo del hombre Editores, Ediciones Uniandes, 2012; co-author: Isabel Cristina Jaramillo Sierra).

Upendra Baxi, now Emeritus Professor of Law at the University of Warwick and Delhi, was Vice Chancellor of the University of Delhi and of South Gujarat. He has contributed widely to comparative constitutional studies, the social theory of human rights, sociology of law, and adjudicatory leadership. His most recent works include *The Future of Human Rights* (Oxford University Press, 2002) and *Human Rights in a Posthuman World: Critical Essays* (Oxford University Press (India), 2007).

Philipp Dann, Professor of Public and Comparative Law at Justus Liebig University Giessen, Germany, is the author of *The Law of Development Cooperation: A Comparative Analysis of the World Bank, the EU and Germany* (Cambridge University Press, forthcoming 2013) and "Federal Democracy in India and the European Union: Towards Transcontinental Comparison of Constitutional Law" (2011) 44 *Verfassung und Recht in Übersee/Law and Politics in Africa, Asia and Latin America* 160.

Julia Eckert, Professor of Political Anthropology at the University of Bern, specializes in legal anthropology, the anthropology of the modern state, conflict theory, and social movements. Her current research interests are in the anthropology of crime and punishment; changing notions of responsibility and liability; security; democracy and citizenship and the transnationalization of legal norms. Recent publications on these issues are *Law against the State: Ethnographic Forays into Law's Transformations* (Cambridge University Press, 2012); "Theories of Militancy in Practice: Explanations of Muslim Terrorism in India" (2012)

36(3) *Social Science History Journal* 47; and "Subjects of Citizenship" (2011) 15(3–4) *Citizenship Studies* 309.

Günter Frankenberg teaches public law, philosophy of law and comparative law at the Goethe University in Frankfurt; he is an associate member of the Cluster of Excellence "Normative Orders" at the Goethe University. His publications in these areas include: "Critical Comparisons – Re-Thinking Comparative Law" (1985) *Harvard International Law Journal*; *Die demokratische Frage [The Democratic Question]* (Suhrkamp 1989, co-author); *Autorität und Integration [Authority and Integration – The Grammar of Law and Constitutions]* (Suhrkamp, 2003); *Normalizing the State of Exception [Staatstechnik* Suhrkamp, 2010*]* (forthcoming 2013). As visiting professor he has taught at the law schools of Harvard University, Boston University, Tulane University, University of Pennsylvania and Phnom Penh. In the 1990s he participated as a legal consultant in law- and constitution-making projects in Central and Eastern European countries.

Roberto Gargarella, Dr. jur., University of Chicago, is a researcher at CONICET, University of Buenos Aires and CMI, Norway and Professor at the University of Buenos Aires and the University of Torcuato Di Tella (Argentina). He is the author of *The Legal Foundations of Inequality: Constitutionalism in the Americas* (Cambridge University Press, 2010) and *Latin American Constitutionalism* (Oxford University Press, forthcoming 2013).

Felix Hanschmann teaches Constitutional and Administrative Law at the Goethe University Frankfurt. His publications include "Das Verschwinden des Grundrechts auf Datenschutz in der Pluralität von Rechtsregimen" in Nele Matz-Lück and Mathias Hong (eds), *Grundrechte und Grundfreiheiten im Mehrebenensystem* (New York and Heidelberg, 2011) 293; "State-Building, Nation-Building, and Constitutional Politics in Post-Conflict Situations: Conceptual Clarifications and an Appraisal of Different Approaches" in Armin von Bogdandy and Rüdiger Wolfrum (eds), *Max Planck Yearbook of United Nations Law* (vol. 9, Leiden and Boston, 2005) 579 (co-authors: Armin von Bogdandy, Stefan Häußler and Raphael Utz).

Jennifer Hendry is a lecturer at the University of Leeds School of Law and the deputy director of the Centre for European Law and Legal Studies. Before joining Leeds, she wrote her doctoral thesis on the topic "Unitas in Diversitate? On Legal Cultures and the Europeanisation of Law" at the European University Institute (EUI) in Florence. She holds an LLB (Hons) in Law and German from the University of Glasgow and an LLM in Law and Society from the University of Edinburgh. During summer 2011 she was a visiting research fellow at the University of Sydney's Department of Philosophy. Her main research interests are in the areas of legal, social and political theory, and in comparative law and legal studies, specifically on the concepts of legal culture and legal pluralism. She is currently writing on issues of legal translation and transfer, and is a principal investigator on an interdisciplinary international research network focusing on "spaces of indigenous justice." Her publications include: "The Double Fragmentation of Law: Legal System-Internal Differentiation and the Process of Europeanisation" in D Augenstein (ed), *Integration through Law Revisited: The Making of the European Polity* (Ashgate, 2012); and "Governance, Proceduralisation & Justice: Some Challenges to the Legal Paradigm" (2008) 19(3) *Law & Critique: Special Issue on Governance, Civil Society & Social Movements* 345.

Stefan Kadelbach teaches Public Law, European Law and International Public Law at the Goethe University in Frankfurt (Germany); he is co-director of the Wilhelm Merton Centre for European Integration and International Economic Order and principal investigator at the Cluster of Excellence "Formation of Normative Orders" of the Goethe University. Recent publications include *Recht ohne Staat? Zur Normativität nichtstaatlicher Rechtsetzung* (editor with K Günther; Campus, 2011) and *Europarecht* (editor with M Zuleeg and R Schulze; 2nd edn Nomos, 2010).

Nora Markard is a postdoctoral research associate at the Collaborative Research Center 597 "Transformations of the State" at the University of Bremen, on leave as a visiting fellow at Columbia Law School for 2012/13. She holds a law degree from Free University Berlin, an MA in International Peace & Security from King's College London, and a Ph.D. in law from Humboldt University Berlin, where she co-founded the Humboldt Law Clinic: Human Rights. She also studied at the Sorbonne and visited the University of Michigan during her Ph.D. Her research areas stretch from human rights law, refugee law and international criminal law to comparative constitutionalism and law and gender. Recent publications include *Kriegsflüchtlinge* (Mohr Siebeck, 2012), a *Parallel Report to the 5th Periodic Report of the Federal Republic of Germany on the Convention against Torture and Other Cruel, Inhuman or Degrading Treatment or Punishment* (2011, co-authored for the Humboldt Law Clinic), and "Asylrecht: Der Stand der Dinge" (2012) *Merkur* 28.

Ralf Michaels is Arthur Larson Professor of Law, Duke University; he teaches Comparative Law, Conflict of Laws, and Law and Globalization. Selected publications include "Global Legal Pluralism" (2009) 5 *Annual Review of Law and the Social Sciences* 243; *Beyond the State – Rethinking Private Law* (edited with Nils Jansen; Mohr, 2008); "The Functional Method of Comparative Law" in *The Oxford Handbook of Comparative Law* (M Reimann and R Zimmermann eds, Oxford University Press, 2006).

H Kwasi Prempeh, Professor of Law at Seton Hall University School of Law, Newark, New Jersey (USA), where he teaches constitutional law and comparative constitutionalism, among others. His current scholarship focuses on the challenges of building constitutionalism in Africa's emerging democracies. He received his Dr. jur. degree from Yale University, where he served as a teaching fellow and an editor of the *Yale Law Journal*. He also holds graduate and undergraduate degrees from Baylor University, Texas, and the University of Ghana, respectively. He was a 2011 Reagan-Fascell Democracy Fellow at the National Endowment for Democracy, Washington, DC. His scholarship has been published in a number of law and social science journals, including the *International Journal of Constitutional Law*, the *Journal of Democracy*, and *Tulane Law Review*. Selected publications include "Presidents Untamed" (2008) 19(2) *Journal of Democracy* 109; "Africa's Constitutionalism Revival: False Start or New Dawn?" (2007) 5(3) *International Journal of Constitutional Law* 469; "*Marbury* in Africa: Judicial Review and the Challenge of Constitutionalism in Contemporary Africa" (2006) 80(4) *Tulane Law Review* 1239.

Ruth Rubio Marín holds a Chair in Constitutional and Public Comparative Law at the European University Institute in Florence, Italy. Formerly, she was Professor of Constitutional Law at the University of Seville, Spain, and a member of the Faculty of the Hauser Global Law School Program at New York University. She has taught at several other academic institutions including Columbia Law School and Princeton University where she was selected as a Fellow for the Program in Law and Public Affairs at Princeton University in 2000–2001. Her interests include migration, minority rights, citizenship, gender justice and transitional justice, areas which she addresses mostly from constitutional, human rights and political theory angles. She is the author and editor of several books, including *Immigration as a Democratic Challenge* (Cambridge University Press, 2000); *The Gender of Constitutional Jurisprudence* (co-editor with Beverley Baines; Cambridge University Press, 2004); *What Happened to the Women? Gender and Reparations for*

Human Rights Violations (ed, Social Science Research Council, New York, 2006); *The Gender of Reparations: Subverting Sexual Hierarchies while Redressing Human Rights Violations* (ed, Cambridge University Press, 2009); *The Struggle for Female Suffrage in Europe: Voting to Become Citizens* (co-editor with Blanca Rodríguez-Ruiz; Brill, 2012) and *Migration and Human Rights* (ed, Oxford University Press, forthcoming 2013).

Margrit Seckelmann, Ph.D. (Dr. jur.), MA, is a senior research fellow and the head of administration at the German Research Institute for Public Administration Speyer. After her studies in history and literature (MA) and law (First State Exam) in Heidelberg and Berlin, she completed her Bar Exam (Second State Exam) in Berlin and her Ph.D. in Law (Legal History) in Frankfurt. Apart from her work at the institute, she also teaches Administrative Law as well as Constitutional and Administrative History at the German University of Administrative Sciences in Speyer. Selected publications include "Autonomy and Accountability" in Sjur Bergan et al (eds), *Leadership and Governance in Higher Education. Handbook for Decision-Makers and Administrators* (Berlin: Raabe, 2012) A.3, 1–24; "From the Paris Convention of 1883 to the TRIPs Agreement of 1994: The History of the International Patent Protection as a History of Propertization?" in Isabella Löhr and Hannes Siegrist (eds), *Intellectual Property Rights and Globalization* (*comparativ*, vol. 21 (2011)) 46–63; "Observations from Germany" in Eberhard Bohne and Charlie Karlsson (eds), *Repositioning Europe and America for Economic Growth: The Role of Governments and Private Actors in Key Policy Areas* (Münster: LIT, 2010) 351–8; *Industrialisierung, Internationalisierung und Patentecht im Deutschen Reich, 1871–1914* (Frankfurt am Main: Klostermann, 2006).

Timo Tohidipur, Ph.D. (Dr. jur.), is a Postdoctoral Research Assistant and Lecturer at the Institute for Public Law, Goethe University in Frankfurt (Germany), where he teaches German Constitutional Law, European Law, Theory of Law, Migration and Refugee Law. Recent publications include "Iran und die Narrative west-östlicher Begegnung" (2012) 45(2) *Kritische Justiz* 178; "Europas Grenzschutzregime" in Martin W Möllers and Christoph van Ooyen (eds), *Migration: Europäische Grenzpolitik und FRONTEX* (2012) 41; "Border Controls at Sea: Requirements under International Human Rights and Refugee Law" (2009) 21(2) *International Journal of Refugee Law* 256 (with Andreas Fischer-Lescano and Tillmann Löhr).

Preface

“Order from Transfer” may have an all too positive ring. Order keeps anarchy at bay and structures social interactions. Transfer moves beyond the horizon of the national everyday. This, however, is not the reading intended here. The title is only meant to suggest that normative orders – constitutional and legal regimes, etc. – are works of construction; and transferred information is used in the process of their making by whoever contributes as maker. Order from transfer neither implies that order is good, nor does it suggest it is evil. Far from precluding or predetermining any questions regarding the nature of an order, the focus on order is only meant to prepare them: how power is allocated and wealth distributed in a society; whether women are discriminated against; which social groups are disfranchised; whether privilege is camouflaged and the subaltern silenced, etc.

To grasp the importance and impact of import/export, borrowing, adaptation, migration, etc. in the constitutional and legal realm it may be helpful to suspend the ultimate decision on whether an order so designed and then established is good or evil (for whom) and, first, look at the situation of transfer – military occupation, colonial rule, post-colonial nation-building, post-socialist reconstruction, economic hegemony or a plurality of competing legal regimes – analyze the transfer process, and *then* return to a critical assessment of the order based on transferred information. Transfer might turn out to be an interesting “take” on the alchemy of truth and deceit, struggle and deliberation, vision and *Realpolitik* in constitution-making.

“Order from Transfer” is a multi-jurisdictional project. It focuses on how constitutions (and laws) in different regions of the world are designed and applied, and how the designers and appliers get hold of their building materials, rearrange and apply them. Once it has been settled that constitutions neither fall from heaven nor spring from the mind of one or the other genius, analyzing constitutional transfers seems to be a sensible option. For this reason the authors here peacefully assembled look from different angles at the import and export of information relating to constitutions: ideas and ideologies, institutions and norms, doctrines and arguments, practices and conventions.

The subtitle promises studies in comparative constitutional design. This calls for a brief explanation. Since the early days of modern constitutionalism, the "making" of constitutions has always already conveyed that they are "not found."[1] They neither fall from heaven nor are they revealed in a mysterious way to founders. Instead, they are drafted, framed, created, constructed, and, yes, designed. The term "constitutional design" has been contested as technocratic or a misleading metaphor; it has been rejected or replaced by "process." And many comparatists preferred or returned to "making."

The architectural concept "design" shifts the attention from the authors of the document and their legitimacy to the making of the document and, more importantly, highlights specific elements of the drafting: the temporal dimension (process), the purpose of the venture (principles, ideology, its premeditation, plan), and the construction or fabrication of an intellectual product based on the available, to a large extent transferred, information. "Framers" accomplish their task usually by drafting a political conception – however ideological or, as it may turn out in the future, ineffective – which contains an institutional arrangement for the shared and separated exercise of power, selects a catalogue of rights to be guaranteed, and distinguishes values fundamental enough to warrant constitutional protection. Like an architect's drawing, sketch or plan, constitutional designers, consultants or engineers produce a more or less detailed intellectual product that delineates the contours and form, and lays down the structures and institutional framework of a normative order. Therefore "design" characterizes quite appropriately what happens when constitutions are made. According to the standard dictionaries,[2] design captures with a fair amount of precision how constitution-making works and is anything but a misleading figure of speech or far-fetched analogy. Accordingly, the contributors to this book were invited, while being under no obligation, to join the conversation about constitutional design.

This book is the result of an inspiring workshop held in September 2011 after which the participants returned to their comparative studies and wrote their contributions to the pathways, politics, and semiotics of constitutional-legal transfer, their analyses of transfers in specific situations (legal pluralism; colonialism; post-conflict) and how transfers

---

[1] Hannah F Pitkin, "The Idea of a Constitution" 37 *Journal of Legal Education* 167–9 (1987).

[2] See "design" in *The American Heritage Dictionary of the English Language*, 4th edn (Houghton Mifflin Co, 2009).

"played out" with regard to specific relationships, such as gender/sex, pregnant woman/embryo/state, and geopolitical mapping (center/periphery).

"Order from Transfer" is an interdisciplinary project. From different theoretical and methodological perspectives, and with different political agendas, some authors ask how transfer can be conceptualized, others trace how constitutional "items" are taken out of a cultural-political-legal context (de-contextualization) and introduced into a different one (re-contextualization). All in all, contributions to constitutional and legal theory, anthropology, legal history and doctrine, post-colonial theory and feminism, normative approaches and empirical analyses are conjoined in this book and continue the conversation we had at a workshop in September 2011, a conversation which Ruth Rubio Marín joins with her chapter in this book.

"Order from Transfer" is also intended to be a critical project. It challenges not only the legal-formalist and positivist conception of "constitution" and "law," but, more importantly, the center/periphery dichotomy, the ethnocentric bias as well as gender/sex subtext still characterizing much of the work done in comparative constitutional law.

The transfer thesis (or "IKEA theory") is presented in the introductory chapter, "Constitutions as Commodities: Notes on a Theory of Transfer" (Günter Frankenberg), which elaborates the commodity theory of constitutional items on the one hand and the (non-)marketability of certain constitutional items on the other hand. This thesis is challenged by the contributions in the first part, introduced by Timo Tohidipur. Margrit Seckelmann qualifies IKEA from a historical perspective, Ralf Michaels from a complex comparative-global law perspective.

Part II, "Ordering Gender," addresses aspects of constitutions that reveal gendered language, structure and reasoning. This part is introduced by Helena Alviar García. Nora Markard then analyzes the constitutional ordering of gender/sex, while Ruth Rubio Marín focuses on constitutional visions of women in abortion cases which traveled from Germany to Portugal.

In Part III, "Ordering Pluralism," the transfer thesis is confronted with insights from and into legal-pluralist regimes from the vantage point of legal anthropology (Julia Eckert) and legal theory (Jen Hendry). They demonstrate how transfers are shaped from within and without.

Part IV, "Ordering the Postcolony," combines Upendra Baxi's scathing comments on the IKEA transfer theory with H Kwasi Prembeh's challenge to the widespread interpretation of the imperial presidency in many African countries as being attributable to the transfer of traditional forms of rulership.

Stefan Kadelbach introduces Part V, "Ordering Hegemony." Philipp Dann analyzes international influence on post-conflict constitution-making in East Timor, Iraq and the Sudan, whereas Felix Hanschmann reconstructs in detail how the German colonial experience left its imprint on German citizenship law.

The last part turns to questions of how Europe was ordered in the constitutional laboratory of the nineteenth century (Günter Frankenberg) and how Europe contributed (or not) to the ordering of Latin America. Helena Alviar García demonstrates how constitutional ideas – i.e. the social function of property – traveled long distances (also from Europe) to Colombia and affected the chances for progressive reform. Roberto Gargarella reconstructs the mixing of constitutional models in Latin America; he analyzes how social rights were grafted upon liberal-conservative constitutions.

Neither the September 2011 workshop nor this publication would have been possible without our generous sponsors: the Fritz Thyssen Foundation and the Cluster of Excellence 'Formation of Normative Orders' at the Goethe University in Frankfurt. For the organization of the workshop and the preparation of this publication I have to thank Helena Lindemann, Cara Röhner, and Yasmina Aznai. Petra Czoik, Asmaa El Idrissi and Lisa Tuchscherer provided valuable research assistance. Tara Gorvine from Edward Elgar Publishing deserves credit and thanks for encouraging us to submit this collection of essays for publication. We are grateful to Virginia Williams and Elizabeth Clack for supporting the project during the production process. We are grateful too for our readers' critique.

Frankfurt, December 2012
G.F.

Constitutions as commodities: notes on a theory of transfer

Günter Frankenberg

1. CONSTITUTIONS AS COMMODITIES

Constitutional information comes packaged and refers to institutions, norms, principles, doctrines, and ideologies. And for more than two centuries, not counting the crucial influence of previous basic laws or *leges fundamentales*, it has crossed national boundaries, social-cultural contexts, and the limits of epistemic communities. Such information has reappeared for application within different constitutional regimes and different political constellations, resulting from the dynamics of social struggles and accommodating specific economic conditions. And the overall result, given the innumerable variations at play, is striking. Constitutions come for the most part in the form of a written document and contain the legal ground rules for life in society: rights and principles, values and duties, provisions for the organization of government and, with regard to the operative quality of the document, ascertaining its authority, openness to interpretive change or legislative amendment, shifting between stability and flexibility. From this general picture I have inferred[1] that most constitutional items – shorthand for ideas and institutions, ideals and ideologies, norms and arguments, doctrines and theories – which are part and parcel of reasoned elaboration in doctrine and theory, of comparative analysis and practical constitution-making have been standardized and circulate like marketable goods among the participants of the local, regional, and transnational

[1] This chapter is based on two earlier publications in which I introduced and elaborated the IKEA theory of legal/constitutional transfer: Günter Frankenberg, "Verfassungsgebung in Zeiten des Übergangs" in idem, *Autorität und Integration. Zur Grammatik von Recht und Verfassung* (Suhrkamp Verlag 2003) 115–35; and Günter Frankenberg, "Constitutional Transfer: The IKEA Theory Revisited" (2010) 8 *International Journal of Constitutional Law* 563–79.

disciplinary discourse and, in particular, among constitutional elites and their consultants as well as social movements with a constitutional agenda.

What reads like one of the many narratives of globalization focuses on the fact that the modern constitutional idiom, though always geared toward and entangled in a specific local and historical context, has proliferated worldwide, with liberal constitutionalism holding a hegemonic position. This (not all that innocent) narrative may be referred to as the globalization of the modern idiom creating a "global constitution." It reflects – and intends to criticize – the dominance of an intensely Anglo-Eurocentric constitutionalism which, incidentally, has shaped and, despite critical voices, still shapes mainstream comparative constitutional studies.

However, in its flat, one-dimensional version, this narrative has very little to say about how such globalization happens, what happens when globalization happens, and whether it is challenged by glocalization – alternatives to the liberal-western paradigm. It needs to consider "subversive reception"[2] and "discursive pathways,"[3] and requires deciphering the gender, class, and race asymmetries it reproduces[4] and the ideological subtext accompanying globalization like a shadow.

For that reason, the IKEA narrative has always accentuated specific items that defy commodification and globalization and remain entrenched in the (local) context they arise from. To complement and also critique the standard line on globalization, I take a closer look at those items – here referred to, somewhat ironically and definitely without any underlying derogatory normative meaning, as "odd details" – which have proven, at least up to a certain point in time, transfer-resistant and therefore challenge the western-liberalist hegemony. The question of how constitutional items (have) turned into commodities for transnational usage will be contrasted here with an analysis of non-marketable phenomena which might or in fact did subvert the dominant paradigm of constitutionalism. This is to say that odd details may superficially seem to be strange items of interest for constitutional tourism; however, they may also and often do constitute moments of anti-hegemonic rebellion and institute alternative constitutional visions and traditions.

---

2 See Chapter 6.

3 See Chapter 9.

4 See Chapter 5.

2. A CRITIQUE OF THE UNITARY PROJECT: FROM TRANSPLANT TO TRANSFER

For quite some time mainstream comparatists have pursued an overwhelmingly western, unitary project[5] by confirming their belief in a cross-culturally coherent body of constitutional law, downplaying differences, proceeding with an eye toward convergence, claiming that there is a significant degree of congruence between social problems and their constitutional solutions, and arguing that the areas of agreement and overlap clearly outweigh significant contextual and functional varieties. This unitary project clearly leaned toward the hegemonic center and supported/sold the Anglo-Eurocentric vision of constitutions and their comparative study. Given the academic pedigree of and political support for this theoretical-methodological venture, it does not come as a surprise that comparatists have looked for "common cores," "unidroit," universal "legal formants," etc. and have explicitly or implicitly assumed that the *transplant* of constitutional and legal items has happened, is possible, and does not create significant theoretical or practical problems.[6]

The concept of transplant appears to have been one of the pillars of this unitary project. Only recently comparatists addressed the question of why and how constitutions, though genealogically and in practice more often than not linked to particular nation-states and cultures, have come to share a modern idiom, and they have confronted the unitary vision with insights into legal pluralism and have accentuated difference.[7]

To move away from congruence and common cores and to challenge the widespread notion of transplant, I once introduced and now still defend the IKEA metaphor, somewhat generously labeled theory. First, it is intended to focus on transfer and set into relief the development and availability of a supranational repertoire of constitutional items. This metaphor is also meant to (a) elucidate the politics and projects of constitution-making by deconstructing the naturalist and idealist mist and myth that generally surround the practice of how constitutions are

---

[5] Recently Morton Horwitz, "Constitutional Transplants" (2009) 10 *Theoretical Inquiries in Law*, available at <http:/www.bepress.com/cgi/viewcontent.cgi?article9>. For critical views see Ruti Teitel, "Comparative Constitutional Law in the Global Age" (2004) 117 *Harvard Law Review* 2570 and Günter Frankenberg, "How to Do Projects with Comparative Law – Notes from an Expedition to the Common Core" in Mauro Bussani and Ugo Mattei (eds), *Opening Up European Law* (Carolina Academic Publishers 2007).

[6] See Chapter 1.

[7] See Chapters 7 and 8.

constructed, and (b) highlight how "framers" are inspired and influenced by, borrow from and, in turn, modify elements of imported constitutional building materials.

Second, and in more difficult step, the IKEA theory addresses the concept and difficulties of transfers of law – a process, activity, and problem – for which the discourse on comparative law has generated a variety of terms: "legal transplants," "reception," "borrowing," "adaptation," "mutation," "influence," "evolution," "translation," and more recently "migration"[8] and so on. At the same time these terms operate as signifiers of different theoretical approaches and projects. Some use transfer or any term considered synonymous with it in support of their unitary agenda; others qualify or reject any legal import/export in support of their theories of legal pluralism or contextualism. Rather than mapping the discourse in comparative constitutional studies on transfer/transplant/reception and so on, I start with a collision of two antagonistic disciplinary projects – legal history versus legal philosophy – and a clash of scientific communities – modern versus postmodern – which originally set off a fundamental (maybe also fundamentally misunderstood) controversy over the (im)possibility of legal transplants. Alan Watson's study on "Legal Transplants"[9] ignited Pierre Legrand's polemical critique; thereafter comparatists have carried on the debate.[10] Considering that there are several approaches to the problem,[11] it may still be worthwhile to briefly recapitulate that initial controversy.

After setting up comparative law as an "independent academic discipline" based on the investigation of the relationship between legal systems, and after elaborating the perils and virtues of a comparative approach, Alan Watson introduced "the strangest paradox" of (private)

[8] From the burgeoning literature see only Sujit Choudry (ed), *The Migration of Constitutional Ideas* (Cambridge University Press 2006) or Vanessa Duss et al (eds), *Rechtstransfer in der Geschichte – Jahrbuch junge Rechtsgeschichte 1* (Meidenbauer 2006).

[9] Alan Watson, *Legal Transplants: An Approach to Comparative Law* (Scottish Academic Press 1974); Pierre Legrand, "The Impossibility of 'Legal Transplants'" (1997) 4 *Maastricht Journal of European and Comparative Law* 111; Alan Watson, "Legal Transplants and European Private Law" (December 2000) 4 (4) *Electronic Journal of Comparative Law* <http://www.ejcl.org/ejcl/44/44-2.html>.

[10] E.g. Michele Graziadei, "Comparative Law as the Study of Transplants and Receptions" in Mathias Reimann and Reinhard Zimmermann (eds), *The Oxford Handbook of Comparative Law* (Oxford University Press 2006); Choudry (n 8); and recently Horwitz (n 5).

[11] See Chapter 2.

law. From a mainly historical perspective, complemented by civil law jurisprudence, he confronted the notion of law as both an emanation of "the spirit of the people" informed by historical experience and of legal transplants.[12] "Savigny plus" one might be tempted to call this project, as it confronts the historical "Volksgeist" with the synchronic existence of norms. Watson went on to identify numerous examples of transplants in the areas of contract, torts, and property, as he traveled from the Ancient Near East to Greece and Rome and from there to Scotland, England, Holland and other countries. Borrowing plus adaptation, we learn, has been the formula for "the usual way of legal development."[13] By way of illustration he compared several provisions from the Laws of Eshnunna and the Babylonian Code of Hammurabi with Exodus concerning the goring of persons or animals by an ox and deduced from the similarities in style and substance that the provisions "probably … share an ultimate common source." From rules dealing with matrimonial property that traveled from the Visigoths via Spain to California he inferred that "legal transplants are already to be found in remote antiquity and were probably not uncommon."[14] He also based his transplant theory on less exotic phenomena and instances such as the selective or sweeping reception of Roman law, Justinian's *Corpus Juris Civilis,* its basic rules, systematic structure and scientific elaboration in the legal regimes of several European host countries as well as the (Puritan) treatment – with significant variations – of the Bible as a source of law.

In the closing chapters of his book Watson offered a list of general reflections on legal transplants that he combined with a few cautionary considerations. On the one hand he argued that "the transplanting of individual rules or of a large part of a legal system is extremely common" and "socially easy." From this statement he inferred that it is, "in fact, the most fertile source of development," and accounts for the "astounding degree" to which "law is rooted in the past."[15] On the other hand he mentioned authority in law as an important variable intervening in any transplanting process[16] and, in the end, found "the mixture" more fascinating than the very act of borrowing.

Against this fairly sweeping message of Watson's transplant thesis, Pierre Legrand launched an equally sweeping attack. Reformulating

---

12 Watson, *Legal Transplants* (n 9).

13 Ibid 7.

14 Ibid 24.

15 Ibid 95.

16 Ibid 96 and *passim.*

Montesquieu's skepticism concerning the simple transfer of legal institutions, Legrand submitted Watson's formalism and comparative functionalism to a biting critique, characterized as legal solipsism Watson's notion of a "nomadic character of rules"[17] and deconstructed the double equation of "law-as-rule" and "rules-as-propositional-statements" by differentiating between the a-contextual meaning emerging from the wording of a rule and the context-dependent meanings ascribed to a legal norm in the processes of application by the interpretive community. Quite persuasively he argued that the latter constitute the ruleness of a rule – or, we might add, the meanings of a right, principle or even preamble – and do not survive (unchanged?) the displacement from one legal regime to another.[18] So the original meaning gets lost in translation, or rather: repetition.[19] Legrand overstated his point somewhat by concluding: "[W]hat can be displaced from one jurisdiction to another is, literally, a *meaningless* form of words. To claim more is to claim too much. In any *meaning-ful* sense of the term, 'legal transplants', therefore, cannot happen."[20]

In consequence he proposed to move away from *l'énoncé* to *l'énonciation.* That is to say, he demonstrated how repetition is conditioned by a particular epistemological framework, by epistemic conventions and a specific *mentalité*, and how repetition, due to the historical-cultural context and power struggles, always involves the repression[21] of alternatives.

Watson's reply to these charges, summed up in Legrand's "Montesquieu minus" position, simplified his critic's point by implicitly restating his own view of law-as-rule: "Where a written statutory law is the same within two countries, its judicial interpretation may well differ because of tradition and ways of legal thinking."[22]

Consequently, he conceded the truth of the trivialized version of the transplant critique that "a transplanted rule is not the same thing as it was in its previous home."[23] Moreover, Watson did not address his critic's

---

[17] Legrand (n 9) *passim.*

[18] Ibid 117–20.

[19] See Eva Hoffman, *Lost in Translation* (Minerva 1991).

[20] Legrand (n 9) 120.

[21] Concerning the connection between repression and repetition, Legrand refers to Gilles Deleuze, *Différence et répétition* (Presses Universitaires de France 1968) 139.

[22] Watson, "Legal Transplants and European Private Law" (n 9) 2.

[23] Ibid and Alan Watson, *Law Out of Context* (University of Georgia Press 2000) 1.

proposal to move from bare text to context, from similarity on the surface to difference at the bottom, and to leave off mechanical analogies, synthetic visions, and unitary thinking in comparative legal studies.[24] Instead, he claimed he could not find any substance in the transplant critique.

Whatever Watson and Legrand may have intended with their comparative projects, they certainly did polarize the field of comparative legal studies and succeeded in elucidating that the transfer of law cannot be treated as a factual given but is deeply problematic and calls for theoretical and methodological assistance that has to move beyond the stand-off between textualism/formalism versus contextualism.[25] Watson tended to receive more support for his transplant thesis in the functionalist camp, from authors defending the unity of law, the convergence of legal regimes, or "the factual approach." By contrast, Legrand's critique was in general supported by anti-formalists and contextualists, who did not deny that quite a few successful institutional transfers have been recorded and that "legal transfers are possible, are taking place, have taken place and will take place,"[26] but who avoided the naturalist fallacy.[27] Some authors have recently suggested other and more apt terms and have praised "migration" as "a helpfully ecumenical concept in the context of the inter-state movement of constitutional ideas," equally amenable to "all movements across systems, overt or covert, episodic or incremental, planned or evolved, initiated by giver or receiver, accepted or rejected, adopted or adapted, concerned with substantive doctrine or with institutional design or some more abstract or intangible constitutional sensibility or ethos."[28]

Transfer[29] appears to qualify as an even more ecumenical concept, unless one wants to analyze how a legal regime is "grafted over" by legal

---

[24] Legrand (n 9) 122–4; Günter Frankenberg, "Critical Comparisons: Rethinking Comparative Law" (1985) 26 *Harvard International Law Journal* 411, 453.

[25] For references to the different critics and supporters see Frankenberg "Constitutional Transfer" (n 1).

[26] David Nelken, "Comparatists and Transferability" in Pierre Legrand and Roderick Munday (eds), *Comparative Legal Studies: Traditions and Transitions* (Cambridge University Press 2003) 437, 442.

[27] See Esin Örücü and David Nelken (eds), *Comparative Law: A Handbook* (Hart Publishing 2007).

[28] Neil Walker, "The Migration of Constitutional Ideas and the Migration of *the* Institutional Idea: The Case of the EU" in Choudry (n 8) 316, 320–21.

[29] See also Rudolf Stichweh, "Transfer in Sozialsystemen: Theoretische Überlegungen" in Duss et al (n 8).

imports.[30] Both migration and transfer refer to movements, capture a wider variety of uses than, say, transplant or borrowing, and qualify such movements as problematic – because of cultural diversity, imperialist structures, hegemonic influence, and so on[31] – rather than socially easy, as artificial rather than natural or organic. As distinct from migration, transfer also is more open to the varieties of conscious and unconscious import-exports over spatial, temporal, social, and cultural distances and differences. Moreover, the concept captures the compactness of the transferred information,[32] its commodification and, more importantly, relates with ease to the constructive dimension of constitution-making, its design and *bricolage* as well as the specific political, socio-economic and economic situation (occupation; colonial regime; postcolony; divided society, etc.).

Hence, assuming that legal transfer is a workable – by no means politically agnostic or neutral – concept, I address in the following not so much its (im)possibility but the mechanisms and conditions that facilitate or preclude import/export. The overall focus will be on pathways – not "one-way streets"[33] – sites and modalities of transfer, and on results, risks and side-effects as well as on the inclusion in or exclusion from the repertoire – the IKEA market center – that can be tapped globally.

3. INITIAL CIRCUMSTANCES OF TRANSFER

In *The World, the Text and the Critic*, Edward Said describes the travels of theory and ideas:

> Like people and schools of criticism, ideas and theories travel – from person to person, from situation to situation, from one period to another. Cultural and intellectual life are usually nourished and often sustained by this circulation of ideas, and whether it takes the form of acknowledged or unconscious influence, creative borrowing, or wholesale appropriation, the movement of ideas and theories from one place to another is both a fact of life and a usefully enabling condition of intellectual activity.[34]

Said distinguishes four stages in the travel of theory that may help to elucidate the pathways and problems of legal/constitutional transfer

30 See Chapter 16.

31 See Chapters 9–12, 15.

32 Stichweh (n 29) 3.

33 As Felix Hanschmann shows in Chapter 13.

34 Edward Said, *The World, the Text, and the Critic* (Vintage 1983) 226–47.

(provided the travel metaphor is itself transferred to the realm of constitutional processes, practices, and ideas, which means to the realm of politics, power, and ideology): "First, there is a point of origin, or what seems like one, a set of initial circumstances in which the idea came to birth or entered discourse."[35] Edward Said's narrative prudently weakens any originalist assumption by considering that the point of origin may only "seem like one" and qualifying and de-privileging the origin as a "set of initial circumstances."

In studies of constitutional transfers any "point of origin" has to be treated with even more skepticism and deconstructed, as it may very likely be fictitious or only the thereafter of something that had happened before.[36] Moreover, it is only for analytical reasons that comparatists have to look for a moment or host environment where transfer could plausibly have begun. So there is no harm in learning that the "government of laws and not of men," often ascribed to the 1780 Constitution of Massachusetts and credited to John Adams, one of its framers, might actually date from Aristotle's political philosophy. Its second coming and not Aristotle triggered its export/import career. And it makes little difference whether the globally illustrious Immanuel Kant, the German celebrity Adam Müller or the fairly obscure and almost forgotten criminal lawyer Harscher von Almendingen fathered the concept "*Rechtsstaat*,"[37] because the study of legal/constitutional transfer is not, one would hope, about ancestor worship and originalism[38] but concerns critical comparisons and contexts.

Hence, the phases of transfer outlined here are not to be taken as a strict sequence of steps but as one of the many possible pathways for the export and import of laws. As a matter of fact, the sequence moving from de-contextualization via globalization to re-contextualization may have to be reversed, if a set of initial circumstances cannot be pinned down – even analytically – or calls for extensive (comparative) research or a

---

35 Ibid 226–7.

36 Unless we return to the constitutional novelties that appeared at the turn of the 18th century; or are able to identify a more recent constitutional innovation, such as the human right to asylum of the 1949 German Basic Law.

37 For a deconstruction of originalist assumptions concerning the *Rechtsstaat* see Günter Frankenberg, *Staatstechnik: Perspektiven auf Rechtsstaat und Ausnahmezustand* (Suhrkamp Verlag 2010) 75.

38 And, incidentally, the conservative proponents of originalism in US constitutional interpretation have unwillingly done their best to deconstruct the very notion of a "fixed and knowable meaning" of texts and intents. See Jack N Rakove, *Original Meanings: Politics and Ideas in the Making of the Constitution* (Vintage Books 1997).

critique of misleading originalist assumptions. Thus, in his informative study of how the imperial presidency proliferated throughout Africa, H Kwasi Prembeh traced its "puzzling persistence" – the results of transfer processes – to authoritarian policies of national integration and development, thereby refuting a widespread "theory" explaining authoritarianism as rooted in the cultural-tribal heritage.[39]

The 1831 Belgian Constitution, widely regarded as one of the leading constitutions of the 19th century in Europe, on closer scrutiny reads like an almost ironic comment on originalism with barely more than 10 percent of the document labeled "Belgian."

4. TRANSFER AS DE-CONTEXTUALIZATION

Unlike travelling theory – "[T]here is a distance transversed, a passage through the pressure of various contexts as the idea moves from an earlier point to another time and place where it will come into new prominence"[40] – constitutional building materials, before they can move to another place and time, transgress cultural borders and the confines of epistemic communities, undergo the complex process of de-contextualization. There is no methodology available to adequately analyze what happens at this open-ended and heterogeneous moment in the transfer of law, when and where national and supranational pathways intersect. So, one is left with an attempt at approximation. Metaphorically speaking, the items are shock-frozen and packaged for the transgressing of time, space, and context. On a more theoretical note, one might add that the transformation of legal and constitutional building materials into marketable commodities presupposes as necessary conditions three operations: it is only after being reified, formalized, and idealized that they qualify for entry into the IKEA showroom where they are on display as universally applicable commodities.

De-contextualization therefore amounts to much more than a mere taking-out of a given context and spatial displacement (or export):

Reification transforms "live" and contested ideas, norms or institutions into objects by stripping them of their historical background and socio-cultural environment. Instead of being phenomena of a specific narrative

[39] H Kwasi Prempeh, "Presidential Power in Comparative Perspective: The Puzzling Persistence of Imperial Presidents of Post-Authoritarian Africa" (September 2007) <http://works.bepress.com/kwasi_prempeh/2> accessed 15 March 2012. See also Chapter 10.

[40] Said (n 34) 227.

and cultural setting, on the surface they turn into commodities that come as a package[41] of information.

Formalization reduces norms to bare texts, which is to say to propositional statements bereft of interpretive debates and epistemic conventions that give them meaning(s). Likewise, institutions are reduced to the propositional content of a document describing one or other organizational arrangement.

Finally, *idealization* transforms the appearance of norms and makes constitutional items look better than they actually are: norms, doctrines and arguments are taken at their face value and presented as meaning (more or less) what they ought to mean. Likewise, institutions are presented as functioning the way they are generally expected to function. Idealization not only distances the idealized object from real existence but turns it into ideology in so far as it camouflages what is the case. In the end, only the official story gets transferred.

To illustrate de-contextualization, the "We the people" formula makes for an instructive example. While there have been myriad instances of "we" and of "the people" throughout history and all over the world, only the US formula was transformed into a package of information and traveled long distances, in fact acquiring a frequent flyer status, disconnected from the original, imaginary "we" plurality in the constitutions of several New England states and their union. De-contextualization meant that it was severed from what was "behind the Federal Constitution" – namely its embeddedness in the founding myth of the former New England colonies, the framers' "efforts to constrain the people" and to contain what Edmund Randolph, one of the framers, feared would be "the fury of democracy."[42] Moreover, removed from its production process and stripped of its contextual connotations, "We the people" has since then become something constitutional elites almost invariably fall back on, very much like proposing a self-congratulatory toast, at the beginning of the document they are about to write and then submit to parliamentary or popular approval.

Likewise, British-style rule of law and the German *Rechtsstaat* as dominant samples of law-rule have traveled a great deal but rarely as what they are: ideologically charged and "contested concepts."[43] Instead they were and still are routinely adopted and applied as abstractions –

---

41 See Stichweh (n 29) 3.

42 See Christian G Fritz, *American Sovereigns: The People and America's Constitutional Tradition* (Cambridge University Press 2008).

43 Walter B Gallie, "Essentially Contested Concepts" (1955–6) 56 *Proceedings of the Aristotelian Society* 169.

abstracted from the historical struggles that informed their development and from their political-legal background – provided in England by the amalgam of tradition, conventions, freedom bills and political compromises and, much later, in Germany by the mix of statism, competing claims to sovereignty and the rather moderate revolutionary agenda of Germany's 19th century bourgeoisie.

More recently, the concept has also been decoupled from theoretical and doctrinal controversies, from implementation problems and deficits before being launched for transfer as a commodity packaged under the label ROL, condensed into "five essential elements" for usage in countries of the periphery under close monitoring by the International Monetary Fund, the World Bank and other non-law-rule organizations:

"Long-term, sustainable economic and social development requires democratic governance rooted in the rule of law. The Rule of Law (ROL) Division provides leadership on rule of law issues to USAID field missions and bureaus …" fostering "1. Order and security … 2. Legitimacy … 3. Checks and balances … 4. Fairness and 5. Effective application."[44]

Similarly, judicial review established in a given country and executed by, say, the US Supreme Court, German Federal Constitutional Court or the French *Conseil constitutionnel*, usually sets out on its journey to the global reservoir as a polished, ideal-typical court (and practice), and not as a more or less successful and influential but also embattled institution.

5. TRANSFER AS INCLUSION IN THE GLOBAL CONSTITUTION

An impression generally sustained by comparatists suggests that constitutions (and constitutionalism as the accompanying meta-text and ideology) have crossed geographical borders and language barriers, transgressed the boundaries of epistemic communities and been accommodated in a diversity of political constellations. As a matter of consequence, constitution-makers everywhere appear to have adopted or at least to have taken notice of the modern idiom: *prima facie* they seem to share the same vocabulary, rules of grammar, style and design. And usually, though not always, they choose from a limited variety of institutional paths, catalogues of rights and values, and follow similar

---

[44] USAID, *Guide to Rule of Law Country Analysis: The Rule of Law Strategic Framework* (updated January 2010).

basic designs. Globalization of the modern idiom, so one is tempted to infer, has streamlined the practices and results of the framing, amending, and interpreting of constitutions. Albert Blaustein's checklist of the essential elements of "the modern constitution"[45] may be read as a fairly accurate, nominalist, albeit superficial, preliminary inventory of the "global constitution" of his time. It inspired rather formalist and naive views regarding the cross-border influence and impact of norms and legal regimes.[46]

The global or globalized constitution is not introduced here by analogy with a national constitution writ large or an "emerging universal" (constitutional) system,[47] nor do I diagnose the existence or advocate the desirability of a novel type of trans-, inter- or supranational regime resulting from an adaptation of national constitutions to global requirements.[48] Instead, I simply claim that the selection of de-contextualized items and their inclusion in the global repertoire can be analytically distinguished as a *third* phase, step or moment in the transfer process. One might object, though, that the globalizing of the modern idiom or some of its parts actually is not a discrete phase or step since it only concludes de-contextualization by integrating marketable items in the IKEA center. However, it can at least be distinguished analytically, as Helena Alviar García demonstrates with regard to the social function of property.[49]

---

45 Albert P Blaustein, *Framing the Modern Constitution: A Checklist* (Rothman & Co 1994).

46 Patricia L Hero, "The Influence of the United States Constitution's Bill of Rights upon the Constitutions of the Countries of the World" (1987–8) 3 *Connecticut Journal of International Law* 31, submitted an exercise in bookkeeping rather than analysis.

47 See P Philipp Allott, "The Emerging Universal Legal System" in Janne Nijman and André Nollkaemper (eds), *New Perspectives on the Divide between National and International Law* (Oxford University Press 2007) 63.

48 Anne Peters describes the various processes of adaptation in "The Globalization of State Constitutions" in Nijman and Nollkaemper (n 47) 251. I will return to and contrast her globalization scenario later with my "odd details" analysis. At this point it may suffice to say that globalization is likely to increase both the convergence and divergence or difference of national constitutional regimes. See Horatia Muir Watts, "Globalization and Comparative Law" in Reimann and Zimmermann (n 10) 579, 586–8; Jonathan Friedman, "Being in the World: Globalisation and Localisation" (1990) 7 (2) *Theory, Culture & Society* 311.

49 See Chapter 15.

Depending on the theoretical register, the global constitution might be referred to as the global reservoir or archive, the collective constitutional consciousness or repertoire, or, for that matter, supermarket. Whatever the designation, the market etc. results from a myriad of transfers: Standardized items are registered, stored, exhibited and available for purchase to constitution-makers around the world. At this IKEA market for constitutional building materials, whoever is about to frame, amend or revise a constitution may – and generally does – tap the vocabulary,[50] grammar, style, and design characterizing the modern idiom. The buyer may shop for a complete political regime, such as a constitutional monarchy or a parliamentary democracy, or items more limited in scope, such as a rights catalogue, a two-chamber system, an institutional arrangement for constitutional review or a presidential system, or only a single item, such as the political-question doctrine or the right to equal treatment. And shoppers have the choice between finished products, *prêt à porter*, disassembled parts to be put together at home, or inspirational ideas requiring a high degree of constructive elaboration.

Once on the shelves of the IKEA market, globalized constitutional items generally do not refer to their (original) production site. Very much like NIKE sneakers not carrying a notice "produced by children in the sweatshops of Mumbai," a constitution would not be labeled "ideological product of the landowning elite." Rights catalogues, models of representative democracy, systems of judicial review, values, amendment rules, and so on are held in store at constitution IKEA as bare descriptions of institutions or texts of norms gleaned from constitutional documents. Moreover, neither do these items come with background information about the contextual prerequisites that make institutions operate smoothly in a specific political setting nor are norms accompanied by elaborate interpretation manuals (for legal reasoning and balancing) provided by the (original) epistemic community.

Inclusion in and exclusion from the global reservoir depend on a virtual and, at times, real threshold test: constitutional building materials, once they have passed through the three-pronged process of de-contextualization, turn into commodities. They may attain the appearance of universal or at least regional applicability and therefore are granted by the open community of constitution drafters, advisors, engineers and scholars the quality seal reserved for the modern idiom and its parts. Constitutional items that have passed or may pass this test abound: the constitution as written text and single document, the archetypes and

---

[50] Comparable to the globalized *lingua franca* of human rights.

the basic architecture of codified constitutions with their typical ingredients[51] – preambles, rights catalogues, organizational provisions, values and duties, meta-rules and conflict rules, etc.[52]

6. DEFYING TRANSFER: ODD DETAILS

There is a reverse or dark side to the narrative of transfer and globalization. And it may be – as a matter of fact, I assume it is – more interesting, albeit more difficult, to recount. It is the story of those ideas, norms, institutions, doctrines, and arguments widely recognized, by the merchants of transfer: constitutional elites, legal consultants, courts, and legal scholars, as either not being amenable to reification, formalization, and idealization or incompatible with the liberal paradigm. Both categories of items are excluded from the global constitution for technical or political reasons.

The first category comprises those items that appear to be too context-specific, particular or parochial and are excluded from the global reservoir. Bereft of universal attire, they do not rise above local prominence and remain, maybe quite happily, at the margin of the transnational discourse of constitutionalism.

Are they irrelevant? Wrong. Obscure, at times strange, always distant from the modern idiom, these "odd details," I argue, deserve special attention and a preferential analytical treatment because they are likely to encapsulate local traditions and experiences, social struggles, anxieties and visions. More than the globalized elements used for constitutional construction, they bring into view local idiosyncrasies, the normative orientations and expectations of social movements, people, and also constitutional elites beyond the pale of Anglo-Euro constitutionalism. Some may be attractive items for constitutional tourism: the 1874 Constitution of the Swiss Confederation, amended in 1991, prohibited the manufacture, import, transport and sale of "the liquor called absinthe" (Art. 32.5 sec. 1). The 1937 Irish Constitution forbids the president to leave the country "save with the consent of the Government" (Art. 12). The 1868 Luxemburg Constitution orders that civil marriage "always must precede the nuptial benediction" (Art. 21). However, others have interesting stories to tell about a people's historical experience, political

---

[51] See Albert Blaustein's checklist (n 45).

[52] See Günter Frankenberg, "Comparing Constitutions: Ideas, Ideals, and Ideology, toward a Layered Narrative" (2006) 4 *International Journal of Constitutional Law* 439, 459.

fears and normative visions. Thus, the 1987 Haiti Constitution expressly forbids, with regard to the despotism and the practices of the Duvalier dynasty, "the cult of the personality" and prescribes that "effigies and names of living personages may not appear on currencies, stamps" etc. (Art. 7). Tonga's 1875 Constitution excludes imbeciles from succession to the throne (Art. 35) to assist the stability of monarchy. One would consider the 1992 Saudi Basic Law's 60 years of gestation to be rather a peculiar duration for constitution-making (disregarding the fact that the Basic Law may not be a constitution).

Also the US right to bear arms according to the Second Amendment qualifies as an odd detail (notwithstanding its modified reappearance in the 1853 Argentine Constitution as an obligation to bear arms).[53] Although it could be copied by other constitutions, it is a highly context-dependent guarantee, derived from the Anglo-American tradition[54] of a common law right to self-defense, dating back to King Henry II's Assize of Arms in the 12th century and the right to resist tyranny informed by the colonial experience of the New England States. Arguably, the Second Amendment was proposed by the Federalists, notably James Madison, to appease the Anti-Federalists' and a widespread popular fear and distrust of central government by allowing for armed citizens and a "well regulated militia,"[55] thus balancing the power of the states and the nation.[56] Despite its English common law pedigree, the right to bear arms is historically informed by the controversies during the founding era concerning the armed forces of the federal government and the colonists' distrust of oppression and a standing army, and their preference for a militia. And it is also intimately linked to the specifically American "regeneration through violence"[57] and the national myth it created. After its metamorphosis into an individual right, the intensely contested[58] Second Amendment is even today – notwithstanding its dark

---

[53] Referring not to militia but compulsory military service in defense "of the fatherland and this Constitution" (chapter I section 21).

[54] Dating back to the English Bill of Rights of 1689. See David H Williams, *The Mythic Meanings of the Second Amendment: Taming Political Violence in a Constitutional Republic* (Yale University Press 2003).

[55] See James Madison, *The Federalist Papers*, No. 46, and Gary Wills, *A Necessary Evil: A History of American Distrust of Government* (Simon & Schuster 1999) 258.

[56] For example Wills (n 55).

[57] Richard Slotkin, *Regeneration through Violence: The Myth of the American Frontier* (Wesleyan University Press 1973).

[58] From *United States v Cruikshank* 92 US 542 (1875) until *District of Columbia v Heller* 128 SCt 2783 (2008), the Supreme Court and commentators

history and the psychopathology of arms bearing – powerful enough to prevent efficient measures of gun control despite a scandalously high death toll in the US every day and recurrent mass killings by berserk gunmen.

Odd details, or strange items, of the *second* category are *rejected* because they run against the orthodoxy of liberal constitutionalism, some qualifying as subversive elements. They articulate the indomitable presence of the local,[59] somehow disconnected from the world at large, both from its brighter side – the prospect of cosmopolitanism – and its darker side – the atrocities of imperialism and colonialism, as well as their supportive comparative studies. Or they formulate a different political agenda. And there are innumerable other constitutional items that resist commodification: the epic 1949 Indian Constitution with its 117,369 words implicitly opposes the dictum that a constitution should be "short and dark." Similarly, the 1988 Constitution of Brazil deviates from the dominant (liberal) paradigm. The extremely elaborate document and its acute sense of detail are illustrated by provisions concerning the economy and labor, for example that workers be "paid weekly preferably on Sundays" (Art. 7 sec. XV). While such a clause may be considered odd in the sense of the first category, the social-democratic design and program would be excluded from IKEA for political reasons.

The 1992 Vietnamese Constitution portrays a unique and complex economic structure – "a multi-component economy functioning in accordance with market-mechanisms under the management of the State

---

have agonized over the meaning(s) of the Second Amendment. See also Mark Tushnet, *Out of Range: Why the Constitution Can't End the Battle over Guns* (Oxford University Press 2007).

[59] The indomitable presence of the local has also shaped the "deviant legislation" recently introduced into the German Basic Law (Art. 72 sec. 3) to accommodate the political interests of the states, by shifting legislative competences from the federal to the state level. Consequently, the states' legislatures may decide to deviate from federal statutes regulating certain enumerated matters such as hunting or the protection of nature. The result is a confusing mix of competencies which does not follow the logic of rational-efficient regulation but the repeated (and ultimately futile) re-allocation of powers within the federalist system to curb centralist tendencies. Too context-dependent, one would think, to be transferable. Yet, the new Iraqi Constitution displays a provision that, on its surface, resembles the Basic Law's Art. 72 sec. 3 (but hardly inspired by it) in that it grants special powers to the regions. However, the equally odd Iraqi Constitution's Art. 112 amounts to more: the right of the regions to nullify federal laws – except in the case of exclusive federal powers – is complemented by a new provision making regional law trump federal law in the case of conflict.

and following a socialist tradition" (Art. 15). State-run, cooperative, family, private, and foreign enterprises are alloyed on the constitutional level by a mixed cluster of heterogeneous values, promotional goals, and guarantees.[60] This peculiar constitutional amalgam hinges upon the leading cadres' decision in the early 1990s to open up the planned economy to private initiative and foreign investors, while preserving both its socialist core and pre-socialist family tradition.[61] It calls for a careful comparative analysis, in particular its historical layers shaped by colonial occupation, imperialist wars, liberation and reconstruction.

Oddity or strangeness, however, is easy neither to identify nor to describe. Non-marketable items may change over time, though, and turn into constitutional building materials that find a market at least in a related geographical, political or ideological region, if only after a certain delay. What appears to be context-specific and peculiar to one country may cross national-cultural boundaries and make its way into other constitutional documents: the constitutional abolition of untouchability in India (1949 Constitution, Art. 17) reappeared in the neighboring constitutions of Bangladesh, Pakistan and Sri Lanka in the guise of a prohibition on discriminating against persons on the grounds of caste. Likewise, the obligation of adult children to provide for their parents, which from the perspective of liberal constitutionalism might seem unusual if not odd, traveled from post-soviet host countries (1991 Uzbekistan, 1993 Russia, 1995 Kazakhstan) to post-colonial constitutions (2005 Swaziland). The right to get married and have a family (1945 Indonesia; 1998 Albania, 2005 Armenia, 2010 Kenya) may embark upon a similar regional career despite resistance from or rather non-compliance on the part of Islamic countries. All these examples – one may want to add the references to historical materialism in socialist constitutions – illustrate the difficulty in differentiating between odd details, regionally marketable items and phenomena that point toward hybrid archetypes complementing the modern idiom.

Finally, oddity or strangeness is a treacherous label. Other than the fact that an item has never been exported and repeated elsewhere and the

---

[60] Connecting the dominant state sector (Art. 19) with the collective sector (Art. 20), the family economy (Arts 21, 64, 66, 67), the private sector (Art. 23, 57, 58), and the sector open to foreign investment (Art. 25).

[61] For a detailed account of legal and economic reform in Vietnam see Michael Blecher and Günter Frankenberg, "Doppelstaat und plurales Recht – Anmerkungen zur Rechts- und Wirtschaftsreform in Vietnam" (1997) 2 *Zeitschrift für Zivilprozeß International* 379.

appearance of context-specificity, there are no reliable criteria to distinguish global(ized) items from constitutional information resisting the push and pull of western-liberal constitutionalism.

7. RE-CONTEXTUALIZATION: THE RISKS AND SIDE-EFFECTS OF BRICOLAGE

In a *fourth* constructive step, the purchased/imported globalized items have to be *re-contextualized* in and *adapted* to a new or "host" environment. There, whatever is transferred meets with "conditions of acceptance or, as an inevitable part of acceptance, resistance."[62] These conditions determine the "grand hazard"[63] not only of constitutional but of any legal transfer: rejection or the complex and complicated, smooth or rough, rapid or lengthy, re-contextualization of the transferred "objects" within the new cultural setting.

Re-contextualization presupposes, first, the unfreezing and unpacking of the transferred item and, second, involves a series of introductory, adaptive, modifying moves in the course of which the imported information is subject to reinterpretation, redesigning, and *bricolage*.[64] At any rate, a simple assembly of the imported parts/information generally does not provide the desired results but involves a great deal of improvisation. Again, along the lines of Said's traveling theory, "the now full (or partly) accommodated (or incorporated) idea"[65] – or constitutional item – has to be inserted in the new constitutional framework by the actors of re-contextualization and then put to use under the new circumstances by the new epistemic community – mostly courts, legal academics. Thus the transferred item undergoes a process of transformation "by its new uses, its new position in a new time and place."[66] Beginning with the making or amending of constitutions and then continuing with their application in

---

62 Said (n 34) 227.

63 Montesquieu, *De L'Esprit des Lois* (Geneva 1748) Book 1, ch 3. See, also, Otto Kahn-Freund, "On the Uses and Misuses of Comparative Law" (1974) 37 *Modern Law Review* 6, and Eric Stein, "Post-Communist Constitution-Making: Confessions of a Comparatist (Part I)" (1992) Jean Monnet Chair Papers – The European Policy Unit at the European University Institute 25.

64 Which may be translated as "tinkering" to convey the makeshift, do-it-yourself character. For a theoretically elaborated concept of *bricolage* as a method of "wild thinking" see Claude Lévi-Strauss, *The Savage Mind* (University of Chicago Press 1966) 16–32.

65 Ibid.

66 Ibid. See Chapters 6, 10, 13, 15 and 16.

constitutional adjudication and interpretation, the imported building materials have to be fitted into the new normative framework, adapted to the political constellations, and cultural setting.

As constitution-makers and their consultants, when they set about re-assembling the imported items, usually have to operate without the original master-plan or meaning – the constructors' intentions or contextual expectations – they may, at best, rely on fairly unreliable and abstract instruction manuals provided by global constitutionalism. This is why transfers come with considerable risks (that experienced IKEA shoppers are well aware of), ranging from "immuno-reactions" by the host culture to a non-adaptable constitutional import to the less dramatic risk of a bad fit and the risk of "missing links."

Immuno-reactions are rare but not unheard of. To insert imported materials into a new normative framework and political-cultural context, and put them to use may fail because the abstract, commodified item meets with political resistance or simply does not make sense in the new environment because there is no methodology available to decode its message nor an ideology to re-invent it. Yet a different outcome of the re-contextualization may be that the operative logic of institutions or procedures remains misunderstood and they just do not even remotely work as was expected.

A case of political resistance happened in 1920 in conjunction with plans to transfer the Swiss federal system to Czechoslovakia.[67] After the "Velvet Revolution," or rather the dismantling of the Soviet Union, the transfer of German-style judicial review to Russia failed because its operative logic was misunderstood.

More commonly, transfer results in a bad fit because the package contains information that can neither be used nor adapted or because it lacks important information. Re-contextualization may furthermore show that institutions have to be redesigned so as to accommodate them to existing power constellations or cultural dispositions. Thus, the model of the German Federal Constitutional Court which could thrive and be reined in in a consolidated democracy, once exported, albeit in a modified version, to post-socialist Hungary, attracted a lot of criticism and opposition as a hypertrophic center of power. Likewise doctrinal items, such as the proportionality principle or the political question doctrine, may need a different twist and norms a different interpretation in a new normative context, or they may have to be revamped altogether.

---

[67] Jana Lachmund, "Paris-Prag: Geschichte eines Verfassungstransfers" in Duss et al (n 8) 322, 325–7.

Correcting the bad fit or finding the missing links may require a return to the IKEA center and the consultation of constitutionalists, unless the parts can be fabricated on-site.

Re-contextualization is likely to produce a variety of results. First, results depend on where the information is contextualized, for example in divided societies, post-colonial situations or post-conflict scenarios.[68] Second, it is crucial which information is selected and purchased, how it is processed, and what risks it entails. Third, transferred items are shaped by both the ignorance and the expertise of those entrusted with the job of re-contextualization, the time-frame for their work, political pressures, etc. The end-product may turn out to be a respectful or ironic imitation or pastiche, a creative hybrid or "naïve novelty,"[69] at best, a modified replica, rather than a genuine copy of what initially was bought as a standardized model.

Despite the semblance of similarity to the propositional statements in constitutions and of designs and structures, one has to bear in mind that transferred items, once contextualized, are invested by their local interpreters with specific meanings according to the prevailing epistemological assumptions (*Vorverständnis*) and conventions. Moreover they are met by local interest groups with specific expectations according to local political circumstances and projects. The open-ended phase of re-contextualization is vastly simplified by the transplant thesis and bears very little resemblance to the transplanting of an organ, let alone a tomato plant.[70] Transfers, if not rejected outright, establish a semiotic relationship between the sender and the recipient, which is usually kept in the dark. Here are some illustrations of the risks and side-effects of transfer:

The preamble of the US Constitution credits its status as an icon of constitutional prose which succinctly captures the spirit of modern constitutionalism in one sentence, and therefore has the charm of tradition and concision.[71] Despite its religious connotations and implicit

---

[68] See Chapters 11 and 12.

[69] The term was introduced by Eric Stein to describe the result of "ignorance of foreign patterns and a romantic, parochial conception of the specificity of local conditions" that may "prevent functional transfers," see Stein (n 65) 25 and Eric Stein, "Uses, Misuses – and Nonuses of Comparative Law" (1977) 72 *Northwestern Law Review* 198.

[70] The rather unfortunate but very telling example of the tomato plant is taken from Watson's defense of his transplant thesis.

[71] "We the People of the United States, in order to form a more perfect union, establish justice, ensure domestic tranquillity, provide for the common

references to the historical context, the preamble is widely reputed as being, at least on the surface, a thoroughly secular and universally applicable text,[72] even if "just beneath this godless surface flows the force of a pure revelation."[73] Despite its elitist origin, the invocation of the (absent) collective has contributed to its high democratic esteem, to its aura as the ultimate source of authority. In the course of constitutional history, "We, the People" has become one of the most prominent items in the global reservoir of constitutionalism, copied and pasted[74] by numerous constitution-makers from Albania to Costa Rica and from Liberia to East Timor. As is illustrated by the traveling "We the people," the formula always reappears as a new creation: a modified replica ("We, the representatives of the people of the Argentine Nation" and "We, the Swiss People and Cantons") or a hybrid[75] imagining of a democratic polity yet to be established ("We the people of Afghanistan" in the post-Taliban constitution). In the framework of a constitutional monarchy (Cambodia 1993), it arguably qualifies as a naïve novelty conjoining the popular we-rule and monarchic I-rule.

Needless to say, as one moves from one strange context to another, "We the People" takes on a different meaning. Despite the repetition of the original propositional formula, constitution-makers invoke and constitution-readers connote a different historical and political "we" depending on the national–cultural environment. The simple "We the People," one may conclude, testifies against the possibility of constitutional "transplants," but illustrates constitutional transfers and the art of *bricolage* and the attribution of meanings in different constitutional settings.

Unlike preambles, which are generally, albeit unduly, dismissed as merely decorative and marginal stuff, rights catalogues, in conjunction with democracy and the rule of law, hold a secure status as central

---

defense, promote the general welfare, and secure the blessings of liberty to ourselves and our posterity, do ordain and establish this Constitution for the United States of America."

72 See Hannah Arendt, *On Revolution* (Viking 1963); Ulrich Rödel, Helmut Dubiel and Günter Frankenberg, *Die demokratische Frage* (Suhrkamp Verlag 1989); Mitchell Meltzer, *Secular Revelations*: *The Constitutions of the United States and Classic American Literature* (Harvard University Press 2005).

73 Meltzer (n 72) 2.

74 For example Cindy Skach, "We, the Peoples? Constitutionalizing the European Union" (2005) 43 *Journal of Common Market Studies* 149.

75 For transfer leading to a hybrid see Michael S Gal, "The 'Cut and Paste' of Article 82 of the EC Treaty in Israel: Conditions for a Successful Transplant" (2007) 9 *European Journal of Law Reform* 467.

chapters in the book of liberal constitutionalism.[76] While constitutions can do without a preamble,[77] the modern constitutional idiom and ideology require that they come with an elaborated bill of rights as well as rule of law and democracy principles. The French *Déclaration* set the tone with its verdict that a society that neither guarantees rights nor establishes the separation of powers does not have a constitution.[78] The first Constitution of Haiti followed in 1801 and sealed the first successful slave revolt in the French colony of Saint-Domingue, as it was then called.[79] Thereafter, numerous other constitutional instruments, political struggles, and philosophical theories have proliferated the idea of rights and have generated, or at least inspired, an indomitable rights-making activity that is partly innovative, but mostly based on transfer. Many of the problems of life in society, such as domination, discrimination, political participation, poverty, access to education, and so on, for which rights are meant to provide the answer, even if they may also be part of the problem,[80] tend to transcend political constellations, economic conditions and socio-cultural settings. And the drafters of rights catalogues, so as not to reinvent the wheel, are tempted to glean the text of norms and the formula of doctrines as well as the design of institutions relating to rights from the global constitution.[81] Again, it would be naïve to assume that all these items are "transplanted" like tomatoes. While rights standardize problems of life in society as well as their legal answers in a manner that appears to be conducive to their transfer across national boundaries, rights also change their meaning in the process. "First

---

[76] Blaustein (n 45).

[77] Such as Austria, Belgium, Denmark, Finland or Botswana. Constitutional monarchies either operate without a preambling "We," or the "We" refers to the monarch as still symbolically embodying the people.

[78] "*Toute Société dans laquelle la guarantie des Droits n'est pas assurée, ni la separation des Pouvoirs determinée, n'a point de Constitution.*" Déclaration des droits de l'homme et du citoyen, Art. 16, 26 August 1789.

[79] CLR James, *Black Jacobins* (2nd edn, Vintage 1989).

[80] David Kennedy, *The Dark Side of Virtue: Reassessing International Humanitarianism* (Princeton University Press 2005).

[81] The wholesale adoption of a rights catalogue is only one way of tapping into the global reservoir. In a less conspicuous manner, national constitutions may declare the Universal Declaration of Human Rights and the International Covenants on Humans Rights as binding within the national legal regime or give priority to other international human rights instruments. Yet, other national constitutional documents explicitly defer more broadly to international law or provide more narrowly for the interpretation and application of the national rights catalogue in accordance with the Universal Declaration of Human Rights.

Amendment" guarantees and rights to equality come with a different doctrinal apparatus, different exceptions, and different connotations in India, Afghanistan, Albania and in socialist constitutions.

That transfer means more than transplant or simple export/import is illustrated, incidentally, by the rather spectacular adoption by the English Parliament, contested by a divided Tory opposition, of the Human Rights Act (HRA) in 1998. The HRA incorporated the European Convention on Human Rights (ECHR) into a constitutional regime widely believed to be unwritten and based on an amalgam of parliamentary conventions and Acts, court decisions, and works of authority.[82] Official recognition of the European Court of Human Rights' jurisprudence as a source of inspiration for the interpretation of the Act ended a long struggle against the Convention and the Court in Strasbourg, carried on by the greater part of the English political and juridical elite who seemed to have forgotten that the ECHR of 1950 was significantly shaped by their fellow countrymen. In the end the HRA was accepted by part of the political elite as a "lawyer's provision for lawyers,"[83] thus changing the "original meaning" of the ECHR, while religiously repeating the two-tiered rights structure, to wit, setting out the right in the first paragraph and limiting it in the second in the name of the interests of the general public: national security, public safety or economic well-being, prevention of disorder and crime, protection of health and morals, and of the rights and freedoms of others.[84] Moreover, the "homecoming" of the ECHR in the guise of the HRA has triggered a series of "juridification" moves regarding the British Constitution: a process of adaptation on the part of the host culture arguably underscored by European integration and globalization.[85] This process has not yet come to an end, as is illustrated by the recent discussion of the desirability of a Supreme Court.[86]

---

[82] Hilaire Barnett, *Constitutional and Administrative Law* (5th edn, Cavendish 2005) 8; Eric Barendt, "Is There a United Kingdom Constitution?" [1997] *Oxford Journal of Legal Studies* 137.

[83] James Young, "The Politics of the Human Rights Act" (1999) 26 *Journal of Law and Society* 27, 37.

[84] The British Institute of Human Rights, "Briefing on the Human Rights Act," 16 May 2006 – www.blink.org.uk/docs/bihr_hra_briefing.pdf.

[85] Peters (n 48) 275.

[86] Gernot Sydow, "Der geplante Supreme Court für das Vereinigte Königreich im Spiegel der britischen Verfassungsreform" (2004) 64 ZaöRV 66; Peters (n 48) 275.

8. THE MERCHANTS OF TRANSFER

To validate the existence of a global constitutional reservoir, an endless list of transfers would have to be and could be provided. At this point it may suffice to summarize that, first, contrary to a widespread belief, constitutions are not "largely invented"[87] by societies or great minds but are largely (re)constructed. Second, the (re)construction is done or supported by the merchants of transfer coming from the "small worlds"[88] of constitutional elites and their advisors, activists of social movements with a constitutional-political agenda, and networks experts within and without academia. They all tap into the global reservoir, where packaged constitutional information is pooled and held in store. Its contents are created and constantly changed by innumerable transnational transfers and the ensuing *bricolage*.

This is why, third, most constitutions have adopted the vocabulary, grammar, style and design of the modern idiom. Rather than desperately trying to be ingenious, the merchants of transfer stick to what they find in the IKEA market – archetypical formats, architectural designs, and semantic paragons. They observe architectural rules that demand the configuration of rights, values, organizational provisions, and meta-rules. Despite the semblance of similarity at the propositional level, one should bear in mind that texts of norms, once they are unpacked, adapted and re-contextualized on-site, are submitted to intensive *bricolage* and then re-invested by local interpreters and appliers with meanings according to epistemological assumptions (*Vorverständnis*), conventions shared by the epistemic community, and political projects to be translated by the constitution into a normative order.

Therefore, the interesting question is not really whether legal transplants are possible (*sensu stricto* of Legrand, they are not) but *how* legal transfer happens and *what* happens when it happens. Which semiotic relationships are established through transfer? How are constitutional items de- and re-contextualized? Which elements are excluded for what reasons from transfer? And so forth.

The IKEA theory has been introduced to help formulate questions and indicate problems arising from and related to constitutional (or other legal) transfer as well as to provoke exactly the kind of inspiring

---

[87] SFC Milsom, *Historical Foundations of the Common Law* (London 1969) ix, quoted approvingly by Watson, *Legal Transplants* (n 9) 8.

[88] "Small worlds" of constitutional elites, experts, engineers or activists facilitate transfer of information, Stichweh (n 29) 7 with further references.

conversation we had during the September 2011 workshop[89] and that we the authors continue here in this book.

[89] The workshop on "Constitutional Transfers" in Frankfurt/Bad Homburg was sponsored by the Fritz Thyssen Foundation (Cologne/Germany) and the Cluster of Excellence Normative Orders at the Goethe University Frankfurt.

PART I

Transplant, transfer, migration, etc. – only words? Problems of theory and method

1. Comparative constitutional studies and the discourse on legal transfer

Timo Tohidipur

1.1. APPROACHING COMPARATIVE CONSTITUTIONAL STUDIES

Debating the relevance of comparative constitutional studies and its vocabulary assumes the existence of a plural international legal order with detectable differences between constitutional constructions and regimes, because "there is no point in comparing what is identical."[1] The law(s) of the world could not easily be described within the frame of a uniform world constitutionalism or a particular blueprint of the world.[2] The myth of modern-style globalization with its inexorable unifying tendencies is not intense enough to generate convincing criteria for an envisaged globally uniform system.[3] The world of constitutions and its studies thus remains colorful.

The law(s) of foreign countries have always attracted legal scholarship and practice. The historical view identifies a long tradition of comparative studies which can be traced back to the ancient western world, where Aristotle examined the constitutions of the Greek (city) states and the customs of the Greeks, the Romans, and the so-called "Barbarians," while the later ideas of Montesquieu in his *Spirit of the Laws* and of John Adams, Alexander Hamilton, and James Madison in their *Federalist*

---

[1] Gerhard Dannemann, "Comparative Law: Study of Similarities or Differences?" in Mathias Reimann and Reinhard Zimmermann (eds), *The Oxford Handbook of Comparative Law* (Oxford University Press 2008) 384.

[2] See Martti Koskenniemi, "The Subjective Dangers of Projects of World Community" in Antonio Cassese (ed), *Realizing Utopia: The Future of International Law* (Oxford University Press 2012) 3.

[3] Werner Menski, *Comparative Law in a Global Context: The Legal Systems of Asia and Africa* (2nd edn, Cambridge University Press 2008) 4.

Papers[4] laid down the foundation of what became the more "modern" approach to comparative law which had its starting point at the First International Congress of Comparative Law in 1900.[5] Finally the emerging processes of transnational governance and economic, political and social interdependence within complex structures of new communication and information technologies expanded interest among political and legal scholars and practitioners in the constitutional laws and institutions of other countries and areas of the world and generated the "rise of comparative constitutional law."[6]

Observing "the other" and developing an understanding of the fundamental (institutional) structure and the constitutional rationale of the state or community in the respective neighborhood and beyond may be of existential relevance for every political community because it eases communication and trade and therefore secures a peaceful coexistence. The systematic study of comparative constitutional law as the "study of constitutional law, jurisprudence and institutions across polities"[7] was the outcome and generated a highly differentiated set of approaches and vocabulary. The wide variety of work in the field of comparative constitutional law could not easily be defined.[8]

1.2. THE COMPLEXITY OF LEGAL TRANSFER

Comparative constitutional studies started by exploring the similarities and dissimilarities of different cultural and social phenomena and regulations,[9] but has tended to go much further. An essential part of the field of comparative constitutional law covers research on the manner and

---

[4] Mark Tushnet, "Comparative Constitutional Law" in Reimann and Zimmermann (n 1) 1226.

[5] For further elaboration see Charles Donahue, "Comparative Law before the Code Napoleon" in Reimann and Zimmermann (n 1) 4.

[6] Ran Hirschl, "The Rise of Comparative Constitutional Law: Thoughts on Substance and Methods" (2008) *Indian Journal of Constitutional Law* 11.

[7] Hirschl (n 6).

[8] Vicki C Jackson and Mark Tushnet, *Defining the Field of Comparative Constitutional Law* (Praeger 2002) draw attention not only to substantial methodological analysis from a North American or European point of view but also to developments in the Near and Middle East, Africa, Asia and Japan. See also Menski (n 3).

[9] Nils Jansen, "Comparative Law and Comparative Knowledge" in Reimann and Zimmermann (n 1) 323.

range of influence or on the interaction between different constitutions and constitutional systems.

Different degrees of influence may be identified, ranging from interested observation and self-determined reception or refusal to complete and unreflecting acceptance of foreign norms and/or general (global-like) principles in the process of constitution-making. The transfer itself might also vary from simple translation of the wording of legal texts or broad principles across content-orientated interpretation to a more demanding attempt of contextualized transfer of norms.

Transfer supposes that people can design institutions and procedures by "reflection and choice."[10] This requires a more active role for those involved, respectively constitutional designer(s), lawyers, judges, but also conceivable is for example a crossing of law(s) by force. Many projects of legal transfer are not least part of a broader hegemonial narrative which was (and still is) often but not necessarily included in development politics and law.[11]

Consequently we find a great variety of vocabulary describing the processes of constitutional transfer, with every term accentuating a specific part of the influential crossing of norms or ideas of norms, examples being migration, reception, adoption, borrowing, diffusion, transplant, to name but a few,[12] or just transfer of norms, while it is difficult to distinguish exactly between the terms and their inherent and/or attributed substance. But this should not be reduced to a simple "battle of metaphors," because it constitutes a search for a theoretical approach which is capable of capturing the complexity of cross-constitutional interaction.[13]

Studying the transfer of constitutional law therefore requires us to look at the circumstances (actors and substantial influences) under which legal

---

[10] Tushnet (n 4).

[11] John Gillespie and Pip Nicholson (eds), *Law and Development and the Global Discourses of Legal Transfers* (Cambridge University Press 2012); David M Trubek and Alvaro Santos (eds), *The New Law and Economic Development: A Critical Appraisal* (Cambridge University Press 2006); Balakrishnan Rajagopal, *International Law from Below* (Cambridge University Press 2003) 24.

[12] See in this volume Margrit Seckelmann, Chapter 2 and Günter Frankenberg, "Constitutions as Commodities: Notes on a Theory of Transfer" for more words and substance.

[13] Vlad Perju, "Constitutional Transplants, Borrowing, and Migrations" in Michel Rosenfeld and András Sajó (eds), *The Oxford Handbook of Comparative Constitutional Law* (Oxford University Press 2012) 1307; Günter Frankenberg, "Constitutional Transfer: The IKEA Theory Revisited" (2010) 8 *International Journal of Constitutional Law* 566.

transfer became relevant at the moment a constitution was made, but also to consider how the transfer of law(s) is relevant in the process of constitutional consolidation and development at the same time.

In Europe, the study of comparative law may refer to the legal tradition of the *ius commune* which established the idea of basic similarity, seeing regional and local laws only as "variations on a common theme."[14] This for example serves today as the basis for the Common Core of European Private Law project which tries to detect what is already common behind the different legal forms of the European Union (EU) member states,[15] assembling hereby parts of a common legal tradition related to a common culture, a project that has been criticized for its methodological approach.[16] While the idea of a public law of Europe seems even more diverse historically,[17] constitutional communication within the supranational framework of the EU has at least access to a shared vocabulary, partly defined by the EU or the Council of Europe and generally by the European Human Rights Convention and the Charter of Fundamental Rights of the EU. But at the same time the EU is far from being a homogeneous constitutional entity. In particular, the different constitutional traditions of eastern and western Europe and the multilevel supranational system of the EU require a broad analysis on vertical and horizontal constitutional transfer.[18]

The international level indeed offers manifold settings of constitutional law and transfer, related to a vast variety of cultural, historical, social, and economic contexts. To understand the other legal systems and mechanisms of transfer requires acknowledging difference as an important category of analysis.[19] The comparative perspective widens its scope

---

[14] Dannemann (n 1) 385.

[15] Mauro Bussani, Marta Infantino and Franz Werro, "The Common Core Sound. Short Notes on Themes, Harmonies and Disharmonies of European Tort Law" (2009) *King's Law Journal* 239.

[16] Günter Frankenberg, "How to Do Projects with Comparative Law: Notes of an Expedition to the Common Core" in Pier Giuseppe Monateri (ed), *Methods of Comparative Law* (Edward Elgar 2012) 120.

[17] See for example Martti Koskenniemi, "The Public Law of Europe: Reflections on a French 18th Century Debate" in Helena Lindemann, Nina Malaviya, Alexander Hanebeck, Felix Hanschmann, Rainer Nickel and Timo Tohidipur (eds), *Erzählungen vom Konstitutionalismus* (Nomos 2012) 43.

[18] For an example regarding the Charter of Fundamental Rights of the EU see Chapter 2 in this volume.

[19] See Günter Frankenberg, "Critical Comparisons: Re-thinking Comparative Law" (1985) 26 *Harvard International Law Review* 441; Pierre Legrand, "The Same and the Different" in Pierre Legrand and Roderick Munday (eds),

from simply detecting similarities to explaining differences and diversity through analyzing constitutional processes and legal transfer in their respective contexts.

1.3. THE SCOPE OF DEBATE: FROM THE RELEVANT/IRRELEVANT DILEMMA TO THE CLAIMED NECESSITY TO IMPLEMENT "GLOBAL" PRINCIPLES

Legal transfer is happening everywhere. Legal rules are extracted from one context, transferred and implanted in another context, or migrate across sometimes fluid borders and so on. So how can one seriously question the relevance or assume the impossibility of legal transplants or transfer?

But constitutional transfer as a theory goes beyond mere phenomenological description and tries to formulate a theoretical basis. The methodological and substantial complexity of analyzing transfer and its surrounding conditions reveals the difficulties of successfully or effectively transferring constitutional law. And successful or effective transfer requires more than a simple trial-and-error method. Two of the most prominent antagonists regarding the appraisal of legal transfer are Pierre Legrand and Alan Watson.

Alan Watson strongly emphasized legal transplants by analyzing English common law and the reception of Roman law in continental Europe.[20] For him, law as rule is not necessarily linked to one sociocultural context and can therefore travel across (legal) borders. Transplants or legal transfer are essential for substantial legal development of a state or a legal community, because only this legal import guarantees new and better (ideas of) law, new and better legal texts. Provided that we can identify a common legal problem, law can be used as a tool to generate an outcome aspired to on each side of the (legal) border. This sets the

---

Comparative Legal Studies: Traditions and Transitions (2003) 240 and Günter Frankenberg "Constitutions as Commodities: Notes on a Theory of Transfer" in this volume for more.

[20] Alan Watson, *Legal Transplants: An Approach to Comparative Law* (Scottish Academic Press 1974).

foundation for the functional method, which plays a significant role in comparative studies but which is as a theory very diverse in itself.[21]

Pierre Legrand in contrast rejects the idea that "law" means only "rules," that law can be removed from one context and repositioned in different countries. He regards constitutional transfer as impossible and somewhat irrelevant because of the impossibility of transferring one legal text with its meaning, context, and/or subtext from one state to another or from one legal system to another. Legrand sees the comparatist as someone who has to "learn to think of law as a culturally-situated phenomenon."[22] The most radical conclusion then would see comparative analysis becoming an abuse if it is only informed by a formal, legalistic spirit that ignores the culture-specific character of law.[23]

The relevance of a possible/impossible debate may be questioned and perhaps does not even begin to describe the profound arguments of Legrand and Watson in depth. Moreover the debate changes its focus if we assume that constitutional transfer is not primarily a bilateral phenomenon but the result of some kind of "transfer market," offering different legal solutions for different legal problems.[24] But that shifts the discussion onto a more global level, emphasizing therefore a global forum of ideas of constitutional law with a clear access code and the absence of sheer (hegemonic) power structures within the process of constitution building.

Although the idea of a single world constitution may still be more or less located within the area of myths, there are already legal texts, legal principles or rules which seem to be a part of an imagined world or global constitution or are relevant within an ideology of global constitutionalism.[25] The debate about human rights and the rule of law leads the way and, whenever a state needs a constitutional update, it seems that the international legal expert has simply to pick up some of the given

---

[21] Ralf Michaels, "The Functional Method of Comparative Law" in Reimann and Zimmermann (n 1) 339; Albrecht Weber, *Europäische Verfassungsvergleichung* (CH Beck 2010) 10.

[22] Pierre Legrand, "The Impossibility of Legal Transplants" (1997) 4 *Maastricht Journal of European and Comparative Law* 124.

[23] Otto Kahn-Freund, "On Uses and Misuses of Comparative Law" (1974) 37 *Modern Law Review* 27.

[24] See Ralf Michaels, Chapter 3 in this volume.

[25] Bruce Ackerman, "The Rise of World Constitutionalism" (1997) 83 *Virginia Law Review* 771; Martti Koskenniemi, *The Politics of International Law* (Hart 2011) 235; Anne Peters, "Are We Moving towards Constitutionalization of the World Community?" in Cassese (n 2) 118.

constitutional vocabulary and norms to modulate a new or improved constitutional text.[26]

But these general rules or principles, which tend to be universally from a European or western point of view, are steadily contested. Modern global law is regarded as deeply rooted in a European (and Christian) oriented law of nations, still inspired by the civilizing mission approach of the colonial period and reflecting (too much) a hegemonic structure of the international legal order.[27] While globalization and the idea of governing the world[28] pretend to support a universal legal (world) community with common basic rules, the opposite viewpoint, which means understanding globalization as the increasing hybridization and pluralization of culture and thus law(s), seems likewise convincing.[29]

1.4. ASPIRATION: WORDS AND SUBSTANCE

The contributions that follow present different ways of handling the discourse on legal transfer as regards words and substance. While Margrit Seckelmann focuses on the European Union as an example of vertical constitutional transfer within a supranational organization and sets this in relation to the term "clotted history," Ralf Michaels risks a provocative view on globalization of (transfer of) laws in the context of the "one size fits all" metaphor as a formalist conception, strongly supporting a certain level of standardization as an imminent factor of perhaps not "best" but "good enough solutions."

---

26 See Günter Frankenberg, "Constitutions as Commodities: Notes on a Theory of Transfer," in this volume for more about his idea of an IKEA theory.

27 See for example Balakrishnan Rajagopal, *International Law from Below* (Cambridge University Press 2003); Sundhya Pahuja, *Decolonising International Law* (Cambridge University Press 2011); Majid Khadduri, "Introduction" in Muhammad al-Hasan Shaybani, *The Islamic Law of Nations* (Johns Hopkins Press 1965) 1; Menski (n 3) 25; William Twining (ed), *Human Rights, Southern Voices* (Cambridge University Press 2009) and Martti Koskenniemi, "International Law in the World of Ideas" in James Crawford and Martti Koskenniemi (eds), *The Cambridge Companion to International Law* (Cambridge University Press 2012) 54 about the colonial legacy.

28 For a differentiated view see Mark Mazower, *Governing the World: The History of an Idea* (Allen Lane 2012).

29 Menski (n 3) 25; Sujit Choudhry, "Rethinking Comparative Constitutional Law: Multinational Democracies, Constitutional Amendments, and Secession" paper presented at the Law and Society Association, Berlin (2007), unpublished manuscript, http://www.allacademic.com/meta/p177524_index.html.

2. Clotted history and chemical reactions – on the possibility of constitutional transfer

Margrit Seckelmann

2.1. IN THE LABORATORY

Can legal principles interact with reality? The German law professor Josef Kohler[1] stated in his 1887 essay on "The Creative Force of Jurisprudence" that:

> As it is the matter of the chemical researcher to find new substances by combining the right compounds [...], so has the [...] legal scholar to dip a [legal] principle in the plenitude of life, and to approximate it to those conditions, in which it brings about the most interesting combinations.[2]

2.2. THE DEBATE: ON THE POSSIBILITY OF LEGAL TRANSFER

The "experimental" nature of law has been subject to many legal considerations.[3] As Oscar von Bülow pointed out in 1885: law is a result of experience,

[1] As for Kohler's biography see e.g. Günter Spendel, *Josef Kohler: Bild eines Universaljuristen* (CF Müller 1983).

[2] Josef Kohler, "Die schöpferische Kraft der Jurisprudenz" (1887) 25 *Jahrbücher für die Dogmatik des heutigen römischen und deutschen Privatrechts* (N.F.); translation by the author of this chapter.

[3] See e.g. Frederick K Beutel, *Die Experimentelle Rechtswissenschaft: Möglichkeiten eines neuen Zweiges der Sozialwissenschaft* (Duncker & Humblot 1971); Rupert Stettner, "Verfassungsbindungen des experimentierenden Gesetzgebers" (1989) 5 *Neue Zeitschrift für Verwaltungsrecht* 806; Reinhold Zippelius, *Die experimentierende Methode im Recht* (Steiner 1991).

> it had to be experimentalized: It is a case-by-case result of bitter legal necessity, which urged to resolve the antagonism of human selfishness and passion, that endangered property and life.[4]

One way in which a national legal system might "learn"[5] would be through the experiences of other legal systems which have dealt with similar (real as well as normative) questions.

2.2.1 From "Reception" to "IKEA": On Different Approaches Concerning Legal Transfer

Whether such "learning" from a strange example is possible has been the subject of major scientific debate. While the "grand"[6] or "classic"[7] narrative of the development of legal systems is characterized by the term "reception,"[8] newer terminology has been developed, with each signifying a specific concept. One can identify – for instance – the organic (and "modern"[9]) term "transplant,"[10] which stands in contrast to a more technical

---

[4] Otto [von] Bülow, *Gesetz und Richteramt* (Duncker & Humblot 1885) 17; translation by the author of this chapter.

[5] On the concept of "learning" by a legal system (but one critical of the possibility of "learning" from other examples): Niklas Luhmann, "Reflexive Mechanismen [1966]" in id (ed), *Soziale Aufklärung* (8th edn, VS Verlag 2009). See also Martin Eifert, "Europäischer Verwaltungsverbund als Lernverbund" in I Spiecker gen. Döhmann and P Collin (eds), *Generierung und Transfer staatlichen Wissens im System des Verwaltungsrechts* (Mohr Siebeck 2008); Margrit Secklemann, Lernen vom fremden Beispiel: Ist Rechtsfransfer möglich?, 2012 (43) *Rechtstheorie* (forthcoming).

[6] Jean-François Lyotard, *La Condition postmoderne: Rapport sur le savoir* (Éditions de Minuit 1979).

[7] Marie Theres Fögen and Gunther Teubner, "Rechtstransfer" (2005) 7 *Rechtsgeschichte* 38, 39.

[8] See for instance Georg von Below, *Die Ursachen der Rezeption des römischen Rechts in Deutschland* (Oldenbourg 1905), but also Mathias Reimann (ed), *The Reception of Continental Ideas in the Common Law World: 1820–1920* (Duncker & Humblot 1993).

[9] Günter Frankenberg, "Constitutional Transfer: The IKEA theory Revisited" (2010) 8 *International Journal of Constitutional Law* 563, 566.

[10] Alan Watson, *Legal Transplants: An Approach to Comparative Law* (2nd edn, University of Georgia Press 1993); id., "Legal Transplants and European Private Law" (2000) 4(4) EJCL <http://www.ejcl.org/ejcl/44/44-2.html> accessed 4 October 2011; Martin De Jong, Virginie Mamadouh and Konstantinos Lalenis, "Drawing Lessons about Lesson Drawing: What the Case Reports Tell Us about Institutional Transplantations" in id (ed), *Lessons in Institutional Transplantation: How Adoption of Foreign Policy Institutions Actually Works* (Kluwer

designation ("transfer"[11]) or the post-modern[12] concept of "IKEA theory."[13] Other expressions used for the relationship between a "giving" and a "receiving" system are "borrowing,"[14] "adaptation,"[15] "mutation,"[16] "influence"[17] or "migration."[18] A skeptical (systems theory) approach uses the term (mere) "irritation."[19] Last but not least, the concept of a "legal"[20] or

---

2002); Peter Mankowski, "Rechtskultur: Eine rechtsvergleichend-anekdotische Annäherung an einen schwierigen und vielgesichtigen Begriff" (2009) 64 *Juristenzeitung* 321, 331.

[11] Margrit Seckelmann, "Im Labor: Beobachtungen zum Rechtstransfer anhand des Europäischen Verfassungsvertrags" (2006) 8 *Rechtsgeschichte* 70; Rudolf Stichweh, "Transfer in Sozialsystemen: Theoretische Überlegungen" in V Duss and others (eds), *Rechtstransfer in der Geschichte* (Meidenbauer 2006).

[12] For post-modern comparative jurisprudence see Anne Peters and Heiner Schwenke, "Comparative Law beyond Post-Modernism" (2000) 49 ICLQ 800.

[13] Frankenberg (n 9) 563; the influence of Lyotard (n 6) can be detected in the concept of a "global constitutional reservoir," from which certain elements can be derived; see e.g. Frankenberg (n 9) 579.

[14] Cindy Skach, *Borrowing Constitutional Designs: Constitutional Law in Weimar Germany and the French Fifth Republic* (Princeton University Press 2009).

[15] See e.g. Przemyslaw Saganek, "The Pre-Accession Adaptation of the Polish Law to the EU Law" in Institute of Comparative Law and Europa Institute Zurich (eds), *3rd Network Conference: Adaptation and Implementation of the EU-Acquis: An Exchange of Experiences* (Europa Institute 2009).

[16] Marc Amstutz and Vaios Karavas, "Rechtsmutation. Zu Genese und Evolution des Rechts im transnationalen Raum" (2006) 8 *Rechtsgeschichte* 14.

[17] See e.g. David S Clark, "The Civil Law Influence on David Dudley Field's Code of Civil Procedure" in M Reimann (ed), *The Reception of Continental Ideas in the Common Law World: 1820–1920* (Duncker & Humblot 1993).

[18] Sujit Choudry (ed), *The Migration of Constitutional Ideas* (Cambridge University Press 2006).

[19] Fögen and Teubner (n 7); Gunther Teubner, "Rechtsirritationen. Zur Koevolution von Rechtsnormen und Produktionsregimes" in G Dux and F Welz (eds), *Moral und Recht im Diskurs der Moderne: Zur Legimitation gesellschaftlicher Ordnung* (Westdeutscher Verlag 2001) after Luhmann (e.g. Niklas Luhmann, *Die Wissenschaft der Gesellschaft* (Suhrkamp 1990) 91). As for the concept of the processing of irritations in Luhmann's systems theory see e.g. Stefan Lange, "Politische Steuerung als systemtheoretisches Problem" in id and D Braun (eds), *Politische Steuerung zwischen System und Akteur* (Leske + Budrich 2000) 59–61.

[20] Lawrence Friedman, "The Concept of the Self in Legal Culture" (1990) 38 *Cleveland State Law Review* 517; Kjell A Modéer, "Lebende Ruinen des

"political culture"[21] is strongly connected to the concept of legal influence, whereas "institutional isomorphism"[22] describes the process by which different (national) legal systems become increasingly similar.

If one wants to systemize the approaches, one can differentiate four main ideas underlying the concepts:

(1) The first, which was made popular by Alan Watson, conceives of institutions as social constructs: thus, legal institutions can be changed by the legislator and – moreover – legal transfer is the "most fertile source of development."[23]

(2) The second perspective is an evolutionary one and resides at the other end of the legal-philosophical spectrum: Pierre Legrand, for instance, emphasizes the historical genesis of rules: legal institutions develop in an evolutionary way. Rules are embedded in a specific context which endows them with a specific meaning. Thus, the initial meaning of a rule does not survive the transplantation; only a meaningless "form of words" can be transferred.[24] For this approach, the term "legal solipcism" (Günter Frankenberg) can be used as well.[25]

(3) The third approach is a systemic one: a (national) legal system is a self-organizing network operating in a recursive way. The observable (receiving) system contains an expectation of its future

---

Rechts. Rechtliche Metaphern in postkolonialen und spätmodernen Rechtskulturdiskursen" (2011) 19 *Rechtsgeschichte* 228; Ingo von Münch, "Rechtskultur: Was ist das?" in id (ed), *Rechtspolitik und Rechtskultur. Kommentare zum Zustand der Bundesrepublik Deutschland* (Berliner Wissenschafts-Verlag 2011).

21 For (slightly different) concepts of "political culture" see e.g. Gunnar Folke Schuppert, *Politische Kultur* (Nomos 2008), Oscar W Gabriel and Bettina Westler (eds), *Politische Kultur: Eine Einführung* (Nomos 2009) and Joachim Wentzel, "Europäische Verwaltungskulturen" in H Hill (ed), *Verwaltungsmodernisierung im europäischen Vergleich* (Nomos 2009). For the concept of "administrative culture" see Stefan Fisch, "Verwaltungskulturen – geronnene Geschichte?" (2000) 33 *Die Verwaltung* 303.

22 John W Meyer, *Weltkultur: Wie die westlichen Prinzipien die Welt durchdringen* (Suhrkamp 2005).

23 Watson 1993 (n 10) 95; see also Watson 2000 (n 10); for a similar position see De Jong et al (n 10).

24 Pierre Legrand, "The Impossibility of Legal Transplants" (1997) 4 *Maastricht Journal of European and Comparative Law* 111, 120, with reference to Walter Benjamin, "Die Aufgabe des Übersetzers" [1923] in id (ed), *Ausgewählte Schriften* (Suhrkamp 1977) 55.

25 Frankenberg (n 9).

operation.[26] The interaction between recursive systems implies a reflection: each input received from external systems forces a system to reorganize itself. The construction of "meaning" is a consequence of this operation and the central observation of systems theory.[27]

(4) The final category for dealing with interaction between two legal systems is the theory of institutional isomorphism.[28] This theory tries to explain the circumstances in which certain similarities arose between different constitutions in the Western world. According to John W Meyer, institutional isomorphism is a "constraining process that forces a unit in a population to resemble other units that face the same set of environmental conditions." Meyer explains this fact through a kind of "coercive isomorphism," that is, a mimetic process which is based on the cultural expectations of societal actors (e.g. professional networks) who exert normative pressure on a legal system.[29]

To sum up, the debate on the possibility of legal transfer is – to borrow from Lawrence Friedman – one "of gaps and hopes,"[30] of modernity and post-modernity, of "normative" and "realistic" approaches.

2.2.2 Clotted History and Legal Culture: An Own Approach to Legal/Constitutional Transfer

Taking this debate into account, a new approach is developed in this chapter. In doing so, we will first understand legal/constitutional transfer as a transfer of information (2.2.2.1). Secondly we analyze how this information is processed by a (national) legal system and will point out

---

[26] Loet Leydesdorff, "Luhmann, Habermas, and the Theory of Communication" (2000) 17 *Systems Research and Behavioral Science* 273.

[27] Niklas Luhmann, "Sinn als Grundbegriff der Soziologie" in J Habermas and id (eds), *Theorie der Gesellschaft oder Sozialtechnologie – Was leistet die Systemforschung?* (Suhrkamp 1971); id., *Soziale Systeme: Grundriß einer allgemeinen Theorie* (Suhrkamp 1984).

[28] Paul J DiMaggio and Walter Powell, "'The Iron Cage Revisited': Institutional Isomorphism and Collective Rationality in Organizational Fields" (1983) 48 *American Sociological Review* 147; Meyer (n 22).

[29] DiMaggio and Powell (n 28).

[30] Friedman (n 20); id. "Some Thoughts on Comparative Legal Culture" in DS Clark (ed), *Comparative and Private International Law: Essays in Honour of John Henry Merryman on his Seventieth Birthday* (Duncker & Humblot 1990) 54.

the limits of legal/constitutional transfer given the prerequisite of legitimacy through the will of the people (2.2.2.2).

2.2.2.1 Legal/constitutional transfer as a transfer of information

2.2.2.1.1 Legal transfer First of all, legal "transfer,"[31] "transplant,"[32] "borrowing,"[33] "mutation,"[34] "influence,"[35] "migration,"[36] "irritation"[37] and the like are *metaphors*. In contemporary legal cultural discourses on globalization, metaphors have experienced a "renaissance."[38] This renaissance is in contrast to the position of legal realism, which holds that metaphors are "transcendental nonsense."[39] The recent reappraisal of the value of metaphors is in part a product of the "law as literature" movement.[40] Given that even the most "technical" (or "cybernetic") sounding term, "irritation," is a (biological, if not medical[41]) metaphor, we will allow ourselves to use metaphors to describe the interrelationship between two systems, a "giving" one and a "receiving" one.

In the course of this chapter, the term "transfer" will be used. As it is a (chemical) metaphor, it fits in with our concept of law as a laboratory. Just as Martin Borowsky calls the institutions of the European Union in Brussels a "value laboratory"[42] and Gunnar Folke Schuppert conceives of the central function of constitutions "as a facilitation framework for

---

31 Seckelmann (n 11); Stichweh (n 11).

32 Watson 1993 (n 10); Watson 2000 (n 10); De Jong et al (n 10); Mankowski (n 10) 331.

33 Skach (n 14).

34 Amstutz and Karavas (n 16) 14.

35 See e.g. Clark (n 17).

36 Choudry (n 18).

37 Fögen and Teubner (n 7); Teubner (n 19) after Luhmann (e.g. Luhmann (n 19) 91). As for the concept of the processing of irritations in Luhmann's systems theory see e.g. Lange (n 19) 59–61.

38 Modéer (n 20) 228.

39 Felix Cohen, "Transcendental Nonsense and the Functional Approach" (1935) 35 *Columbia Law Review* 809.

40 See e.g. Modéer (n 20) 228, with reference to Thomas Grey, *The Wallace Stevens Case: Law and the Practice of Poetry* (Harvard University Press 1991) 6.

41 As for biological metaphors see Otto Kahn-Freund, "On Uses and Misuses in Comparative Law" [1974] in id (ed), *Selected Writings* (Stevens 1978).

42 Martin Borowsky, "Die Grundrechtecharta als normatives Fundament der Europäischen Union" in O Leiße (ed), *Die Europäische Union nach dem Vertrag von Lissabon* (VS Verlag 2010).

conflicts,"[43] we perceive the national legal systems as *laboratories* where normative rules and real life interact, enriched by *information* from other legal systems.[44]

Legal transfer is conceived of as a transfer of information.[45] Information "is a difference which makes a difference,"[46] meaning that the information received has a certain importance to the receiving system.[47] To give an example, the British and US-American case law systems with their *stare decisis* rule fundamentally differ – at least in theory[48] – from German legal positivism with its "descending steps of the legal order" ("*Stufenbau der Rechtsordnung*"[49]). The "strange" information must, therefore, cross certain (spatial, temporal) boundaries.[50]

As explained earlier, systems theory perceives the central activity of social systems as being the production of "meaning." Thus, "incoming" information (e.g. about other laws/constitutions) is filtered through the symbolic structures of the medium of language and the related social system.[51] The "incoming" information causes irritation in the receiving system. In its attempt to construct "meaning," the receiving system selects one possible way of understanding a piece of information out of the "excess of possibilities" ("*Möglichkeitsüberschuß*").[52]

In order to facilitate a transfer process, certain "facilitators" have to exist. The piece of information needs certain macrostructures if it is to be received by the other system. These "facilitators" can be supranational

---

43 Schuppert (n 21) 478.

44 On the concept of "law as a catalyst" see Seckelmann (n 11) 73; id. (n 5); id. *Industrialisierung, Internationalisierung und Patentrecht im Deutschen Reich* (Klostermann 2006) 1–56.

45 Stichweh (n 11) 2 after Luhmann 1984 (n 27).

46 Gregory Bateson, *Steps to an Ecology of Mind: Collected Essays in Anthropology, Psychiatry, Evolution and Epistemology* (Palatin Books 1973) 315; Luhmann 1984 (n 27) 68; Stichweh (n 11) 2–3.

47 Stichweh (n 11) 2.

48 For a counter-example see the new German "casebooks,", e.g. Andreas Voßkuhle and Christian Bumke, *Casebook Verfassungsrecht* (5th edn, Beck 2008).

49 Hans Kelsen, *Reine Rechtslehre. Das Problem der Gerechtigkeit* (2nd edn, F Deuticke 1960).

50 Stichweh (n 11) 3; Seckelmann (n 5).

51 Manfred Aschke, "Einheit: Theoretische Aspekte des Großtransfers von Recht und juristischem Personal" (2005) 7 *Rechtsgeschichte* 13, 23; see also Stichweh (n 11) 3.

52 Luhmann 1984 (n 27) 66-67; id. 1971 (n 27).

organizations or (expert) networks (this is how the "small world theory"[53] explains *institutional isomorphism*[54]). A good example is the role of (social) media in the so-called "Arab spring" which was used to transmit information about democratic ideas.

2.2.2.1.2 Methodological questions In the course of this chapter, a "*bricolage*" approach will be followed.[55] Although a systemic approach will still be the main one taken, the complexity of the observed processes requires a multi-perspective approach:

> Each Theory, that deals with a complex, multi-faceted issue is thus selective, both in the questions through which it poses the issue as well as the explanations which it puts in the foreground.[56]

Legal/constitutional transfer is mainly a *hermeneutical problem*: information always encounters certain preconceptions ("*Vorverständnis*," Hans Georg Gadamer)[57] on the part of the receiver. Moreover, analysis of the "*Vorverständnis*" leads to understanding of a "deeper semantic" (Paul Ricœur),[58] for example of the cultural context of the receiving system. It can lead to an understanding of the "collective memory"[59] and the

---

53 Albert-László Barabási, *Linked: How Everything Is Connected to Everything Else and What It Means for Business, Science, and Everyday Life* (Plume 2003); Manfred Kochen (ed), *The Small World* (Ablex Publishing Cooperation 1989); Stichweh (n 11) 7. On the central role of the concept of (construing) meaning within systems theory see Luhmann 1971 (n 27); Luhmann 1984 (n 27).

54 Meyer (n 22).

55 Claude Lévi-Strauss, *La Pensée sauvage* (Plon 1962); see also Frankenberg (n 9) 575; Seckelmann (n 5).

56 Renate Mayntz, "Zur Theoriefähigkeit makro-sozialer Analysen" in id (ed), *Akteure – Mechanismen – Modelle – Zur Theoriefähigkeit makro-sozialer Analysen* (Campus 2002) 39, translation by the author of this chapter.

57 Hans-Georg Gadamer, *Wahrheit und Methode. Grundzüge einer philosophischen Hermeneutik*, vol I (6th edn, Mohr Siebeck 1990). See also Hein Kötz, "Alte und neue Aufgaben der Rechtsvergleichung" (2000) 57 *Juristenzeitung* 257, 259; Mankowski (n 10).

58 Paul Ricœur, *Verstehende Soziologie: Grundzüge und Entwicklungstendenzen* (WL Bühl 1972).

59 Schuppert (n 21) 596.

"cultural codes"[60] of the giving as well as the receiving legal system and – moreover – to the "constitutional unconscious."[61]

Thus, in this chapter, a "legal culture" approach will be followed, based on a modified evolutionary perspective. This approach takes into account the historical genesis of legal institutions. Just as Dieter Grimm states after Max Weber that law is "clotted politics,"[62] we understand "legal culture" as "clotted history."[63] The historical approach takes not only the genesis and to some extent – contingency – of the law into account, but also its "temporality."[64] Furthermore, it also establishes the institutional framework[65] for new developments.[66] Therefore, we will – in the sense of Talcott Parsons – understand "culture" as "not only a set of symbols of communication but a set of norms for action."[67] This framework also sets the limits for a "path dependent"[68] development.

The "path dependency" in the societal subsystem of the law provides an explanation for the difference between "general" and "legal" hermeneutics.[69] Legal hermeneutics have to take – according to Philippe Mastronardi – the special prerequisites of the legal system into account:

> The material law gives us the criteria for legal hermeneutics. For the circle of understanding has to serve the realisation of legal norms. Equality and reliability of law as well as justness demand an optimal rationalisation in the sense of an inter-subjective revisable argumentation. The prohibition against

---

60 Ibid 595.

61 Günter Frankenberg, "Comparing Constitutions: Ideas, Ideals, and Ideology. Toward a Layered Narrative" (2006) 4 *International Journal of Constitutional Law* 439.

62 Dieter Grimm, "Recht und Politik" (1969) 9 *Juristische Schulung* 501.

63 For a similar approach, see Fisch (n 21).

64 Mankowski (n 10) 324.

65 Paul A Hall and David Soskice, *Varieties of Capitalism: The Institutional Foundations of Comparative Advantage* (Oxford University Press 2001).

66 Schuppert (n 21) 478.

67 Talcott Parsons and Edward A Shils (eds), *Towards a General Theory of Action* (Harvard University Press 1951), 106.

68 Paul A David, "Clio and the Economics of QWERTY" (1985) 75 *American Economic Review* 332; W Brian Arthur, "Competing Technologies, Increasing Returns, and Lock-In by Historical Events" (1989) 99 *Economic Journal* 116.

69 Friedrich Müller, *Normstruktur und Normativität. Zum Verhältnis von Recht und Wirklichkeit in der juristischen Hermeneutik, entwickelt an Fragen der Verfassungsinterpretation* (Duncker & Humblot 1966).

arbitrariness ["*Willkürverbot*"] and duties of legal justification are positive legal norms illustrating that obligation to rationality.[70]

2.2.2.1.3 Constitutional transfer as a transfer of symbols What we have pointed out about how the symbolic structures of law can highlight the "collective memory"[71] and the "cultural codes"[72] of the giving as well as the receiving legal system applies even more to constitutions. These supply not only "a facilitation framework for conflicts,"[73] but are also a means of integrating citizens into a nation (Rudolf Smend).[74] Thus, they contain the fundamental information about a legal system (i.e. the protection of human dignity, the fundamental rights and the fundamental organizational principles as seen in Art. 20 of the German constitution). Together with the preamble, these core principles form one of the fundaments of "legal culture."

2.2.2.2 Some screws are always missing – or: what is happening in the "black box"?

As outlined above, transferred laws or dogmatic principles (jurisdiction) are a reservoir for possibilities which can be used as information and adopted in one variant or another by the receiving system.[75] Legal culture is thus a permanent process of the "fabrication of order."[76] But how exactly does that fabrication take place? In the cybernetic model of the political process, which underlies this chapter, political "demands" undergo – according to David Easton et al – a process in which information is processed by the political system through a "black box"

---

70 Philippe Mastronardi, *Juristisches Denken* (2nd edn, Haupt 2003) 52, translation by the author of this chapter.

71 Schuppert (n 21) 596.

72 Ibid 595.

73 Ibid 478.

74 Rudolf Smend, "Verfassung und Verfassungsrecht" [1928] in id (ed), *Staatsrechtliche Abhandlungen und andere Aufsätze* (3rd edn, Duncker & Humblot 1994); see for this approach Michael Stolleis, *Geschichte des öffentlichen Rechts in Deutschland*, vol 3 (Beck 1999) 174–5.

75 Aschke (n 51).

76 Schuppert (n 21) 70.

(giver → information → *black box*[77] → receiver).[78] "Learning"[79] by a legal system takes place precisely within that "black box."

But this procedure is not a unidirectional one. On the contrary, if one follows the IKEA metaphor,[80] one can say that the assembly instruction will be interpreted by the receiver of the information – and (even though one tries to follow the assembly step-by-step) in the end some screws may be missing or superfluous.[81]

This goes back to the fact that misunderstanding is possible,[82] but even if present, can still lead to (continued) productive processing. Nonetheless, the danger exists, that a purposeful "legal transfer" (e.g. by the transposition of EU directives) leads to the continuity of former structures in the guise of new ones ("*formal structures*"[83]).

So the most that one can say is that receiving information about a strange constitution or law irritates the receiving system in such a way that it has to construe "meaning" out of the given information, but one cannot predict the exact outcome of this process of understanding.

However, one can outline a specific manner in which a certain transfer will unfold: when a transfer will lead to a change of the constitution or "fundamental" questions (such as fundamental rights) are touched upon, a *lawmaking procedure* will – following the jurisdiction of the German constitutional court[84] – be the outcome. This "hard" prerequisite for any legal transfer goes in the direction of what Fran Olsen calls "the drama of

---

77 David Easton, *A Systems Analysis of Political Life* (Wiley & Sons 1965); Luhmann 1984 (n 27) 156 (with more literature on this subject).

78 See e.g. Easton (n 77); Werner Jann and Kai Wegrich, "Phasenmodelle und Politikprozesse: Der Policy Cycle" in K Schubert and NC Bandelow (eds), *Lehrbuch der Politikfeldanalyse 2.0* (2nd edn, Oldenbourg 2009).

79 Luhmann (n 5) 118; Eifert (n 5); Secklemann (n 5).

80 For the IKEA theory see Frankenberg (n 9).

81 At this point, I want to express my opinion that the IKEA metaphor does not work (particularly) well regarding screws that are missing or do not fit well. If and when this occurs, one gets missing screws for free at any IKEA store. Also, I have also experienced missing or ill-fitting screws in the case of other furniture stores. And, finally, I have many happy memories of my student (and that means: IKEA) life.

82 Paul Watzlawick, Janet H Beavin and Don D Jackson, *Menschliche Kommunikation* (Hans Huber 1971).

83 See DiMaggio and Powell (n 28).

84 See for instance the decisions of the German constitutional court printed in its official volume: BVerfGE 33, p. 125; 47, p. 46; 49, p. 89.

comparative law":[85] if one is to predict certain outcomes of a transfer procedure, the imagination of the legal scholar is "fenced" within the gates of the legal prerequisites of the receiving culture. Constitutions and institutions (such as expectations) form a "framework"[86] for legal transfer.

One of the central issues of the constitution (at least a German one) is the need for any decision of a public authority to be legitimized by the will of the people. This results from the principle of the sovereignty of the people (Art. 20 section 2 of the German constitution), which along with Art. 20 section 1 of the German constitution forms the *Demokratieprinzip*. According to the German constitutional court, this principle leads (in combination with the *Rechtsstaatsprinzip* of Art. 20 section 3 of the German constitution) to the conclusion that every "important" legal issue needs an act of parliament (when the constitution is changed or fundamental rights or other "fundamental" questions are touched upon).[87] This jurisdiction sets limits on the simple convergence of law through professional networks[88] – though this is to some extent different in the case of civil law[89] (if no "important" issues such as fundamental rights are touched upon).

2.3. THE DISTILLATE: THE CHARTER OF FUNDAMENTAL RIGHTS OF THE EUROPEAN UNION

In order to "put flesh on the bones," one example of legal transfer will be examined here. The "distillate" being analyzed (to stick to the metaphor

---

[85] Fran Olsen, "The Drama of Comparative Law" (1997) *Utah Law Review* 275–80, 277.

[86] Schuppert (n 21) 478.

[87] See for instance the decisions of the German constitutional court printed in its official volume: BVerfGE 33, p. 125; 47, p. 253; 49, p. 89; 77, p. 1; 83, p. 60; 93, p. 37.

[88] Meyer (n 22). Here too a certain difference from civil law (and one which Fögen and Teubner (n 7) analyze) can be seen. Regarding the problems with the judicial determination of networks see Christoph Möllers, "Netzwerk als Kategorie des Organisationsrechts – Zur juristischen Beschreibung dezentraler Steuerung" in J Oebbecke (ed), *Nicht-normative Steuerung in dezentralen Systemen* (Franz Steiner 2005).

[89] Which was analyzed by Fögen and Teubner (n 7).

of the laboratory) is Art. 41 of the Charter of Fundamental Rights of the European Union.[90]

The Charter was solemnly proclaimed on 7 December 2000 by the European Parliament, the Council and the Commission. Seven years later it was (with few modifications) incorporated into the Treaty of the European Union (TEU) through recognition in Art. 6 section 1 (Lisbon Version, 13 December 2007). The Charter is one of the "columns" of the EU fundamental rights (along with the European Convention on Human Rights (recognized in Art. 6 section 2 TEU) and the European "Fundamental Rights," which are recognized by the jurisprudence of the Court of Justice of the European Union as well as the "constitutional traditions common to the member states" Art. 6 section 3 TEU).

The addressees of Art. 41 sections 1 and 2 of the Charter of European Fundamental Rights are – following the wording of this article – the "institutions and bodies of the Union." Nonetheless, some authors see the first two sections of Art. 41 of the Charter as binding upon the member states of the European Union – at least when they implement European law.[91] In any case, the member states are bound to the "constitutional

---

[90] Art. 41 Charter EUFR – Right to good administration:

1. Every person has the right to have his or her affairs handled impartially, fairly and within a reasonable time by the institutions and bodies of the Union.
2. This right includes:
   a the right of every person to be heard, before any individual measure which would affect him or her adversely is taken;
   b the right of every person to have access to his or her file, while respecting the legitimate interests of confidentiality and of professional and business secrecy;
   c the obligation of the administration to give reasons for its decisions.
3. Every person has the right to have the Union make good any damage caused by its institutions or by its servants in the performance of their duties, in accordance with the general principles common to the laws of the Member States.
4. Every person may write to the institutions of the Union in one of the languages of the Treaties and must have an answer in the same language.

[91] Ralf Bauer, *Das Recht auf eine gute Verwaltung* (Peter Lang 2002); Martina Lais, "Das Recht auf eine gute Verwaltung unter besonderer Berücksichtigung der Rechtsprechung des Europäischen Gerichtshofs" (2002) 5 *Zeitschrift für Europarechtliche Studien* 447, 457; in opposition to this understanding: Kai-Dieter Classen, *Gute Verwaltung im Recht der Europäischen Union: Eine Untersuchung zur Herkunft, Entstehung und Bedeutung des Art 41 Abs. 1 und 2 der Europäischen Grundrechtecharta* (Duncker & Humblot 2008)

traditions common to the member states" (Art. 6 section 3 TEU)[92] which might be influenced by Art. 41 of the Charter.[93] Thus, the possibility exists that it can influence either the jurisdiction of the European courts or even that of the national courts.[94]

2.4. POSSIBLE REACTIONS

2.4.1 Brussels as a "Value Laboratory"

The "right to good administration" is by no means a given term. On the contrary, it is itself part of the Brussels "value laboratory":[95] thus, its interpretation is highly debated. It is currently under discussion whether Art. 41 of the Charter of European Fundamental Rights contains an original subjective right aside from its specifications within sections 1 and 2.[96] Some authors hold the view that the term "right to [a] good administration" contains an overall entitlement,[97] while others vehemently oppose this view.[98]

Another question is what characterizes a good administration. One view takes it as read that it should be "efficient" and "effective,"[99] while

---

74; Hans-Werner Laubinger, "Art. 41 GRCh (Recht auf eine gute Verwaltung) im Lichte des deutschen Verwaltungsrechts" in V Mehde, U Ramsauer and M Seckelmann (eds), *Staat – Verwaltung – Information, Festschrift für Hans Peter Bull zum 75. Geburtstag* (Duncker & Humblot 2011) 660.

[92] For more information see Theodor Schilling, "Bestand und allgemeine Lehren der bürgerschützenden allgemeinen Grundsätze des Gemeinschaftsrechts" (2000) 27 *Europäische Grundrechte-Zeitschrift* 3.

[93] Siegfried Magiera, "Die Bedeutung der Grundrechtecharta für die Europäische Verfassungsordnung" in DH Scheuing (ed), *Europäische Verfassungsordnung* (Nomos 2003) 128–9; Laubinger (n 91) 661.

[94] See e.g. M Mahlmann, "Die Grundrechtscharta der Europäischen Union" (2000) 3 *Zeitschrift für Europarechtliche Studien* 419, 425–6; Magiera (n 93) 128–9; M Seckelmann, "Good Governance – Importe und Re-Importe" in V Duss et al (eds), *Rechtstransfer in der Geschichte* (Meidenbauer 2006); id. (n 5) (n 11) 74–80; Laubinger (n 91) 659–60.

[95] Borowsky (n 42).

[96] Opposed by Laubinger (n 91) 682.

[97] Martin Bullinger, "Das Recht auf eine gute Verwaltung nach der Grundrechtecharta der EU" in CE Eberle (ed), *Der Wandel des Staates vor den Herausforderungen der Gegenwart, Festschrift für Winfried Brohm zum 70. Geburtstag* (Beck 2002) 31.

[98] Laubinger (n 91) 662.

[99] Bullinger (n 97) 30–31.

others reply that the term "good administration" is completely arbitrary and cannot function as a "signifier of a certain stock of fundamental rights."[100]

From a German viewpoint, the relative "vagueness" of this term "causes a hard-boiled German scholar of administrative law certain stomach troubles."[101] This is because the "right to good administration" stems from the Scandinavian (and – to a lesser extent – the Benelux and the British) tradition (namely the *god forvaltningssstandard* of Swedish and the *god forvaltningsskik* of Danish law).[102] Those traditions follow a "legal process ideal type" or "substantive (material) ideal type,"[103] which is in opposition to the German and French "formalist ideal type"[104] that binds all political power within the framework of fundamental rights (Art. 1 section 1 of the German constitution) and to the "constitutional order" (Art. 20 section 3 of the German constitution).

Another question regarding the Charter of European Fundamental Rights is the question of who will be the "custodian of the fundamental rights" of the Charter? Most likely, this safeguarding role will fall to the European courts (European Court of Justice and European Court) and indeed, the European Court has already adjudicated over matters regarding the Charter.[105] But how can a broad interpretation of the "right to good administration" (i.e. a binding commitment upon the member states and a subjective right, safeguarded by the European courts) fit into the principle of limited authorization of the European Union? As the German constitutional court recently stated, the "responsibility for integration" falls to German governmental bodies, which – in the course of Europeanization – have to safeguard fundamental German principles such as the fundamental rights and principles of Art. 20 of the constitution.[106]

Thus, the "right to good administration" can be a method by which the European courts may influence the "administrative culture"[107] of the member states. This development is in accordance with the European Commission's attempts to influence the administrative culture of the member states by establishing core demands concerning the composition

---

[100] Classen (n 91) 429; Laubinger (n 91) 662–3.

[101] Laubinger (n 91) 662.

[102] Classen (n 91) 100 ff.

[103] Schuppert (n 21) 711.

[104] Ibid 710.

[105] Decision as of 4 October 2006 – Rs. T-193/04, Ls. 3 und Rn. 127.

[106] See for instance the "Lisbon" decision of the German constitutional court, printed in BVerfGE 123, p. 267.

[107] On "administrative culture" see e.g. Wentzel (n 21).

of their administration, as seen with the European Directive on services in the internal market.[108] This directive ignores the fact that the EU does not have the competence to regulate the composition of the administration in the member states and thus to an extent conflicts with the principle of limited authorization of the European Union.

2.4.2 The "Margin of Appreciation" Doctrine

One possible solution to reconcile different legal cultures is the "margin of appreciation" doctrine of the European Court of Human Rights. This doctrine takes into account that the European Convention on Human Rights will be interpreted differently in the member states due to their cultural and religious circumstances.

Due to its relative vagueness, Mireille Delmas-Marty sees in the "margin of appreciation" doctrine a kind of "fuzzy logic"("*logique floue*")[109] that she appreciates as an appropriate means of dealing with the post-modern "new complexity."[110] Others, such as Lord Lester, are more critical of the "margin of appreciation" doctrine, seeing it as "as slippery and elusive as an eel" and thus opposed to the *rule of law* doctrine.[111] A German "answer" to the "fuzzy logic" of the "margin of appreciation" doctrine would also point out[112] that the German

[108] Directive 2006/123/EC of the European Parliament and of the Council of 12 December 2006 on services in the internal market, *Official Journal of the European Union* of 27 December 2006, L 376/36 (EN).

[109] Mireille Delmas-Marty, *Vers une autre logique juridique: à propos de la jurisprudence de la Cour européenne des droits de l'homme* (Dalloz 1988); Mireille Delmas-Marty (ed), *The European Convention for the Protection of Human Rights: International Protection Versus National Restrictions* (Martinus Nijhoff Publishers 1992); Siegfried Gottwald, *Fuzzy Sets and Fuzzy Logic: Foundations of Application – from a Mathematical Point of View* (Vieweg 1993); Jerzy Wróblenski, "Fuzziness of Legal System" in U Kangas (ed), *Essays in Legal Theory in Honour of Kaarle Makkonen* (The Finnish Lawyer's Society 1983); Jerzy Wróblenski, "Legal Language and Legal Interpretation" (1985) 4 *Law and Philosophy* 239.

[110] Jürgen Habermas, *Die neue Unübersichtlichkeit* (Suhrkamp 1985).

[111] Lord Lester of Herne Hill QC, "The European Convention on Human Rights in the New Architecture of Europe: General Report" in Council of Europe (ed), *Proceedings of the 8th International Colloquy on the European Convention on Human Rights* (Council of Europe 1995).

[112] Therefore, the German critics of the "margin of appreciation doctrine" mostly demand a further specification; see e.g. Annette Rupp-Swienty, *Die Doktrin von der margin of appreciation in der Rechtsprechung des Europäischen*

Rechtsstaat[113] requires a certain predictability of legal decisions that sets limits on fuzzy logic. Ingo von Münch, for instance, counts "reliability of law and trust of the citizen in the law"[114] as central to Western European as well as US legal culture.

2.5. RATIONALE: LEGAL CULTURE, CLOTTED HISTORY, AND THE POSSIBILITY OF CONSTITUTIONAL TRANSFER

2.5.1 Clotted History and the Transfer of Information

To sum up, this chapter has posed the question of whether legal/ constitutional transfer is possible. In the course of the chapter, we developed an idea of legal culture as the historical genesis of legal institutions which we have called "clotted history."[115] National legal systems have certain "*Geltungsgeschichten*"[116] or "layered narratives"[117] which tell the stories of constitutional as well as legal practise (in the sense of Clifford Geertz' "thick descriptions"[118]).

Gerichtshofs für Menschenrechte (Florenz 1999) 260–75. On the British reception of the idea see Onder Bakircioglu, "The Application of the Margin of Appreciation Doctrine in Freedom of Expression and Public Morality Cases" (2007) 8 *German Law Journal* 711. See also Oren Gross and Fionnula Ní Aoláin, "From Discretion to Scrutinity: Revisiting the Application of the Margin of Appreciation Doctrine in the Context of Article 15 of the European Convention on Human Rights" (2001) 23 *Human Rights Quarterly* 621, 648 who plead for a more narrow understanding of this doctrine in order to enhance the protection of human rights. For an argument along the same lines see also Rupp-Swienty 260 ff.

113 On the German Rechtsstaatsprinzip see Philip Kunig, *Das Rechtsstaatsprinzip. Überlegungen zu seiner Bedeutung für das Verfassungsrecht der Bundesrepublik Deutschland* (Mohr Siebeck 1986).

114 Münch (n 20) 53.

115 See also Fisch (n 21).

116 Schuppert (n 21) 373; Hans Vorländer, "Integration durch Verfassung? Die symbolische Bedeutung der Verfassung im politischen Integrationsprozess" in H Vorländer and G Melville (eds), *Integration durch Verfassung* (Westdeutscher Verlag 2002).

117 Frankenberg (n 61) 439.

118 Clifford Geertz, *The Interpretation of Cultures* (2nd edn, Basic Books 2000) 14.

More so than the "simple" law, constitutions have a "symbolic function."[119] But the symbolic function is harder to transfer than an "ordinary" legal principle. A danger exists that "only words," in the sense of Pierre Legrand, are transferred,[120] resulting in a "decoupling" of the "formal" and the "real structure."[121]

Legal elements and (parts of) constitutions form "units of information"[122] that can be transferred. Such transfer takes place via "bridges," which can be formed by international organizations or the European Union as well as by professional networks.

The central activity of social systems is the production of "meaning." Thus, the receiving system evaluates and processes "incoming" information in a "black box."[123] In the process of constructing "meaning," the system selects one possible way of understanding out of the "excess of possibilities" ("*Möglichkeitsüberschuß*").[124]

The term "transfer" used as a (chemical) metaphor (not a medical one such as "transplant"[125]) is comparable to an irritation process, understood as "chemical interference" (Josef Kohler[126]) with uncertain outcomes, but which is, nonetheless, a process of productive irritation.[127]

However, law is not only the subject and object of legal transfer but also the framework within which it occurs. Thus, the issue of (public) legitimacy arises when it comes to (material) changes to constitutional law or other "important" issues (as outlined in the jurisdiction of the German constitutional court).[128] The need to go back to the will of the people sets limits (except in certain aspects of civil law) upon a simple convergence through international organizations or professional networks. Thus, the outcome of productive irritation of the receiving (legal and political) system will be an act of parliament that, at the very least, follows the procedure of the receiving system. One aspect of construing

---

119 Schuppert (n 21) 373.

120 Legrand (n 24) 120, with reference to Benjamin (n 24) 55.

121 DiMaggio and Powell (n 28); Meyer (n 22).

122 Stichweh (n 11) 3; Seckelmann (n 5).

123 Easton (n 77); Luhmann 1984 (n 27) 156 (with more literature on this subject).

124 Luhmann 1984 (n 27) 66–7; Luhmann 1971 (n 27).

125 On the different kind of metaphors see Kahn-Freund (n 41).

126 Kohler (n 2) 271.

127 On the concept of "law as a catalyst" see Seckelmann (n 11) 73; id (n 44) 1–56.

128 See for instance the decisions of the German constitutional court printed in its official volume: BVerfGE 33, p. 125; 47, p. 253; 49, p. 89; 77, p. 1; 83, p. 60; 93, p. 37.

"meaning" is to integrate the received legal principle into the existing system, which means that the system has to stick to its own rules (path dependency, e.g. with Art. 3 of the German constitution (the principle of equality before the law) or the German *Rechtsstaatsprinzip*).

2.5.2 Necessity of Staff in the Laboratory?

One last question remains to be answered, one which (also) differentiates the approach adopted in this chapter from one based on "pure" Luhmannian systems theory. Again, we want to quote Renate Mayntz by saying that

> Each Theory that deals with a complex, multi-faceted issue, is thus selective, regarding both the questions through which it poses the issue as well as the explanations which it puts in the foreground. The theoretical eclecticism thus lies – unavoidably – in the eye of the beholder. Even theories which claim to grasp the wholeness of social phenomena, as e.g. the systems theory of Niklas Luhmann, remain selective, as they only capture certain fundamental principles.[129]

Thus, legal transfer does not simply emerge. On the contrary, the legal laboratory needs a certain "staff" that comes from the political as well as the legal system: the first is the parliament and the second are the (constitutional) courts as corporate actors. Thus, an "enrichment" of systems theory by an actor-centered perspective[130] is proposed in this chapter.[131] The assumption of collective actors and the parliament as a corporate actor in the sense of a "manager,"[132]

---

129 Mayntz (n 56): 39, translation by the author of this chapter.

130 Namely actor-centered institutionalism; see Renate Mayntz and Fritz W Scharpf, "Steuerung und Selbstorganisation in staatsnahen Sektoren" in id (eds), *Gesellschaftliche Selbstregelung und politische Steuerung* (Campus 1995); Fritz W Scharpf, *Interaktionsformen: Akteurzentrierter Institutionalismus in der Politikforschung* (Leske + Budrich 2000). For another important attempt to combine systemic with actor-centered approaches see Helmut Willke, *Supervision des Staates* (Suhrkamp 1997).

131 As to the manifold attempts to combine systemic approaches with actor-centered ones see Dietmar Braun, "Politische Steuerung zwischen System und Akteur" in S Lange and id (eds), *Politische Steuerung zwischen System und Akteure* (Leske + Budrich 2000).

132 Philipp Genschel and Bernhard Zangl, "Metamorphosen des Staates – vom Herrschaftsmonopolisten zum Herrschaftsmanager" (2008) 36 *Leviathan* 430.

"pilot,"[133] "mediator"[134] or moderator[135] or – at the very least a "supervisor"[136] – can guarantee a "controlled explosion"[137] in the "laboratory."

Therefore, we want to conclude our remarks with a statement made by Carl Gareis in 1910 on "the influence of inventions on legal development":

> Beneficial as the might of the fire are inventions, if the human being watches over them.[138]

133 Jan Ziekow, "Wirtschaft und Verwaltung vor den Herausforderungen der Zukunft: Auswirkung von Europäisierung und Globalisierung für die Wirtschaftsverwaltung" in id (ed), *Wirtschaft und Verwaltung vor den Herausforderungen der Zukunft* (Duncker & Humblot 2000) 33–4.

134 Steffen Augsberg, "Der Staat als Informationsmittler. Robin Hood oder Parasit der Wissensgesellschaft?" (2007) 122 *Deutsches Verwaltungsblatt* 733.

135 Margrit Seckelmann, "Keine Alternative zur Staatlichkeit – Zum Konzept der 'Global Governance'" (2007) 98 *Verwaltungsarchiv* 30, 53.

136 Willke (n 130).

137 Seckelmann (n 94) 124.

138 Carl Gareis, "Der Einfluß der Erfindungen auf die Rechtsentwicklung" (1910) 15 *Deutsche Juristen-Zeitung* 35, 41, translation by the author of this chapter.

3. "One size can fit all" – some heretical thoughts on the mass production of legal transplants

Ralf Michaels

3.1. INTRODUCTION

The World Bank likes global solutions. In the first of its annual "Doing Business" reports, it suggested that, in law reform, "one size can fit all – in the manner of business regulation."[1] What the Bank means is that best practices can be identified that would improve the legal system of every country, regardless of its legal and general culture, economic system, level of development, etc.[2] This idea – that what matters is the quality of a legal institution law determined in the abstract, not its fit – is widespread in business law reform, but not confined to this area. Recent studies on transfer of constitutional norms show similar developments. David Law and Mila Versteeg mention "generic rights" that exist in virtually all constitutional texts.[3]

This idea of "one size fits all" is a provocation for comparative lawyers.[4] The presumption that the success of legal transplants is

---

[1] International Financial Corporation (IFC) and World Bank, "Doing Business in 2004: Understanding Regulation" (2004) xvi.

[2] The report does suggest that underdeveloped countries should adopt simpler versions. See ibid xvi, xvii.

[3] David S Law and Mila Versteeg, "The Evolution and Ideology of Global Constitutionalism" (2011) 99 *California Law Review* 1163, 1199–2002.

[4] For a critique, see, especially, Kevin E Davis, "Legal Universalism: Persistent Objections" (2010) 60 *University of Toronto Law Journal* 537. For a summary of French reactions, see Anne-Julie Kerhuel and Bénédicte Fauvarque-Cosson, "Is Law an Economic Contest? French Reactions to the *Doing Business* World Bank Reports and Economic Analysis of Law" (2009) 57 *American Journal of Comparative Law* 811. The World Bank, in face of this pressure, later dropped the "one size fits all" idea.

independent of the conditions of the recipient countries runs against longstanding convictions in comparative law. Some of these convictions are empirical and theoretical: the inadequacy of viewing laws as mere words (law in action versus law in the books); the interplay between different legal rules within one legal system, the groundedness of all law in local legal culture. Others are ideological: an opposition against legal hegemonialism through Western laws and concepts, against a Western preference for formal rules over substantive justice.

In fact, amongst comparative lawyers, "one size fits all" has long been used as an ironic depiction of unsophisticated attempts at law reform that is to be rejected.[5] Another metaphor, similarly scathing, is "cut and paste"[6] – the (critical) observation that legal reformers merely copy textual bits and pieces from one constitution to another, with little regard for context. But the critique of comparatists has long been, to some extent, a matter of faith more than experience. We observe that universal solutions are in fact sought more and more – whether they fit or not. And if we took the "cut and paste" metaphor seriously, we would have to admit that it is not incompatible with context-specificity. When you choose "paste" in your word processing program, it will likely give you three options: "Keep source formatting; match destination formatting; keep text only." Transposed to legal transplants, we can not only try to implement rules in the same fashion in which they exist in the source country – which will likely yield strange results. We can also yield to the demands of comparatists and adapt the rule to the "formatting" of the destination country, so it will match indistinguishably. And, most mysteriously perhaps, we can also transfer rules as "text only" – and then they will, like a chameleon, suddenly become compatible with any new surroundings. How can we explain this?

---

[5] E.g. Randall Perenboom, "Toward a Methodology for Successful Legal Transplants" (2012), http://ssrn.com/abstract=1981887. But see also JP Verheul, "Così fan tutte," in K Boele-Woelki (ed), *Comparability and Evaluation: Essays on Comparative Law, Private International Law and International Commercial Arbitration in Honour of D. Kokkini-Iatridou* (M Nijhoff Publishers 1994).

[6] Richard Zajac Sannerholm, "'Cut-and-paste'? Rule of Law Promotion and Legal Transplants in War to Peace Transitions" in Antonina Bakardjieva Engelbrekt and Joakim Bergelius (eds), *New Directions in Comparative Law* (Edward Elgar 2009) 56; Michal Gal, "The 'Cut and Paste' of Article 82 of the EC Treaty in Israel: Conditions for a Successful Transplant" (2007) 9(3) *European Journal of Law Reform* 467; Holger Spamann, "Contemporary Legal Transplants: Legal Families and the Diffusion of (Corporate) Law" (2009) *Brigham Young Law Review* 1813, 1840, citing Kenneth L Karst and Keith Rosenn, *Law and Development in Latin America: A Case Book* (1975) 67.

We need a more sophisticated account, and here, Günter Frankenberg's recent work can help. Frankenberg takes the idea of "one size fits all" more seriously and develops a whole "IKEA theory of legal transplants" around it – though one that he views critically.[7] For Frankenberg, transplants do not take place directly between domestic systems; they are mediated through a global constitution. But that global constitution is not a real one. Instead, it is "a supermarket, where standardized constitutional items – grand designs as well as elementary particles of information – are stored and available, *pret-à-porter*, for purchase and reassemblage by constitution makers around the world."[8]

I sympathize with the comparatists' reservations about the one-size-fits-all idea. How could I not? But I think the critique is not only exaggerated but actually, in part, misdirected. This is so for several reasons. A first reason is that critics like proponents conflate a formalist and a functionalist understanding of law. However, whereas "one size fits all" is deficient as a functionalist position, it proves to be surprisingly successful as a formalist conception. A second reason is that the critique of legal transplants often insists on what can be called a "best law" approach, whereas in law reform, what we sometimes need is law that is just good enough. "One size fits all" will not create the best law, but it can sometimes create law that is good enough in situations in which a best law is not available. Just as IKEA brings affordable design into households that cannot afford tailor-made furniture, so a one-size-fits-all approach to law reform may create good-enough legal solutions that are at least as adequate for globalization as would be purely local rules. A third reason is that legal transplants no longer happen in isolation but rather on a global scale, a process that encourages formalization and standardization. Context-specific rules make sense as local rules only as long as the context remains local. Under conditions of globalization, such locality becomes questionable.

The chapter proceeds as follows. In section 3.2, I recapitulate Frankenberg's IKEA theory of legal transplants. In section 3.3, I put this theory into context by juxtaposing it with three theories of transplant –

---

[7] Günter Frankenberg, "Constitutional Transfer: The IKEA Theory Revisited" (2010) 8 *Journal of International Constitutional Law* 563; see already Günter Frankenberg, *Autorität und Integration: Zur Grammatik von Recht und Verfassung* (Suhrkamp 2003) 124–32; Günter Frankenberg, "Constitutions in Transfer – Territoriality and Extra-territoriality" in Gunther Handl, Joachim Zekoll, and Peer Zumbansen (eds), *Beyond Territoriality: Transnational Legal Authority in an Age of Globalization* (Brill 2012) 261, 278–83.

[8] Frankenberg, "IKEA Theory Revisited" (n 7) 565.

instrumentalism, culturalism, and formalism – and demonstrate that formalism, not functionalism, is most in accordance with it. In sections 3.4 and 3.5 I expand on the idea of an IKEA theory by comparing in more depth IKEA's success in the consumer market with the success of legal transplants. First, in section 3.4, I discuss standardization and economies of scale as factors of success. In section 3.5, I look at globalization as an underestimated element in transfer analyses. A short conclusion follows.

3.2. THE IKEA THEORY OF LEGAL TRANSPLANTS

It should be clear from the beginning: "One size fits all" is not just an innocently naïve view of law reform and of legal transplants. Behind the idea lie both a certain concept of law and a certain ideology of law reform. Most analysts view transplants as a two-stage process: a rule is taken from law A, and implemented in law B. Frankenberg, by contrast, helpfully unearths the implications involved in the one-size-fits-all approach as a multistage process that he borrows from Edward Said.[9] Instead of summarizing the theory, I want to represent it here both graphically and in a consecution of steps slightly different from the one Frankenberg draws himself.

In its original version, the IKEA theory includes four steps, but I find it more instructive to recreate the theory as a five-stage process. In the first stage, a legal rule is found in the specific context of a legal system and its underlying legal and political culture. The transfer from stage 1 to stage 2 represents a decontextualization of the rule. This includes three elements: rules are "reified as marketable commodities, then formalized, that is, stripped of their contextual meanings, and, finally, idealized as meaning what they are meant to mean and functioning in the way they are meant to function."[10] Here, the rule is still understood as belonging to legal system A, but this belonging is merely formal – the rule has no context-specific meaning. It can be called an empty rule.[11]

The step from stage 2 to 3 captures the transfer from the local to the global reservoir. Frankenberg, quite ingeniously, realizes that rules are

[9] Frankenberg, "IKEA Theory Revisited" (n 7) 570–76. For Said's own theory, see Edward Said, *The World, the Text, and the Critic* (Vintage 1983) 226–47.

[10] Ibid 571.

[11] Frankenberg, following Legrand, calls it a "propositional statement"; ibid 567.

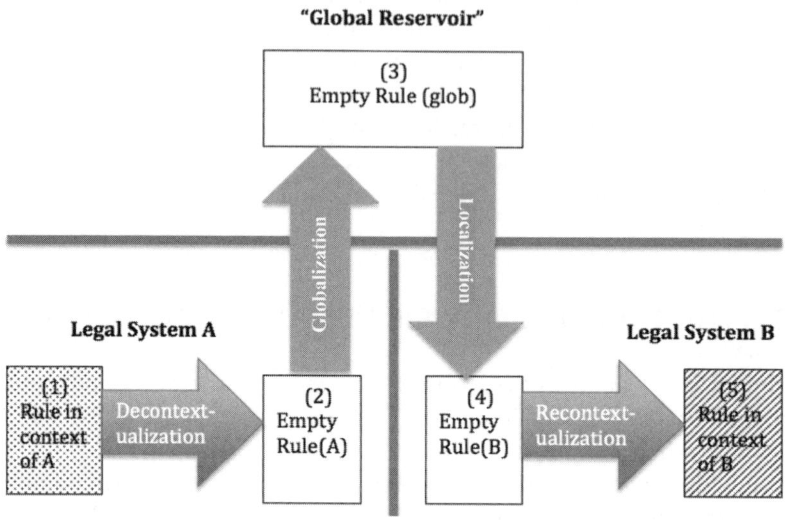

Figure 3.1 The IKEA Theory of Legal Transplants (after Frankenberg 2010)

rarely transferred directly from one system to another. Where they are identified as "best practices," they are no longer viewed as properly belonging to a legal system; they are part of "a reservoir or, for that matter, a supermarket, where standardized constitutional items – grand designs as well as elementary particles of information – are stored and available, *prêt-à-porter*, for purchase and reassemblage by constitution makers around the world."[12] As such, a rule belongs to no legal system; the legal rule can be transferred back into a different legal system B – the move from stage 3 to stage 4. As in stage 2, the rule may look as though it belongs to a legal system, but it is a mere empty rule without any contextual meaning. In fact, except for the formal integration into a new legal system, the legal rule looks no different in stage 4 than it did in stage 2 (or 3): its commodification enables it to travel.

Context-specific meaning is added in the contextualization which leads from stage 4 to 5. This last step, Frankenberg suggests, presents far greater risks than are usually acknowledged: rules may require complicated adaptations, reinterpretations, *bricolage*, and parts that make such adaptation possible may be missing. The recontextualization may or may not be successful. The rule may meet with resistance. It may be a bad fit

---

[12] Ibid 565.

for the new system. And it may face what Frankenberg, invoking his IKEA metaphor again, calls "the risk of 'missing links' – institutional parts, doctrinal screws, ideological hooks, and the like."[13] Recontextualization thus creates technical problems that are underplayed by law reformers. But recontextualization also creates ideological concerns. The foreign rule may function as an irritant, to use Gunther Teubner's term;[14] it may put considerable pressure on the recipient legal system. Such irritation can sometimes be desirable, as Wilhelmsson has argued with regard to pressures that EU law exerts on domestic law.[15] Even then, this is where the threat of hegemonialism and imperialism becomes most virulent.

There are, thus, three different critiques involved in the IKEA theory. The first of these, the one most familiar from the general literature, concerns recontextualization – the step from stage 4 to 5. Here, Frankenberg does not add much to what we already know in theory (though we do not always pay enough attention to it in practice) – the fact that law reformers are often insensitive to the actual requirements of the recipient country. A second critique is less common, though it too exists in the literature.[16] This is the critique concerning decontextualization, the step from stage 1 to 2. Here, Frankenberg draws on Legrand's critique against

---

[13] Ibid 575.

[14] Gunther Teubner, "Legal Irritants: Good Faith in British Law or How Unifying Law Ends Up in New Divergences" (1998) 61 *Modern Law Review* 11, 12.

[15] E.g. Thomas Wilhelmsson, "Private Law in the EU: Harmonised or Fragmented Europeanisation?" (2002) 1 *European Review of Private Law* 77, 91–3; cf. Ralf Michaels, "Why We Have No Theory of European Private Law Pluralism" in Leone Niglia (ed), *Pluralism and European Private Law* (Hart 2013) 139, 154.

[16] It has been made by Frankenberg before, too. In an early text, he already laid the foundation for his critique of the IKEA approach to transplants:

> How solutions can be "cut loose" from their context and at the same time be related to their environment, how law can be "seen purely" as [a] function satisfying a "particular" need escapes me. It seems to require two contradictory operations: first, suppressing the context and considering it; and then moving from the general (function) to the specific without knowing what makes the specific specific. The functionalist negates the interaction between legal institutions and provisions by stripping them from their systemic context and integrating them in an artificial universal typology of "solutions." In this way, "function" is reified as a principle of reality and not taken as an analytical principle that orders the real world. It becomes the magic carpet that shuttles us between the abstract and the concrete, that transcends the

Watson's theory of legal transplants, in particular the distinction between laws as text versus laws as propositional statements. The third critique is, I think, the most novel and the most illuminating. It concerns the steps between stages 2, 3, and 4, where a rule travels freely between (different) local levels and a global level. This travel is made possible by the commodification of the legal rule – treating it as a commodity that can be bought and sold in a global public market for laws.[17] Here, Frankenberg's critique is not merely practical, like that of many other opponents of legal transplants. Rather, it goes directly against the capitalist ideology underlying the "one-size-fits-all" approach.

3.3. INSTRUMENTALIST, CULTURALIST AND FORMALIST TRANSPLANTS

Frankenberg's critique of decontextualization as a step in the transplant process finds some inspiration in the so-called Watson-Legrand debate on legal transplants.[18] This provides a helpful framework for discussions of legal transplants, but I worry that the discussion is inexact in one important respect. Frankenberg, like Legrand and many others before him, criticizes Watson for both formalism and functionalism; he suggests, in fact, that functionalists should agree with Watson.[19] But such an

---

> boundaries of national legal concepts, that builds the system of comparative law, the "universal" comparative legal science or "the general law."

Günter Frankenberg, "Critical Comparisons: Re-thinking Comparative Law" (1985) 26 *Harvard Journal of International Law* 411, 440 (internal citation omitted).

[17] Ralf Michaels, "Make or Buy – A Public Market for Legal Transplants?" in Horst Eidenmüller (ed), *Regulatory Competition in Contract Law and Dispute Resolution* (Hart 2013).

[18] Frankenberg, "IKEA Theory Revisited" (n 7) 565–70. Alan Watson first presented his thesis in his *Legal Transplants* (1974), and in numerous iterations since. Pierre Legrand's reply is entitled "The Impossibility of 'Legal Transplants'" (1997) 4 *Maastricht Journal of European and Comparative Law* 111–24; republished without significant changes as Pierre Legrand, "What 'Legal Transplants'?" in David Nelken and Johannes Feest (eds), *Adapting Legal Cultures* (Hart 2001) 68. Alan Watson responded to Legrand in his Ius Commune Lecture: "Legal Transplants and European Private Law" (December 2000) 4(4) *Electronic Journal of Comparative Law*, http://www.ejcl.org/ejcl/44/44-2.html.

[19] Frankenberg, "IKEA Theory Revisited" (n 7) 569.

equation of formalism and functionalism, although not infrequent,[20] is problematic. When functionalism was developed as an approach to law, this happened in explicit opposition to formalism.[21] The critique against formalism is that it does not care about consequences, whereas the critique against functionalism is that it cares only about consequences. An approach that tries to be both functionalist and formalist would thus be internally contradictory. I therefore discuss first functionalism (and within it the variant most at play in the one-size-fits-all approach, namely instrumentalism), then the culturalist critique, and only at the end formalism.

3.3.1 The Instrumentalist Failure

Although both Legrand and Frankenberg direct their critique against Alan Watson's position, I think the main culprits, in their view, are law reform institutions like the World Bank and scholars like La Porta et al, who develop single best solutions for the problems of each society.[22] Such law reformers have an instrumentalist understanding of law; they view laws as means towards an end. Their approach has three elements. First, "law matters": law has predictable consequences on society. Second, those effects are, in principle, the same in any society. Third, based on this knowledge, law reformers can pick the best laws in order to bring such consequences about.

Note that, among the three elements of this approach, the first and the last are less controversial than the second. The first element, namely that law has an impact on society, can hardly be denied in general (though Alan Watson does deny it, at least for private law). The third, namely that law reformers can pick the best laws in order to bring about the best consequences, is more contentious, but still widely supported. Without this assumption, law reform would be futile. It is the second step – the

---

[20] Kerry Rittich, "Functionalism and Formalism: Their Latest Incarnations in Contemporary Development and Governance Debates" (2005) 55 *University of Toronto Law Journal* 853; Peer Zumbansen, "Law after the Welfare State: Formalism, Functionalism and the Ironic Turn of Reflexive Law" (2008) 56 *American Journal of Comparative Law* 769; also in Nils Jansen and Ralf Michaels (eds), *Beyond the State – Rethinking Private Law* (Mohr Siebeck 2008) 349.

[21] Felix S Cohen, "Transcendental Nonsense and the Functional Approach" (1935) 35 *Columbia Law Review* 809.

[22] Rafael La Porta et al, "The Economic Consequences of Legal Origins" (2008) 46 *Journal of Economic Literature* 285.

idea that laws yield the same outcomes anywhere, and that therefore one solution is the best for any society, that is the most problematic.

This is a kind of legal functionalism, even if that is not always said openly.[23] But it is a very peculiar kind of functionalism. First, in insisting that one solution fits the problems found in every legal situation, it ignores one core element of functionalism in comparative law, namely functional equivalence – the insight that, in different systems, different legal solutions may respond to similar problems.[24] Second, in viewing law as a tool, it represents a specific kind of functionalism, namely instrumentalism.[25] Functionalism takes an observer's perspective on the relation between institutions and societal needs; it incorporates also unrealized needs and unrealized ("latent") functions. Instrumentalism, by contrast, adopts a participant's need: here, the societal need is necessarily known, and a legal rule is aimed at responding to this need – whether successfully, or not. Third, although instrumentalism could develop different solutions for different societies, the one-size-fits-all approach, in proposing one solution for every society, must deny the relevance of context, or of the specific character of the legal problem to respond to. This is sometimes called the law of the hammer ("If all you have is a hammer, everything looks like a nail").[26]

3.2 The Culturalist Critique

Such a functionalist and instrumentalist understanding of law for legal transplants has often been criticized by comparative lawyers.[27] The most radical critique of transplants has been voiced by Pierre Legrand. In opposition to both functionalism and instrumentalism, Legrand represents what can be called a culturalist approach to legal transplants. He suggests

---

23 Ralf Michaels, "The Functionalism of Legal Origins" in Michael Faure and Jan Smits (eds), *Does Law Matter? On Law and Economic Growth* (100 Ius Commune Europaeum, Intersentia 2011) 21.

24 Ralf Michaels, "The Functional Method of Comparative Law" in Mathias Reimann and Reinhard Zimmermann (eds), *The Oxford Handbook of Comparative Law* (Oxford University Press 2008) 339, 376–8.

25 See ibid 351.

26 Cf. Abraham Kaplan, *The Conduct of Inquiry: Methodology for Behavioral Science* (Chandler Publishing Co 1964) 28–9 ("the law of the instrument"); cf. Abraham H Maslow, *The Psychology of Science* (1966) 15.

27 For a collection of such arguments, see Ralf Michaels, "Comparative Law by Numbers? Legal Origins Thesis, *Doing Business* Reports, and the Silence of Traditional Comparative Law" (2009) 57 *American Journal of Comparative Law* 765.

that legal transplants are both impossible and undesirable. His main argument is that rules are inseparably connected with their local/national culture and society and thus cannot be taken out of one society and transplanted to another without losing, or changing, their meaning. Moreover, Legrand argues, transplants need to be rejected vigorously because they threaten the integrity of legal cultures.

Legrand's thesis is sometimes viewed as exaggerated but generally sound, at least among comparative lawyers. And indeed, Legrand's suggestion that law is cultural fits well our desire in comparative law to focus on law in action rather than in the books, and to see law in context. We know (or we think we know) that legal rules alone do not do much work, that the real life of the law is in its interaction with society and culture.

We should note, however, a certain inconsistency between the two critiques. Recall that Legrand voices two arguments against the transplant theory: first, they are impossible (thus the title of his article); second, they are to be rejected because they lead to undesirable outcomes. Actually, these two arguments are inconsistent:[28] something cannot be without an effect and harmful at the same time. Either legal cultures are robust, then transplants are impossible. Or, legal transplants do change cultures, then they cannot be impossible.

This suggests two weaknesses in the culturalist critique of legal transplants. The first concerns the object of critique, in particular the conflation of functionalist and formalist conceptions. One part of Legrand's critique is directed against a formalist understanding of legal rules as mere propositional statement, which, precisely because they have no meaning, have no impact on society. Another part of his critique, by contrast, is directed against an instrumentalist understanding, which is aimed at having an impact on society.

The other weakness is the underlying assumption of legal cultures as relatively isolated entities. In reality, we can see that legal rules often receive their meaning, in part, from inspiration by foreign legal systems. This is so not only where comparative law is used explicitly – a strategy that culturalists regard with justifiable suspicion.[29] It is also true where societies have forgotten that they once borrowed both an institution and its underlying rationale. One example is the concept of "militant

---

[28] As has been noted by Annelise Riles, "Comparative Law and Socio-Legal Studies" in *The Oxford Handbook of Comparative Law* (n 24) 775.

[29] Pierre Legrand, "Comparative Legal Studies and the Matter of Authenticity" (2006) 1 Journal of Comparative Law 365, 404–25.

democracy"– developed by Loewenstein after his emigration in the US context, and later imported into Germany.[30]

3.3 The Formalist Challenge

Now, insofar as the culturalist critique is directed against instrumentalism, it does not apply to Watson's thesis. Watson's thesis is not that laws are transplanted as instruments to improve society. Rather, he suggests that a connection with society is irrelevant. Laws are transplanted all the time; over centuries and between vastly different societies. Chinese, Ecuadorian and French rules on minute details of contract law are almost verbatim, despite the great differences between societies.

It is usually overlooked that Watson – in that sense in perfect agreement with Legrand – is explicitly antifunctionalist and anti-instrumentalist. He suggests, repeatedly, that legal transplants do not matter. This is so because, in his view, law – at least private law – does not matter. To go back to the IKEA theory, because Watson denies any relevance of context for legal rules, he would deny that stage 1 plays any role – and, consequently, also that stage 5 could play any role. His focus is only on the transitions between stages 2 and 4. Legrand, by contrast, focuses only on a direct transition from stage 1 to stage 5 and thus, because he ignores stages 2 to 4, considers transplants impossible. Neither of them offers a meaningful concept of translation.

This seems, at first, an uninteresting theory. Watson has little to offer, it appears, beyond the observation that rules as mere propositional statements are borrowed and transferred all the time. His suggestion that legal rules are detached from society seems extreme, even if (as Bill Ewald suggests)[31] it is an implication and not a precondition of his views on transplants, leaving us only with a negative but not independent theory of law. And his project – to look at texts of rules regardless of their purpose or impact – seems, intellectually and aesthetically, deeply unattractive.

The theory gets more exciting, however, if we view it in light of the IKEA theory. Since neither functionalism nor formalism can explain the "empty rule" element of that theory, it seems Watson's formalism seems most compatible both with theory in the form of the IKEA theory and with experience. When laws are transferred, they are transferred as mere forms, largely devoid of meaning. They receive their meaning in the local

---

[30] See also Markus Thiel (ed), *The "Militant Democracy" Principle in Modern Democracies* (Ashgate 2009).

[31] William Ewald, "Comparative Jurisprudence (II): The Logic of Legal Transplants" (2005) 43 *American Journal of Comparative Law* 489, 502–3.

context, but they retain their denationalized, abstract character. They do represent "propositional statements," but, amazingly, as such they suddenly transcend national contexts and therefore are able to travel.

This phenomenon is looked down upon in traditional legal scholarship, which has become profoundly antiformalist. But such disdain for form is not shared by other disciplines, especially (legal) anthropology. Marilyn Strathern has suggested the constraint of form as a valid object of ethnographic analysis,[32] as known from anthropology, in particular from science and technology studies. Bruno Latour has suggested that standardized forms make it possible, effectively, to travel far without leaving home: the form is capable of traveling and of referencing its origin, without the need to carry meaning with it.[33] Annelise Riles has applied such insights to legal anthropology. In her ethnology of financial markets, she finds that forms and documents are what is transplanted and what keeps global law together – complex legal documents with no relevance other than their symbolic role.[34]

Indeed, it seems fruitful to view the empty rules that travel so easily, detached from any contextual meaning, less as propositional statements, and more as artifacts.[35] Fuchs praises artifacts for much the same things that legal transplants are supposed to accomplish: they "make little room for skepticism, especially when they generate rather predictable uniform outcomes across a variety of settings, occasions, times or operating personnel."[36] It is their character as artifacts that enables rules to travel. And it is that character that enables their commodification, too.

---

[32] Marilyn Strathern, *The Gender of the Gift: Problems with Women and Problems with Society in Melanesia* (University of California Press 1988) 180–82.

[33] Bruno Latour, *Science in Action: How to Follow Scientists and Engineers through Society* (Harvard University Press 1987); see also, e.g., Stefan Timmermans and Marc Berg, "Standardization in Action: Achieving Local Universality through Medical Protocols" (1987) *Social Studies of Science* 273.

[34] Annelise Riles, "The Anti-Network – Private Global Governance, Legal Knowledge, and the Legitimacy of the State" (2008) 56 *American Journal of Comparative Law* 605, and in Jansen and Michaels (n 20) 183.

[35] Annelise Riles (ed), *Documents – Artifacts of Modern Knowledge* (2006).

[36] Stephan Fuchs, *Against Essentialism: A Theory of Culture and Society* (2001) 306.

3.4. IKEA REVISITED 1: ECONOMIES OF SCALE IN LAW REFORM

This may explain how one size fits all, and the IKEA theory presupposes the possibility of a purely formal understanding of legal rules, of rules as artifacts. But how can "one size fits all" work? It is worth going back to Frankenberg's IKEA metaphor and expanding on it, maybe taking it more seriously even than its creator. I want to look at what makes IKEA so successful in the marketplace, and what we can learn from this for legal transplants. I do this in two steps – first by focusing on local consequences, then on global ones.

3.4.1 Standardization and Adaptation as Complementary Strategies

When companies go global (as IKEA has), they have, it is often said, two alternative possible strategies.[37] One is *adaptation* to local contexts – the willingness to sell, in each country, products tailor-made for that country. In comparative law, adaptation seems most analogous to calls to make legal transplants fit the respective local context. But whereas such adaptation is often viewed as the only possible strategy for legal transplants, in international marketing, a different strategy has proven popular, too. That strategy is *standardization*. Here, the idea is to establish a worldwide standard that can be used for every country. The great advantage of standardization lies mainly in cost efficiency: research and development costs are reduced (because fewer products need to be developed); large numbers of its product for worldwide markets enable economies of scale; global marketing strategies enhance the value of the brand. This approach is analogous to universalism in comparative law.[38] Notably, because the standard is not, ideally, drawn from one background

---

[37] John K Ryans Jr, David A Griffith, and D Steven White, "Standardizations/Adaptations of International Marketing Strategy: Necessary Conditions for the Advancement of Knowledge" (2003) 20 *International Marketing Review* 588; Marios Theodosiou and Leonidas C Leonidou, "Standardization versus Adaptation of International Marketing Strategy: An Integrative Assessment of the Empirical Research" (2003) 13 *International Business Review* 141.

[38] Mark Tushnet, "Some Reflections on Method in Comparative Constitutional Law" in Sujit Choudhry (ed), *The Migration of Constitutional Ideas* (Cambridge University Press 2006) 67, 69–72; cf. Ran Hirshl, "On the Blurred Methodological Matrix of Comparative Constitutional Law" in Choudhry 39, 43–6 ("concept formation through multiple description"); Günter Frankenberg, "Stranger than Paradise: Identity and Politics in Comparative Law" (1997) *Utah Law Review* 259, 264–5.

but instead incorporates worldwide differences, such a strategy can be successful, too.

IKEA's global strategy is clearly one of standardization.[39] IKEA's official business idea is "to offer a wide range of well-designed, functional home furnishing products at prices so low that as many people as possible will be able to afford them."[40] Billy, the famous bookshelf, has been sold at least 41 million times worldwide.[41] IKEA products fit in a vast variety of places. And we find the same products, by and large, in Sweden, the United States, and Hong Kong – an extreme standardization of products. Although IKEA does offer slightly different products in different countries, the layout of its stores is the same everywhere, and many of its most successful products can be bought anywhere in the world. Such standardization extends even to standards of quality, efficiency, and socially responsible behavior[42] – in a sense, IKEA comes with its own IKEA law. IKEA's "one size fits all" is not accidental; it follows a deliberate company strategy.

This global success is made possible by a second element: the quality and style of IKEA products. IKEA products are relatively durable. Moreover, they are not completely without style. In its early days, IKEA sold what we foreigners took to be Swedish design. Later, IKEA adopted – aped, one might say – other styles, became more minimalist in its design, and indeed often looked like a cheap copy of "real" design.

---

39 This has been established in several Swedish university theses; see, e.g., Damien Badier and Carole Rousset, "Strategies Adopted in the International Market – The Case of IKEA in France" (Bachelor Thesis, University of Skövde, 2007); David Eskander and Mohamed Kotaiba Abdul Aal, "Does IKEA Culture Apply Abroad? A Study of IKEA in Saudi Arabia" (Master's Thesis, Karlstad University, 2010); Sofiya Gilyazova and Alina Gogunova, "IKEA and Volvo Marketing Strategies in the Italian Market" (Jönköping International Business School, Spring 2012). Standardization is not absolute; IKEA also adapts to local circumstances: Ulf Johansson and Åsa Thelander, "A Standardised Approach to the World? IKEA in China" (2009) 1 *International Journal of Quality and Service Sciences* 199.

40 http://inter.ikea.com/en/about-us/purpose.

41 "Billy, the World's Most Versatile Bookcase Turns 30!" (2009), http://www.ikea.com/ms/en_CA/img/pdf/Billy_Anniv_en.pdf, 2, 7.

42 Suzanne Konzelmann, Frank Wilkinson, Charles Craypo, and Rabih Aridi, "The Export of National Varieties of Capitalism: The Cases of Wal-Mart and IKEA" in Wolfram Elsner and Hardy Hanappi (eds), *Varieties of Capitalism and New Institutional Deals: Regulation, Welfare and the New Economy* (Edward Elgar 2008) 123.

Today, one might well speak of a distinct IKEA style. Of course, this is a strange style, reminiscent of the bizarre imaginary buildings on Euro notes – a style that suggests a number of local references but remains strangely ephemeral, placeless, global. It is, in Frankenberg's words, decontextualized. But it would not be successful if it were genuinely decontextualized. By contrast, a large part of IKEA's success derives from its presentation as genuinely Swedish[43] – it uses the national colors, Swedish names for its products, Swedish dishes in its cafeterias. This Swedishness may be an idealization – "bereft of its local, theoretical, and doctrinal elaborations and controversies." We now know that some of the genuinely Swedish furniture was actually produced by political prisoners in East Germany.[44] But, in the end, this matters little to consumers.

The same seems to be true of legal transplants. A globalized rule may, in substance, be stripped of any link to the national context from which it once emerged. But it will not be successful unless it appears to be "from somewhere" – for example, the Torrens system of land registration from Australia (though it may in reality emerge from Hamburg).[45]

3.4.2 "Best Solutions" and "Good Enough Solutions"

Such standardization will, of course, never create optimal furniture. IKEA products will never represent the same quality as high-price furniture. Nor will they ever fit their surroundings as well as tailor-made furniture pieces would. What makes them so successful in the world are two additional characteristics that play a role in law reform as well: their price is low, and customers can assemble them on their own. Now, in law reform, price is rarely considered: we care about quality and disregard,

---

[43] http://www.ikea.com/ms/en_US/about_ikea/the_ikea_way/swedish_heritage.

[44] "Ikea Admits Forced Labor Was Used in 1980s" *New York Times*, 18 November 2012; see also "Ikea – Die Legende vom ehrlichen Möbelhaus" *Der Spiegel*, Issue 51, 17 December 2012.

[45] Antonio Esposito, "Ulrich Hübbe's Role in the Creation of the 'Torrens' System of Land Registration in South Australia" (2003) 24 *Adelaide Law Review* 263; Esposito, "A Comparison of the Australian ('Torrens') System of Land Registration of 1858 and the Law of Hamburg in the 1850s" (2003) 7 *Australian Journal of Legal History* 193; Horst Lücke, "Ulrich Hübbe and the Torrens System: Hübbe's German Background, his Life in Australia and his Contribution to the Creation of the Torrens System" (2009) 30 *Adelaide Law Review* 213; for a critique of the thesis, see also Greg Taylor, "Is the Torrens System German?" (2008) 29 *Journal of Legal History* 253; Taylor, "The Torrens System – Definitely not German" (2010) 30(2) *Adelaide Law Review* 195.

more often than not, what such law reform costs and how easily it is implemented.[46] But of course law reform is not costless. Good tailor-made law reform requires great expertise on the specific societal and institutional conditions for which a law is made. Obviously, where such expertise is available, tailor-made law reform can be successful. Often, however, sufficient expertise is lacking in the recipient country of law reform, and law reformers from the first world cannot substitute for it. Undoubtedly, the first world law reformer with insufficient interest in the recipient country will not bring about good reforms; he will try to replicate his home law, and fail. But the context-sensitive law reformer will often fail as well, realizing, at the same time, the need to go native and her inability to do so.[47]

It may seem crude to present the problems of interculturality and transplants in mere economic terms as costs. But ultimately, this is one way in which they materialize. First world law reformers would undoubtedly provide better service if they were schooled in the culture and law of the recipient country for several years. Law reformers in the recipient country would benefit from multi-year interdisciplinary studies in comparative law. Law reform would be easier if lawyers in recipient countries were paid higher salaries and had access to more legal materials. But, in the end, the costs of all of this would be prohibitive – or, at least, law reform institutions are not willing to provide for them.

And it may also be idealistic to ask that all these resources be spent to create a perfect law, when in reality the resources are not available. IKEA may be ultracapitalist, but its project to offer furniture that is both functional and affordable has progressive roots in the Bauhaus and its effort to bring quality not just to the rich few but to the masses. If we want to achieve the same for law reform, then we may want to learn from the Bauhaus and from IKEA that perfect law reform, in the sense of providing a perfect fit, may not be what is necessary. To take an example from the current work of the World Bank,[48] it may not be clear how the regulation of access to electricity for small businesses should be handled. Under some circumstances, a one-stop-shop solution, in which only one comprehensive application is handed to one authority, which is then responsible for dealing with all the other relevant authorities, may be preferable. Under other circumstances, it may be preferable for the applicant to be in charge of dealing with several relevant authorities

---

46 See also Michaels (n 17).

47 Frankenberg, "IKEA Theory Revisited" (n 7) 266–70.

48 IFC and World Bank, *Getting Electricty: A Pilot Study by the Doing Business Project* (2010).

individually. It seems clear, however, that a situation in which applicants have to deal with 27 authorities and need an average 233 days to be connected is deficient. In such a situation, it may not make much sense to wait until a perfect, tailor-made legal solution is established. It may be more helpful to develop a "best practice" – an IKEA-like cheap solution that fits, relatively well, most contexts – that provides a solution that is not a "best solution" but that is "good enough."

3.4.3 The Adaptability of Formal Solutions

Something more is relevant. As a matter of fact, the thought that laws must necessarily be tailor-made for the societies in which they should perform is somewhat unrealistic. It rests on an ultimately romantic idea of a perfect fit between law and society.[49] But just as people have, since time immemorial, imported their furniture from foreign countries and then put it to use in their homes, so legal transplants can come from afar and be put to new use in a new home. Laws cannot meaningfully be reduced to propositional statements, that much is true. At the same time, the fact that laws come in the form of words means that they can remain a constant source of reference that enables alterations in meaning.[50]

And sometimes laws that are *more* formal, less rich in intrinsic meaning, less "odd,"[51] are actually to be preferred – not just because they travel more easily, but also because they are more open to changes in meaning within one society. It is true, as critics of transplants have pointed out, that legal rules will often acquire a different meaning in the recipient country than they do in the donor country. An attempt to replicate the meaning and effects from the donor country in the recipient country is thus doomed to fail. But it seems to me that especially those who insist on the context-sensitivity of legal rules should then praise those legal rules that can acquire different meanings in different contexts. If we find the same IKEA shelves and tables in student apartments, designer lofts, coffee bars, and entrance lounges, this suggests their flexibility, their ability to function differently in different contexts.

---

[49] Thus the friendly critique by James Q Whitman, "The Neo-Romantic Turn" in Pierre Legrand and Roderick Munday (eds), *Comparative Legal Studies: Traditions and Transitions* (Cambridge University Press 2003) 312.

[50] Cf., in a different context, H Jefferson Powell, "Parchment Matters: A Meditation on the Constitution as Text" (1985) 71 *Iowa Law Review* 1427.

[51] Cf. Frankenberg, "IKEA Theory Revisited" (n 7) 572–4.

And then, of course, even IKEA furniture need not necessarily remain the same. One new emergent trend is IKEA hacking.[52] People take IKEA furniture and assemble it differently from the producer's intention. And then they share their new constructions on the internet and can thus inspire other users.[53] Such creative re-use may not be favored by IKEA – just as the creative re-use of legal rules in a recipient country may not be what the donor country intended. But it may well serve the needs of the recipient country.

3.5. IKEA REVISITED 2: TAKING GLOBALIZATION SERIOUSLY

So far, I have assumed that legal rules travel from one legal system to another. This leaves out what Frankenberg calls the global constitution – the global reservoir from which solutions can be dispatched to very different contexts. It is a major achievement of his theory to account for globalization, since any theory of legal transplants that ignores globalization must remain deficient.

3.5.1 Global Product Lines

The first aspect is not strictly one of globalization but can most fruitfully be discussed here. One element that guarantees IKEA's success is that it offers matching pieces. IKEA furniture may not match its new surroundings perfectly, but in return it will match other pieces from IKEA. IKEA pieces are not just individual; they are part of a whole series. The purchaser of a chair from a series knows that he can also buy a table and a shelf from IKEA that will match the chair.

The same is true of law reform. Take, for example, law reform for OHADA, the organization of French-speaking countries in Africa.[54] Here, a new, and Western-inspired contract code may not immediately match African peculiarities (though contract law has proven remarkably

---

[52] Daniela Rosner and Jonathan Bean, "Learning from IKEA Hacking: 'I'm Not One to Decoupage a Tabletop and Call It a Day'" (2009) *CHI '09 Proceedings of the SIGCHI Conference on Human Factors in Computing Systems* 419–22. I thank Rebecca Myers for alerting me to the practice of IKEA hacking.

[53] E.g. www.ikeahackers.net.

[54] Claire M Dickerson, "Harmonizing Business Laws in Africa: OHADA Calls the Tune" (2005) 44 *Columbia Journal of Transnational Law* 17.

adaptable to local circumstances). But it matches other law reform projects, also inspired by Western laws: corporate codes, bankruptcy codes, etc. It is not clear, a priori, which match is more important.

This has at least two consequences. For the global reservoir of legal rules, it means that its rules do not stand in isolation from each other. Rather, the global reservoir becomes attractive as a package solution. And for the legal system, it results in what is sometimes called bricolage:[55] an amalgam of legal rules, often from different contexts, fitting sometimes the local context, sometimes the global reservoir of legal rules. A romantic understanding of legal systems as coherent would be alarmed by such a result. But arguably, bricolage represents quite well the situation of postmodern law. Legal systems display internal inconsistencies as a consequence not just of globalization and legal transplants but also of conflicting internal rationalities. Legal transplants are thus not only a cause of internal fragmentation, they are also in accordance with such fragmentation as a typical feature of current law.

3.5.2 Transformation

This is not all. Ali Yakhlef, a scholar teaching in Sweden, has suggested – using IKEA as his example – that adaptation and standardization are not the only alternatives for international strategy.[56] In fact, both adaptation and standardization suffer from the same shortcomings: they assume that local contexts are a given that global companies have to accept as it is. (We see similar shortcomings in comparative law, where legal culture is often viewed as static and immune to change.[57]) In reality, however, global companies do change local circumstances, and they often do so quite deliberately. In China, consumers are not used to assembling their furniture themselves. Yet rather than give up its cost-efficient do-it-yourself approach, IKEA is teaching the Chinese how to assemble

---

[55] Mark Tushnet, "The Possibilities of Comparative Constitutional Law" (1999) 108 *Yale Law Journal* 1225, 1229; Michele Graziadei, "Legal Transplants and the Frontiers of Legal Knowledge" (2009) 10 *Theoretical Inquiries in Law* 693, 694.

[56] Ali Yakhlef, "The Trinity of International Strategy: Adaptation, Standardization and Transformation" (2010) 9 *Asian Business & Management* 47.

[57] Ralf Michaels, "Legal Culture" in Jürgen Basedow, Klaus Hopt and Reinhard Zimmermann (eds), *Max Planck Encyclopedia of European Private Law* (Oxford University Press 2012) 1060.

their furniture. Thus, instead of adapting the product (and its assembly) to the context, IKEA is adapting – transforming – the context to its product.[58]

Yakhlef suggests that it is therefore necessary to add a third strategy, that of transformation. This may be novel for global marketing, but it is well known in the context of legal transplants. After all, transformation is an explicit goal of law reform. Where Western institutions support law reform, they invariably do so in the hope of changing society: they want to secularize and democratize it; they want to increase the protection of human rights or the rule of law; they want to bring about economic prosperity. If transplants alter legal cultures, this is often desired.

Of course, such transformation is problematic, both empirically and normatively. Empirically, transformation through law reform was largely unsuccessful in the first wave of law and development; whether the current wave can be more successful remains to be seen.[59] Normatively, such transformation smacks of Western hegemonialism and parochialism: either Westerners know better what is right for developing countries, or, worse, they try to transform those countries for their own benefit.[60]

However, such a story may again be too bleak. Or, rather, it may be apt for the instrumentalist but not for the formalist concept of legal transplants. Formal legal rules may occasionally transform societies in ways that we find quite desirable. Or, put more appropriately, they may provide societies with instruments that help them to transform themselves. Rather than impose new and foreign concepts on a society, such law reform may provide the powerless with new tools to challenge those in power. Thus, Sally Merry reports how women in India use human rights in what has effectively become a fragmented legal system in order to tap into a discourse that strengthens their position – often without having a clear idea of what human rights actually are.[61]

---

58 Yakhlef (n 56) 58–9.

59 Kevin E Davis and Michaels J Trebilcock, "The Relationship between Law and Development: Optimists versus Skeptics" (2008) 56 *American Journal of Comparative Law* 895.

60 James Q Whitman, "Western Legal Imperialism" (2009) 10 *Theoretical Inquiries in Law* 635.

61 Sally Engle Merry, *Human Rights and Gender Violence: Translating International Law into Local Justice* (Chicago University Press 2006).

3.5.3 Globalization

The insight that transplants enable recipients of legal rules to tap into a global discourse leads to a final aspect of globalization. If IKEA transforms Chinese culture by teaching the Chinese to assemble their own furniture, it thereby also helps make Chinese culture less genuinely Chinese (if such genuineness were ever possible in the first place) and more global. What IKEA creates, through standardization and transformation, is a global IKEA culture.

The same seems to be true in law reform. Frankenberg, in developing his IKEA theory, explicitly ignores, "if only for the time being," the idea of a global constitution as an actual body of legal rules;[62] in his presentation the global constitution is a mere reservoir that feeds the "real" legal systems. In the end, even on his own terms, this seems insufficiently informed by globalization. The idea of legal transplants between legal systems A and B, whether direct or mediated through a global constitution, still suggests that legal systems A and B remain distinct entities. In reality, they no longer are (if they ever were). Even in developed countries, constitutions are now more and more in interaction with those of other countries. This is even more so in less developed countries, the most frequent recipients of constitutional transplants. There may not be an actual global constitution – what we find is at best a somewhat loose network. And yet, the existence of this network makes it seem inadequate to treat national constitutions as self-sufficient entities, just as though the network were no more than an add-on.

The global character of the "reservoir of rules" that Frankenberg describes as his stage 3 is thus mirrored by the global character of the emerging world of national constitutions. The uniformity offered by the warehouse bot presupposes and results in, unsurprisingly, a uniformity of emerging constitutional texts. Frankenberg is correct to point out that this uniformity is only superficial – below the propositional level, meanings of seemingly similar legal rules and concepts can differ dramatically from one context to the next. But he seems to assume that these differences exist, largely, between, not within, national legal systems. In reality, however, it seems that the uniformity of the propositional level has helped spur a truly global discussion on legal concepts, and that, as a consequence, similarities of meaning exist no longer predominantly within national legal systems, but often also transcend such contexts. Whether constitutions could remain separate if their texts looked very

---

62 Frankenberg, "IKEA Theory Revisited" (n 7) 564–5.

different is an open question. But once their texts look similar, increased interaction among them appears almost inevitable. The global constitution is no longer just a reservoir or a supermarket; it is also an emerging network of local constitutions and actors.

We may, of course, oppose globalization, including legal globalization, because we believe that it facilitates the exploitation of developing countries. By installing laws in these countries that are made more for Western investors than for indigenous needs, we prioritize the interests of global commerce over those of indigenous culture. Pierre Legrand's critique of legal transplant undoubtedly has such a culturalist and anticapitalist bent. But we should be aware that such attempts to protect local cultures can also be paternalistic and thus, in an ironic way, hegemonialist as well. Developing countries depend on investment, and it seems questionable whether we even can, let alone should, try to isolate them from globalization and thereby from investors.

6. CONCLUSION

Let there be no doubt – the IKEA theory, just like its inspiration the furniture producer, is both an emanation and an accelerator of global capitalism. Legal transplants in the IKEA theory mode not only increase global flows of legal rules; they also help turn laws into commodities. One may therefore argue that they represent everything that we fear about globalization: they threaten to help exploit developing countries. They are often as lopsided as the legal systems in the developed countries from which they are borrowed, focusing on the liberalization of markets rather than social welfare, on negative rights rather than positive rights and access, on overall economic efficiency rather than substantive equality and justice.

Regardless of one's normative position, however, it seems necessary for understanding, let alone critique, to have an adequate understanding of the processes of legal transplantation. Analytically, the IKEA theory seems to me to provide a very helpful structure for analyzing legal transplant processes. The theory is superior to other models not just because it focuses on the transplant from one system to another, but also because it includes de- and recontextualization. It is superior also because, by introducing a global level, it transcends the mere horizontal relation between legal systems and thus makes it possible to properly conceptualize the current "one-size-fits-all" revival in comparative law. If the theory has one descriptive deficiency, then maybe it is that it does not take the globality of current law sufficiently seriously, that it still insists too much, for conceptual analysis, on treating national legal systems as distinct.

As regards our critique of current practice of legal transplants, however, I think we must be wary of misunderstanding the phenomenon we are dealing with. There exists, of course, a naïve instrumentalism or functionalism in law reform that deserves criticism. However, what emerges from the IKEA theory as a much more powerful agent of global legal change is not functionalism but formalism. Rules that are tied to one legal function will be ineffective in societies with different functional needs; their transplant is often a waste of time and resources, but not much more. The truly powerful rules are those formal rules that, precisely because they carry so little inherent meaning, can become active in very different legal systems – and, at the same time, link different legal systems to each other.

What we are observing, under conditions of globalization, is a move towards more formal, less context-specific legal rules. This new formalism is not a neoliberal strategy or ideology; it is a consequence of a globalizing world, in which the creation of meaning and context is no longer a national affair, and in which a fragmented society makes rules with fixed and unitary meaning impossible – on any level, whether global, national, or local. In the face of this, insisting on the cultural specificity and locality of legal rules, as we comparative lawyers are used to doing, may be both romantic and elitist. It may be romantic because it overestimates local cultures – their localness, their persistence, their desirability. And it may be elitist because it suggests that only best law solutions are good enough. If we comparative lawyers want to be relevant, we must take the return to form and standardization seriously. And we may, grudgingly, have to admit that Alan Watson is not, in the end, as uninteresting as we make him out to be.

PART II

Ordering gender – comparing the casting and recasting of women and gender relations in constitutional contexts

4. Gender structures and constitutional law

Helena Alviar García

In the last four decades, countries around the world have drafted new constitutions and created new government institutions and laws. As a matter of fact, more than half of all written constitutions in the world were made after 1974.[1]

From a traditional perspective, there is a convergence in global constitution-making processes. According to this view, most contemporary constitutions include a similar vocabulary and basic values such as fundamental freedoms, human rights, and separation of powers. In addition, and due to international trends and treaties which are a product of globalization, most constitutions have included gender equality provisions.

Günter Frankenberg in the introduction to this book describes this mainstream interpretation of constitution-making in the following terms:

> What reads like one of the many narratives of globalization focuses on the fact that the modern constitutional idiom, though always geared toward and entangled in a specific local or regional and historical context, has proliferated worldwide, with liberal constitutionalism holding a hegemonic position. This (not all that innocent) narrative may be referred to as the globalization of the modern idiom creating a "global constitution." … However, in its flat, one-dimensional version, this narrative has very little to say about how such globalization happens, what happens when globalization happens, and whether it is challenged by glocalization – alternatives to the liberal-western paradigm.[2]

---

[1] Kristin Van der Leest, "Engendering Constitutions: Gender Equality Provisions in Selected Constitutions" http://www.unifem.sk/uploads/doc/Constitutional%20publication%20Nov%2020071.pdf, accessed 12 November 2012.

[2] Günter Frankenberg, "Constitutions as Commodities: Notes on a Theory of Transfer," in this volume.

An example of this style of analysis is Kristin Van der Leest in her study: "Engendering Constitutions: Gender Equality Provisions in Selected Constitutions." Her paper groups gender issues in constitutions if they form part of different sections of the constitution in the following form:

(1) *Preamble*: Preamble/Founding Principles;
(2) *Civil and Political Rights*: Citizenship and/or Nationality Provisions; Gender Equality Provisions; Discrimination Clauses; Equality before the Law; Positive/Affirmative Action Provisions; Political Participation; Rights of Women; Right of Association;
(3) *Economic, Social and Cultural Rights*: Employment Equality/Equal Pay for Equal Work; Marriage/Family/Pregnancy; Children/Abortion; Religious/Customary Law; Right to Property/Inheritance;
(4) *International Responsibilities/Oversight Mechanisms/Customary Law*: International Treaty Obligations; Remedial and Oversight Mechanisms; States of Emergency/Non-Derogability of Human Rights.[3]

When taking into account this division, many contemporary constitutions include the objective of achieving gender equality. In some cases, there is a clause that establishes it directly and in other cases it is combined with a non-discrimination provision. In addition, the goal of gender equality is not only achieved through a specific clause but also through the establishment of both general affirmative action provisions and specific clauses that promote political participation.

Although it is not my intention in this introduction to provide a detailed account of how equality is understood in constitutions worldwide, it is worthwhile pointing out that another recurring factor is the linking of gender equality to marriage, family and protection during pregnancy. These provisions mostly state that women have the right to have special protection from the state when they are pregnant, and that marriage entails the equal sharing of responsibilities.

A different perspective, which brings more depth into the analysis, is the one proposed in the book: Comparative Constitutional Law, Gender Equality and Constitutional Design.[4] In it the different chapters analyze the issue of gender equality not only according to where in the constitution it is included (which is the Van der Leest proposal) but according to

---

3 Van der Leest (n 1).

4 Susan H Williams, *Constituting Equality: Gender Equality and Comparative Law* (Cambridge University Press 2009); see the chapter "Comparative Constitutional Law, Gender Equality and Constitutional Design."

what institutional design promotes greater gender equality, which conceptual understanding of rights provides powerful tools and how the interaction between culture, religion and equality as well as the relationship between constitutional provisions and international law limit or give force to gender equality provisions.[5] Along these lines Ruth Rubio Marín presents in Chapter 6 yet another style: in her thick description of abortion decisions in Germany and Portugal she compares how normative visions of women underlying the arguments of the judges have traveled and changed from Germany to Portugal.

A first conclusion that one could draw from these two styles of analysis would be that there have been enormous advances around the globe in terms of gender equality. Nevertheless, the objective of the chapters included in this volume is to provide a different take on this interpretation of how constitutional provisions travel: one that doesn't flatly look at where they are situated or what institutional design and interaction benefits them more, but rather a view that brings in the dynamics of transfer. Professor Frankenberg announces the objective in the following terms:

> Transfer appears to qualify as an even more ecumenical concept … Both migration and transfer refer to movements, capture a wider variety of uses than, say, transplant or borrowing, and qualify such movements as problematic … rather than socially easy, as artificial rather than natural or organic. As distinct from migration, transfer also is more open to the varieties of conscious and unconscious import-exports over spatial, temporal, social, and cultural distances and differences. Moreover, the concept captures the compactness of the transferred information, its commodification … The overall focus will be on pathways … sites and modalities of transfer, and on results, risks and side effects as well as on the inclusion in or exclusion from the repertoire – the IKEA market center – that can be tapped globally.[6]

Nora Markard's chapter does not analyze the issue of equality between men and women but between same-sex couples. Her proposal sheds additional light on how constitutional provisions migrate. In her chapter she argues that when guaranteeing the rights of same-sex couples, the equality framework provides full citizenship participation. The right to privacy, on the other hand, greatly limits citizenship. She effectively proves, by analyzing a range of cases, that there are important differences when a judge protects equality rather than privacy. In a sense, she is

[5] Ibid.

[6] Frankenberg (n 2) xx.

arguing that convergence is not the trend; constitutions, constitution-making processes and interpreters face choices which are not neutral and which have engrained possibilities or limitations. This last idea is linked to another objective of her chapter which is to question Günter Frankenberg's assumption that rights will behave differently once they are de-contextualized and set in alien legal, social, cultural and economic contexts. The author argues that some commodities found in the IKEA center are prone to produce different limitations and uses than others.

I would disagree somewhat with this last argument. I agree that different rights and right protection travel differently. Nevertheless, in my opinion, local context greatly determines their strength and force. In order to argue this I will provide an example from the Colombian Constitution and I will briefly describe how the legal environment has determined and weakened the search for equality across gender lines.

Even though the Colombian Constitution includes an equality clause, a nondiscrimination provision and the equal sharing of family obligations among men and women, women are poorer, continue to be discriminated against, have less political representation and fewer job opportunities. As a matter of fact, a growing percentage of women experience higher levels of extreme poverty, 60 percent have informal jobs, receive lower pay than men, and their access to formal, well-paid jobs is limited because they have to care for their children. In a poll published in 2010, 80 percent of the mothers surveyed said that their situation as main carer had led them to accept lower wages, and 75 percent stated that they had fewer job opportunities, among other things, because they had less control over their time.[7]

It is my opinion that context makes the promise of equality elusive. Context means that there are local competing views about how to define inequality and what to do about it. In addition, context means that any constitutional clause has to interact with a range of national legal regimes that in the end are going to limit the potential of any IKEA commodity brought into a local context.

Feminists in Colombia have fought for a range of legal transformations, depending on their interpretation of what lies at the heart of the uneven distribution of power and resources across gender lines. Broadly speaking, there are three trends that have characterized Colombian feminist legal reforms: the liberal, the socialist and the cultural. According to the liberal explanation, for historical and cultural reasons, women

---

[7] Tatiana Munévar B, "Ellas prefieren hijos antes que pareja" *El Tiempo*, 7 March 2010, www.eltiempo.com, accessed 12 November 2012.

do not have equal access to the law, regardless of how neutral they are. As a result, the legal system doesn't really establish a balance between the rights and opportunities for men and women, which results in effective discrimination. In this sense, to level this historical and cultural inequality, laws should be reformed to specifically include women; this means that neutral regulation is not enough. This legislation should clearly establish the rights of women and should regulate in a particular way, with equal opportunities in areas such as education and access to work.[8] The prime example of this approach would be the right to equality established in Article 43 of the Colombian Constitution which states:

> Women and men have equal rights and opportunities. Women may not be subjected to any kind of discrimination. During pregnancy and after delivery, women shall enjoy special protection and assistance of the state, and will receive an allowance from it if unemployed or homeless. The State shall provide special support to the female head of household.

An alternative perspective is provided by cultural feminists. According to this view, men and women reason differently. Due to their capacity to have children, women value the connection with others and personal relations have greater significance for them. As a result, their values are determined by the needs, desires and interests of others. For women the most important ideals are caring, relationships and responsibility. Men on the other hand, due to biological differences, value autonomy, independence and individuality. In Colombia this view has been supported in the privileged protection of women as mothers, through maternity leave (which is 12 weeks), a daily rest of 20 minutes in the morning and 20 in the afternoon for breastfeeding and the prohibition of dismissal during pregnancy.

Finally, another view that attempts to attack gender inequality is socialist feminism. According to this perspective, what determines the discrimination of women is their lack of economic opportunities, which

---

[8] For more examples, see Helena Alviar García and Isabel Cristina Jaramillo Sierra, *Feminismo y Crítica Jurídica: el análisis distributivo como alternativa crítica al legalismo liberal* (Siglo del Hombre Editores, Ediciones Uniandes 2012); Helena Alviar García, *Derecho, Desarrollo y Feminismo* (Ediciones Uniandes 2008); Dirección Nacional de Equidad Para las Mujeres, Presidencia de la República, *40 años del Voto de la Mujer en Colombia – Leyes y Jurisprudencia* (1st and 2nd supp, 1998); Aixa Ansorena M, "Negotiating Women's Legal Equality: Four Versions of a Law" in Ilse A Leitinger (ed), *The Costa Rican Women's Movement: A Reader* (Pittsburgh University of Pittsburgh Press 1997) 111–18.

in turn is a result of their obligations as main care givers. Therefore, as long as reproductive work is not socialized and until it becomes the responsibility of all members of society, women will continue to see their job opportunities, education and participation in public life being greatly limited. In Colombia, there is an experiment with the socialization of reproductive work through a program called "Hogares Comunitarios." In this project, a mother takes cares of the children of her neighbors during the workday and municipal authorities provide space, food subsidies and a small salary for the community care provider.

Colombian feminists have focused on legal and constitutional reforms, but from my perspective have ignored two issues that are fundamental to structuring the environment in which the equality clause develops: administrative regulation and the interaction between different legal regimes. By administrative regulation I mean everything that happens once a law is set in place. For example, what are the consequences of not following the law? What types of sanctions are established? Is there adequate regulation issued by the Executive Branch that allows their application? What institutions are set in place in order to make equality a reality? Are they well funded and staffed? Is there horizontal and vertical integration in the government in terms of equality ideals? On the other hand, interaction between the different legal regimes greatly limits any progressive regulation. For example, not having a right to child care will determine access to paid work. Formal paid work, in turn, determines access to social security (pension, health and children's benefits).

In conclusion, there is much more to constitutional transfer than the establishment of one clause or the other. Context, understood as the different ways in which equality is defined as well as its interaction with administrative regimes and institutions, will greatly determine how constitutional commodities travel.

5. Private but equal? Why the right to privacy will not bring full equality for same-sex couples[1]

Nora Markard

The gender order remains one of the more contested sites of the constitutional order, despite the fact that sex equality has become one of the standardized commodities available at Günter Frankenberg's global IKEA center.[2] Notwithstanding the proliferation of constitutional and human rights guarantees ever since the 1948 Universal Declaration of Human Rights made the move from the equality of "all men" to that of "all human beings," the meaning of sex equality remains contested both locally and at the international level. More recently, gender has been understood as encompassing a number of dimensions: not only the male/female binary in terms of both (biological) sex[3] and (social) gender, but also the match between the two (gender identity[4]) and the matching –

[1] I am indebted to the participants of the September 2011 workshop for their comments, and to Anna Katharina Mangold and Anuscheh Farahat for further criticism. I have done my best to do them justice. I dedicate this chapter to Laura Adamietz, who inspired me to write it.

[2] See Günter Frankenberg, "Constitutions as Commodities: Notes on a Theory of Transfer," in this volume.

[3] The biological binary is challenged by intersexed bodies whose primary and secondary sexual characteristics – gonads, chromosomes, outer appearance, etc. – do not all point to the same sex in the male/female binary. Some transgendered individuals also change their bodies to such an extent that it eludes classification.

[4] Gender identity refers to the non-/identification with a body's assigned sex. The normative expectation of a match between sex and gender is challenged not only by transsexuals who identify with the "other" sex and (or) gender, but also by intersexuals who do not wish to be standardized, or by transgendered individuals who assume a position beyond the binary. The concept of "passing," also applied to a race context, is used to describe the extent to which an

opposite-sex – desire (sexual orientation[5]). These expectations, as Adamietz[6] calls them, are of course not universal: they are age-specific, racialized, dependent on bodily dis/abilities, etc., as gender always already intersects with other social inequalities.[7]

Among the many contested issues related to the gender order, this chapter will turn to those relating to sexual orientation. More specifically, it will examine how the framing of these legal issues in terms of constitutional rights affects their resolution. Considering constitutional court or supreme court decisions from different jurisdictions and times, it will trace the specific dynamics of privacy arguments as opposed to equality arguments by analyzing two topics: the decriminalization of same-sex sexual activity, and same-sex marriage. This chapter will focus on the arguments made, rather than delineating each jurisdictional context,[8] in order to compare the dynamics of a privacy vs. an equality approach.

In doing this, the chapter presents two arguments: firstly, the claim that the right to private life tends to deny full citizenship in a thick sense, meaning full and free participation in society,[9] while an equality framework provides for full inclusion. In granting something less than full inclusion while pretending to grant full rights, the right to private life offers a logic similar to "separate but equal,"[10] which I call "private but equal." Secondly, this chapter questions Günter Frankenberg's assumption that these rights will tend to work quite differently in different constitutional, social, cultural contexts, having been stripped of their specific meaning in the process of their de-contextualization on the way

---

individual is accepted in their gender role, typically facilitated by a gender-typical appearance; see, inter alia, Judith Butler, *Bodies that Matter: On the Discursive Limits of "Sex"* (Palgrave 1993).

5 The expectation of opposite-sex desire has been termed heteronormativity.

6 Laura Adamietz, *Geschlecht als Erwartung: Das Geschlechts-diskriminierungsverbot als Recht gegen Diskriminierung wegen der sexuellen Orientierung und der Geschlechtsidentität* (Nomos 2011).

7 The intersectionality paradigm has always been a topic of marginalized feminist movements; as an academic concept, it has been introduced by Crenshaw, see e.g. Kimberlé Crenshaw, "Mapping the Margins: Intersectionality, Identity Politics, and Violence against Women of Color" 43 *Stanford Law Review* 1241.

8 On the method of constitutional comparison in a more detailed sense, see Günter Frankenberg, "Critical Comparisons: Re-thinking Comparative Law" (1985) 26 *Harvard International Law Journal* 411.

9 Diane Richardson, *Rethinking Sexuality* (Sage 2000) 71–115.

10 This is the infamous formula coined in *Plessy v Ferguson* 163 US 537.

to the global IKEA center.[11] Instead, it seems that some of the commodities on the IKEA center shelf cannot be used any which way; their specific design resists certain uses and invites others. To give an example from the world of commodities, bus stop benches with individual seat molds cannot be used for rough sleeping but only for sitting, whereas water buckets can be used not only for water, but also for any other type of liquids or solids, or even – turned upside down – for sitting.

5.1. SEXUAL ORIENTATION BETWEEN THE RIGHT TO PRIVACY AND THE RIGHT TO EQUALITY

The issue at hand is presented very clearly in *HJ (Iran)*, a refugee law case decided by the UK Supreme Court in 2010.[12] In dealing with access to the host state based on an understanding of unacceptable treatment in the home state, refugee law is constantly engaged with deciding on "same" and "other": to what extent do we accept differences in dealing with otherness, and where do we draw the line required by an appeal to universal human rights standards?[13] The question posed to the Law Lords was whether refugee protection was engaged if persecution could be avoided by secrecy. Both claimants feared persecution in their respective home countries, Iran and Cameroon, where sexual activity between males is criminalized. The lower courts had denied the claim, suggesting the claimants could live safely if they acted "discreetly," keeping their sexual

---

[11] See Günter Frankenberg, "Constitutional Transfer: The IKEA Theory Revisited" (2010) 8 *International Journal of Constitutional Law* 563.

[12] *HJ (Iran) and HT (Cameroon) v Secretary of State for the Home Department* [2010] UKSC 31.

[13] Following James C Hathaway, *The Law of Refugee Status* (Butterworths 1991), it is now widely accepted that persecution is a human rights violation of a certain gravity. A well-founded fear of being persecuted confers refugee status if it occurs "for reasons of race, religion, nationality, membership of a particular social group or political opinion" (Article 1(A)(2) of the 1951 Geneva Convention on the Status of Refugees, 189 UNTS 150). It is also widely accepted that homosexuals can form a "particular social group." See e.g. UNHCR, *Guidance Note on Refugee Claims Relating to Sexual Orientation and Gender Identity* (UNHCR 2008). For a discussion of gender-based persecution in armed conflict, see Nora Markard, *Kriegsflüchtlinge: Gewalt gegen Zivilpersonen in bewaffneten Konflikten als Herausforderung für das Flüchtlingsrecht und den subsidiären Schutz* (Mohr Siebeck 2012).

orientation "in the closet."[14] The Supreme Court allowed the claim, based on a human rights argument: "In short, what is protected is the applicant's right to live freely and openly as a gay man."[15] What place, then, does homosexuality have in human rights law, in constitutional law, in EU law? How private is it; how equal is it?

Two issue areas dominate constitutional and human rights case law on sexual orientation: (1) the decriminalization of same-sex sexual activity and (2) the inclusion, full or in part, of same-sex couples in the existing framework of rights, especially the rights cluster of marriage. In both issue areas, whether or not courts frame the issue as a privacy issue or as an equality issue has a lot to do with how we think about the issue.

Both equality and privacy come with their own problems. Equality is a basic right against unfair discrimination that requires justification for any unequal treatment. While the stringency of the justification standard differs, at a minimum there has to be a legitimate reason for differentiation, one that is then open to evidence-based challenges.[16] Where the privilege cannot be withheld for lack of such justification (and cannot be abolished for constitutional reasons, or is maintained for policy reasons), the right to equality can even turn into a right to inclusion into existing privilege.[17] At the same time, equality is usually understood as the right to be treated as equal to something else, and this comparison sets the privileged "something else" as the normative standard. Moreover, minorities have found that it is easiest to be granted inclusion into privilege if one can show that one belongs to a small, clearly defined group of similar people and will not open the floodgates. While it is a right that

---

[14] On the concept of the "closet" as the metaphorical hiding place of sexual desires seen as deviant, see Eve Sedgwick, *Epistemology of the Closet* (University of California Press 1990). On *HJ (Iran),* see Nora Markard and Laura Adamietz, "Keep it in the Closet? Flüchtlingsanerkennung wegen Homosexualität auf dem Prüfstand" [2011] *Kritische Justiz* 294.

[15] *HJ (Iran) and HT (Cameroon) v SSHD* (Lord Rodger).

[16] As I note in my conclusion, this claim leaves out religion-based justificatory arguments in constitutional systems based on the primacy of religious tenets. Here, challenges of justification would have to be based on religious counter-arguments, e.g. from other parts of the scripture.

[17] In legal gender studies, discrimination and privilege have been discussed as two sides of the same coin. The distinction I make here is whether the legislator is obliged to extend the privilege or is free to dispose of it – "[e]quality … is as well pleased by graveyards as by vineyards." Douglas W Rae, *Equalities* (Harvard University Press 1981) 129.

can be mobilized against discrimination based on difference, equality therefore also has at the same time a homogenizing, assimilating tendency.[18]

The right to private life also has problematic connotations. Understandings of this right differ: it encompasses the right to autonomy, the right to make choices and to live by them without interference from the state, but it is also often understood as protecting a private space of some sort – in a building or even a phone line – to the exclusion of others and especially of the state. As such, it tends to be limited to the right to keep things *away* from the public or from the state, especially in relation to matters sexual, famously coined as "the right to be let alone."[19] Privacy thus extends to both a protected territorial space, where one can be unobserved, be oneself, and to a "personal and psychological space within which each individual develops his or her sense of self and relationships with other people."[20] The territorial aspect is strongly connected with the privacy of the home. The relational aspect, as this chapter will show for same-sex relationships, has a tendency to be read as the right to keep such relationships secret from the public, to keep them in the domestic sphere, that is, "in the closet." This understanding of privacy as a sphere of non-intervention and secrecy, in the area of gender, is ambivalent. Feminists have long struggled against such a separation of the public and the private sphere[21] and have identified the private sphere as a site of violence and discrimination. However, for those not conforming to

---

[18] In feminist jurisprudence, this has been called the feminist dilemma, or difference dilemma; see Martha Minow, *Making All the Difference: Inclusion, Exclusion, and American Law* (Cornell University Press 1990) 20.

[19] "The makers of our Constitution undertook to secure conditions favorable to the pursuit of happiness. They recognized the significance of man's spiritual nature, of his feelings and of his intellect. They knew that only part of the pain, pleasure and satisfactions of life are to be found in material things. They sought to protect Americans in their beliefs, their thoughts, their emotions and their sensations. They conferred against the government, *the right to be let alone* – the most comprehensive of rights and the right most valued by civilized men." *Olmstead v United States* 277 US 438 (Brandeis); emphasis added.

[20] *Countryside Alliance and others, R (on the application of) v HM Attorney General & Anor* [2007] UKHL 52 (Baroness Hale).

[21] See e.g. Nancy Fraser, "Rethinking the Public Sphere: A Contribution to the Critique of Actually Existing Democracy" in Craig Calhoun (ed), *Habermas and the Public Sphere* (MIT Press 1991); Frances E Olsen, "The Family and the Market: A Study of Ideology and Legal Reform" (1983) 96 *Harvard Law Review* 1497.

gender norms, the private sphere can also be a site of reprieve from the violence and discrimination experienced in the public sphere.

Against this backdrop, what happens if sexual orientation is considered a privacy issue; what if it is considered an equality issue? The following sections will address the issues of decriminalization of same-sex sexual activity (5.2) and of same-sex partnerships (5.3).

5.2. DECRIMINALIZATION OF SAME-SEX SEXUAL ACTIVITY

First, then, let us turn to the issue of decriminalization of same-sex sexual activity. Homosexuality is often not illegal as such; what is illegal is sexual activity between individuals of the same sex. Such activity is sometimes criminalized by reference to the sex(es) and age(s) of those engaged in it. Often, it is criminalized in the form of specific prohibited sexual practices, which are deemed to be "against the order of nature," or which are labelled as "sodomy."[22] These specific sexual practices are generally associated with sex between men, and it is often male couples who are mainly affected by such criminalization.

5.2.1 Privacy: "A Most Intimate Aspect of Private Life"

The European Court of Human Rights (ECtHR) stands for a strong privacy approach in protecting sexual orientation.[23] In its first case concerning the question of sexual activity, *Dudgeon v UK*,[24] the claimant had challenged the criminalization of sexual activity between consenting male adults in Northern Ireland.[25] After Dudgeon's house had been searched for drugs, the Ulster Constabulary had questioned him about

---

22 This term is used to refer to forms of penetration other than vaginal, such as oral or anal sex, but also to sexual acts between humans and animals. Stemming from a contested reading of the biblical story of Sodom and Gomorrah (Gen. 14, 18 and 19), whose inhabitants incurred the wrath of God, it carries a strong derogatory note. It will therefore be avoided, or used in scare quotes.

23 This has been brilliantly analyzed by Paul Johnson, "'An Essentially Private Manifestation of Human Personality': Constructions of Homosexuality in the European Court of Human Rights" (2010) 10 *Human Rights Law Review* 67.

24 *Dudgeon v UK* Series A, No. 45 [1981] ECHR 5.

25 By that time, the Sexual Offences Act 1967 had already abrogated much of the criminalization of same-sex sexual activities in Great Britain, with the exception of Scotland and Northern Ireland. After the *Dudgeon* judgment, the Homosexual Offences (Northern Ireland) Order 1982 was passed.

the same-sex sexual activities which his personal papers had revealed. This case set the tone for the Court's subsequent jurisprudence: "The present case concerns a most intimate aspect of private life."[26] The Court found such laws – even if they were unenforced[27] – to be an unjustified interference with the right to respect for the applicant's private life, protected by Article 8 of the European Convention on Human Rights (ECHR).[28] The Court has generally declined to make (additional) findings under the equality guarantee of Article 14 of the Convention in cases relating to same-sex sexual activity,[29] with the exception of plain sex discrimination in relation to the age of consent.[30] In this, the Court did not follow the example of the Human Rights Committee, which, in *Toonen*,[31] had found so-called "sodomy" laws to be a violation not only of the right to privacy (Article 17 of the International Covenant on Civil and Political Rights (ICCPR)) but also discrimination on the basis of sexual orientation as a form of sex discrimination (Articles 2 and 26 ICCPR).

The Court's privacy approach becomes clearer in the cases of *Laskey, Jaggard and Brown* and *A.D.T.* While *Dudgeon* had concerned forms of intimacy that were only revealed in the claimant's diaries and private correspondence, these cases involve a certain degree of publicity, as well

---

26 *Dudgeon v UK* [52].

27 *Norris v Ireland* 10581/83 [1988] ECHR 22; *Sutherland v UK* 25186/94 European Commission of Human Rights (unreported) [36].

28 "In the personal circumstances of the applicant, the very existence of this legislation continuously and directly affects his private life … : either he respects the law and refrains from engaging (even in private with consenting male partners) in prohibited sexual acts to which he is disposed by reason of his homosexual tendencies, or he commits such acts and thereby becomes liable to criminal prosecution." *Dudgeon v UK* [41].

29 Article 14 ECHR can only be taken with another, substantive Convention right, such as Article 8 ECHR ("The enjoyment of the rights and freedoms set forth in this Convention shall be secured without discrimination on any ground such as sex, race, colour, language, religion, political or other opinion, national or social origin, association with a national minority, property, birth or other status."); nonetheless, the Court does sometimes jump right into the conjoined analysis, as it did in the same-sex marriage case of *Schalk and Kopf v Austria* 30141/04 [2010] ECHR 995 (see below). A free-standing equality guarantee has been introduced in Protocol No. 12 to the ECHR in 2000, in force since 2005 and ratified by 18 out of 47 Council of Europe member states (as of March 2013).

30 *Sutherland v UK*: higher age of consent as sex discrimination against men, Art. 14 taken with Art. 8 ECHR.

31 *Toonen v Australia* Communication No. 488/1992 CCPR (1994).

as less common sexual practices. In *Laskey*,[32] three men had been convicted of assault, based on videotapes of bondage and sado-masochistic activities (BDSM) between consenting adults. The applicants had been members of a close circle practicing BDSM and taping it for later viewing; tapes were only circulated among the members. The seizure of these tapes had been part of a large-scale British police operation called "Operation Spanner" which was conducted in search of alleged homosexual snuff movies (of which none were in fact discovered). The Court found that the interference with the applicants' right to private life by the prosecution was justified on the basis of public health, declining to make a finding on the protection of morals. However, the Court insinuated that it was doubtful whether "private life" covered sexual activities that involved a considerable number of people, for which "new members" were recruited, and which were videotaped for later viewing by the members. The Court therefore seemed to consider not the sexual nature of the activity, but the private nature of the sexual activity "most intimate" and worthy of protection, indicating that this protection might meet limits as the activity becomes publicly noticeable.

A few years later, the case of *A.D.T.*[33] also involved videotapes of sexual activity between adult men. The applicant had been convicted under the Sexual Offences Act 1967 because the taped incidents involved more than two men at a time. The Court decided that the taping alone did not move the facts outside the scope of the right to private life, but in the same move confirmed its privacy approach by stressing the fact that – unlike in *Laskey* – the tapes were not *meant* to become public, that in fact the applicant wished no outing: "The Court finds it most unlikely that the applicant, who had gone to some lengths not to reveal his sexual orientation, and who has repeated his desire for anonymity before the Court, would knowingly be involved in any such publication." (Dudgeon, 1981) It is because of this very private setting that the Court, then, finds the interference not "necessary in a democratic society," the justification standard of Article 8 ECHR.[34] Again, no finding is made under Article

---

32 *Laskey, Jaggard and Brown v United Kingdom* 21627/93; 21628/93; 21974/93 [1997] ECHR 4.

33 *A.D.T. v United Kingdom* 35765/97 [2000] ECHR 402.

34 Article 8(2) ECHR: "There shall be no interference by a public authority with the exercise of this right except such as is in accordance with the law and is necessary in a democratic society in the interests of national security, public safety or the economic well-being of the country, for the prevention of disorder or crime, for the protection of health or morals, or for the protection of the rights and freedoms of others."

14, although the Sexual Offences Act 1967 only criminalizes homosexual activities, and only between men. Privacy, in the Court's approach, is not so much the freedom of autonomous choices, but the ability to keep intimate things away from the public.

As a side note, Great Britain, the respondent state in all of these cases, had exported its "sodomy" laws throughout the British Empire, where they survived long after the Sexual Offences Act 1967, and long after *Dudgeon*. In 2005, taking guidance from international and comparative jurisprudence, the Fijian High Court found these laws to be a violation of the constitutional right to privacy. Affirming the colonial heritage of the law, it quoted the Wolfenden Report[35] which had ended criminalization in Britain itself: "[T]here must remain a realm of private morality and immorality, which is, in brief and crude terms, not the law's business."[36]

The ECtHR's jurisprudence shows how closely related the spatial and the relational aspects are in the case of homosexual behavior: homosexual activities are protected if no one finds out.

The German Federal Constitutional Court (FCC) has also referred to the right to private life for the protection of same-sex sexual activities, with the exception of the issue of sex discrimination between male and female homosexuals. In its infamous 1957 decision, it found the criminalization (only) of sexual acts between men to be no violation of the sex equality clause, since it was clear that "male homosexuality" was more dangerous than "lesbian love."[37] It also found no violation of the

---

35 Report of the Departmental Committee on Homosexual Offences and Prostitution, published 4 September 1957 (Wolfenden Report). The Committee had found that "homosexual behaviour between consenting adults in private should no longer be a criminal offence" and recommended the age of consent of 21. The Report eventually resulted in the decriminalization of homosexual acts in private between two men over 21 by the Sexual Offences Act 1967.

36 *McCoskar and Nadan v State* High Court Fiji at Suva (2005). The case arose because of disagreement between a male Australian tourist and his Fijian male sexual partner of two weeks over payment of modeling fees for nude photographs, which McCoskar had reported as stolen. The digital photographs served as evidence.

37 BVerfGE 6, 389 (1957). S 175 of the German Criminal Code (*Strafgesetzbuch*) sanctioned the prohibition of sexual acts between men. Nazi Germany had extended this to any acts of a "prurient nature" between men and increased the punishment. Eastern Germany ceased to apply the norm in the late 1950s and in 1968 only retained criminalization of same-sex sexual acts with (male or female) minors, also scrapped in 1988. Western Germany decriminalized sexual activity between males over 21 years of age in 1968, over 18 in 1973. The age limit for sexual activities between females and for heterosexual sex was 14.

right to self-determination. This jurisprudence was confirmed in passing in 1973, when the Court upheld the then remaining criminalization of male-male sex with minors under 18 for the protection of youth.[38] These judgments were obviously passed in times much more morally restrictive than today. As morals became more liberal, however, the Court did not have an opportunity to reconsider its jurisprudence in light of sex equality before the provision was finally abrogated in 1994. Unlike the ECtHR, the FCC therefore did not contribute to the decriminalization of same-sex sexual activities.

The remainder of the FCC same-sex cases – up until the introduction of civil unions[39] – concern the protection of homosexuals against outing, confirming the tendency of the Strasbourg Court to interpret privacy as the right to remain private. In the 1973 *Lebach* case, the FCC found the revelation of homosexual contacts in a TV documentary about a convicted murderer a violation of his right to privacy, especially with a view to his chances of reintegration upon release. The Court was worried not only about the added stigma, but also about the fact that such a revelation would stump his chances of finding a female partner, an important factor for the success of reintegration.[40] In 2005, the Court halted investigations into an asylum seeker's lesbian history in her native Lebanon, which would have outed her to her family.[41] A robust equality jurisprudence in same-sex matters has not developed until quite recently; as it relates to same-sex marriage, it will be addressed below.

The opposition between a privacy analysis and an equality analysis is most striking in the 2003 US case of *Lawrence v Texas*.[42] The case concerned a Texan statute criminalizing "deviate sexual intercourse with another individual of the same sex."[43] Two men had been convicted on the basis of this statute, following a manufactured charge of weapons disturbance (a black man "going crazy with a gun").[44] In 1986, in *Bowers v Hardwick*, the Court had upheld a Georgian statute that criminalized oral and anal sex, denying a "constitutional right of homosexuals to

[38] BVerfGE 36, 41 (1973).

[39] See below, at 5.3.1. and 5.3.3.

[40] BVerfGE 35, 202 – *Lebach* (1973).

[41] BVerfGK 5, 60 = NVwZ 2005, 681.

[42] *Lawrence and Garner v Texas* 539 US 558.

[43] Texas Penal Code s 21.06, adopted in 1973, downgraded male homosexual acts to Class C misdemeanors which are punishable by a fine: s 12.23 of the Code.

[44] Apparently the call was an act of jealousy; see Dale Carpenter, *Flagrant Conduct: The Story of Lawrence v. Texas* (Norton 2012).

engage in acts of sodomy."[45] In *Lawrence,* the majority of the Court relied on the right to privacy, arguing that it also covers the choice of partners. It called this one of "the most intimate and personal choices a person may make in a lifetime, choices central to personal dignity and autonomy," quoting a line from the abortion case of *Casey* that had related to family and procreation matters.[46] It also made express reference to the British Wolfenden Report of 1957 and to *Dudgeon.* The Court constructed privacy as a broad liberty right, in contradistinction to the insular approach in *Bowers v Hardwick* of a "right to sodomy" (the existence of which the Court had denied). It called this frame demeaning, "just as it would demean a married couple were it to be said marriage is simply about the right to have sexual intercourse."[47] Despite the fact that the petitioners were not actually a couple nor possibly even having sex the night they were arrested,[48] the case became a story of love and intimacy, of the possibility of nurturing a relationship in the home.[49] As

---

[45] *Bowers v Hardwick* 478 US 186 [191]. A heterosexual couple had also claimed they had been "chilled and deterred" from engaging in oral or anal sex, but had been denied standing by the lower courts. As their challenge was not upheld, the Supreme Court case was limited to same-sex couples; see ibid, note 2.

[46] "Our law affords constitutional protection to personal decisions relating to marriage, procreation, contraception, family relationships, child rearing, and education. ... Our cases recognize 'the right of the *individual,* married or single, to be free from unwarranted governmental intrusion into matters so fundamentally affecting a person as the decision whether to bear or beget a child.' ... These matters, involving the most intimate and personal choices a person may make in a lifetime, choices central to personal dignity and autonomy, are central to the liberty protected by the Fourteenth Amendment. At the heart of liberty is the right to define one's own concept of existence, of meaning, of the universe, and of the mystery of human life. Beliefs about these matters could not define the attributes of personhood were they formed under compulsion of the State." *Planned Parenthood of Southeastern Pennsylvania v Casey* 505 US 833 [851] (O'Connor, Kennedy, and Souter JJ; quotations omitted, original emphasis). In *Bowers v Hardwick,* the Court had rejected any association with such matters.

[47] *Lawrence v Texas* [567] (Kennedy J).

[48] It is hard to believe that the police, breaking into Lawrence's house, actually witnessed Lawrence engaging in sexual intercourse with his (black) friend Garner, and the witness accounts actually differ in this respect. However, Lawrence and Garner did not dispute the facts, basing their challenges on constitutional grounds only. Carpenter (n 44).

[49] *Lawrence v Texas* [567]: "When sexuality finds overt expression in intimate conduct with another person, the conduct can be but one element in a personal bond that is more enduring. The liberty protected by the constitution allows homosexual persons the right to make this choice" (Kennedy J).

in *Dudgeon,* this privacy framework therefore left the issue in the bedroom and did not address the pervasive violence and discrimination encountered in public – very much unlike the equality framework relied on by Justice O'Connor.

5.2.2 Equality: Stigma and Discrimination

Justice O'Connor, in her concurring opinion in *Lawrence*, puts the emphasis on equality. She finds the prohibition of sodomy to make "homosexuals unequal in the eyes of the law,"[50] because it criminalizes a conduct closely related with being homosexual. She emphasizes the stigma this produces and adds, "there can hardly be more palpable discrimination against a class than making the conduct that defines the class criminal."[51] Given that the statute is rarely enforced, "the law serves more as a statement of dislike and disapproval against homosexuals than as a tool to stop criminal behavior,"[52] Justice O'Connor thus brings in wider issues of discrimination in society at large. While sexual orientation is not only about having sex, just as heterosexual orientation (or marriage) is not only about sex, criminalizing the form of sex that is commonly *associated* with gay men stigmatizes them as a group in *all* forms of expression.

The South African Constitutional Court had also relied on these arguments in *National Coalition*,[53] where it considered prohibitions of sexual activity between males a violation of the equality clause.[54] It strongly highlighted the symbolic effect and stigma that such laws carry, encouraging blackmailing and gratuitous police violence. Adding dignity to the mix, it found that the prohibition of anal sex punishes "a form of sexual conduct which is identified in our broader society with homosexuals. Its symbolic effect is to state that in the eyes of our legal system all gay men are criminals"[55] – degrading and devaluing gay men in society.[56]

---

[50] Ibid [581] (O'Connor J, concurring).

[51] Ibid [583], quoting *Padula v Webster* 822 F2d 97 [103] DC Cir. (1987) from *Romer v Evans* 517 US 620 [641] (Scalia J, diss.).

[52] *Lawrence v Texas* [583].

[53] *National Coalition for Gay and Lesbian Equality and Another v Minister of Justice and Others* [1998] ZACC 15; 1999 (1) SA 6; 1998 (12) BCLR 1517.

[54] At issue were s 20A of the Sexual Offences Act 1957 that prohibits male-male acts of sexual stimulation where more than two people are present, as well as the common-law prohibition of anal sex ("sodomy") which had only been applied to anal sex between males.

[55] *National Coalition* [28] (Ackermann J).

[56] For the dignity reasoning, see below.

The Delhi High Court, in *Naz Foundation*, follows this line of reasoning in relation to a law that criminalized oral and anal sex regardless of the sex of those involved. It found the law effectively to be criminalizing an identity, denying "a gay person full personhood."[57] Emphasizing stigma, it finds that the law pushes gays underground, leaving them vulnerable to violence and police harassment. Relying heavily on comparative law, including Justice O'Connor's concurring opinion and *National Coalition*, it finds a violation of the right to equality, recognizing sexual orientation as a ground of discrimination analogous to those explicitly prohibited, but also of the right to privacy, implicit in the Constitution, and of the right to dignity.

Before considering the triangle[58] of equality, dignity and privacy, the case of *Leung*[59] indicates the slippery slope of an equality analysis. In this case, the Hong Kong High Court frames "buggery" – anal sex, criminalized up until the age of 21 while other forms of intercourse are legal from the age of 16 – as a denial of the "right to sexual expression in the only way available to them [scil: homosexual men] … ."[60] It holds this to be "discriminatory when persons of a majority class are permitted the right to sexual expression in a way that is natural to them … It is disguised discrimination founded on a single base: sexual orientation."[61] In *Leung*, the conduct is thus made central to a group's identity; it is both likened to traditional forms of heterosexual intercourse, and – surprisingly – identified as the only "real" form of sex available to "them," implicitly making penile/vaginal intercourse the standard. Unlike Justice O'Connor, the High Court does not only refer to *others* identifying homosexuals with a specific form of sex, it perpetuates this identification.

---

57 *Naz Foundation v Govt of NCT of Delhi and Others* 160 Delhi Law Times 277 Delhi High Court at New Delhi, India (2009). The challenge against s 377 of the Indian Penal Code ("carnal intercourse against the order of nature"), also inherited from the British Empire, was allowed by the Supreme Court as public interest litigation. The High Court developed the right to privacy and dignity from Article 21 of the Indian Constitution, which is very similar to the US Due Process Clause.

58 Susanne Baer, "Dignity, Liberty, Equality: Aspects of a European Constitutional Triangle" (2008) 59 *Toronto Law Journal* 417.

59 *Leung v Secretary for Justice* High Court of the Hong Kong Special Administrative Region, Court of Appeal (2006).

60 Ibid.

61 *Lawrence v Texas*.

5.2.3 Privacy vs Equality and the Role of Dignity

In both *Lawrence* and *National Coalition*, equality-based arguments strike at the core of the problem: discrimination against homosexuals. The criminalization of same-sex sexual activities, between males in particular, is not just about being allowed to engage in specific sexual practices, or about being able to have sex with a partner of one's choice. Framing the issue in this way reduces homosexuality to specific sexual practices, thereby implicitly sexualizing homosexuals. What "counts" out of the whole spectrum of activities in a same-sex love relationship is sex; it is *seen* as "defining the class." This tendency is of course innate to the concept of "sexual orientation," which attracts the main attention not to whom you love and plan your life with and have children with, but to who you have sex with (and how). Equality arguments show that the question of whom you sleep with is only part of the larger question of whether you are accepted as an equal in society, or whether you count as deviant, a prey to violence and ostracism.

Privacy, on the other hand, protects just that freedom of who you sleep with. It reduces this to an individual problem and does not address the discrimination and devaluation that underlies the prohibition of "sodomy" in general or of sex between men in particular. To an extent, it even perpetuates this stigma by using it to justify the protection against outing, signaling that same-sex sexual activity is shameful and must be kept secret in the area of the home. Even where constructed as an autonomy right – as in *Lawrence* – the right to privacy tends to be reduced to a territorial sphere of privacy. Privacy says: in your bedroom, you can do what you like (as long as you don't harm or recruit anyone). Privacy says: if you don't want to, you don't have to tell anyone. Privacy says: don't ask, don't tell.

While privacy is the right to *do* something different (have "deviant sex"), equality is the right to *be* different, or rather – and less essentializing – the right not to be discriminated against because one is *perceived to be* different ("being a homosexual"). Justice Sachs points this out in his concurring opinion in *National Coalition*: "[P]eople are subject to extensive prejudice because of what they are or what they are perceived to be, not because of what they do."[62]

The claimants in *National Coalition* concisely pointed out the failings of a privacy approach: It suggests, they argued,

---

[62] *National Coalition* [109] (Sachs J).

> that homosexuality is shameful and therefore should only be protected if it is limited to the private bedroom; it tends to limit the promotion of gay right to the decriminalisation of consensual adult sex, instead of contemplating a more comprehensive normative framework that addresses discrimination generally against gays; and it assumes a dual structure – public and private – that does not capture the complexity of lived life, in which public and private lives determine each other, with the mobile lines between them being constantly amenable to repressive definition.[63]

Sachs J disagrees with this analysis, considering privacy *in conjunction with* equality and dignity. He defends privacy against the reduction to a territorial space, extending it to a "sphere of private intimacy and autonomy."[64] He thereby highlights the emancipatory dimension of privacy in terms of free decision-making. This dimension is also present in the ECtHR jurisprudence (e.g. in the assisted suicide case of *Pretty*[65]) and in the German Basic Law (as the right to free development of one's personality in Article 2(1)). But by leaving aside equality considerations in sexual orientation matters, both the ECtHR and the FCC restrict the right to privacy to an autonomy in the non-public sphere.

Sachs J, on the other hand, conceives of privacy and equality as intersecting rights, in that "the gross interference with privacy will bear strongly on the unfairness of the discrimination, while the discriminatory manner in which groups are targeted for invasions of privacy will destroy any possibility of justification for such invasions."[66] And lastly, both concepts are linked by dignity[67] – not the kind of dignity that one earns by good behavior, but a concept of dignity which denounces the devaluation of a person that is implicit in discrimination, the insecurity which people experience in a society where they are threatened with violence and criminalization, effectively reducing their sphere of autonomy. Taken with equality, this concept of dignity is not paternalistic, as in sexual harassment cases,[68] or individualized as in the majority

---

[63] Ibid [110] (Sachs J).

[64] Ibid [32] (Ackerman J); Sachs J, quoting the US Supreme Court, reiterates that "privacy protects people, not places" [116], and also prefers the term autonomy [117].

[65] *Pretty v United Kingdom* 2346/02 [2002] ECHR 427.

[66] *National Coalition* [114] (Sachs J).

[67] Ibid [120]–[129] (Sachs J).

[68] Susanne Baer, *Würde oder Gleichheit* (Nomos 1995) 220 et seq. argues that framing sexual harassment as an invasion of dignity confirms hierarchical gender roles, while equality is a right against hierarchies.

opinion in *Lawrence*, it is emancipatory. This is also true for the case of *Naz Foundation.*

These cases demonstrate that equality de-individualizes the issue and takes on larger structures of discrimination, and that it has the potential to point beyond sex. However, it carries the tendency to liken a minority group to the majority group, and to limit advances to areas which are comparable. This is obvious in the case of *Leung:* seeking to emphasize the disenfranchisement produced by "sodomy" laws, the High Court likens anal sex between men to the implicit norm of heterosexual penile-vaginal penetration, thereby depicting male anal sex as both inferior and as central to male homosexuality.

5.3. SAME-SEX MARRIAGE

The privacy/equality divide also structures court cases on same-sex claims to legally recognized partnerships or marriage. The starting point, where such a right is codified, is the right to marry. This is sometimes protected for "men and women," sometimes for "everyone," or it merely protects the institution of "marriage" as such.

5.3.1 Privacy: Some Sort of Partnership

The rejection of the right to marry a same-sex partner is usually the starting point for a privacy analysis of such claims. Consider the 2010 case of *Schalk and Kopf*:[69] the ECtHR first notes that the right to marry in Article 12 ECHR – unlike in the more recent EU Charter of Fundamental Rights (CFR)[70] – is not granted to "everyone" but to "men and women." Given that it cannot establish a European consensus on the matter, it concludes that the Convention does not impose an obligation on the state parties to grant same-sex couples access to marriage.[71] The Court then moves on to barring an equality analysis, arguing that where a right such as that in Article 12 is expressly limited to a specific situation, equality arguments cannot be used to claim it for another, albeit

---

[69] *Schalk and Kopf v Austria.*

[70] Entered into force in 2010, the Charter only applies to acts of the European Union and to acts of its member states in application of EU law, Article 51 CFR. The EU competence on family law matters, however, is limited to according benefits that ensure free movement of Union citizens, and to non-discrimination.

[71] *Schalk and Kopf v Austria* [54]–[63].

comparable, situation.[72] It also does not consider discriminatory those alternative forms of recognition that grant a lesser status than marriage.[73]

What is left, then? Privacy, the right to live with whom you wish – not the right to be included, not the destruction of heterosexual privilege. A throw-back in this respect, the Court advances gay rights by extending the right to family life to same-sex couples for the first time[74] and indicates that it may consider it necessary to provide these couples with an "alternative means of legal recognition" at some point in time, given the rapidly emerging consensus.[75] However, it also becomes clear that the Court has in mind only those couples that are comparable to "proper" heterosexual couples: two people in a stable, hopefully monogamous relationship, living together.[76]

In a 1993 decision, the German FCC used a very similar analysis, although the German Basic Law speaks of the protection of "marriage," not of the right to marry for "men and women." The Court rubber-stamped the statutory exclusion of same-sex couples from the institution of marriage, having found no fundamental change of the concept of marriage as a different-sex union.[77] Therefore, neither the constitutional right to equality nor the general right to develop one's personality could be used to access marriage.

However, following the introduction of the civil partnership in 2001 which withholds important benefits attached to marriage, especially in the area of tax breaks,[78] the FCC has considered that there must be some

---

[72] Ibid [96]–[103].

[73] Ibid [107]–[109].

[74] Ibid [94].

[75] Ibid [104]–[106]. See para. 105: "The Court cannot but note that there is an emerging European consensus towards legal recognition of same-sex couples. Moreover, this tendency has developed rapidly over the past decade. Nevertheless, there is not yet a majority of States providing for legal recognition of same-sex couples. The area in question must therefore still be regarded as one of evolving rights with no established consensus, *where States must also enjoy a margin of appreciation in the timing of the introduction of legislative changes*" (emphasis added).

[76] Ibid [95]: "[T]he Court would start from the premise that same-sex couples are just as capable as different-sex couples of entering into *stable committed relationships*" (emphasis added).

[77] BVerfG-K NJW 1993, 3058 (1993); decision of non-acceptance.

[78] Life partnerships (*Lebenspartnerschaften*), as they are called, were excluded from a number of financial and tax benefits, as well as the right to adopt as a couple. In particular, they cannot participate in "spousal splitting" for

sort of recognized partnership available. The 2005 *Transsexualism V* case concerned a male-to-female transsexual who had changed her first name but not her registered sex and was then caught between, on the one hand, not wanting to marry (as this legally entailed losing the female first name) and, on the other hand, not being able to enter a partnership with her female partner (which was reserved to same-sex partners only).[79] The Court finds that the legislator is free to bar access to marriage for transsexuals that have not changed their registered sex, in order to avoid the impression that same-sex marriage is available. However, it finds it unacceptable that the applicant has to forego recognition of her gender identity in order to access the only form of recognized partnership available to her.[80] The Court thus implies a right to access to some sort of partnership, but does not locate it in terms of specific constitutional rights, basing its finding on the protection of gender identity alone.[81]

In 2002, the Court had rejected a sex discrimination claim, since both men and women were equally able to marry a partner of the opposite sex, or conclude a partnership with a partner of the same sex.[82] In a 2007 case, a chamber of the Court cheekily rejected discrimination based on

---

tax purposes, which saves married couples with very different income levels hundreds of Euros in taxes each month.

79 At the time, under the Transsexuals Act (*Transsexuellengesetz*), transsexuals were able to change their first name ("small solution") much more easily than their legal gender ("big solution"), which required a surgical sex change and loss of procreative abilities. The Court found that recent research had shown that not all transsexuals hated their genitals and that some were quite happy to remain in the "small solution." However, marriage led to a loss of the new first name, since the legislator had considered this a return to the "old" gender, assuming that transsexuals were only truly transsexuals if they wanted to be heterosexuals in the "new" gender. The Court found that recent research had shown that transsexuals could also be homosexuals in their "new" gender. In 2011, the FCC declared the surgery requirement unconstitutional: BVerfGE 128, 109 – *Transsexualität VIII* (2011).

80 BVerfGE 115, 1 – *Transsexualität V* (2005) MN [55] et seq. See Laura Adamietz, "Transgender ante portas? Anmerkungen zur fünften Entscheidung des Bundesverfassungsgerichts zur Transsexualität" [2006] *Kritische Justiz* 368.

81 The right to gender identity has been found to be part of the right to a personal identity (*allgemeines Persönlichkeitsrecht*), developed from the right to personal development in conjunction with the right to dignity, Basic Law s 2(1) and 1(1).

82 BVerfGE 105, 313 (2002), MN [104]–[106].

sexual orientation: Since heterosexuality is not a precondition for getting married, it argues, access to marriage is not based on sexual orientation.[83]

These cases, based on privacy, thus do acknowledge the need for an institutionalized, legally and socially recognized form of partnership. But they do not grant access to actual marriage, or even to the full benefits of marriage.[84] They grant something similar but lesser: "Private but equal."

5.3.2 Equality "of the Vineyard, Not of the Graveyard"

This is different with cases that employ an equality analysis. In *Lawrence v Texas*, Scalia J had expressed concern that Justice O'Connor's equality reasoning would open the door to same-sex marriage: "This reasoning leaves on pretty shaky grounds state laws limiting marriage to opposite-sex couples … [because] 'preserving the traditional institution of marriage' is just a kinder way of describing the State's *moral disapproval* of same-sex couples."[85] And so it is: equality cases tend to grant full access to marriage or its benefits.

In Canada, the province of Ontario started a sort of domino effect with *Halpern v Canada*;[86] within a few years, the courts in eight out of ten provinces and one of three territories[87] declared the common-law definition of marriage as the "union of one man and one woman to the exclusion of all others" to be in violation of the equality clause of the Canadian Charter of Fundamental Rights and Freedoms, opening up marriage to same-sex couples. In 2005, the federal legislator tipped over the remaining dominoes by introducing a statutory definition of marriage as a union of two "persons," which had been upheld by the Supreme Court in *Reference re Same-Sex Marriage* in 2004. Absent a right to

---

83 BVerfG-K FamRZ 2008, 487; decision of non-acceptance. The Court has more recently adopted the equality framework, see below at 5.3.3.

84 The exception being pre-existing (formerly opposite-sex) marriages of transsexuals: BVerfGE 121, 175 – *Transsexualität VII* (2008).

85 *Lawrence v Texas* [601] (Scalia J, diss.).

86 *Halpern v Canada (Attorney General)*, 2003 CanLII 26403 (ON CA).

87 *Hendricks v Quebec* [2002] RJQ 2506 Quebec Superior Court; *Barbeau v British Columbia* 2003 BCCA 251; *Dunbar & Edge v Yukon (Government of) & Canada (A.G.)* 2004 YKSC 54; *Vogel v Canada* [2004] MJ No 418 Man. Q.B; *Boutilier v Nova Scotia (Attorney General)* [2004] NSJ No 357 (QL); *W. (N.) v Canada (Attorney General)* 2004 SKQB 434, [2004] SJ No 669; *Pottle et al. v Attorney General of Canada et al.* 2004 O1T 3964 Supreme Court of Newfoundland and Labrador; *Harrison v Canada (Attorney General)* [2005] NBJ No 257 (QL).

marry in the Charter, the Supreme Court had confirmed that the common-law definition of marriage violates the Charter's equality clause.[88] By excluding same-sex couples, the common-law definition constituted a distinction based on sexual orientation, a grounds of discrimination that is analogous to those enumerated in the Charter,[89] and thereby withheld benefits in a way that denied human dignity:

> In this case, same-sex couples are excluded from a fundamental societal institution – marriage. The societal significance of marriage, and the corresponding benefits that are available only to married persons, cannot be overlooked. Indeed, all parties are in agreement that marriage is an important and fundamental institution in Canadian society. It is for that reason that the claimants wish to have access to the institution. Exclusion perpetuates the view that same-sex relationships are less worthy of recognition than opposite-sex relationships. In doing so, it offends the dignity of persons in same-sex relationships.[90]

The Court expressly rejected arguments that marriage must remain as it is for the sake of tradition, and that its limitation to opposite-sex couples is necessary to encourage "natural" procreation and childrearing, given that same-sex couples do bear and raise children by other means:

> We fail to see how the encouragement of procreation and childrearing is a pressing and substantial objective of maintaining marriage as an exclusively heterosexual institution. Heterosexual married couples will not stop having or raising children because same-sex couples are permitted to marry. … Similarly, a law that restricts marriage to opposite-sex couples, on the basis that a fundamental purpose of marriage is the raising of children, suggests that same-sex couples are not equally capable of childrearing. … In the absence of cogent evidence, it is our view that the objective is based on a stereotypical assumption that is not acceptable in a free and democratic society that prides itself on promoting equality and respect for all persons.

The same common-law definition was the subject in the South African case of *Fourie*.[91] Just like the Canadian Charter, the South African Bill of Rights does not contain a right to marry. However, it does list sexual orientation as a prohibited ground of discrimination. The Constitutional Court uses this non-discrimination clause to find that the limitation of the

---

[88] *Reference re Same-Sex Marriage* 2004 SCC 79, [2004] 3 SCR 698.

[89] *Egan v Canada* [1995] 2 SCR 513, 1995 SCC 49.

[90] *Reference re Same-Sex Marriage* [107].

[91] *Minister of Home Affairs and Another v Fourie and Another* [2005] ZACC 19; 2006 (3) BCLR 355 (CC); 2006 (1) SA 524 (CC).

Marriage Act to opposite-sex couples is under-inclusive and discriminatory.[92] It leaves the resolution of this issue to the legislator, albeit with two caveats: firstly, the solution cannot be lowering the standard of rights, as the issue "calls for equality of the vineyard and not equality of the graveyard."[93] Secondly, there cannot be a solution that reproduces marginalization, a "separate but equal" approach.[94] Just like the Jim Crow race segregation laws in the US that had been found inherently discriminatory in *Brown v Board of Education*,[95] a recognition of "same-sex unions in desiccated and marginalized forms" makes a distinction that is exclusionary and that implies a different worth of one group in comparison with the other.[96] In the wake of *Fourie*, South Africa passed laws allowing same-sex marriage,[97] as well as polygynous customary marriage and Muslim marriage.

Similar arguments by analogy have also been made in some US cases. The first leading case on access to marriage was a segregation case, *Loving v Virginia*.[98] While non-whites, too, were allowed to marry, they were not allowed to marry whites, in order to "preserve the racial integrity of [the State's] citizens."[99] Building on its rejection of "separate but equal" in *Brown*, the US Supreme Court found: "There can be no doubt that restricting the freedom to marry solely because of racial classifications violates the central meaning of the Equal Protection Clause."[100] Can the introduction of civil partnerships for those excluded from marriage based on their sexual orientation be likened to this situation? It can. In several federal states, an equality analysis has led US

---

92 "The conclusion is that when evaluated in the context of the legal regime as a whole, the common law definition and section 30(1) are under-inclusive and unconstitutional to the extent that they make no appropriate provision for gay and lesbian people to celebrate their unions in the same way that they enable heterosexual couples to do." Ibid [82].

93 Ibid [149].

94 Ibid [150].

95 *Brown v Board of Education of Topeka* 347 US 483 (1954) at 495: "We conclude that, in the field of public education, the doctrine of 'separate but equal' has no place. Separate educational facilities are inherently unequal." (Warren CJ).

96 *Fourie*, ibid.

97 The Civil Union Act 2006 (Act No. 17 of 2006) permits civil unions between two partners of same or different sex, concluded either as a marriage or as a civil partnership.

98 *Loving v Virginia* 388 US 1 (1967).

99 Ibid [6], citing from *Naim v Naim,* 197 Va. 80, 87 S.E.2d 749 (1965).

100 Ibid [12] (Warren CJ). The Court also found a violation of the due process clause.

courts to find the exclusion of same-sex couples unconstitutional. In fact, it appears that once the equality argument is made, it is hard to escape its compelling argumentative force.

Courts are declaring unconstitutional not only the *total exclusion* from recognition, such as in Vermont or Massachusetts. In 1999, the Vermont Supreme Court had found the exclusion of same-sex couples to be in violation of the state constitution's equality clause (common benefit clause), leaving it up to the legislator to either open marriage or grant equivalent status and privileges.[101] Vermont introduced civil unions in 2000 and upgraded to same-sex marriage in 2009. In 2003, the Massachusetts Supreme Court argued in *Goodridge* that the state's constitution "forbids the creation of second-class citizens" by denying same-sex couples access to marriage, calling upon the legislator to make amends;[102] Governor Mitt Romney ordered the issuance of marriage licenses.

US courts have also taken issue with the *withholding of some of the benefits* attached to marriage.[103] In 2003, New Jersey introduced domestic partnerships for same-sex couples with a much more limited array of rights than marriage. In 2006, the New Jersey Supreme Court struck this down under the state constitution's equal protection clause, leaving it to the legislator whether to open marriage or introduce civil partnerships with a similar rights standard.[104] The state opted for civil unions and has made efforts to introduce same-sex marriage in line with the recommendations of the Commission charged with reviewing the implementation of the judgment.[105] In Connecticut, the state's Supreme Court equally found that the inferior status of civil unions in relation to marriage violates equality and liberty rights of the state's constitution.[106] A similar decision followed in Iowa.[107] Benefits are also being withheld at the federal level:

---

101 *Baker v Vermont* 744 A2d 864 Vt.

102 *Goodridge v Dept. of Public Health* 798 NE2d 941 Mass.

103 On German life partnerships, see below.

104 *Lewis v Harris* 188 NJ 415; 908 A2d 196.

105 In 2010, there was no majority; in 2012, Governor Christie vetoed the act and announced a constitutional amendment; see http://www.nytimes.com/2012/02/18/nyregion/christie-vetoes-gay-marriage-bill.html. In *Garden State Equality v Dow* (pending, docket no. MER-L-1729-11), plaintiffs claim that the denial of marriage licenses still violates the equal protection clause; see http://www.lambdalegal.org/in-court/legal-docs/gse_nj_20110629_complaint-for-declaratory-and-injunctive-relief (all links last accessed 14 September 2012). In February 2012, the Superior Court of New Jersey has allowed the claim to go forward.

106 *Kerrigan v Commissioner of Public Health* 289 Conn 135 (2008).

107 *Varnum v Brien* 763 NW2d 862 Iowa (2009).

the Defense of Marriage Act (DOMA) denies recognition to same-sex marriage for the purpose of federal benefits. State courts, joined by the Department of Justice, have found no justification for this, even on a rational basis review.[108] The Supreme Court has granted certiorari to review whether DOMA violates the Equal Protection Clause of the Fifth Amendment.[109]

Finally, even where the rights are identical, the *social recognition as marriage* makes a difference. In California, domestic partnerships between "two adults" had gradually acquired all rights but the designation of marriage.[110] In 2008, in *In Re Marriage cases*, the California Supreme Court found a statutory amendment limiting recognition to opposite-sex couples[111] to be a violation of the right to marry and of the right to equality, subject to strict scrutiny, under the Californian Constitution.[112] Shortly after, a similar constitutional amendment was introduced, Proposition 8. After the California Supreme Court had upheld the amendment under the state constitution,[113] the District Court found a violation of the *federal* Constitution, namely the due process clause and the equal protection clause:[114] it was confirmed by the Ninth Circuit Court of Appeal in 2012 on equal protection grounds. This judgment, in *Perry v Brown*,[115] is remarkable in the way it emphasizes the recognition provided by full access marriage, and its symbolic effect:

---

108 *Gill v Office of Personnel Management* 682 F3d 1 1st Cir. (2012); *Massachusetts v HHS* 698 F Supp 2d 234 1st Cir. (2012); *Golinski v Office of Personnel Management* 824 F Supp 2d 968 ND Cal. (2012); *Windsor v United States* 833 F Supp 2d 394 2nd Cir. (2012). *Windsor* was the first time intermediate scrutiny was applied at this level.

109 *Windsor v United States, cert. granted* (No. 12-307, 2012 Term); the Court added questions on jurisdiction and standing. The case was argued on 27 March 2012. Petitions were also filed in *BLAG v Gill* (No. 12-13); *Massachusetts v. HHS* (Nos. 12–15, 12–97); *OPM v Golinski* (Nos. 12–16).

110 A gradual approximation was followed by an express regulation in 2003: Cal. Fam. Code § 297.5(a).

111 Cal. Fam. Code § 308.5 as amended in 2000 (Proposition 22). Since 1977, the marriage statute had provided that marriage is a contract between one man and one woman.

112 *In Re Marriage Cases* 43 Cal4th 757 (2008).

113 *Strauss v Horton* 46 Cal4th 364, 93 CalRptr3d 591, 207 P3d 48 (2009). The Court let same-sex marriages stand that were concluded post-*In Re Marriage cases*.

114 *Perry v Schwarzenegger* 704 F Supp 2d 921 ND Cal. (2010).

115 *Perry v Brown* 671 F3d 1052 9th Cir. (2012).

> Newspapers run announcements of births, deaths, and marriages. We are excited to see someone ask, "Will you marry me?", whether on bended knee in a restaurant or in text splashed across a stadium Jumbotron. Certainly it would not have the same effect to see "Will you enter into a registered domestic partnership with me?". Groucho Marx's one-liner, "Marriage is a wonderful institution ... but who wants to live in an institution?" would lack its punch if the word "marriage" were replaced with the alternative phrase. So too with Shakespeare's "A young man married is a man that's marr'd," Lincoln's "Marriage is neither heaven nor hell, it is simply purgatory," and Sinatra's "A man doesn't know what happiness is until he's married. By then it's too late." We see tropes like "marrying for love" versus "marrying for money" played out again and again in our films and literature because of the recognized importance and permanence of the marriage relationship. Had Marilyn Monroe's film been called *How to Register a Domestic Partnership with a Millionaire*, it would not have conveyed the same meaning as did her famous movie, even though the underlying drama for same sex couples is no different. The name "marriage" signifies the unique recognition that society gives to harmonious, loyal, enduring, and intimate relationships [...]

Moreover, while the Court of Appeal frames the issue as one of existing rights taken away, it implies that *not* granting them would have been unconstitutional: as Proposition 8 could not be justified as merely reverting to the *status quo ante In Re Marriage cases* if that meant re-establishing discrimination. Quoting *Lawrence v Texas* and *Loving v Virginia*, the Court confirms that a tradition of discrimination does not "save a law ... from constitutional attack."[116]

The Court also rejects arguments that the 11th Circuit had accepted to uphold a popular amendment of the Constitution of Nebraska that forbids recognition of same-sex marriages or partnerships.[117] Given that Proposition 8 affects neither family law nor school curricula nor the freedom of religious communities to discriminate on the basis of sexual orientation, it finds that denying same-sex couples marriage licenses cannot advance the upbringing of children in stable family structures, nor be reasonably believed to be encouraging or strengthening opposite-sex marriages, nor that it violates religious freedom. Twice citing *Romer v Evans,* the Court concludes: "Proposition 8 is 'so far removed from these particular justifications that we find it impossible to credit them.'" Overall, "Proposition 8 serves no purpose, and no effect, other than to lessen the status and human dignity of gays and lesbians in California, and to officially

---

[116] Ibid [1093], quoting *Lawrence v Texas* [557]–[78] (2003) and *Loving v Virginia,* 388 US 1 (1967) which had noted the historical pedigree of anti-miscegenation laws but not even considered this a possible justification.

[117] *Citizens for Equal Protection v Bruning* 455 F3d 859 8th Cir. (2006).

reclassify their relationships and families as inferior to those of opposite-sex couples. The Constitution simply does not allow for 'laws of this sort.' … "[118]

A petition for certiorari to the US Supreme Court has been granted.[119] Should the Supreme Court not deny standing to the defenders of Proposition 8, it will have to decide whether it is time to apply *Loving v Virginia* to same-sex couples, endorsing the equality argument made by Justice O'Connor in *Lawrence v Texas.* Such a decision would have an effect throughout the United States that would go far beyond the issues raised in the DOMA challenges.[120] While the DOMA "merely" disregards same-sex marriages introduced at the state level, this case could lead the Supreme Court to find that *not* introducing same-sex marriages is a violation of the Equal Protection Clause – an outcome that, despite recent trends at the polls,[121] is very unlikely given the current political dynamics within the Court.

5.3.3 Federalism as Equality Motor

While the US Supreme Court has not recently been known for liberal avant-gardism, such movements from the de-centralized level to the national level have worked in other states, such as in Argentina and Mexico.

The city of Buenos Aires introduced civil unions for same-sex and different-sex couples in 2002 and put them on an equal footing with marriage on the state level;[122] inheritance and adoption rights, federally regulated, could not be extended to civil unions. In 2009, seized with an

---

118 *Perry v Brown* [1063]-[64].

119 *Hollingsworth v Perry, cert. granted* (No. 12-144, 2012 Term): "Whether the Equal Protection Clause of the Fourteenth Amendment prohibits the State of California from defining marriage as the union of a man and a woman."

120 The court added a question on the standing of the initiators of Proposition 8 as plaintiffs; a dismissal on these grounds would also invalidate *Perry v Brown,* but not *In Re Marriage Cases.* Affirming *Perry v Brown* on its own narrow grounds would only affect California, affirming it on the grounds that withholding (only) the label of marriage is generally discriminatory would affect eight states. The Court could refrain from deciding the case by dismissing it as improvidently granted.

121 At the 2012 presidential elections, voters in three states (Maine, Maryland, Washington) approved same-sex marriage by ballot, and in one state (Minnesota) rejected a constitutional amendment against same-sex marriage.

122 *Ley de Unión Civil* N° 1.004, Boletín Oficial de la Ciudad de Buenos Aires No. 1617 of Jan 27, 2003; Article 4: equality with marriage with respect to

acción de amparo against the denial of civil marriage to a same-sex couple, the Buenos Aires administrative court decided that the marriage law was in violation of the prohibition of discrimination on the basis of sexual orientation (Articles 16 and 19 of the Argentine Constitution).[123] Four other same-sex couples followed this example. LGBT activists managed to put the issue on the national agenda, and in 2010 the Argentinian Senate passed a law to open marriage to same-sex couples on the national level.[124]

Mexico City, a *distrito federal*, introduced a civil partnership in 2006[125] and legalized same-sex marriage in 2009.[126] Conservative parties, the Catholic Church and the *Procuraduría General de la República* filed a constitutional complaint with the Mexican Supreme Court of Justice.[127] In 2010, the Court found the reform to be constitutional, including the extension of the right to adoption, by a large majority. Moreover, marriages and adoptions concluded in the *distrito federal* were declared valid throughout Mexico. In 2012, the Court went one step further: based

---

"... derechos, obligaciones y beneficios que emanan de toda la normativa dictada por la Ciudad ... ."

[123] *Freyre Alejandro c/CGBA–sobre amparo* (expte. no 34.292/09), Contencioso Administrativo y Tributario No 15 de la Ciudad Autónoma de Buenos Aires (2009). The Court affirms the importance of freedom and recognition for human dignity, quoting Theodor W. Adorno's "true injustice is always to be found at the precise point where you put yourself in the right and other people in the wrong," after Judith Butler, *Giving an Account of Oneself* (Fordham University Press 2005) 104.

[124] Law on Equal Marriage (*Ley de Matrimonio Igualitario*), Ley 26.618 of 21 July 2010.

[125] Law on Cohabitation Unions for the Federal District (*Ley de Sociedades de Convivencia para el Distrito Federal*), Gaceta Oficial del Distrito Federal of 16 November 2006. These partnerships enjoyed inheritance rights but no right to adoption.

[126] Act Reforming Several Provisions of the Civil Code for the Federal District and of the Civil Procedure Code of the Federal District (*Decreto por el que se Reforman Diversas Disposiciones de Código Civil para el Distrito Federal y del Código de Procedimientos Civiles para el Distrito Federal*), Gaceta Oficial del Distrito Federal of 29 December 2009.

[127] *Acción de Inconstitucionalidad 2/2010, promovente: Procurador General de la República*, Tribunal Pleno de la Suprema Corte de Justicia de la Nación (2010); session transcripts available at http://supremacorteinforma.blogspot.com/2010/08/discusion-del-caso-sobre-matrimonio.html.

in part on the IACHR's judgment forbidding sexual orientation discrimination,[128] it declared the exclusion of same-sex couples from marriage in the state of Oaxaca unconstitutional,[129] a decision that will have an impact nationwide.

As in the US, it appears to be easier to achieve institutional recognition of same-sex couples at the local or state levels. Equality arguments can then be used in court to "upgrade" rights and benefits, and even status, and to start a dynamic that will eventually reach the national level.

5.3.4 Privacy vs Equality

What we see is: where partnership issues are resolved within the equality framework, full marriage rights tend to be granted, since "equality of the graveyard" is not an option – be it because the institution of marriage is constitutionally protected, because it is required to provide for some sort of recognized partnership anyway, or because it would just be unacceptable to get rid of marriage. Where they remain within the privacy framework, only some sort of partnership has to be granted which can be substantially inferior to marriage, especially in matters such as adoption or – in the German case – taxes.

What we also see is: once an equality argument is made, it appears hard to escape its force. Privacy asks: is it necessary for a relationship to be institutionally recognized? Equality asks: is there a rational justification for denying access to marriage? Once a justification for a differentiation between same-sex and opposite-sex couples is required, given that there is no rational basis for it, there is no stopping the dynamic, all the way to the designation of marriage as in *Perry v Brown*.

This is also observable in the case of the German FCC. In *Maruko*, a preliminary ruling on whether Germany could deny a widower's pension to a civil partner, the European Court of Justice (ECJ) decided in 2008 that member states who introduce same-sex partnerships have to grant equal rights in all areas where partnerships and marriage are comparable.[130] It based its judgment on the anti-discrimination Framework Directive which proscribes discrimination on the grounds of sexual

---

[128] *Atala Riffo y Niñas v Chile*, Inter-Am. Comm. HR, Case 12.502 (2012). The claimant had been denied custody based on her same-sex relationship.

[129] Amparos 457/2012, 567/2012 y 581/2012, Suprema Corte de Justicia de la Nación (2012).

[130] Case C-267/06 *Tadao Maruko v. Versorgungsanstalt der deutschen Bühnen* [2008] EUECJ C-267/06, [2008] IRLR 450 [73]: The Framework Directive (see below) precludes legislation that denies a survivor's benefits to a

orientation.[131] In *Römer*, it confirmed that there is direct discrimination where (opposite-sex) marriage and same-sex partnerships exist side by side and same-sex partners are treated differently in matters where they are "in a legal and factual situation comparable to that of a married person."[132] As a result, litigation is moving from one benefit to the next in the member states, such as in Germany.

The German FCC first changed course in 2009.[133] It decided that a mere reference to the special protection of marriage is not enough to justify the differentiation in relation to survivors' pensions. It found that the inability to procreate "naturally" made no difference, since childless marriages were also protected and children also grew up in same-sex households. Also, it applied *Maruko* by finding that the purpose of the benefit – honoring the contribution of the spouse to the productivity of the worker by providing a stable private life based on care and support – also applied to same-sex partners. The FCC applied its version of strict scrutiny, considering sexual orientation close to the grounds listed in Article 3 section 3 of the German Basic Law.[134] In the years that followed, the FCC applied this jurisprudence to the unequal treatment of registered civil partners and spouses under the Gift and Inheritance Tax Act,[135] in relation to family allowance for public servants,[136] and to conveyance duty.[137]

It is becoming clear that there will be hardly any benefits attached to marriage which serve a purpose which does *not* apply to same-sex life

---

same-sex life partner, although life partners and married spouses are in the same situation as far as the benefit is concerned.

131 Council Directive 2000/78/EC of 27 November 2000 establishing a general framework for equal treatment in employment and occupation (Framework Directive).

132 Case C-147/08 *Römer v Freie und Hansestadt Hamburg* [2011] EUECJ C-147/08. This case indirectly touched on the "spousal splitting" issue, a tax break in connection with tax category III, reserved to married couples. In *Römer,* the supplementary retirement pension was calculated in reference to tax categories.

133 BVerfGE 124, 199 – *Hinterbliebenenversorgung* (2009).

134 Article 3 section 1 of the Basic Law (*Grundgesetz*) contains a general equality clause, section 2 a sex equality clause, and section 3 a specific prohibition of discrimination on the basis of "sex, parentage, race, language, homeland and origin, faith, or religious or political opinions [or] disability."

135 BVerfGE 126, 400 – *Erbschafts- und Schenkungssteuergesetz* (2010).

136 BVerfG 2 BvR 1397/09 – *Familienzuschlag* (2012); not yet published in the official collection.

137 BVerfG NJW 2012, 2719 – *Grunderwerbssteuer*.

partners as well. This will also apply to the remaining financial discrimination: income tax breaks for married couples ("spousal splitting") save them hundreds of Euros each month.[138] Important voices in the ruling conservative party[139] and in government[140] as well as the *Länder* chamber of the Parliament[141] therefore started pushing for a legislative initiative to pre-empt yet another defeat in Court. A draft bill from the Ministry of Justice seeks to put life partnerships on an equal footing with marriage in a number of other respects.[142] As statuses approximate each other and same-sex couples gain recognition in the Court's jurisprudence, exclusion not only from tax breaks but also from joint adoption will become ever harder to justify, especially since single-parent adoptions by homosexuals are permitted as well as step-parent adoptions of biological children by same-sex partners.[143] And once all things are equal, who can really justify the need for a different designation?

5.4. EQUALITY VS. PRIVACY APPROACHES TO SEXUAL ORIENTATION

In the area of the decriminalization of same-sex sexual activities, the private nature of the activity has helped recognition, but in a way that is exclusionary at the same time. Judgments emphasize that the sexual activities are taking place in private between consenting adults – implying that any publicization of such activities might lead to a different

---

138 Cases pending before the FCC: 2 BvR 909/06, 2 BvR 1981/06 und 2 BvR 288/07.

139 http://www.spiegel.de/politik/deutschland/ehegattensplitting-cdu-abgeordnete-wollen-gleichstellung-der-homo-ehe-a-848570.html.

140 Family Minister Kristina Schröder (http://www.sueddeutsche.de/politik/gleichstellung-mit-der-ehe-familienministerin-schroeder-unterstuetzt-homosexuelle-lebenspartnerschaften-1.1433831) and Minister of Justice Sabine Leutheusser-Schnarrenberger (http://www.sueddeutsche.de/politik/gleichstellung-von-homopaaren-justizministerin-fordert-schaeuble-per-brief-zum-handeln-auf-1.1439115).

141 Bundesrat Drs. 302/12 (Beschluss), Stellungnahme des Bundesrates: Entwurf eines Jahres steuergesetzes 2013, 6 July 2012 [127]–[28].

142 http://www.sueddeutsche.de/politik/eingetragene-lebenspartnerschaft-homo-ehe-wird-gesetzliche-normalitaet-1.1446875.

143 The prohibition on successive adoption of adopted children by a same-sex life partner is being challenged before the FCC on equality grounds; request for a preliminary ruling from the second-instance civil court of Hamburg, HansOLG FamRZ 2011, 1312 (2010).

assessment. Other judgments emphasize the comparability of same-sex and different-sex sexual activities – implicitly limiting recognition to those areas where homosexuals are "the same as" heterosexuals, strengthening heteronormativity as it is being challenged. At the same time, the privacy framework reduces the issue to sex, rhetorically turning sex into what homosexuality is all about, thereby sexualizing homosexuals. The equality framework, on the other hand, can reach beyond a mere comparison to heterosexuals and address larger issues of discrimination in society. It locates sexual activity in a larger "right to live freely and openly as a gay man," as the British Supreme Court puts it in relation to male homosexuals.[144]

In the area of same-sex partnerships, the privacy framework tends to lead to a "separate but equal" type of non-marriage that is generally some sort of lesser status. The equality framework, on the other hand, tends to open up all the benefits that a marriage would have, up to marriage itself. This inclusion, of course, is by definition limited to an inclusion into the heteronormative framework of marriage. But it leads to citizenship in a thick sense: full participation in all areas of society without fear or exclusion.

The advantages of an equality approach also apply in the case of gender identity. Transsexuals who feel that they belong to the "other" sex often wish this identity to be recognizable by their first name and registered sex, whether or not they also wish to surgically or hormonally alter their body. The issues related to such legal recognition are usually resolved within a privacy framework. The right to live a gender identity and to express it through the choice of a matching first name is seen as a private choice, protected by the right to develop one's personality, and more generally by the right to privacy. An equality approach, instead of individualizing gender identities as a personal choice (or even as an illness[145]), could show that everyone has the right to live their gender identity without legal inhibitions – just as most of us do, every day. Here, too, equality reveals its potential to achieve full participation in society, citizenship in a thick sense, as opposed to the mere toleration of deviant individual choices.

---

144 *HJ (Iran) and HT (Cameroon) v SSHD* [78] (Lord Rodger).

145 In order to receive support from health insurance or have access to prescription pharmaceuticals – such as hormones that will affect the shape of the body, hair growth and the voice – or even to be recognized in their wish for a legal status change, transsexuals usually have to submit to medical assessment procedures that qualify their gender identity as pathological, a problematic double-bind.

Equality thus has the potential to address gender as a structural hierarchy that places some of us on the privileged side – our sex life and our gender identity conform to the normative expectations based on the categorization of our body – while others are confronted with discrimination, ostracism, and violence. Making their plight an individual problem leaves this hierarchy untouched.

As Catharine MacKinnon indicates, recognizing an inequality is the first step to addressing it.[146] Recognizing the multiple ways in which people are oppressed by the binary, heteronormative gender system goes beyond a mere individual wish fulfillment. It addresses the inequality gender causes at its core. It widens the view to full citizenship, understood as the ability to participate in all areas of life without fear of discrimination or violence.

5.5. OBSTINATE IKEA GOODS

This chapter started with Günter Frankenberg's argument that constitutional modules lose their context as they are made available globally and then built into another constitutional system and context. This would imply that they will also turn out to work quite differently in different contexts. However, it seems that privacy and equality have specific "built-in" dynamics that are not altogether context-specific.

The right to privacy carries two meanings, autonomy and domesticity. While a combination with dignity can strengthen its autonomy meaning, this freedom remains individualized, and it is a minimum freedom that is amenable to differentiations and exclusions.

The right to equality, on the other hand, not only takes larger patterns of discrimination into view. It also requires justification for privilege and discrimination. The decisions on same-sex marriage show: once the need for justification is recognized, there is no going back. There is no escaping the compelling force of an equality argument, because none of the justifications given for forbidding same-sex marriage holds up to rational analysis: same-sex marriages will not prevent opposite-sex couples from getting married, nor will they destabilize opposite-sex marriages. Since marriage is protected even if there are no children, or none can be had, and since same-sex couples can also procreate or adopt children, procreation cannot make the difference. Moreover, same-sex

---

[146] Catharine MacKinnon, *Toward a Feminist Theory of the State* (Harvard University Press 1989) 242: " … once equality is meaningfully defined, the law cannot be applied without changing society."

marriages do not negatively affect childrearing in stable family settings, and there is no evidence that children raised by two parents of the same sex suffer from developmental disadvantage, outside of discrimination against their parents.[147] And lastly, same-sex marriages also do not negatively impact on the religious freedom of those that reject homosexuality on religious grounds. As the cases show, using this line of argument leads to a sort of domino effect all the way to same-sex marriage.

Of course, this does not mean that courts will actually follow rational argument. The 2009 decision of the Portuguese Constitutional Tribunal on the statutory limitation of marriage to "persons of different sexes" is a case in point.[148] The Tribunal extensively examines comparative jurisprudence, only to reject the equality argument, based on the fact that the constitutional legislator introduced the prohibition of sexual orientation discrimination without expressly amending the right of "everyone" to marry. While this argument has little force given that such an amendment would not have been necessary, the Court goes on to argue that, although marriage is not based on procreation alone, it is a way for the legislator to *promote the value* of procreation within marriage, and so it would be up to Parliament to choose between this view of marriage and one of marriage "as a private relationship between two adult persons that essentially seeks to fulfil their own needs."[149] The "value" bit appears to be a way for the Tribunal to back out of a decision it does not want to take – especially when it adds that "there is nothing to prevent the appellants from being able to form a 'family', even if they are not able to legally enter into marriage."[150]

And a last caveat – the equality analysis will work differently in a setting which prioritizes values that are deemed to be incompatible with what an equality claim seeks to achieve. In a country where religion is set above the constitution, constitutional rights will offer limited protection where they start to clash with religious tenets. As many believers see maintaining the gender order in a broad sense as important to their religion, this can make a major difference in the cases here discussed.

---

[147] For a German context, cf. Marina Rupp (ed), *Die Lebenssituation von Kindern in gleichgeschlechtlichen Lebenspartnerschaften* (Bundesanzeiger Verlag 2009), a study conducted for the Federal Ministry of Justice.

[148] Tribunal Constitucional Portugal, Ruling No. 359/2009, Case no. 779/07.

[149] Ibid, official translation.

[150] Ibid.

That said, I believe that these cases strongly point to the compelling force of an equality argument across constitutional contexts. If you take it off the global IKEA shelf, it will force you to use it in a specific way, and reveal all efforts to avoid this use as flawed.

6. Legal transfer of women and fetuses: a trip from German to Portuguese abortion constitutionalism

Ruth Rubio Marín[1]

6.1. INTRODUCTION

Abortion legislation in Europe has experienced a common and gradual liberalizing trend since the 1960s. More and more European countries have by now departed from indication models (such as those allowing women to have an abortion to protect their life and health, in case the fetus has serious malformations, when the pregnancy results from rape or when the woman lacks social means), and embraced a periodic model or time-phase solution, allowing women to freely decide during a period of time whether or not to go through with their pregnancies, with or without a mandatory reflection period, and a counseling procedure seeking to ensure either women's informed decision-making, or to dissuade women from having an abortion.[2] Pioneered by Scandinavian countries, the liberalization of abortion became a unifying issue of the feminist movement in the Europe of the early 1970s, especially in countries with a strong Catholic tradition. Among the factors accounting for a change in public opinion and press coverage in favour of liberalization were the high number of illegal abortions, the fact that in many countries the number of prosecutions was minimal, as well as the discriminatory impact of criminalization on poor women who could not travel abroad to

[1] My thanks to Tiago de Freitas for his valuable assistance, to Miluska Kooij for her editorial help and to the editors of this volume for pertinent comments.

[2] See "Abortion Legislation in Europe," published by International Planned Parenthood Federation Network, in www.ippfen.org.

have an abortion.[3] Both feminist ideas challenging the patriarchal family, and broader health concerns linked to the high mortality of illegal abortions, were prompting the liberalization of abortion legislation in the US around the same time.[4] As the abortion movement gained momentum in both Europe and North America, anti-abortion forces were generated, supported by the Catholic Church and conservative parties claiming a right to life of the fetus against the woman's claim to self-determination.

In this context, pressure forced governments to act, but the strongly emotive-symbolic content of the abortion issue made a political compromise difficult to reach in some countries, and the opposition asked Constitutional Courts to step in and curb liberalizing attempts.[5] Thus, it was during this time that abortion constitutionalism was born in both North America and Europe, although the basic framing of the abortion question differed radically.

The American constitution was from the beginning interpreted as giving protection to the aborting woman, with abortion constitutionalism becoming a woman-centered rights debate. The pioneering decision in this respect was of course *Roe v. Wade*,[6] the landmark 1973 US Supreme Court decision, which read women's reproductive freedom into a silent constitutional text, endorsing a trimester framework and affirming a woman's and her practitioner's right to decide whether or not to terminate her pregnancy, banning any kind of state interference in the first trimester, and allowing but not imposing a limit or a ban on abortion after the point of viability.[7] Later case law, especially *Planned Parenthood of Southeastern Pennsylvania v. Casey*,[8] departed from *Roe*'s strict trimester scheme, affirming that, so long as the law did not impose an "undue burden" on the pregnant woman's decision, the state could assert an interest in protecting unborn life throughout the term of a pregnancy.[9] Still, for the European audience, the *Roe* paradigm has continued to symbolize the basic framing of the abortion question, in constitutional terms, as one of letting women freely decide whether to continue with

---

[3] Machteld Nijsten, "Abortion and Constitutional Law: A Comparative European-American Study," European University Institute, 1990, 37–8.

[4] Reva Siegel, "The Constitutionalization of Abortion" in Michel Rosenfeld and Andras Sajo (eds), *The Handbook of Comparative Constitutional Law* (Oxford University Press 2012) 1060.

[5] Nijsten (n 3) 39 and 43.

[6] 410 U.S. 113 (1973).

[7] Ibid 164–5.

[8] 505 U.S. 833 (1992).

[9] Ibid 877.

their pregnancy up to a certain point, basically free from both state interference and state assistance.

Around the time of *Roe*, Europe saw its first constitutional abortion litigation as well. Thus, between 1974 and 1975, constitutional decisions on abortion saw the light of day in Austria, France, Italy, and Germany. In contrast with the US Supreme Court, and with the exception of Austria, where the Constitutional Court refused to give unborn human life any constitutional standing,[10] most Constitutional Courts in Europe relied from the beginning on different provisions and doctrinal constructions to "read in" the protection of the fetus into silent constitutional texts. Thus, from the beginning, for most European Courts protecting unborn human life became a constitutional *must*, not just a *may*. And although some Courts, such as the French *Conseil Constitutionnel*, were able to read the protection of the fetus out of a silent constitutional text without striking down progressive legislation,[11] it was the German Federal Constitutional Court's 1975 abortion decision striking down a legislative attempt to embrace a periodic model by decriminalizing abortion during the first 12 weeks of pregnancy which came to exercise symbolic hegemony in European abortion constitutionalism.[12] Unlike the French decision, which had basically legitimated a balancing of constitutional values as performed by the legislator to justify its non-interference, and had done so on extremely succinct reasoning, the German decision contained a very elaborate doctrinal construction to back its rejection of the periodic model, and framed abortion constitutionalism as primarily concerned with the protection owed to the fetus, normalizing a pregnant woman's duty of motherhood. As we shall see, over time, the German constitutional doctrine evolved and came to validate the periodic model, but did so mainly as a concession to the inefficiency of criminalization in deterring abortions.

In more recent times, however, we see the emergence of a constitutional doctrine of abortion, which, on the one hand, explicitly recognizes the German (and refuses the US) legacy in accepting the constitutional protection of unborn human life as constitutionally grounded and as the starting point of the reasoning in abortion constitutionalism; but, on the other hand, assigns wider discretion to the legislator regarding how unborn life is to be protected, accepting the periodic model, not only for

---

[10] See [1974] *Erklaerungen des Verfassungsgerichtshofs* 221, decision of October 11, 1974.

[11] See *Conseil Constitutionnel* [1975] D.S.Jur. 529 [1975] A.J.D.A. 134 (of January 15, 1975).

[12] Bundesverfassungsgericht February 25, 1975, 39 BVerfGE 1.

strategic considerations, but also as duly expressing women's constitutionally protected dignity and autonomy in the reproductive domain. This doctrinal shift has, as its primary consequence, the de-normalization of pregnant women's duty of motherhood. So far, the most articulate expression of this process, which I identify as *subversive legal reception* (whereby the main legal framing is received from abroad but domesticated through a doctrine that fundamentally alters the system of meanings), has been provided by the Portuguese Constitutional Court in a 2010 decision. This decision validates Portugal's recent adoption of legislation allowing women to choose within the first ten weeks whether to have an abortion, without first forcing them to undergo dissuasive counseling. It draws on the German constitutional materials, both the majority and dissenting views expressed in the German case law, but also in German academic work, and it interprets what it sees as the exceptionalism of the German doctrine to justify its departure from it. Moreover, both the German model, as it has evolved over time, and the Portuguese subversive reception of it, rely heavily on epistemic assumptions about the fetus and women which cannot be automatically derived from the constitutional texts.

It is still too soon to tell how widely this new abortion doctrine will travel, including in areas of the world such as Latin America, where the abortion debate is extremely lively, the indications model is still dominant, and the strong Catholic tradition makes it likely that the right to life, and the meaning attached to unborn life, will play a crucial role in constitutional abortion debates. This is especially so because, in many of these countries, constitutions are silent on abortion and reproduction matters, so that abortion constitutionalism inevitably consists of jurisprudentially led processes of reading women and/or fetuses "in" or "out" of the constitutional text. The purpose of this chapter is to describe the abortion constitutionalism doctrine from Germany and Portugal characterized as a journey of subversive legal reception. I first describe the German framing and doctrine on abortion constitutionalism as it has both remained constant and evolved throughout the period between the two landmark abortion constitutional cases. I then describe Portugal's doctrine as both drawing from, and departing from, German constitutional materials. In each step, I explore the underlying epistemic assumptions, which explicitly or implicitly give content to the different meanings of the fetus/unborn human life and pregnant women which transpire in the case law.

6.2. PREGNANT WOMAN AS DUTIFUL MOTHERS VERSUS FETUSES AS HELPLESS OTHERS: *ABORTION I*

In 1975, the German Federal Constitutional Court struck down legislation proposing the reform of the criminal code (article 218c), decriminalizing abortion during the first 12 weeks of pregnancy, provided that mandatory counseling took place to inform women of available public and private assistance in the decision-making process (henceforth, *Abortion I*),[13] a decision which provoked the bombing of the Court's siege by feminist opponents. In building the basic abortion construction around the protection of unborn life, this landmark decision became a crucial point of reference for other European Courts, probably because the German decision was the first one to articulate a full-fledged doctrine with the unborn deserving constitutional protection, and the German Constitution had been taken by many countries as a referent in their own constitution-making process.

Basing its reasoning to some extent on legislative history, the German Court held that, as an "unborn human being," the fetus enjoyed the protection of the right to life (article 2.2.1 GG) from the 14th day after conception, which is when, according to what it took to be established biological and physiological findings, human life began. For the Court, this ruled out the possibility of signaling different stages in the process of development of the fetus that could be taken as relevant to determining different degrees of constitutionally required protection.[14] In determining this, the Court noticed that it was not necessary to decide whether or not the fetus had to be considered a rights-holder, strictly speaking.[15] Rather, instead of going for a "rights-centered" approach, the Court anchored the entire discussion in the realm of "duties," focusing primarily on those vis-à-vis the fetus. The move was rendered possible through a theory of fundamental rights in which these duties are not to be interpreted only as expressing subjective interests, which the state must respect and not interfere with, but rather also as embodying an objective value system

---

[13] Bundesverfassungsgericht February 25, 1975, 39 BVerfGE 1.

[14] Ibid C.I.1b. Contrary to this, the representatives of the *Bundestag* defending the legislation had argued that the question of when human life begins cannot be answered with religious, medical, or philosophical arguments, but only through social and legal reasoning; and that it was rational to consider the unborn at an early stage of development as being different from life at later stages of development.

[15] Ibid C.I.3.

that the state must foster: fundamental rights as guidelines and impulses for state action.[16]

But the Court went further. Thus, besides deriving protection from the right to life clause, the Court held that the fetus also enjoyed the protection of human dignity (article 1.1.2 GG).[17] Connecting both life and dignity, the Court elevated human life to the category of supreme value, and argued, on the basis of it, that the life unfolding in the womb of the mother had an independent legal value that the government had a constitutional duty to protect, even, if necessary, against the woman's will.[18] Consequently, women were introduced into the constitutional scene as a threat to unborn life.

In supporting the elevation of human life to the category of supreme value, the Court referred to Germany's history. Interpretive context was the key. For the Court, the express incorporation of the self-evident right to life into the Basic Law, in contrast to the Weimar Constitution, could be explained principally as a reaction to the "destruction of life unworthy of life," to the "final solution" and "liquidations," carried out by the National Socialist Regime.[19] German history also justified, according to the Court, Germany's exceptionalism in resisting the influence of evolving standards in other democratic countries of the Western world, which had by then "liberalized" or "modernized" their abortion legislation.[20] This in fact echoed conservative Catholic opponents of abortion reform, which also invoked Nazism.[21] The irony lay in that, as the Court itself recognized when describing the regulation of abortion under the National Socialist period, during the specified regime abortions were in fact punished severely as "attacks on the vital energy of the people" and "attacks on race and heredity."[22] This was something which the dissent

[16] This allowed the Court to escape taking a final position on whether or not the fetus is strictly speaking a bearer of fundamental rights, deducing the state obligation to protect developing life from the objective-legal content of the "right to life" and "dignity" provisions in the GBL.C.I.3.

[17] Ibid C.I.2.

[18] Ibid C.II.2.

[19] Ibid C.I.1.

[20] Ibid D.IV.

[21] See Siegel (n 4) 1063 citing Manfried Spieker, *Kirche und Abtreibung in Deutschland: Ursache und Verlauf eines Konflikts* (2nd edn, Ferdinand Schöning 2008) 22–3.

[22] *Abortion I* A.4.c. Interestingly, what the Court does not mention is the Nazi legacy regarding the role of women in society, which can be synthesized as the triple K, *Kinder*, *Küche* and *Kirche* (children, kitchen and Church), and which would inspire its sex equality doctrine at least until the early 1990s. See

by Justices Rupp von Brunnek and Simon picked up on as they argued that the "decisive renunciation completed with the Basic Law of the totalitarian National Socialist state" actually advised the opposite, that is, restraint in employing criminal punishment.[23] In fact, in Italy, where abortion prohibition up to 1978 was part of Fascist legislation, the striking down of this provision and the liberalization of abortion was seen as a reaction against Fascism.[24]

For the Court, this process of reading the life of the fetus into Germany's Constitution, and turning it into a paramount object of constitutional protection, ruled out the possibility of any sort of balancing with a pregnant woman's reproductive autonomy, taking into account the stage of development of the fetus. Proportionality analysis was therefore out of the question. Although the Court admitted that the constitutionally enshrined right to the free development of one's personality embraced a woman's option to decide against parenthood and the responsibilities flowing from it,[25] it also specified that this could not mean that pregnant women had a right to have an abortion, for abortion simply entailed the annihilation of the unborn, a constitutionally protected good. A hierarchical ordering of the rights and values at stake was needed, and for the German Court it was the primordial value of *dignity* that tilted the matter in favor of the life of the fetus. It was this life that had to be granted priority as a matter of principle, and for the entire duration of the pregnancy.[26]

The decision to center the constitutional reasoning around the protection due to the unborn had clear implications for the constitutional status of pregnant women, a matter to which the Court devoted only 20 lines in a decision of almost 60 pages. The Court recognized in passing that, in theory, women's self-determination could be impaired by pregnancy, birth and childrearing. However, this did not prevent it from asserting that pregnant women had, prima facie, a constitutional duty to carry a pregnancy to term.[27] In other words, the Court seemed to suggest that a woman's reproductive freedom went as far as the beginning of pregnancy only. Once pregnant, women did not have a right to arbitrarily reject their

---

Blanca Rodríguez Ruiz and Ute Sacksofsky, "Gender in the German Constitution" in Beverley Baines and Ruth Rubio-Marín (eds), *The Gender of Constitutional Jurisprudence* (Cambridge University Press 2005) 149.

23 *Abortion I* A.II.2.

24 Nijsten (n 3) 190.

25 *Abortion I* C.II.2.

26 Ibid.

27 Ibid C.III.1.

natural maternal duties and the self-sacrifices that came along with them.[28] Instead, public authorities had a duty to protect the unborn against what the Court described as the search for "unlimited pleasure" and "comfort" by pregnant women.[29] Pregnant women unwilling to accept the "ordinary" burdens of motherhood were thereby naturally turned into selfish beings who had lost connection with their natural calling as mothers. Identified as "mothers," pregnant women entered the constitutional scene primarily as *potential threats* to the fetus, portrayed as an "independent human being" in need of protection.[30] In other words, the main consequence of this fetus-centered framing of the abortion question was to turn women, constitutionally and reproductively speaking, into duty-bearers, through a process of normalizing and naturalizing their motherly obligations.

This did not have to be so. In deciding the precise reach of a state's duty to protect unborn life, including which forms of protection are conceivable and/or necessary and upon whom the ensuing obligations fall, we can in theory distinguish at least between four forms of protection of unborn life: *preventive* (seeking to prevent undesired pregnancies), *promotional* (seeking to assist women who do not necessarily reject the prospect of motherhood, but lack the means to accept responsible motherhood), *dissuasive* (seeking to persuade women to abandon abortive plans), and *punitive* (relying on deterrence of the practice of abortion through the threat of punishment). In the first two, it is the state that assumes the primary responsibility, whereas in the punitive and dissuasive models, the state lays its responsibility primarily on women, and then assumes only the subsidiary responsibility of convincing, or coercing, women into accepting their primary duties of motherhood.

In *Abortion I*, the Court started by recognizing that, in principle, it falls to the legislator to decide what the effective protection of unborn life requires. However, in setting the minimum standards, which the Court took to be its own responsibility, it explicitly endorsed that the state must assume a duty to carry a pregnancy to term. A duty which it takes for granted, yet can only fulfill by shifting its weight onto women. That this was not something the Court perceived as problematic from the perspective of assigning gender roles is clear, for the Court bluntly recognized

---

[28] Ibid D.III.2.

[29] Ibid C.III.3.

[30] Ibid C.II. For the Court, because the embryo cannot be seen as a part of the maternal organism only, the termination of pregnancy cannot be regarded as falling within the sphere of protection of the right to bodily privacy.

that "reawakening and strengthening of the maternal will to protect the unborn life where it has been lost [is] the most noble end of the state's endeavor to protect life."[31] Beyond this, the Court recognized that it is for the state to decide whether to favor preventive and promotional measures (such as social, political and welfare means for securing developing life) over repressive measures (seeking to coerce women). Whatever the specific regulation, the legislator had to ensure that termination of pregnancy was *perceived* as a *wrong*. The legal order *had to* express its disapproval.[32] The state *had to* make a value judgment and reflect that abortion is unjust, even if it decides to rely on means other than the threat of punishment. This gave punitive means a privileged position, for such means had to remain an option, if it was shown that the protection of life could not be achieved through any other means in an equally effective way.[33]

Once pregnant women's "normal" or "a priori" constitutional duty to carry their pregnancies to term has been affirmed, the question becomes whether, in view of women's constitutional interests, there might be "extraordinary circumstances" which would allow (or even force) the legislator to exempt the woman from her ordinary reproductive and motherhood obligations. For the Court, this *must only be* the case when the life or grave impairment of the woman's condition is at stake. Beyond that, the legislator can decide freely which other categories of extraordinary burdens should not be imposed on pregnant women.[34] But even in these cases, if the legislator opts to exempt women from punishment, the state has the obligation to offer counseling and assistance to a woman, not only to reduce hardship, but also to "remind her of the fundamental duty to respect the right to life of the unborn, and to

---

[31] Ibid. C.III. 1.

[32] The dissent by Justices Rupp von Brunnek and Simon challenges the Court's failure to explain how the requirement of condemnation as an independent duty is constitutionally derived. In a pluralistic, ideologically neutral, and liberal democratic community, the task of the state is only to protect the legal values guaranteed and recognized by the constitution. See ibid II.2.

[33] Ibid C.III.2.

[34] Ibid C.III.3. The Court thus seemed to suggest that the criminality or non-criminality of abortion depended only on the situation of the pregnant woman and had nothing to do with the status of the unborn, which is to be equally protected since the beginning of human life. In fact, it does take the stage of development of the fetus into account. As has been noted, the differentiated time limit adopted in the amended abortion law, distinguishing times for fetal and social or ethical indications, in fact shows that the fetus is treated differently according to stage of development. See Nijsten (n 3) 113.

encourage her to continue the pregnancy."[35] In other words, other than in order to protect their own life or health, women always have a constitutional duty to carry to term a pregnancy, with a distinction made only between *normal hardship* linked to pregnancy, labor, and child upbringing, and *extraordinary hardship* (which the legislator must define, but which could possibly include a fetus carrying severe malformations, the pregnancy being the result of rape, or the lack of social and financial means to face motherhood), only for the purpose of allowing the legislator *to not exact the punishment.* In all cases falling outside the "extraordinary hardship" category, the legislator could only dispense with criminal law punishment if it identified other means capable of emphasizing the unjust character of the act, and which were shown to be as effective as punitive means in preventing the interruption of pregnancies.[36]

Applying these standards to the legislation under review, the Court had no difficulty striking it down. Combining a periodic model with mandatory medical and social counseling to inform women about public and private services to assist pregnant women, mothers, and children, was simply considered insufficient to live up to constitutional standards. Adopting a time-phase rule in the interests of preserving an allegedly higher number of lives was incompatible with the obligation of giving individual protection to every single actual life. The goal of containing the abortion epidemic could not take priority over fundamental legal protection in individual cases. The legislator was always under an obligation to signal that abortion is wrong. Thus, abortion counseling necessarily had to be fetus-centered and dissuasive.[37] Moreover, there had to be a waiting period of at least two days before abortion could be performed. Preventive and promotional forms of protection were therefore deemed insufficient.

6.3. THE REFINEMENT OF THE PARADIGM: FROM SELFISH TO VULNERABLE MOTHERS UNDER *ABORTION II*

Following the first abortion decision, a revised version of the Abortion Reform Act was passed on May 18, 1976, reproducing the indications

[35] *Abortion I* E.3.

[36] Ibid.

[37] Ibid D.II.2.

model that had been suggested by the Court, permitting abortions for medical, eugenic, ethical, and serious social reasons. However, the legislatively embraced indications solution failed to satisfy anyone. Pro-choice activists considered the regulation too burdensome, ineffective, and unnecessarily restrictive of a woman's decision to choose in early pregnancy. Anti-abortionists objected to the high number of abortions being performed under the social hardship indication, as well as to the public insurance coverage of such abortions. Moreover, there was a lot of geographical variation depending on the prevailing religious ethos of the state or region charged with administering the law.

This is how things stood when reunification triggered the need to come to a compromise solution. Since East Germany had for a long time recognized abortion on demand within the first trimester, in the 1990s, the abortion issue became entangled in negotiations over reunification, and this led to the enactment of more liberal abortion legislation, which supplemented the indications model with a time-phase solution decriminalizing abortion in the first trimester after an open-ended counseling procedure and a three-day waiting period. The new model retained the concept that abortion should only be allowed if the continuation of pregnancy would result in an unreasonable burden for the woman because it destroyed life. At the same time, it reflected the view that, instead of through punitive means, the state's duty to protect developing life could be better served by improving the social environment for women and families with children, and in the individual case of an unwanted pregnancy, by comprehensive information and dissuasive counseling. Consequently, the new legislation contained a voluminous package of general social measures on education, birth control, and state assistance in matters of family planning and pregnancy.[38]

Once again, the Act was constitutionally challenged, providing an opportunity for the German Constitutional Court to refine its jurisprudential model in a second landmark decision (henceforth, *Abortion II*),[39] striking down the legislation. This time around, while the Court accepted the strategic policy shift towards a periodic model, it was still not satisfied with the specific counseling procedure foreseen in the law, a procedure it thought to be insufficiently dissuasive and hence insufficiently protective of the unborn. However, underlying *Abortion II* was a shift in the perception of the woman who typically goes for an abortion

---

[38] Susanne Walther, "Thou Shalt Not (but Thou Mayest): Abortion after the German Constitutional Court's 1993 Landmark Decision" in *German Yearbook of International Law* 36 (1993) 387.

[39] 88 BVerfGE 203 (1993).

from that of a selfish or whimsical woman to that of a desperate and vulnerable (and thus malleable) potential mother. Women as responsible and sexed human beings deciding autonomously on reproduction matters were still nowhere to be found.

Abortion I had noted that affirming the state's constitutional obligation to protect the unborn was not tantamount to mandating punitive protection, but that equally effective means of protection of each individually conceived fetus had to be identified.[40] But it was *Abortion II* which clearly articulated an expanded legislative realm of options, primarily taking into account efficiency considerations in view of the persistent reality of illegal abortions performed with risk to a woman's health. Like *Abortion I*, *Abortion II* started from the duty of the state to protect human life, including that of the unborn, specifying that this protection was due not only in general, but to each individually conceived fetus.[41] In other words, the protection of unborn life could not be reduced to an expressive act; it had to be about saving individually conceived human lives. As in *Abortion I,* the Court recognized that women had an a priori duty to carry their pregnancies to term,[42] and that this duty could not be generally suspended, even within a limited time frame. However, this time around, the German Constitutional Court granted the legislator much greater discretion to abandon ineffective punitive means, not only because it accepted that criminal law must always be an *ultima ratio*,[43] but also in recognition of the special link tying the fetus to the woman, a relationship described now by the Court as one of "duality within unity,"[44] distancing itself from the adversarial relationship opposing women and threatened fetuses that *Abortion I* had portrayed. The new framing did not however entail a move towards a constitutional anchoring of a pregnant woman's right to decide, à la *Roe v. Wade*. For the Court, indications exceptions were permissible in some cases and even required in some,[45] but the German legal system simply could *not* turn abortion into a right. It had to convey the message that abortion was wrong, and, in particular, that unjustified abortions were never legal.[46] Because of

---

[40] Ibid D.III.2.

[41] Ibid D.I.1.b.

[42] Ibid D.I.2.

[43] Ibid D.I.2c.dd.

[44] Ibid D.I.2.

[45] Ibid D.I.2c.aa.

[46] In this particular case, the Court suggested that this could be done through strictly regulated mandatory dissuasive counseling, as well as through limiting public funds to those abortions considered legal (i.e. backed by a

this, the constitutionality of a system of non-punitive forms of protection depended on the other forms of chosen protection being sufficiently protective of the fetus.[47]

On the other hand, the Court clearly recognized that neither dissuasive nor punitive means of protection were sufficient. Assistance was also necessary to enable motherhood for women who would in principle embrace it, but either lacked the means to do so, or were rightly concerned about the toll of motherhood on their social and professional development. For the German Court, the duty of protection of the right to life had to be interpreted in the light of the duty of protection of the family enshrined under articles 6.1. and 4 of the German Basic Law. This meant that the responsibility to protect life could not *entirely* fall on the woman but was to be shared, with motherhood and the care of children being portrayed as a service done for the benefit of the entire community.[48] Among the many protective actions that were called for to overcome this, the Court mentioned state assistance in case of need, but also legislation to ensure a child-friendly society, including a prohibition on ending rental agreements because of the birth of a child; legislation ensuring the equality between men and women in employment; facilitating the compatibility between education, profession and family responsibilities; as well as compensating for the losses that ensue for the person primarily in charge of raising children.[49] In spite of this, the Court did not go as far as to link pregnant women's a priori duty of motherhood to the actual verification of the conditions for the reproductive responsibility to be a truly shared one. Pregnant women's duties remained constitutional duties which could be criminally enforced if the legislator chose to do so. Wider family and societal support for human reproduction remained, from a woman's point of view, a non-enforceable constitutional imperative seeking a more equitable distribution of the costs of human reproduction.

---

tolerated exception) or for poor women. See ibid D.II and D.III.1 and D.I.15–16 and E.V.2.

[47] Ibid D.I.2c.dd.

[48] Tellingly, in spelling out what it considered some of the most common causes for abortions, the Court included lack of adequate housing; the lack of means to raise the children while furthering an educational project or an economic activity; lack of material means and social discrimination against single mothers. Ibid D.I.3.

[49] See ibid D.I.3.

The move away from the punitive protection model, under *Abortion II*, therefore entailed the recognition of the importance of enabling conditions for human reproduction and reflected a change in perception of the "by-default" aborting woman (no longer seen as selfish or hedonistic, but as vulnerable), but was also a concession to strategy, i.e. the need to identify means that could better succeed in minimizing the total number of abortions. The normative understanding of women remained fundamentally unchanged, as it was not their reproductive autonomy that made the abandoning of criminalization necessary. The prevalence of strategic considerations explains the emphasis placed in *Abortion II* on spelling out the precise nature and objectives of the mandatory counseling procedure which, according to the Court, had to accompany a woman's decision-making process, a procedure which still had to express the constitutional value system.

If we take a step back here, and think about the conceivable aims of a counseling procedure that is to accompany a woman's decision-making process, we can imagine a four-step scale ranging from the goal that a woman's decision be one, "informed"; two, "thoughtful and responsible"; three, "persuasion- resistant"; or four, "coercion-resistant". Only the first aim seems perfectly compatible with the goal of allowing pregnant women to make an autonomous (meaning free and informed) choice, whereas the last simply denies women's autonomy. Women can be presumed to make "informed" decisions, if, at the moment of facing pregnancy and with the possibility of either continuing or discontinuing it, they are aware of the likely course of events connected to their decision to have an abortion or to carry on with the pregnancy, childbirth, and childrearing. A free decision is arguably also one in which women are aware of the existence of *relevant alternatives* to abortion, such as adoption procedures or assistance and protection measures enabling motherhood. Philosophically, regulation enabling this type of decision-making process is fully compatible with taking women as fully autonomous moral agents. Counseling aimed at ensuring women's "thoughtful" decision, though not necessarily violating women's autonomy, starts from the dubious assumption that women lack full moral competence, considering it a necessity to inform women about the moral arguments that can be brought to bear in favor of their continuing the pregnancy to full term.

Because the refined 1993 Germanic model was not primarily grounded on the recognition of women's reproductive autonomy and the need to render it meaningful by putting in place enabling measures for motherhood and parenting, it is not surprising that it made *persuasion-resistant* consent, and not just *informed consent*, the mandatory constitutional threshold for abortions on demand. Thus, whereas the Court portrayed this model as one that seeks protection of the fetus "with the mother and never against the mother" (i.e. collaborating with her instead of forcing or threatening her), it was clearly the need to protect the unborn it was mainly concerned about.[50] It was only bothered by the reality that women go for illegal abortions, and that it would defeat the purpose of allowing women to truly and openly disclose their reservations about going through with a pregnancy (thereby rendering impossible their change of mind) if the ultimate decision was not placed in their hands after counseling.[51] As a consequence, as a condition for validating the "abortion on demand plus dissuasive counseling" option, the Court required counseling that would, firstly, inform women about social assistance options for both mother and child;[52] secondly, strengthen their sense of responsibility by reminding them of the right to life of the unborn and their corresponding duty of motherhood;[53] and thirdly, actively encourage them to continue their pregnancies.[54] Moreover, the procedure had to contemplate the possibility of involving or excluding from the process all those who could exercise a negative influence on women (such as the doctor, the father or other people from the family or social environment). According to the Court, all of these actors *should* encourage and support the woman in her choice to carry the pregnancy to term, but could in fact unduly influence her in the opposite direction, disrespecting not only her responsibility, but also their own co-responsibility in the matter.[55] In light of this, the Court struck down the legislation under review, which it regarded as having focused too exclusively on allowing women to overcome a situation of need and conflict instead of positively encouraging women to continue with the pregnancy, reminding them of the fundamental rank of the right to life of the unborn and her subsequent duties.[56] More explicit dissuasion was required.

In the end, the assigned gender roles under the refined German model, accepting periodic abortion regulation mainly on strategic grounds, did not fundamentally change. The basic assumption remained. Pregnant women must want motherhood, and therefore they must be helped and comforted by others in making that choice when conflicted. They must also be protected from selfish others who would discourage, instead of

---

50 Ibid D.II.3.
51 Ibid D.II.5 and D.III.1.c.
52 Ibid D.III.1.d; D.IV.1.C.
53 Ibid D.III and D.IV.
54 Ibid D.III.1.a.
55 Ibid D.III.1.b; D.IV.1.d; D.VI.
56 Ibid E.II.

help them, to follow their natural calling.[57] It falls to the legislator to decide how best to achieve this, and it may be justified to think of forms of protecting the unborn *with* and *through* the pregnant woman rather than *from* and *against* her, for, typically, women who go for an abortion are neither necessarily selfish nor frivolous, but rather desperate, vulnerable, and therefore, malleable. A combination of the necessary persuasive arguments, as well as adequate material support, and a child-friendly society are then considered the means most conducive to changing a pregnant woman's mind. However, identifying efficient ways of convincing women to resume their natural obligations of motherhood in order to save fetuses remains the primary aim, not the recognition of pregnant women's reproductive autonomy as equal citizens free to pursue their vision of a good life.[58]

6.4. THE EMERGENCE OF A COMPETING PARADIGM: FROM SAVING FETUSES TO RESPECTING LIFE AND RESPONSIBLE WOMEN

Recently, we have started to observe a paradigm shift in which the abandoning of punitive measures and the endorsement of preventive and promotional measures in the early stages of pregnancy are conceptualized not mainly as a concession to strategy, but rather as an articulation of principles that challenge the German paradigm at its core, including by lending more importance to the recognition of pregnant women's constitutionally protected reproductive autonomy, thereby unsettling the normalization of women's maternal duties. This is achieved by recognizing that, even if constitutional significance were to be attached to it, the life of the fetus does not enjoy an automatic constitutional priority over a

[57] Literally, for the Court, "the conflict which arises from a pregnancy usually stems from knowing that one carries inside human life worthy of protection and the desire to have the child, on the one hand, and, on the other, the fear not to be able to face the task, be immersed in a serious personal conflict, or have to renounce to one's own life plan. Counseling which tries to avoid this inner split and tries to overcome the obstacles to the desire to have a child, encouraging women to carry the pregnancy to term, does not imply that the decision is externally taken. That women [thus conflicted] need help is confirmed by the psychological problems that often follow from an abortion." Ibid D.IV.1.

[58] In the wake of the 1993 decision, abortion in Germany remains criminally prohibited except under indications, but a woman who completes counseling can receive a certificate granting her immunity from prosecution for an abortion during the first 12 weeks of pregnancy (German Penal Code, StBG, para. 218a).

woman's reproductive autonomy; that the state cannot automatically discharge its duty to protect life by transforming it into an ordinary duty of motherhood to be borne by the pregnant woman; and that both a pregnant woman and the unborn deserve some form of constitutional protection, which means that the legislator is necessarily bound to perform an act of balancing, relying on proportionality techniques, probably taking into account the developmental phase of the fetus. To this day the most accomplished expression of this new paradigm can be found, as we shall see, in the recent jurisprudence of the Portuguese Constitutional Court.

6.4.1 The Seeds from Inside: From Dutiful Mothers to Sexed and Responsible Beings

In fact, the seeds of this paradigm shift can be found in the dissent expressed by Mahrenholz and Sommer in *Abortion II.* For the dissenting justices in *Abortion II*, every abortion regulation must take into account not only the state's duty to protect unborn life, but also women's rights respecting her dignity, physical integrity, and the free development of her personality. Proportionality *must* therefore come into play, as the affirmation of a constitutional good cannot imply the full sacrifice of the other. Not surprisingly, instead of starting from pregnancy, and the assumption that all pregnant women unquestionably desire motherhood, the dissent takes us one step further back. Setting the scene in a radically different manner, the dissent recognizes as a basic feature of the human condition that sexuality and the desire to have children do not necessarily coincide, and that the consequences of such a divergence fall mainly to women. It then refers to the fact that women have throughout time sought ways to escape this situation by having abortions, whether legal or illegal, when they considered that their life circumstances did not enable them to responsibly assume motherhood. This does not mean that the state does not have the constitutional duty (and not just the prerogative) to protect human life from the very beginning, but, crucially, this is a duty which falls primarily to the state and cannot simply displace women as right bearers.[59] Rather, every abortion regulation must take into account not only the duty of protection of unborn life, but also women's right to the protection and respect of dignity (article 1.1 GG); physical integrity (article 2.2 GG); and free development of her personality (article 2.1 GG), and live up to proportionality standards.

---

59 Ibid I.1 and 2.

This vision has implications for the interpretation of the "periodic plus dissuasive counseling model." In concrete terms, the dissenting justices argue that when the legislator opts for such a form of protection, more than strategy is at stake. Rather, this option recognizes that with regard to the early stages of pregnancy, and after the woman has gone through a primarily fetus-focused dissuasive counseling, the decision belongs to her as an exercise of her fundamental rights. When the human dignity of unborn life and that of the pregnant woman collide, it falls to the legislator to reach a proportionality based solution. The legislator may take into account that, in the "duality within unity" which the status of pregnancy represents, as the pregnancy advances, the duality dimension gains in strength. Not surprisingly, the preconception of the aborting woman embodied in the dissent is also a radically different one from the one which can be distilled from the majority decision. According to the dissent, the point of departure of the legal regulation must be that pregnant women are, in general, perfectly able to make responsible and justified decisions on this matter. The best protection of the unborn life must be truly with and not against women, and the state must trust women's capacity to make responsible decisions, for, in general, women do not go for abortions lightly and without good reasons.[60]

After Germany's *Abortion II*, other European Constitutional Courts started to endorse the constitutional validity of mandatory dissuasive counseling as an alternative to punitive protection in ways which suggested that principle – i.e. the recognition of women's reproductive autonomy – and not just strategy – i.e. greater efficiency in sparing the lives of fetuses – must be taken into account, thereby confirming the beginning of a paradigm shift.[61] However, the most accomplished expression of the paradigm shift is to be found in a 2010 decision by the

---

60 See ibid II.1.

61 See Alkotmánybíróság (AB) [Constitutional Court], Decision 48/1998 (XI.23), Official Gazette (Magyar Közlöny) MK 1998/105 (Hung.), 26 available at www.mkab.hu/admin/data/file/710_48_1998.pdf.), where the Hungarian Constitutional Court acknowledged that decriminalization of abortion, coupled with abortion dissuasive counseling, would be a constitutionally valid method of protecting unborn life, which was also respectful of women's rights. See also the 2006 decision by the Constitutional Court of the Slovak Republic (PL-US 12/01-297), upholding legislation supplementing an indications model with a periodic model, which allowed women non-funded abortion on request during the first 12 weeks, subject to consultation with their physician on the basis that sufficient protection to the unborn could be provided by the deterrent effects of the costs of the procedure and dissuasive counseling of the type that may be

Portuguese Constitutional Court, which does not even make acceptance of the periodic model conditional on explicitly dissuasive counseling.[62] It is interesting to observe that this new paradigm is coming about not through a process of formal rupture with the dominant German framing, which places the fetus center stage, but through a process of what we might call *subversive legal transfer*, in which the basic framing of the abortion debate (fetus- and duty-centered) is still taken from Germany (and contrasted with that of the US (women- and rights-centered), but, at the same time, the doctrine developed under it is significantly re-shaped. The re-shaping takes place through doctrinal bricolaging with constitutional materials, which include those contained in the dissents of the German cases, but interestingly, in German academic works too, showing that the symbolic power of the German referent goes beyond the Court's doctrine. Also, departure from the point of reference justifies itself in doctrinal distinctions linked to a reading of Germany's exceptionalism, which does not necessarily coincide with the German Court's understanding of Germany's exceptionalism. Worth noticing are the different "extra-constitutional" epistemological assumptions – in this case about either women or the meaning of protecting unborn life – underlying, and probably accounting for, the different doctrinal choices. Let us take a closer look.

6.4.2 Receiving and Re-shaping the German Paradigm: From Saving Fetuses and Helping Mothers to Respecting Human Life and Responsible Motherhood

Portugal has a rich history of abortion constitutionalism. By tradition a deeply Catholic country, abortion was entirely banned in Portugal under the criminal code until May 1984, when an indications model was first introduced declaring abortion non-punishable when performed to protect the life of a woman, or her physical and/or mental health; in case of severe abnormalities of the fetus; or when the pregnancy resulted from

expected from doctors who are professionally bound to express ethical condemnation of abortion.

[62] See Acórdão do Tribunal Constitucional n.º 75/10, upholding legislation supplementing the indications model with one more exception to punishment for abortions in the first ten weeks of pregnancy, after a counseling process destined only to provide women with the information needed to make a free, conscious and responsible decision (and hence not explicitly dissuasive), and a three-day reflection period.

rape.[63] This legislative reform triggered the first constitutional litigation, with two decisions, one from 1984 and one from 1985, validating the indications model.[64] On both occasions, the Court upheld the indications model in a move which can be described as one of *nuanced reception* of the German model: even though the basic German framing was transferred, and placed in opposition to the US framing, the exact doctrine was clearly not.

Although the first decision, that of 1984, started with a section devoted to comparative law, presenting both the legislation in France, Germany, and Italy, and the jurisprudence of the Constitutional Courts in these countries, the only referent that the Court used throughout the entire decision, to express both agreement and disagreement, was Germany's. Explicitly mentioning Germany's *Abortion I*,[65] the first Portuguese cases started from the protection owed, not to pregnant women, but to what the Portuguese Court called "intra-uterine life," which it considered covered by the constitutional right to life (article 24(1) of the Portuguese Constitution) and personal integrity (article 25), both interpreted in harmony with the principle of human dignity.[66] In doing so, the Court vaguely invoked the "nature of things," and noted that scientific progress had shown that intra-uterine life is human life, a reasoning which, according to the Court, had also guided the German Court in the *Abortion I* decision, even though the German Constitution, in its right to life provision, referred to the word "everyone," as opposed to the Portuguese Constitution's wording in article 24, which more broadly declares that "Human life shall be inviolable."

However, unlike the German Court, which had declared the question open and, ultimately, irrelevant in *Abortion I*, the Portuguese Court specified, in both its 1984 and 1985 decisions, that this did *not* make the unborn a rights-holder, for under the Portuguese Constitution only persons, not fetuses, could be holders of fundamental rights. Thus, the protection owed to intra-uterine life was a protection due to unborn life as an "objective value" worthy of constitutional promotion.[67] For the Court, the doctrinal implications were not minor, as they meant that the

---

[63] Lei no. 6/84, of May 11, amending the Código Penal.

[64] Acórdão do Tribunal Constitucional n.º 85/85 (published in *Acórdãos do Tribunal Constitucional*, V, Lisboa, pp. 245 ff.) and Acórdão do Tribunal Constitucional n.º 25/84 (published in *Acórdãos do Tribunal Constitucional*, II, Lisboa, pp. 7 ff.).

[65] Acórdão do Tribunal Constitucional n.º 25/84 cfr. VII, § 1.

[66] Acórdão do Tribunal Constitucional n.º 25/84 cfr. VII, § 1.

[67] Acórdão do Tribunal Constitucional n.º 85/85, cfr. 2, § 2.

hierarchical placement of the value of unborn life over women's autonomy could not be accepted.[68] Instead, it was acknowledged from the start that the objectified constitutional value of intra-uterine life might have to give way when in conflict with women's subjective constitutional rights, including the right, not only to life, health, and reputation (all of which might support the need for criminal indications), but also to dignity and conscientious motherhood.[69] Moreover, unlike what had been suggested in *Abortion I*, and just as Otto Bachof had defended in criticizing the German Court, great discretion was to be granted to the legislator, in deciding which protective means to opt for in protecting unborn life.[70] On these premises, the Portuguese Court validated the proportionality analysis exercised by the legislator when introducing the criminal exceptions in the abortion regulation in both its 1984 and 1985 decisions.

However, it was not until 1998[71] that the Portuguese Court was given the opportunity to confirm the constitutionality of a reform embracing a periodic model which would allow abortion on demand during the first ten weeks of pregnancy. This reform was (unsuccessfully) put to a referendum, first in 1998 and then in 2007, following yet another positive decision by the Constitutional Court in 2006.[72] Both decisions were adopted by the closest margin of votes but were to no avail as in the first referendum the "no" votes outweighed the "yes" votes and neither referendum had achieved the necessary participation quorum to be

---

68 Acórdão do Tribunal Constitucional n.º 25/84 cfr. VII, *in fine*.

69 Acórdão do Tribunal Constitucional n.º 85/85, cfr. 2, § 2.

70 Acórdão do Tribunal Constitucional n.º 25/84 cfr. V, § 1. It is thus not surprising that the dissenting opinion by Justice Cardoso da Costa calls on Germany's *Abortion I* to support that the subjective/objective reading of the right to life provision should not be interpreted as allowing for different degrees of protection of human life (2), and to insist on the importance of punitive protection (4).

71 Acórdão do Tribunal Constitucional n.º 288/98. In this decision, after describing the difficult position of women facing abortion (§ 27), the doctrinal reasoning starts once more from the protection owed to intra-uterine life under article 24 of the Portuguese Constitution (§ 43). However, once more, the Court cites Otto Bachof's criticism of *Abortion I* to support the legislator's discretion in deciding how to adequately balance competing constitutional goods (§§ 43 and 51). Although validating the option of non-punitive protection and the periodic solution, the Court makes clear that it is not endorsing the *Roe v. Wade* framework, which assigns women a constitutional right to have an abortion (§§ 44–5).

72 See Acórdão do Tribunal Constitucional n.º 617/2006.

binding. Interestingly, it has been observed that among the main factors accounting for the failure of liberalization through referendum was the strong and successful fight put up by civil society groups; and, more fundamentally, the Catholic Church, as the most engaged actor, which succeeded in having bishops and priests seize both the pulpits of rural areas and national mass media to aggressively combat liberalization, including by drawing comparisons between abortion and the Nazi Holocaust.[73]

The path to reform through referendum having failed on two consecutive occasions, legislation was finally passed in April 2007 amending Portugal's Criminal Code, supplementing the indications model with one more exception for abortions upon request by the pregnant woman during the first ten weeks of pregnancy and after mandatory counseling to provide women with the information needed to make a "free, conscious and responsible" decision and a three-day reflection period.[74] Notably, explicit dissuasion of the kind that the German Constitutional Court had made a precondition for accepting the periodic model in *Abortion II* was not contemplated in the legislation.

In February 2010, the Portuguese Constitutional Court arrived at its decision upholding the legislation.[75] The basic framework of the decision reproduced the essential features of the Court's prior doctrine: the life of the unborn had to be protected as an objective value, and this protection had to be balanced against the fundamental rights of the pregnant woman.[76] Also, citing not only Otto Bachof this time, but also Robert Alexy, when deciding on the concrete abortion regulation, the legislator enjoys wide discretion, for, unlike negative duties (i.e. duties to not infringe on constitutional rights or values), positive duties (i.e. duties to actively promote such rights or values, or protect them from third-party interference), even when constitutionally derived, are much more undetermined in nature.[77] In this regard, the Court clarified, two considerations are, however, important. Firstly, that it is comprehensively considered that positive measures must be said to provide adequate protection of fundamental rights or constitutional values.[78] Secondly,

[73] André Freire and Michael A. Baum, "Partidos políticos, movimentos de cidadãos e referendos em Portugal: os casos do aborto e da regionalização" (2001) XXXVI (158–9) *Análise Social* 23, 29.

[74] Law no. 16/2007 of April 17.

[75] Acórdão do Tribunal Constitucional n.º 75/2010 (23.10.2010).

[76] Cfr. § 14.4.2.

[77] Cfr. § 11.4.3.

[78] Cfr. § 11.4.4.

that, in deciding how to properly harmonize the duty to protect intra-uterine life and women's fundamental rights, the legislator may take into account the gestational phase of the fetus. This, the Court claimed, was a widely accepted axiom, which duly reflects the special type of connection between a woman and the fetus inside her. Explicitly borrowing from Germany's *Abortion II*,[79] the Court referred to this relationship as a relationship of "duality within unity,"[80] yet attached to it the meaning proposed not by the majority, but by the dissenting Justices Mahrenholz and Sommer instead,[81] which the Court cited when stating that the relationship "does not remain static throughout the pregnancy, instead 'during the first weeks the woman and the *nascituro* (…) fully appear as unity, whereas with the growth of the embryo the "duality" becomes more apparent'."[82]

In spite of this, to avoid misunderstandings, the Court pushed the *Roe* specter away, clarifying that at no point during the pregnancy, including at its earliest stages, could the legislator give absolute priority to women's rights, thereby entirely sacrificing the value of life, for this would amount to an absolute and unconditional recognition of a woman's right to have an abortion,[83] a right which the Court claimed the American, but not the Portuguese legal order, recognized.[84] Within this framework, the crucial question then became whether the state had fulfilled its obligation of minimum protection of intra-uterine life.

In discussing the sufficiency of the protective means contemplated by the proposed legislation, the Portuguese Court, like the German Court, recognized that to protect the life of the unborn, the state is obliged not only to refrain from actions threatening the unborn life, but also to safeguard it against potential threats by third parties, including the pregnant woman.[85] However, unlike the German Court, the Portuguese Court did not see the need for punitive or, alternatively, explicitly dissuasive protection to be put into place. Instead, for the Portuguese Court, in performing its constitutional duties, the state is under an obligation to undertake measures to avoid unwanted pregnancies (such as family planning and other forms of preventive measures) and measures

79 See 88 BVerfGE 203 (1993).
80 Ibid.
81 Ibid. 338, 342.
82 Cfr. § 11.4.4.
83 Ibid.
84 Cfr. §§ 11.4.5 and 11.4.6.
85 Cfr. §11.4.3.

intended to stop abortive intentions,[86] recognizing that, among the latter – aside from punitive measures – and especially worthy of consideration, are *promotional* measures, such as those seeking to encourage women to consciously accept and exercise motherhood.[87] There was thus no obligation of punitive protection.[88] Rather, it was for the legislator to decide if, and when, criminal punishment measures were adequate and necessary, bearing in mind that criminal punishment must always be an *ultima ratio*.[89] In fact, in this particular case, the adequacy and necessity of criminalization was rather difficult to justify in view of the proven inefficiency of criminal punishment as a deterrent, and the end result of abortions being performed illegally with great risk to the woman's health and life.[90] Additionally, evidence about the under-enforcement of the criminal system showed that, for the most part, the crime was no longer socially perceived to be such.[91]

Seen from this angle, the Court clarified that the new legislative model could not be interpreted as an expression of the state entirely giving up its duty to protect unborn life at an early stage. Rather, again paraphrasing the Mahrenholz and Sommer dissent in Germany's *Abortion II*, the Court referred to the fact that the "duality within unity" that pregnancy represents lends itself to a better understanding of the nature of the conflict faced by a pregnant woman, its inherently personal character, and the reasonableness of assuming that the legislator understands that, at an early stage, the protection of the unborn is most efficient *through* the protection of the woman (i.e. relying on her sense of responsibility and trusting her judgment), making sure only that the decision is both informed and deliberate.[92] According to the Court, a sort of "soft law," more promotional than repressive in nature, is more conducive to altering a woman's motives and making her reconsider the decision in the few cases wherein the woman has not entirely made up her mind, that is, in the only cases in which abortions can be stopped.[93]

Not surprisingly, underlying this construction is a perception of the pregnant woman facing the decision, which the Court affirmed to be backed by German sociological data cited in *Abortion II*, according to

---

86 Ibid.
87 Ibid.
88 But see dissenting opinion of Justice Benjamin Rodrigues (§ 3).
89 Cfr. §§ 11.4.6 and 11.4.7.
90 Cfr. § 11.4.7.
91 Cfr. §§ 11.4.7 and 8.
92 Cfr. § 14.9.9.
93 Cfr. § 11.4.10.

which women seeking an abortion cannot be presupposed to follow hedonistic reasons and act selfishly.[94] Rather, the decision to have an abortion is taken, in spite of the anxiety it generates, out of a genuine conviction that this is the right course of action, after pondering responsibly the value of unborn life as well as the existence of other types of harms to oneself and others which must be avoided.[95] Not surprisingly either, this understanding of women encouraged the Portuguese Court to go beyond efficiency considerations, dominant under *Abortion II*, and justify the legislative solution, as the Sommer and Mahrenholz dissent had done, as *also* expressing women's constitutional status, including her dignity.[96] Women's constitutional interests could not simply be compromised, especially taking into account that, for women, what is usually involved is not only a negative obligation, namely to not interfere in a natural gestational process, but also the positive obligation of taking care of a person for many years, at the expense of burdening her own entire existence.[97]

For the Court, this conflict between goods of a personal nature to a rights-holder, on the one hand, and the objective protection of the social good of respect for life, on the other, cannot be resolved in an all or nothing fashion. The legislator may therefore find, on grounds of both efficiency *and* principled considerations related to the woman's dignity, that it is adequate to consider that the best solution is to allow a woman's responsible decision for a certain period of time at an early stage of pregnancy.[98] It still remained to be seen whether the actual legislation would live up to the minimum standards of required protection. While the dissenting voices did not think this was the case, the Court assessed, and ultimately validated, the sufficiency of non-punitive protective measures.

Much of the weight of the plaintiffs' argumentation had relied on the fact that the counseling and three-day reflection period contemplated by the 2007 Act was not sufficiently *dissuasive* and hence protective of the fetus. The counseling procedure, they claimed, was primarily informative, only helping women to make informed decisions. But only seeking women's informed consent, the Portuguese plaintiffs argued, was not a sufficiently fetus-centered procedure. As the Court acknowledged in

---

94 Ibid.

95 Ibid.

96 Ibid § 11.4.11. Notice therefore the implicit reference and contrast with *Abortion I*, which had called on dignity only to strengthen the protection of the unborn, not of pregnant women.

97 Ibid.

98 Ibid.

passing, the hope of the plaintiffs had been to have the Portuguese Court follow the German Court in *Abortion II*, and make the departure from a proven inefficient criminalization/indications model, and the partial embracing of a periodic system, contingent on it being supplemented by an explicitly dissuasive counseling model.

The Portuguese Constitutional Court approached the question of whether the specific counseling model in the 2007 Act constituted sufficient protection of the unborn in two steps. As a first step, it relied on comparative law to show both the increasing prevalence of the periodic model, as well as the widespread variation with regard to the endorsement (or not) of mandatory counseling across Europe.[99] Secondly, it reflected on the German model, which the plaintiffs had pushed as the relevant comparator, to conclude that in fact it constituted more the exception than the norm. For the Portuguese Court, what justified the imposition of such a model by the German Constitutional Court, and hence what lay behind Germany's exceptionalism, was the Court's doctrine of recognizing the unborn as a rights-holder, something the Portuguese constitutional order had refused to do from the beginning.[100] In fact, *Abortion I* had simply left the question open as irrelevant.

In what is probably the most vociferous dissent in the decision, Chief Justice Rui Manuel Moura Ramos challenged the doctrinal relevance that the Court attached to the status of the unborn. According to Justice Moura Ramos, the protection constitutionally due to intra-uterine life, whether considered as a rights-holder or not, can never be reduced to a protection of life as a concept or a notion, but rather required the protection of the existential reality of each individually conceived fetus, through at least minimally effective means, including during the first ten weeks of pregnancy.[101] This is, in fact, what the majority in *Abortion II* had affirmed. Non-dissuasive counseling and the general existence of preventive and incentivizing measures therefore could *not* satisfy the minimum protection owed to the existing fetus, because these measures fail to intervene directly in the mental decision-making process of the woman and discourage her from having an abortion.[102]

The majority, instead, seemed satisfied with a counseling procedure seeking women's informed and thoughtful consent, both on efficiency and principled grounds. In essence, for the Court, the fact that the procedure was not explicitly dissuasive did not mean that it was "merely

---

99 § 11.4.13.

100 §§ 11.4.13-14 and 11.4.17.

101 See dissent by Justice Rui Manuel Moura Ramos (§§ 2–3).

102 Ibid.

informative," as the plaintiffs had claimed. Rather, the very existence of mandatory counseling implied a procedure seeking women's thoughtful and responsible conduct.[103] Moreover, one could expect promotional measures to have a dissuading effect, especially on women with a low socio-economic profile.[104]

What the Portuguese legislator, unlike the German legislator, had clearly not included in the procedure was any language or requirement which could be experienced by women as an external judgment or imposition. This was explicitly granted by the Portuguese Court. Granted also was that the legislator could have embraced more explicit language celebrating the importance of the value of life, or, along the lines of the German model under *Abortion II*, charged the agents involved in the process with the task of dissuading women, including through the explicit repudiation of abortion. Once again, according to the Court, the difference hinged on the fact that the German Court, unlike the Portuguese, had considered that the unborn had a subjective right to life.[105] But for an external observer it is obvious that the difference hinged not only on the understanding of the fetus, but also on the understanding of the pregnant woman.

According to the Court, the dissuasion of women through the explicit repudiation of abortion could not be supported, either for efficiency considerations or on principled grounds.[106] For the Court, a model which assumes the responsible choice of the pregnant woman and her inclination to cooperate with the state's duty to protect life cannot easily be reconciled with one that creates a largely unfavorable context of choice for her, putting pressure on her by interfering in her decisional process, and making inroads into her emotional and psychological vulnerability.[107] In fact, a pressuring environment could actually provoke the opposite of the desired end result.[108] There was no empirical evidence to show that the German dissuasive counseling system was a particularly efficient one, the Court noted.[109] More fundamentally, leaving aside efficiency considerations and focusing on the constitutionally protected dignity of women, the Court maintained that an understanding of women as "responsible and sensitive to the reasons that speak against abortion" was

---

103 § 11.4.15.
104 Ibid.
105 § 14.4.17.
106 § 11.4.16.
107 Ibid.
108 Ibid.
109 § 11.4.18.

not compatible with an infantilizing and paternalistic counseling system. In other words, the dignity of women also had to have an impact on how the mandatory counseling was shaped.[110] This, however, was rejected by those dissenting justices who insisted that explicit dissuasive counseling should be constitutionally required.[111]

Instead, in assessing whether the legal system grants due protection to the value of unborn life, it was essential to bear in mind that such a protection is articulated not only through legal regulation of abortion. Rather, "it falls to the state to fight against 'risk factors' … through education, and to adopt social policies favoring responsible conception as well as willingness to continue pregnancy" as essential tools to reduce the number of abortions.[112] Providing sexual education and family planning services, as well as ensuring living and working conditions, through social policies in favor of motherhood and family life, are all necessary in order to ensure responsible conception, as well as to allow women the ability, and encourage their willingness, to carry pregnancies to term. The Court referred to some such measures already contained in the Portuguese legal system, mostly in employment and social security legislation, as well as to sexual education in the schooling system. The existence of these measures, the Court argued, showed that the Portuguese state was not indifferent to abortion as a phenomenon.[113] More could still be done to attain the levels of sexual education and the protection of motherhood of the most advanced countries.

6.5. CONCLUDING THOUGHTS: FRANKENBERG'S THEORY OF TRANSFER VALIDATED

This journey from Germany's to Portugal's abortion constitutionalism confirms many of the features of a theory of transfer described in Frankenberg's introduction to this volume. Constitutional information and items travel across boundaries and social-cultural contexts, but the relevant actors who borrow from one country's constitutional repertoire, in turn, modify elements of imported constitutional building materials. Thus, the Portuguese Constitutional Court, when confronted with abortion as a constitutional matter, explicitly borrowed the German framing

[110] § 11.4.16.

[111] See dissenting opinion of Justices José M Borges Soerio, Lucia Amaral and Rui Manuel Moura Ramos.

[112] § 11.4.18.

[113] Ibid.

(and rejected the US framing, which was also available), locating the value of unborn human life at the center of its reasoning, and turning it all into a conversation about the kind of protection that the state owes to it. At the same time, the Portuguese Court adapted the doctrine by explicitly spelling out that it did not consider the unborn a constitutional rights-holder, thereby justifying its deviation from the German doctrine, which had affirmed the hierarchical superiority of the value of unborn life over women's reproductive interests. This allowed the Portuguese Court to embrace proportionality analysis, which the German Court had rejected, affirming that human life deserved some form of protection from inception, but was to be seen as an evolving process with qualitatively relevant milestones, a process which may call for different degrees and forms of protection, and which has to be balanced against women's constitutionally protected reproductive interests primarily by the legislator.

Interestingly, the German Court had its own views about Germany's exceptionalism, accounting for its difficulty in accepting a periodic abortion model, and these did not coincide with those the Portuguese Court relied upon. For the German Court, it was the historical context of the constitution-making process and its reaction against the Nazi legacy that justified reading the constitutional dignity clause as a ground for the hierarchically superior value of human life, including unborn human life. By justifying the difference on the grounds of doctrine rather than in the specific historical circumstances – i.e. on whether the unborn is, or is not, considered a rights-holder – the Portuguese Court was able to de-contextualize the German referent. This then facilitated what I have called a process of *subversive legal transfer*, in which the main framing, or the original point of departure, was accepted, but the doctrinal implications fundamentally altered through a bricolaging exercise. This allowed the Court to retain the narrative appeal and symbolic strength of placing "human life" at the center of its reasoning, something which was likely to appeal to the larger public in an overwhelmingly Catholic country, yet – at the same time – letting women, who carry human life inside them, be placed with it, next to it, instead of being erased by it. Interestingly, in its bricolaging activity, the Portuguese Court did not hesitate to draw from materials provided by the dissenting voices of the German Court itself, as well as by critical scholarship, thereby indirectly challenging essentialist understandings of the winning German doctrine. The matter could have been decided differently even in Germany, and in fact some were critical of how it was actually decided.

In shaping the profile of its distinctive doctrine, the Portuguese Court, at the same time, affirmed and challenged the hegemonic position of

German abortion constitutionalism in Europe: affirmation in the sense that, in each step, the Court considered it relevant to dialogically include the German referent, whether to embrace it or to depart from it; challenge in the sense that, in its own decisions, the Portuguese Court pointed out the existence of relevant alternatives, showing that, as far as abortion goes, the German legal/constitutional model should, in European terms, be seen as the exception rather than the norm.

As framing and doctrine travel, their meaning does not remain unchanged. Under the German model, the meaning of the protection due to the fetus/unborn life has remained tied to the goal of maximizing the actual number of fetuses that make it into full human beings (the means chosen for this being more of an instrumental question, as long as, under the refined German model of *Abortion II*, women are not left alone to bear all the costs). Instead, under the Portuguese model, the centrality attached to intra-uterine life (*together with* the respect owed to women's reproductive autonomy) has basically been affirmed as requiring the recognition of the central importance of human reproduction, something which a state can do by adopting preventive and promotional means (i.e. education policies seeking deliberate and responsible conception, and state measures aimed at encouraging motherhood and parenting), yet allowing women to freely decide whether or not to go through with the pregnancy at the very early stages.

This exercise of reception has, therefore, allowed the rhetoric centrality of the value of unborn human life to be maintained, while re-defining what it means in terms of concrete obligations to respect and protect on the part of the state and others. In Germany, *Abortion I* rejected the periodic model; and *Abortion II* accepted it conditionally: it had to be duly supplemented by preventive and promotional measures, as well as dissuasive counseling. In Portugal 2010, the periodic model was accepted on the condition that it was duly supplemented by preventive and promotional measures, but without the need for dissuasive counseling. Underlying this jurisprudential evolution, from Germany (*Abortion I* and then *II*) to Portugal, are epistemic assumptions and shifting perceptions of pregnant women in general, of the relationship between the woman and the fetus inside her, and of the "by-default" aborting woman. The antagonistic relationship between woman and fetus, seen as two existentially separate entities, and the need to protect the latter from the selfish or whimsical motives of the former by forcing her to accept her destiny as a mother, have gradually been replaced by a perception of the pregnant woman as a single entity (a duality within unity), as well as a responsible decision-maker. This woman is constructed not as somebody inclined to take the decision whether to proceed with or discontinue her pregnancy lightly, or out of selfish or hedonistic reasons, but rather as influenced by the existence of adequate means and support (or lack thereof), or out of the conviction that she must avoid inflicting serious harm onto others and herself. This construction does not recognize women as having an ultimate right to be left alone in their choice, granting them a time-limited but absolute decision-making power, à la *Roe v. Wade*. Instead, it supports the periodic abortion model both on efficiency and principled grounds, in the conviction that punitive measures are not adequate means to fight against abortions, and that, instead, in the early stages of pregnancy, the best protection of the unborn can only be the protection of the pregnant woman. It requires both trust in a woman's judgment, and ensuring that her decisions are free and informed, including through the provision of means and relevant alternatives. It also requires duly taking into account that what is at stake for women when confronting the decision is typically not just the biological process of pregnancy and delivery, but the lifelong task of mothering; and that this task must not be biologically determined, but autonomously chosen.

PART III

Ordering pluralism – alternative normative orders challenging the state-centeredness of constitutionalism

7. Legal pluralism and normative transfer

Jennifer Hendry

The transfer, transplant and translation of legal norms from one locus, context or culture to another is a topic with which comparative legal scholars are well-acquainted, it having been one of the issues central to the fledgling discipline at its inaugural Paris congress in 1900.[1] Although in the intervening period it could be said that these concerns receded somewhat from the academic limelight, the past thirty years have seen a resurgence of interest, no doubt due to the particular questions raised by a patent increase in globalization, Europeanization and governance operations, as well as by the recognition, reconciliation and "decolonization" processes occurring in many post-colonial societies. While legal norms have always crossed borders, be these national, cultural or functional ones, recent legal and social changes and developments have served to make the study of this transfer of law more important than ever before.

It is not only issues of legal transfer that global, supranational, and post-colonial developments in society and society's law have brought to the forefront of the debates among proponents of comparative legal studies, however, but also the similarly topical matter of legal pluralism. Legal pluralism introduces the idea of there being spaces of normativity that may or may not be congruent with the recognized boundaries of specific legal orders, promoting a fragmentation of "law" within and across jurisdictions formerly understood as monist or even monolithic. An increasingly popular approach, legal pluralism has been described as a "key concept in a post-modern view of law,"[2] and has been employed in

[1] This refers, of course, to the famous congress on "Les Méthodes du droit comparé," held by the Société de Législation Comparée in Paris, 1900.

[2] Boaventura de Sousa Santos, "Law: A Map of Misreading. Toward a Post-modern Conception of Law" (1987) 14 *Journal of Law and Society* 279–302, 297.

a wide variety of endeavors including, among others, questioning the very character of law, challenging the bias that saw the nation state as the sole legal source, and making sense of the connections and interactions that gave rise to new post-national constellations.[3] Alongside legal transfer, legal pluralism has starred in debates concerning the importance of locality and context in understanding legal features and practices, while also – and this is certainly as a result of their shared history within the discipline of legal anthropology – finding themselves inextricably linked by their conceptual relevance to different legal orders and to issues of conflict, contestation and interaction in terms of law, society, culture and legal culture.

Legal transfer suggests the movement of legal norms between closed legal or normative orders, which has often tended to concern nation state legal orders.[4] This chapter contends that framing legal transfer in terms of legal pluralism introduces another dimension to this debate, namely the possibility of a reciprocal interaction of normative orders occupying a new "space" that has the potential to give rise to a newly contextualized form of the "transferred" legal norm, detached as it is from both of its original contexts. The chapter will attempt to illustrate this by focusing specifically on the normative *locus* of state-internal legal pluralism vis-à-vis post-colonial societies with indigenous communities.[5] This selection is driven by the particular challenges this presents in terms of

---

[3] This term was first employed by Jürgen Habermas in *The Postnational Constellation* (Polity Press 2000).

[4] This is more noticeable in terms of its employment in debates on *constitutional* borrowing or transfer; for a comprehensive account, see Günter Frankenberg, "Constitutional Transfer: The IKEA Theory Revisited" (2010) 8 *International Journal of Constitutional Law* 563–79, and also *Autorität und Integration: Zur Grammatik von Recht und Verfassung* (Suhrkamp 2003). David Nelken raises a similar point, noting that "given the way it often sets boundaries of jurisdiction, politics and language, the nation state will often serve as a relevant starting point for comparing legal culture." See David Nelken, "Defining and Using the Concept of Legal Culture" in D Nelken and E Örücü (eds) *Comparative Law: A Handbook* (Hart 2007) 109–32, 119.

[5] There are, of course, alternative *loci* also pertinent to such an analysis, of which this is necessarily a selection. These alternatives include trans-state, supra-state, inter-state interactions and constellations, such as (and perhaps most obviously) the European Union (EU), but these will need to be the focus of another paper. For more on the multiplicity of legal orders or "systems" in the EU, see: Julie Dickson, "How Many Legal Systems? Some Puzzles Regarding the Identity Conditions of, and Relations between, Legal Systems in the European Union" (2008) 9 *Problema* 9–50; and Martijn W Hesselink, "How Many Systems of Private Law are there in Europe? On Plural Legal Sources,

how state-internal normative borders and boundaries are (re)presented, consideration of which is of course key to the concept of legal transfer, along with how these boundaries affect interaction among and across normative orders. It is the selection of intra-state legal transfer as the focal point of the investigation that necessitates a discussion of both legal and normative pluralism.

7.1. ORDERING PLURALISM

The title of this section, which was appropriated from the conference that gave rise to this volume, tends to conjure images of luckless legal-comparatists attempting to herd cats or undertake other equally unenviable tasks, for little appears to be less "ordered" than legal pluralism, whether this is in terms of its (contested) conception or (diverse) application. Mireille Delmas-Marty makes a similar point in her book of the same name, observing the inherent contradiction between the two words and stating that, while pluralism "refers to dispersion or free movement … ordering evokes structure, even constraints."[6] What is being referred to here is, in essence, the tension at the heart of any discussion of legal unity and legal, or normative, diversity. As Sionaidh Douglas-Scott notes:

> With its associations of order, regularity, proportionality and equality, there is something geometric or architectonic about the Rule of Law – a contrast with the "chaos of surfaces" and "rhetorical fronts" of postmodernity and pluralism. And yet, the very fact of complex trajectories and perspectives might suggest a reason why this structural component is needed more than ever … as a means of containing the chaos of the legal universe.[7]

If it is assumed that such a structural component is required, how, then, can the perceived benefits of formal law mentioned in this quotation be given effect without perpetuating violence against legal-cultural alterity? Is it even possible to provide legal plurality with a semblance of order or structure without reducing it to (a hegemonically dictated) uniformity? In

---

Multiple Identities and the Unity of Law" (2012) Amsterdam Law School Legal Studies Research Paper 59.

[6] M Delmas-Marty, *Ordering Pluralism: A Conceptual Framework for Understanding the Transnational Legal World* (Hart 2009) 63.

[7] Sionaidh Douglas-Scott, "Pluralism and Justice in the Contemporary European Legal Space" (2012) University College London Current Legal Problems Lecture Series 11.

terms of the *locus* mentioned above, the intra-state or intra-systemic issues raised by the interaction of indigenous normative orders and institutionalized post-colonial state legal systems concern the idea of legal character (or what counts as law), and as such the discussion is arguably more accurately described as one of *normative* pluralism as opposed to legal pluralism. Clarity concerning this distinction is essential and so, before proceeding further with this investigation, it is necessary to explain and justify the definitions of legal and normative pluralism, and the resultant conception of alternative normative order that will be employed throughout this chapter.

7.1.1 Legal / Normative Pluralism: Contestation and Interaction

As discussed earlier, legal pluralism has become increasingly popular since its genesis in 1986[8] and now tends to crop up in a wide range of postmodern approaches, many of which conceptualize both it and law very differently.[9] The potential and scope of the concept of legal pluralism lend it a malleability that operates as a double-edged sword: on the one hand it is flexible enough to be discussed from many different perspectives, while on the other it appears to lack any real defining contours, other than being premised upon contestability. While not necessarily crossing over into outright conflict, a plural constellation nonetheless only manifests if there are alternative paths or processes available within a pre-defined legal space, in contrast to the monist situation (or jurisdiction) which offers no such potential for selection. Issues of selection, or choice, of course, introduce their own considerations of authority and enforceability but, leaving those to one side for the moment, suffice to say that the presence of different normative options within the same legal space constitutes those circumstances generally accepted as being legally plural.[10] Writ large, therefore, legal pluralism can be said to come into existence when there is a dispute, disagreement or some other form of contestation about the "law" that applies in particular circumstances. Importantly for the purposes of this

---

[8] John Griffiths, "What is Legal Pluralism?" (1986) 24 *Journal of Legal Pluralism and Unofficial Law* 1.

[9] For a more in-depth account of this issue, see Brian Z Tamanaha, "A Non-Essentialist Version of Legal Pluralism" (2000) 27 *Journal of Law and Society* 2.

[10] As Emmanuel Melissaris puts it, "the conception of the law in terms of shared normative experiences reflects the fragmentation of our identities and memberships." See Emmanuel Melissaris, *Ubiquitous Law* (Ashgate 2009) 125.

chapter, moreover, wherever there is normative contestation, there is also *interaction* between (or among, to bypass the "pervasive binary"[11] that tends to attach itself to the discourse on indigeneity and, by association, intra-state legal pluralism) normative orders, as this is a pre-requisite of legal transfer.

Another aspect that is interesting about this notion of contestability as fundamental to plurality is that, as long as legal pluralism can be defined in this broad sense, in essence, simply as the opposite of legal monism or centralism, without qualification, then contestability itself comes to represent the full spectrum of legally pluralist possibilities. The definition *contra* monism[12] has the effect of casting the net very wide, meaning that a huge variety of normative orders could arguably raise a plausible claim to existing in circumstances of legal plurality; indeed, it could be argued that this gives rise to a spectrum of legal plurality, with differences in positioning across this spectrum being premised upon conditions of contestability that could range from absolute normative conflict and even non-recognition, to an altogether far milder form that manifests as mutual recognition and compromise. Under these circumstances, then, the definition of an alternative normative order becomes a rather straightforward exercise, for the only features that appear necessary for inclusion in this category are that such an order is, in fact, normative, and that these (constituent) norms are at variance with the hegemonic, usually state, legal order. In essence the definition can be reduced to the simple observation that there exists within a single legal space, to use John Griffiths' term, a situation of "normative heterogeneity."[13] By way of contrast, however, legal pluralism is a more unwieldy concept both to employ and to rely upon. Much of the difficulty, this chapter submits, can be attributed to both the popularity and malleability of legal pluralism, which have resulted in it becoming rather stretched and "thin" and, moreover, that this dilution has occurred in two main areas, namely its character and its utilization.

---

[11] This phrase is used courtesy of Mark McMillan (Melbourne Law School, University of Melbourne).

[12] The fundamental basis of legal pluralism, and perhaps the sole characteristic that unifies all proponents, is a rejection of the "false ideology" of legal centralism as recognized by John Griffiths, whereby "law is and should be the law of the state, uniform for all persons, exclusive of all other law, and administrated by a single set of state institutions". See Griffiths (n 8) 3.

[13] John Griffiths, "The Social Working of Legal Rules" (2003) 48 *Journal of Legal Pluralism and Unofficial Law* 84, 23.

The next section will investigate both of these areas: in terms of the former, the character or *object* of legal pluralism, the focus will rest upon the distinction that can be drawn between legal and normative pluralism, while engagement with the latter will revolve around the emancipatory potential implicit in the instrumental approach adopted and the motivations underpinning said adoption. By separating out these two aspects of the concept of legal pluralism it is hoped that some further light will be shed on the idea of transfer – be it legal or normative – across state-internal, contextually determined boundaries and normative spaces. At this juncture it should be noted that, while the focus of this chapter rests specifically upon intra-state arrangements pertaining to the interaction of state and indigenous normative orders, different legal spaces and arenas – supra-state, trans-state, inter-state, even (and perhaps controversially) *non*-state – offer further avenues for future investigation.

7.1.2 The Object of Legal/Normative Pluralism

At the outset of this discussion concerning the character (object) of legal pluralism, it should be stated that this issue involves less consideration of the aspect of plurality and more of that of legality. That is to say, the focus rests on the distinction that can be drawn between legal and normative pluralism or, rather, on the requirements that social norms are expected to meet in order to achieve the status of law within a particular jurisdiction. While different commentators impose different standards and set different thresholds for this,[14] Sarah Engle Merry's famous observation is no less pertinent here than it was twenty-five years ago, for "[w]here *do* we stop speaking of law and find ourselves simply describing social life, [and] is it useful to call these forms of ordering law?"[15]

To explain the importance of this point in terms of the overall argument it is necessary to revisit the categories established by the concept's founding father, John Griffiths, namely weak and strong legal pluralism. The weak form supersedes a legally monist form but in a rather half-hearted kind of way – Griffiths describes it as "the messy compromise [that] the ideology of legal centralism feels itself obliged to make with recalcitrant social reality."[16] This weak form, which tends to be associated both with the intra-state paradigm and with post-colonial

---

[14] See, for example, Boaventura de Sousa Santos, *Towards a New Legal Common Sense* (2nd edn, Butterworths 2002).

[15] Sarah Engle Merry, "Legal Pluralism" (1988) 22 *Law & Society Review* 869, 878, emphasis added.

[16] Griffiths (n 8) 7.

societies, has three main features: first, that it always remains in the gift of the (hegemonic) state; second, that the state receives some benefit from this compromise situation; and third, that it is invariably envisaged as being impermanent, a temporary solution for a difficult situation, which is fine in the meantime but only until a preferable alternative can be found.[17] Griffiths actually rejects this weak form as constituting legal pluralism at all – indeed, he dismisses all but the strong form, his understanding of which is extremely broad, effectively boiling down to the idea that *all self-regulation is law*. To put this notion another way, his understanding of law is that it is co-extant with self-regulation within the social.

While this is an intriguing point in terms of normativity, it appears, however, that such a drastic move has the effect of undermining any claim to legality that could be raised by an alternative normative order or, rather, that it empties out any *legal* claim. Strong legal pluralism in the Griffiths sense thus represents what is more accurately described as *normative* plurality because, within his conceptualization, law does not require any validation such as that demanded by the major proponents of the liberal (statist) legal-theoretical enterprise, in the form of either a Kelsenian *Grundnorm* or Hartian rule of recognition.[18] Weak and strong legal pluralism, as conceptualized by Griffiths, are thus differentiated by the extent to which alternative (social) norms are recognized by the state or not and, in terms of the latter, the degree to which these norms can exist at variance to those of the state without compelling it to act upon them in some way. The differences between Griffiths' two categories, therefore, concern plurality and plurality alone, with no specific consideration of legality; by designating the legal as co-extant with regulation in the social, he appears deliberately to signify a conceptual break with legally monist theoretical approaches and those predicated upon "state

---

[17] James Tully discusses this idea in terms of "internal colonization" in James Tully, *Public Philosophy in a New Key, Vol. 1: Democracy and Civic Freedom* (Cambridge University Press 2008) 261–76.

[18] In a more "modest" account of legal pluralism, Nick Barber argues that a legal order can "contain multiple rules of recognition that lead to the order containing multiple, unranked, legal sources". See NW Barber, *The Constitutional State* (Oxford University Press 2010) 145.

consent-centred formalism."[19] This approach, by means of de-privileging the legal, causes the distinction between the legal and the normative to collapse.

While innovative, it is submitted that it is this broad conception of strong legal pluralism that has caused it to be such a contested and scrutinized concept,[20] which has in turn contributed to the "stretching" or dilution mentioned above. Other subsequent proponents of legal pluralism have come at the issue from the opposite perspective, seeming to prefer the expansion of a specifically legal character to include certain social norms and suggesting that such alternatives as, for example, soft law, social practices and self-regulation exist along a *spectrum* of legality. Indeed, this standpoint is often adopted in spite of the concession that forcing a legal character onto social norms has the effect of causing "violence to be done to common understandings" and a loss of distinction between the law and other social rules, such as customs, practices and morals.[21] It is submitted that these two perspectives – on one hand the de-privileging of the legal and, on the other, its extension[22] – are representative of ideologically driven instrumental approaches to this issue, and that the standpoint adopted as to the *object* of legal pluralism is premised undeniably upon the way the concept is intended to be used. This utilization, or method, is the focus of the next section.

1.3 The Method of Legal/Normative Pluralism

In terms of legal pluralism's conceptual *method*, it seems rather futile to engage with anything other than an instrumental approach, although arguably the empirically grounded descriptive approach also remains an option. Descriptive approaches, which in disciplinary terms are perhaps

---

[19] Ming-Sung Kuo, "The Concept of 'Law' in Global Administrative Law: A Reply to Benedict Kingsbury" (2009) 20 *European Journal of International Law* 997.

[20] The vital difference here is between the identification and the application of an order or feature as legal instead of merely normative. For an excellent overview of the debate on this issue, see Emmanuel Melissaris, *Ubiquitous Law* (Ashgate 2009), specifically chapter 2.

[21] Brian Z Tamanaha, "The Folly of the Social Scientific Concept of Legal Pluralism" (1993) 20 *Journal of Law and Society* 192.

[22] Tamanaha takes issue with both of these approaches, arguing that state and non-state law norms are fundamentally dissimilar and thus cannot be accurately compared: "Properly seen in terms of their different criteria of existence, state law norms and non-state law 'norms' are two starkly contrary phenomena, not at all alike. Stated more strongly, they are ontologically distinct." Ibid 209.

more anthropological than jurisprudential, tend to be neutral in their assessment, merely intending to identify instances of normative plurality and thus recognizing the existence of conflicting rules in different socio-legal spaces without engaging with issues of resolution or action. By contrast, instrumental approaches employing the concept of legal or normative pluralism are naturally more ideological, even political in nature, with the motivation and aims of the theorist often apparent from the outset.

While this variety of impetus and intention can be cited as a contributory factor in the increasing fragmentation of the debates on legal and normative pluralism across a variety of *loci*, whereby incompatible theoretical applications are compared and contrasted despite being fundamentally at cross-purposes with each other, this is actually not the main focus here. Rather, the more interesting point concerning instrumental approaches concerns the extent to which they facilitate the identification of (a certain degree of) emancipatory potential within the very notion of legal plurality. Implicit within the legal pluralist challenge[23] to the state-centered formalist conception of the monist legal order is a claim to the counter-hegemonic – the minority, the marginalized, the indigenous, the "Stranger" and the "Other" – which necessarily involves the rejection of the western, Westphalian, statist, liberal, authoritative, centralist and monist conception of law and legal order.

There are a number of ways of conceptualizing the issues raised by a pluralist conception, even if the arena is restricted to that of state internal situations as it is in this chapter. For example, and as discussed above, John Griffiths' argument is targeted at undermining the perceived hierarchy of the state legal order vis-à-vis alternative normative orders with the aim of removing state law from its elevated position in favor of a heterarchical constellation within a specific legal space. More concretely, and more recently, Keith Culver and Michael Giudice employ a legally pluralist approach to present their inter-institutional idea of "intra state legality," which is "a legal analogue of an internal political minority – insiders who nonetheless retain something of their outsider status,"[24] and is theorized as existing within the state jurisdiction. In a third example, Iris Young utilizes legally pluralist reasoning to argue in favor of

---

[23] Interestingly, this challenge to law appears to take the *form* of law (however much that may be distorted), thus suggesting a turn *towards* law and a claim upon its emancipatory potential instead of a rejection of the legal paradigm.

[24] Keith Culver and Michael Giudice, *Legality's Borders* (Oxford University Press 2010) 149–55.

representation rights for minority groups, making the claim that such groups have been oppressed and silenced in democratic debate, and that representation rights ensure not just a voice but also an ear, thus facilitating participation in the shaping of state institutions.[25] While these examples are not intended to be exhaustive, it is hoped that they illustrate the range of challenges laid at the door of the legally monist modern nation state, for so long untroubled in its hegemony, unopposed within its borders, and untrammelled in its employment and control of its own legal identifiers, structures, contours and practices. These challenges not only tug at the boundaries and contours of the state but also attack it at its very foundation, which is to say, the consensual basis upon which its power, authority and legitimacy are established.

This section on legal and normative pluralism has endeavored to emphasize the importance of distinguishing between the legal and the normative, to illustrate some of the possible applications of pluralist approaches, and to outline the extent to which these are motivated by the outcomes sought by the theorists employing them. At the heart of the concept, however, is the idea of normative contestation between and among normative orders within the boundaries of the nation state, *normative orders which are in themselves bounded*, whether that be on the basis of identity, community, nation, or participation. It is these intra-state normative borders that the next section will consider, with the aim of ascertaining the extent to which communication, interaction and transfer across these is possible.

7.2. NEGOTIATING BOUNDARIES

If it is to be posited that alternative normative spaces exist within the boundaries of the nation state, then subsequent boundaries or borders delimiting the interior and exterior of such spaces must be identifiable. "Space" is used here in the loosest sense of the term, which is to say that it does not specifically correlate with a geographical, territorial or jurisdictional *locus* but rather with a context or place that is constitutive of meaning, itself constituted by means of a boundary that separates this

---

[25] Iris M Young, "Hybrid Democracy: Iroquois Federalism and the Postcolonial Project" in D Ivison, P Patton and W Sanders (eds), *Political Theory and the Rights of Indigenous Peoples* (Cambridge University Press 2000) 237–58.

normative space from its environment or surroundings.[26] The establishment of a boundary is premised upon the drawing of a distinction, although this assertion of alterity remains to all intents and purposes a neutral one until one side is selected or "marked,"[27] whereby We are distinguished from Them, for example, and Them from Us. It is this "marking" of the different spaces on each side of the border that gives rise to the context and thus the meaning. While this arises by means of a simple dichotomy, the "distinguishing" and "marking" of subsequent distinctions can result in innumerable spaces and contexts; indeed, it is the detachment of the notion of space from that of geography that represents the vital step here. This attenuation each from the other has the effect of providing for context as opposed to situatedness, thus allowing for overlaps and interpenetrations by and of these normative spaces from the perspectives of the individuals who operate within their context/s and boundaries.[28] This section will contend that it is the instigation of such boundaries that serves to represent those counter-hegemonic assertions that are facilitative of a normatively pluralist situation. To elucidate this point vis-à-vis the selected example of state-internal normative plurality and normative transfer across intra-state normative orders, it is necessary to look back on the genesis of those states now referred to as "post-colonial" and the circumstances that gave rise to the situation now being critiqued.

From one perspective, the originary violence of the colonial project can be understood in terms of an omission, which is to say that there was a severe lack of participation by indigenous or subaltern actors within the circumstances of the foundational. The effective dismissal of indigenous societies by their lands' colonizers as being insufficiently complex and

---

[26] Roger Cotterrell makes a similar distinction in terms of the delineation of boundaries in legal interpretation, which can refer to "the fixing of boundaries of *meaning* … or the extent of the *authority* of law or a legal system." See Roger Cotterrell, "Interpretation in Comparative Law" in *Law, Culture & Society: Legal Ideas in the Mirror of Social Theory* (Ashgate 2006) 148.

[27] This echoes the construction used in Luhmanian systems theory; see Niklas Luhmann, *Social Systems* (Stanford University Press 1995).

[28] As Duncan Ivison observes, "since individuals are situated in a range of different social, political and cultural contexts, some with significant moral and normative effects, these contexts must … be acknowledged and accommodated." See Duncan Ivison, *Postcolonial Liberalism* (Cambridge University Press 2002) 161.

sophisticated even to warrant recognition of their existence is well known,[29] with the disgraceful legal fiction of *terra nullius* being given as the justification for what amounted to a barefaced land grab. A different view, however, is that the originary colonizing violence was the absorption of the indigenous normative order into that of the legally monist colonial state. This process was a twofold one, combining the misconception of indigenous norms as (functionally) equivalent to the alien state norms and the a-contextual imposition of those norms on practices and relationships that were "ontologically distinct."[30] Even the subsequent halfway-house arrangements that come under the umbrella of the "weak" form of legal pluralism maintained and perpetuated that initial subsumption – as discussed above, this was nothing more than a pragmatic solution given effect by the state in order to remove irreducible issues of legal conflict between itself and the indigenous normative orders.

Nevertheless, and in spite of colonial motivations concerning legal and administrative practicalities, it is submitted that this "weak" step along the spectrum opened the door to the (re)assertion of a genuinely subaltern normative order within that alternative, newly delimited "space" of indigenous normativity. While this state-sanctioned practice lacked any genuine emancipatory character or potential, it can nonetheless be conceptualized as representative of a limited form of compromise between the two normative orders. That is not to say that recognition of the alternative normative order by a hegemonic one is required (or vice versa, however unlikely); neither recognition nor acknowledgement is a criterion of existence for either order, of course, but they are necessary for *interaction* and, importantly for the purposes of this investigation, for transfer. It is the boundary that is important here, for it is within and under these "borderline conditions,"[31] on the margins, that normative transfer occurs. As Niklas Luhmann puts it, "boundaries do not mark a break in connections. [...] The concept of boundaries means ... that processes which cross boundaries ... have different conditions for their

---

29 "Some tribes are so low in the scale of social organization that their usages and conceptions of rights and duties are not to be reconciled with the institutions or the legal ideas of civilized society. Such a gulf cannot be bridged." Per Lord Sumner speaking for the Privy Council in *Re Southern Rhodesia* (1919) 60 AC 211, 233–4.

30 Brian Z Tamanaha, "The Folly of the Social Scientific Concept of Legal Pluralism" (1993) 20 *Journal of Law and Society* 209.

31 Homi Bhabha uses the term "borderline conditions"; see Homi Bhabha, *The Location of Culture* (Routledge 1994) 9.

continuance after they cross the boundaries."[32] It is to this movement or transfer of normative processes and/or features that the focus of this investigation will now turn.

7.3. DISTINGUISHING TRANSFER

The three terms mentioned at the outset of this chapter – transfer, transplantation and translation[33] – related as they are by the common etymological root of the prefix *trans* – all connote a movement or "crossing" from one position to another. However, despite this basic definitional commonality encompassing one form or another of the "transformation through travel" of legal norms,[34] these terms have substantial differences in terms of their conceptual employment within the comparative law discussion, not least as "signifiers of different theoretical approaches and projects."[35] While admittedly there may be a general and widespread guilt within the discipline in terms of becoming overly entangled with metaphors and semantics, the ongoing debates concerning the most fitting phrase to encapsulate these diverse processes of legal normative "movement" at the very least draw attention to their complexity and variety. This volume engages with many of these well-known debates and so this section shall endeavor to avoid repeating any of these at length, short of what is required for clarity; nevertheless, the conceptual differences between the three terms – transfer, transplantation and translation – do necessitate some further explanation in order adequately to justify the selection of transfer for employment within this investigation. This justification can be simply stated: not only does the concept of transfer have a more universal character and application than either that of transplant or translation, but also, by incorporating a translation component within its process(es), it provides a more nuanced option for the purposes of investigating an area as complex as intra-state normative plurality. This conceptualization of transfer will be explored by means of comparison with the other two, starting with transplantation.

---

32 Luhmann (n 27) 17.

33 While there are many other associated terms, namely transformation, transmission and transportation, the three listed above have been most frequently employed by comparative legal scholars and thus these three will form the basis of this discussion.

34 Julia Eckert, Chapter 8 in this volume, xx.

35 Günter Frankenberg, "Constitutions in Transfer: Notes on a Theory of Transfer," in this volume, xx; see also Frankenberg 2010 (n 4) 566.

7.3.1 Legal Transplantation

As Ralf Michaels explains earlier in this volume, the idea of "copy/paste" intrinsic to the notion of transplantation is different from that of "cut/paste," for the original feature remains unaffected by its recreation elsewhere,[36] regardless of whether the "copying" can be viewed as a success or failure. Indeed, the extent to which the retention of original "copied" features in the newly established legal norm constitutes success is a question for another paper, although most comparative law proponents would argue that the processes of acceptance, reception and recontextualization occurring subsequent to the "pasting" necessitate some degree of alteration or adaptation.[37] That said, the transplantation of legal norms cannot be equated with their translation, for transplantation has a unilateral nature.[38] Whether law is conceptualized either as an instrument for social engineering or as a commodity to be sold,[39] there is rather an element of "trumps" to the idea of transplantation, a sense of victory in competition, the vanquishing of an inefficient or outmoded legal feature in favor of a conquering champion – a Law 2.0, as it were. To put this a different way: while transplantation is interactive, it is not *mutually* so, which is to say that it lacks genuine reciprocity within the process of interaction.[40] For the interaction between normative orders to be reciprocal it must by definition be bi- (or even multi-) lateral, a requirement that transplantation, it is submitted, falls short of. By way of contrast, both transfer and translation can be said to meet this condition, although these must also – for the moment – be distinguished as distinctive concepts or, perhaps more accurately, as different processes.

---

[36] R Michaels, Chapter 3 in this volume, xx.

[37] In his seminal text on legal transplants, Alan Watson goes as far as to state that the "usual way of legal development" is that of copying or "borrowing" plus adaptation: Alan Watson, *Legal Transplants. An Approach to Comparative Law* (Scottish Academic Press 1974) 7; for a more contemporary debate see also Pierre Legrand, "What 'Legal Transplants'" and Roger Cotterrell, "Is There A Logic of Legal Transplants?", both in D Nelken and J Feest (eds), *Adapting Legal Cultures* (Hart 2001).

[38] (n6).

[39] This arguably remains the case within a marketplace or "law as product" conception whether or not the commodity is being bought or sold, as there is no requirement that the "seller" be dominant and the "purchaser" or recipient subservient.

[40] This issue is most overt in Alan Watson's "rule-emphasizing" conceptualization of legal borrowing and legal transplantation, whereby law is detached from society; see Watson (n 37).

7.3.2 Legal Translation

Legal translation can be differentiated from transplantation and transfer by means of its core requirement – namely, translation entails that there be a translating *subject* situated in the space between the normative orders. The process of translation, by definition, requires the active and constructive input of a translator, this abovementioned translating subject, who operates as a conduit, a connection, or a mediator between two texts or spaces.[41] By means of the process of translation, therefore, the translator becomes the *de facto* "author" of the new version of the legal feature, and it is this active additional *creative* aspect that separates translation, conceptually, from transplantation, which neither involves nor requires such a medium – that is to say, the position of the translating subject in the space between the "selling" or "sending" and "purchasing" or "receiving" normative orders means that the two processes are markedly different from what they would have been were such features merely transplanted from donor to recipient. The vital point here to note is the idea of an "in-between space" as it were, a liminal or third space,[42] separate from either context A or context B, for it is here that the translator must necessarily be situated.

In terms of understanding these various forms of interaction between normative orders, the language of systems theory might be useful here, for through this it is possible to separate out the component parts of the interaction or communication.[43] Luhmann's theory of autopoietic systems utilizes communications as its systemic elements and presents these as a

---

[41] This is not to say that the task of translation is a straightforward one – on the contrary, it is an act of extreme complexity, as explained by Gilles Deleuze and Felix Guattari: "Translating is not a simple act: it is not enough to substitute the space traversed for the movement; a series of rich and complex operations is necessary […]. Neither is translating a secondary act. It is an operation that undoubtedly consists in subjugating, overcoding, metricizing smooth space, in neutralising it, but also in giving it a milieu of propagation, extension, refraction, renewal, and impulse without which it would perhaps die of its own accord: like a mask without which it could neither breathe nor find a general form of expression." See Gilles Deleuze and Felix Guattari, *A Thousand Plateaus* (Continuum 1987) 486.

[42] H Bhabha, *The Location of Culture* (Routledge 1994).

[43] Communication in this sense is between social systems, of course, and not normative orders – this point is intended more as an explanation of a particular construction rather than as a genuine application of systems theory.

synthesis of three aspects, namely information, message and understanding,[44] which may of course be an inaccurate understanding or even *mis*understanding. By separating out these aspects, Luhmann serves to neutralize the central component, the message, decontextualizing it from its original setting and/or function and thus facilitating its understanding – in the form of its receipt, interpretation and recontextualization – within an alternative system. Leaving aside for the moment the questionable neutrality of the feature in and of itself, it is arguably possible to observe equivalences between this systems-theoretical conception of communication and the processes of transplantation and transfer. This does not, however, hold true for the process of translation, which is *specifically* facilitated by a translator or translating subject within a liminal space.

7.3.3 Legal Transfer

The aspect that distinguishes transfer from transplantation, therefore, is the additional "step" of translation inherent in it. More nuanced and sensitive than transplantation, more dynamic than mere translation, the concept of transfer has the characteristics of a *process*. Instead of a mere instance of movement, transfer rather denotes a reciprocal and interactive relationship that is simultaneously both place and progression – this final section will endeavor to explain this notion, starting with the idea of "place" or, rather, "space".

It is the involvement of a translating medium *within* the process of transfer that facilitates its conceptualization not only as an interactive process but also as a reciprocal one. Indeed, it is submitted that this has the effect of making the concept of transfer even more "ecumenical" by *liberating* it from the binary construction of import/export and similar.[45] Avoiding this "pervasive binary," as mentioned above, is particularly important within an intra-state situation where the interacting normative orders are those of the state and indigenous peoples and societies, with their attendant power differential. It is, for example, this inequality in terms of the respective power-positions – the dominance of non-indigenous legal categories and concepts compared to indigenous ones – that contributed to the criticisms encountered by Noel Pearson and his

---

[44] "*Information, Mitteilung, Verstehen*"; see Luhmann (n 27).

[45] Günter Frankenberg 2010 (n 4) 570, and Günter Frankenberg's IKEA theory generally, where there is a showroom, supermarket, or "reservoir" of constitutional features ready to be picked off the shelf, could arguably also be thought of as avoiding the usual binary construction, although the idea of a "storage space" is very different from the liminal space argued for here.

concept of a "recognition space" in respect of native title in Australia.[46] Although admittedly his argument did not concern legal transfer or any other movement between normative orders or contexts, Pearson argued that legal recognition was constituted within an *overlap* between the two distinct fields of Aboriginal law and Australian law, to wit, native title. While this is an interesting idea, it generated concern about the transformative potential of recognition and thus the effects of state law recognition of and upon indigenous norms,[47] in spite of arguments that this transformation was a two-way process and would lead to indigenous norms also having an effect upon the non-indigenous Australian common law. Instead of arguing for a recognition space that remains within or, at least, bonded to each of these separate normative orders and contexts, therefore, this chapter proposes an interactive and reciprocal space, discrete from both (or all) original contexts. This in-between space is delimited by boundaries but *negatively* so – it is neither the marked nor the unmarked space but rather something and somewhere different. This translating space, as it were, introduces a more interactive aspect to the concept of normative transfer, and this exists in addition to that of "progression" or "movement" across boundaries.

These boundaries, of course, exist between and among intra-state alternative normative orders, and thus generate a situation of normative plurality replete with issues of contestation and interaction. While the translation "step" inherent in the process of transfer creates a new liminal space, the "movement" aspect of transfer itself generates those circumstances necessary for that space to become *productive*. This may not, on the face of it, seem to be a particularly substantial conceptual gain; nevertheless it is proposed that focusing not only on the outcomes of a process of transfer but also on the circumstances leading to such a process taking place provides additional insight – to make use once more of the terminology of the "marketplace", what if it is not only the norm on the shelf that is worthy of attention but also the reciprocal and respective behaviors of the buyer and seller? Recognizing this

[46] Noel Pearson, "The Concept of Native Title at Common Law" in G Yunupingu (ed), *Our Land is Our Life: Land Rights – Part, Present and Future* (Queensland UP 1997) 150–62, discussed in Duncan Ivison (n 29) 146–51.

[47] See BR Smith, "Towards an Uncertain Community? The Social Effects of Native Title in Central Cape York Peninsula" in BR Smith and F Morphy (eds), *The Social Effects of Native Title: Recognition, Translation, Coexistence* (ANU E-Press 2007) 117–34, 118–20.

dual-aspect process of transfer is, consequently, more important than ever in circumstances of normative plurality, particularly where there is a power-differential asymmetry.

8. Who is afraid of legal transfers?

Julia Eckert

8.1. INTRODUCTION

Who is afraid of legal transfers? While it seems (to a lay outsider) that scholars in comparative law have often feared for (their) laws, legal anthropologists have feared for those who were subjected to them; they have focussed on the relations between different legal orders, their normative effect on each other and on people whose affairs were governed by them. Common to both perspectives on legal transfers is the question about the conflicts of laws, and, implicit in it, the question about a conflict of "culture". Common to both thus also seems to be a notion of authenticity, and, related to this, a skepticism about change as a divergence from authenticity. If we focus on the fate of laws, that is: their possible transformation along their journeys, we are faced with the question about the "original," the question how systemic "legal systems" are as well as the question what laws "mean" or what they "are" after their travels. If we explore the effects of traveling law on the social relations of those receiving them, the question about the relation between law and the social arises: in what way does a transfer as such make law different in terms of its effects on the social; what do we mean by a law being "foreign"; what do we assume about law and about its relation to the social if we separate "foreign" from "autochthonous" laws? Is "foreignness" an issue for the social and political effects of law, or rather: for whom is it an issue, when and in what respect? And if so, what does it mean both for the norm and for social relations if the norm is applied to relations that it is foreign to?

The latter question has been central to the anthropological debate. Recently the travels of laws and norms have been critiqued in terms of their impact on the very self-understanding of those induced (by whatever means) to apply them to their circumstances.[1] This direction of exploration rests on the assumption that, just as with any other norm, law shapes our understanding of what we are and how we relate to others and to things, what is at issue in our conflicts, what is of value and what is right. Law, by slicing up our reality in specific ways, categorizing our experiences in accordance with specific aims, will impact on our understanding of social relations and our subjectivities as much as materially structuring them, effecting one by the other.

Because the assumption that the social significance of law reaches far beyond the official arenas of law, such as courts or contracts, and that law not only regulates the material world but affects how we perceive this world and the relations that link us to others, to the past and the future and to things, is central to anthropological concerns, anthropological accounts often concentrate on the social significance of law; the fate of the legal norms themselves, their transformation through travel that is at the center of the comparative law discussion, is of interest to anthropologists in as much as it provides insights into the social constitution of legal norms, the assumption being that the way that norms change throughout their travels is inextricably linked to the social situations they encounter. This points to the dialectic of the two sides of the sociality of law: first, law's formative impact on social perceptions; and secondly, its very constitution in the social.

Hence, in many ways, anthropological debates show the same sensibilities as those perceptible in Pierre Legrande's outright refutation of the possibility of legal transplants,[2] in that they assume that laws will not be the same in different circumstances; however, anthropological perspectives focus less on the fate of the norms as on the transformations effected among those subjected to "foreign" norms.

Several authors have proposed theories of what actually happens when law travels and is, for better or for worse, transported, transplanted, transmitted or translated from one context to another. For the adoptions of globally circulating legal concepts, the term "vernacularization" has been used in legal anthropology.[3] Vernacularization here means the

---

[1] E.g. Jane Collier, Bill Maurer and Liliana Suarez-Navaz, "Sanctioned Identities: Legal Constructions of Modern Personhood" (1995) 2 *Identities* 1.

[2] Pierre Legrand, "The Impossibility of Legal Transplants" (1997) 4 *Maastricht Journal of European and Comparative Law* 111.

[3] Sally Merry, "Transnational Human Rights and Local Activists: Mapping the Middle" (2006) 108 *American Anthropologist* 38; Peggy Levitt and Sally Merry, "Vernacularization on the Ground: Local Use of Global Women's Rights in Peru, China, India and the United States" (2009) 4 *Global Networks* 441.

adaptation of legal norms, institutions or simply terms to locally valid normative languages and institutions. A "universal" norm is translated into "local language." Levitt and Merry[4] distinguish situations of "replication," in which only the name of an imported norm or institution is changed in order to create the semblance of conformity with existing norms, and the content remains for the most part unaltered. At the other end of the spectrum is "hybridization", a merging of imported transnational norms or institutions with local ones. An extreme form of hybridization is subversion, in which the recognized "global name" is adopted, but it is applied to a practice that is fundamentally in keeping with existing cultural practices. In such cases, while the name is retained, the transnational institution or norm is fundamentally transformed.[5]

Theories of vernacularization thus assume the meeting of two (or more) distinct normative systems. New and alien norms are adopted according to existing normative models into which people are socialized and within which they think and feel. Such adoptions and adaptations appear as a result of the fact that people live within one distinct normative system that is shared by a given community. These communities are – in a slight tautology – defined by such shared norms and are presumed to be normatively integrated and rather homogeneous. We can distinguish between those positions that consider all "cultures" to be homogeneous in this sense, i.e. as relying on shared norms, and those who attest to such high degrees of normative homogeneity particularly in non-western, so-called traditional societies, which are assumed to be less differentiated.[6]

Such perspectives assume a rather close fit between law and the social. By focussing on the relation between two or more different normative orders, they neglect the heterogeneity of normative orientations *within* social groups; they exclude from their analyses the struggles over the meaning of norms *within* normative orders that are a defining feature of all social interaction. They thus often do not come to assess the social processes by which certain norms gain dominance within particular social relations, or by which normative homogeneity or consensus is actually produced. In these perspectives, law, normativity, and social action fall into one. The assumed systemic nature of law is conflated with the assumed normative integration of those to whom specific normative orders are attributed. This restricts the analysis of legal transfers: it

---

4 Levitt and Merry (n 3).

5 Merry (n 3) 44.

6 Cf. Anthony Giddens, *The Consequences of Modernity* (Polity Press 1990).

privileges the differences between normative orders over contestations within them without necessity, thereby neither reflecting on the role of such contestations for the processes of transfers or vice versa, nor coming to a more general theory of normative change. Thus, neither normative integration nor difference can really be understood.

The concept of culture that lies at the base of such notions has long been problematized. The ontological concept of coherence and in this sense of normative integration disappeared with structural functionalism – and with this a fundamental change of the concept of culture has emerged. A "pragmatic notion of culture"[7] stresses the continuing process of synthesis, distinction, differentiation and articulation, which produces "culture". Culture thus is an explanandum, not an explanans.

Such a perspective could inform our thinking about normative change as both the change in norms as well as the changes of normative orientations; it can further the understanding of the intertwining of norms[8] by overcoming not only a dichotomous notion of authenticity and alienness, but also a restrictive notion of legal combination or hybridization. It might lead us instead to a theory of normative change that relies less on the notion of mixing than on processes of transformation.

8.2. TRANSCULTURATION

I want to develop this idea with the help of a story, the case of a small dispute that took place in a slum in Mumbai, and hook onto that my claims.

Amita and Vikram, who lived in Dharavi, a large slum in Mumbai, got married in 2001. Amita was eighteen at the time and Vikram nineteen – at least that is what was said. Their parents had arranged the marriage, dowry had been paid in the form of pots and other kitchen utensils, and they conducted the wedding according to Hindu ritual. The marriage was not registered and, according to members of the Jamaat council, it might not have conformed to the standards that need to be met in order to make for a valid marriage under the Hindu Marriage Act of 1955. Somehow nobody was quite sure at the time that it seemed to matter. In March

---

7 Werner Schiffauer, "Anthropologie als Kulturwissenschaft" in Friedrich Jaeger, Burkhard Libsch and Jürgen Straub (eds), *Handbuch Kulturwissenschaften*, Band 2 (Metzler 2004).

8 Sally Merry, "Legal Pluralism" (1988) 22 *Law & Society Review* 869; Franz von Benda-Beckmann, "Who's Afraid of Legal Pluralism?" (2002) 47 *Journal of Legal Pluralism* 37.

2002 Vikram wanted to divorce. He said that Amita was unfit for marriage because of mental illness and that the marriage had never been consummated.

Amita's mother Tara agreed to the divorce. (Amita's father had long disappeared.) Tara feared the worst: that her daughter might be physically harmed. She knew of so many cases in which girls had been severely ill-treated by their in-laws. The disagreement thus was not about whether or not to divorce, but about the rights over the dowry. Tara insisted on its return. Tara, always speaking for Amita, who never spoke herself because she was evidently in a state of severe depression, claimed that Amita's mental instability was due to the way Vikram had treated her during the marriage, in particular his adultery. Vikram refused to return the dowry, claiming that he had been tricked into marrying a mentally ill woman. In this he felt affirmed by the counsel of the Jamaat, the caste council, who affirmed that it was in accordance with the stipulation of the Hindu Marriage Act of 1955 that marriage partners must be free of any mental disorder which could make them unfit for marriage.[9] They were not willing to make a further statement on the matter. To me they said that they saw their role not as adjudication; they could only help where the parties involved were willing to come to an amicable conclusion. They had counseled the two young people to mend their differences and stay together.

Vikram, however, turned to the local Shakha Pramukh of the Shiv Sena party,[10] who threatened to drive Amita's family out of Dharavi. Tara was afraid of the Shakha Pramukh, and of being driven away from her home. So she went to a local NGO (non-governmental organization) to find help. In response, the NGO, incidentally staffed by Muslim women and men, threatened to file a case of "dowry harassment" against Vikram, a threat that would inevitably lead to police investigations. Although many "dowry harassment" and "dowry death" cases are not solved and might

---

9 According to the Act, if after the solemnization of the marriage it is found that the bride could not have given her valid consent because of the unsoundness of her mind, the groom can get the marriage nullified through the court. If voidable marriages are not challenged in court, they remain valid for all legal purposes.

10 Shakha Pramukhs are the heads of the local branches (Shakha) or party offices of the Shiv Sena (the RSS also uses the term). Shakha Pramukhs organize the activities and finances of the Shakhas with a relatively high degree of autonomy from the movement's leadership. Like the local big men of other political parties or gangs, they take on the role of adjudicator.

not even be taken seriously by the police,[11] who often consider deaths related to dowry disputes to be domestic accidents, a police investigation means being brought to the attention of the police and made vulnerable to police harassment, and is thus a serious threat.

However, a few weeks after, Amita's mother, in a meeting of the parties now involved in the case, declared that she now wanted not only the pots and pans, but also 135,000 rupees for "maintenance."[12] When all the other parties responded with surprise, she declared that she had heard that women were entitled by state law to maintenance after divorce.

A rumor was behind this sudden demand and her sudden increase in self-confidence; indeed one that was based on a misunderstanding. Tara told me that she had discussed the fate of her daughter with some of the women in her neighborhood. At first she discussed it only grudgingly – she had wanted to keep the affair hushed up because she was afraid it would jeopardize the prospects of a second marriage for her daughter. But the case was making the rounds anyway, partly because Vikram's family were also going around telling their version of the story so as to establish it as fact; partly because such stories can hardly be kept secret in the dense living conditions of a slum. So one day, Tara said, someone had told her that the Indian Supreme Court – an entity well known and equally mysterious in the slums – had awarded a Muslim woman a large settlement that was to be paid to her by her ex-husband, who had divorced her. If a Muslim woman could get this, then surely it was also Amita's right. Everyone knew that Muslim women had at least as hard a lot as themselves.

I assumed then and still assume today (but cannot ascertain it) that this was the story of Shah Bano, the case that achieved notoriety because of the severe political upheavals that followed it. In the end, Rajiv Gandhi overturned the court's judgment granting alimony to Shah Bano when the Muslim Personal Law Board protested that the judgment was an infringement of minority rights and their legal autonomy. Shah Bano not only lost her alimony rights, but her case also came to symbolize the conservative politics of some representatives of Indian Muslims and their claims for minority rights, which in turn served to justify Hindu nationalists in their diatribes against Islam and the Muslims of India.

None of this was known to Amita's mother. She did not know the name of the Muslim woman she had heard about and did not know who

---

11 Subhadhra Butalia, *The Gift of a Daughter* (Penguin 2002).

12 I was so surprised by Tara's sudden confidence that I never asked how she came up with this precise sum, a sum that was well-nigh impossible for Vikram to pay as he earned only about 1000 rupees per month.

exactly had first mentioned her. None of her neighbours knew of Shah Bano either, but all started talking about the right to maintenance and that the legendary institution that was the Supreme Court had given a Muslim woman a lot of money and had taken this money from her estranged husband. Tara also wanted to write to this court (or rather, to have someone write a letter to the court for her) and tell the story of her daughter to whom such injustice had been done. The other "rumor" – this time widespread and based in fact, but "known" in the vague ways that rumors are – was that anyone can write to the Supreme Court and tell of their plight.

In the course of talking with her neighbors about the fate of Amita, her position changed from one of trying to save her daughter from harm but being at the same time ashamed of the affair, to one where she assertively augmented her protective feelings with certain demands. "Maintenance" seemed to become the name for hopes and feelings that had found none before.

This transformation emerged somewhat collectively and was highly contingent upon local factors of sympathy, solidarity, friendship and alliances that cannot be known in full, but are very specific to the case.

8.3. INTERLEGALITY

Tara's adoption of the women's rights notion of maintenance could be said to be a classic case of "forum shopping," a case of her choosing the legal forum and the normative order most suitable to her interests. However, from a perspective of "forum shopping" we would not be able to see how these "interests" emerged and thus how her opting for one rather than another normative order could be explained. After all, her "interests" might have been best served by keeping her daughter married – and avoiding the burden of having to marry her off again or of having an unmarried daughter. The notion of "interests" is far from straightforward in this regard: the transition of Tara from her first role as a mother relieved of her duty towards her daughter upon marriage, to one worried about the safety of her daughter, to one adopting the category "woman" as grounds for rights, exemplifies the various possible "interests" in conflict here, and the shift in roles that Tara underwent.

If considered in a systematic way, the normative systems that Tara draws upon do not fit together: Tara was never opposed to dowry as such, never considered its illegality in Indian law, and never saw women's rights violated or denigrated thereby. Nor was she opposed to divorce, even if that principally violated the sacramental character of marriage in religious law. For her, the sequence of a "customary" marriage ritual with a legal divorce in which certain rules as to the question of the right over dowry (and particularly the *stridhan*[13]) applied, and that she reasoned with reference to the "guilt" of the husband, was unproblematic; her perspective already merged several normative systems, and overrode the contradictions between them as well as those within them.[14] At the center of this perspective was the feeling of injustice that had been committed against her daughter because Vikram had been a "bad husband" on any normative perspective; he had brought about all that led to the dissolution of the marriage. This central concern of Tara was like the "melting pot" into which the normative elements of the different legal orders that were in operation in this case were poured. Tara did not break with the customary norms that had guided her in arranging the marriage of her daughter, and which she knew as a way of practice rather than as "law". Rather, she merged them with various other normative aspects in order to have them interpreted in the way proper to the specific circumstances. This she battled for by drawing on norms provided, in a way, by other normative systems. The particular situation determined the relevance of these normative aspects and their validity. Tara, in her insistence on maintenance, not only integrated into her own normative repertoire the maintenance rules of the Hindu Adoption and Maintenance Act, but applied a notion of "women's rights" to the situation, thus introducing a novel category into the interpretation of the social relations at issue in the case. The distinction between them, however, did not matter and was not even evident to her. This points us to the question as to whether what is of importance is possibly simply the perception of actors of something as law, and of something as plural.[15] Tara did not see pluralism; to her, there

---

[13] *Stridhan* is the part of a woman's property which she can sell, give away, mortgage, lease or exchange. Besides the jewellery, clothes and bedding given at marriage, *stridhan* also includes the gifts to the woman before, during and after marriage. It includes property inherited by the woman from her family or husband's family; property received by her under a compromise or in lieu of maintenance; and property bought using the proceeds of *stridhan*. Section 27 of the Hindu Marriage Act of 1955 stipulates that refusal to return *stridhan* upon divorce makes a husband liable to prosecution.

[14] The regulation of the return of dowry by state law contradicts the illegalization of dowry by this very same state law.

[15] Cf. Baudouin Dupret, "Legal Pluralism, Plurality of Laws, and Legal Practices: Theories, Critiques, and Praxeological Re-specificcation" (2007) 1(1) *European Journal of Legal Studies*, <http://www.ejls.eu/1/14UK.pdf>.

was no conflict of laws. She knew (by rumor[16]) of one law that attributed the right to maintenance, and this she considered to express what she, for many different reasons, felt to be "right." In fact also the distinction between "law" (of whatever source: religious, state or customary) and other norms did not matter to Tara that much: she fused all under norms that prescribed certain forms of action. Indeed, defining law seems to be not necessarily productive for the analysis either of what people perceive as law and how they treat that which they perceive as law, or for the role of norms.[17]

8.4. CONSTELLATIONS AND FIGURATIONS

Of course, it does not suffice for Tara to evoke a hearsay law to "make it happen." The conditions for it to be recognized as valid and as relevant to the dispute in question are embedded in complex contextual interdependencies. In Tara's case it was the empathy of her female neighbors, the precise reason for which cannot be known. It was also the fact that, when faced with the wrath of the local women, the Shakha Pramukh lost interest in the case. For him, there was not much to gain from it, and more to lose, especially as he suddenly found himself in opposition to the women of his own party, members of the Mahila Aghadi. The women of the Mahila Aghadi here seemed to want to assert their prerogative in counseling marital disputes in the locality against the Shakha Pramukh; thus they were in a party-internal competition shaped by the general male dominance within Shiv Sene party affairs. Moreover, they needed to reclaim their supposed "pro-women stance" on women's questions: in competition with the Muslim-led NGO that had taken Tara's side, they pleaded strongly for the maintenance payment. They presented this as the age-old Hindu tradition of maintenance to destitute dependents (this being the origin of the maintenance provisions entailed in the Hindu Adoption and Maintenance Act, 1956). Although they had in many cases of marital conflict counseled against separation – like most other authorities active in conflict mediation – here their situational interpretation of what Hindu tradition *is* points us again to the frame that different normative orders provide for each other, either as source of further

---

[16] Cf. Julia Eckert, "Rumours of Rights" in Julia Eckert et al (eds), *Law against the State: Ethnographic Forays into Law's Transformations* (Cambridge University Press 2012).

[17] Brian Tamanaha, "A Non-essentialist Concept of Legal Pluralism" (2000) 27 *Journal of Law and Society* 296.

reasoning and inspiration or, as in this instance, as a bogey against which one can positively distinguish oneself. It also points us to the fact that no normative system simply "is," but that it always "is" in relation, and therefore it "is" in a specific situation.

This further points us to the political constellations that were decisive in determining the conclusion of the case: the Shakha Pramukh withdrew because in his "game", namely democratic competition for support, that is for numbers of voters, he had nothing to gain from siding with the wrong party. Norms did not play a part in his calculation.

Vikram suddenly stood alone with his version of the story; he grudgingly agreed to return the *stridhan,* and even to pay the maintenance sum of 135,000 rupees, a sum that he needed ten years to earn according to his own calculation.[18] The NGO refrained from accusing him of "dowry harassment", and Tara did not have a letter written to the Supreme Court.

Many strands of interdependence thus shaped the relationship between Tara and Vikram and led to this outcome. It was, for example, shaped by the competition between the NGO and the Shakha Pramukh for clients. That competition was in itself shaped by their differing dependence on the support of people, i.e. their different embeddedness in the realm of democratic politics. The particular ways in which Indian democracy works determined the behavioral logic of the Shakha Pramukh. It also propelled the discourse of women's rights to a certain prominence in a context in which chauvinist movements such as the Shiv Sena use the discourse of women's rights to distinguish themselves from their "dangerous other," namely Muslims and Islam. Hence, the currency of women's rights was constituted by various movements within what could be called a global public in a historical moment at which Islam is perceived as most hostile to women's rights and the global security discourse also legitimates itself by claiming to protect women. (Of course, this line of justification itself rests on the very currency of women's rights that have been struggled for by diverse women's movements across the globe.)

These figurations are all constituted by the often contradictory efforts to be heard, to distinguish oneself against another, to gain dominance and to forge alliances. They are also shaped by the means with which such

[18] I have no information on whether Vikram even started to pay this sum. It seems very unlikely that, given his own meager income, he would ever be able to comply with this demand.

dependencies and alliances are sustained through rules of majorities, brute force, money, a common enemy, law or a combination of the above.

8.5. THE PRAGMATICS OF NORMS

Several observations from Tara's and Amita's story seem pertinent to the questions that legal transfers bring up, namely the two main concerns about the fate of laws and the fate of those subjected to them, anchored as they are in the wider debates of the respective disciplines.

It seems that what we learn from Tara is that when people turn towards legal norms to express their hopes and strive for their future, they interpret norms in the light of these aspirations – rather than simply in terms of existing normative orders. Of course, these aspirations are shaped by the normative orders that prevail in the historical situation within which they live; their perception of the world, of what it should be and what is wrong with it, is structured by their moral parameters that relate to what Bourdieu has called *doxa*,[19] that which is not questioned and cannot be named because it is taken as the given natural order beyond reflection. There are limits to interpretation that lie in the norm itself, but also in pre-existing norms that shape people's interpretations of norms. Much has been written about the structuring effects of liberal law, the ways in which its categorizations and classifications impact on what is sayable, and how we can think about ourselves.[20] Of course, any other normative system has similarly forceful effects on one's scope of self-perception. However, people's habitual normative orientations, their subjectivities in another theoretical language, always entail a measure of openness: situations demand interpretation; they entail alternatives even within habitually restricted realms of normative orientation.[21] A practice-oriented perspective points to the dynamic between normative or habitual orientation which shapes the understanding of a situation, and the open-endedness of action that is possible because of the singularity of each situation. This implies that every normative orientation is to some degree open to new interpretations, and that such interpretations are inherent in the application of a norm in a specific singular situation.

---

19 Pierre Bourdieu, *Outline of a Theory of Practice* (Cambridge University Press 1977).

20 E.g. Collier et al (n 1).

21 Bourdieu (n 19) 225.

Judith Butler, too, proposes that "agency exceeds the power by which it is enabled."[22]

To Tara there was no conflict of laws. There was no issue of legal pluralism. Neither did she reflect on histories and pathways of legal transfer, of either maintenance laws, divorce laws, or women's rights. Rather, there was an amalgamation of different norms that was interpreted as an amalgamation only from an analytic outside, but that was one to her and as such was pertinent to the situation as she perceived it. The "origins" and ways of travel were oblivious and irrelevant to her. In fact even the distinction between "law" and other social norms was not of relevance: Tara treated them as one: one normative prescriptive that she considered supported by that mythical entity, "law". Law in this situation was perceived as the ultimate source of legitimacy – this raising a host of questions that I cannot enter into here.[23] What is of relevance here is the struggle to have a particular normative vision accepted as "law" by the actors involved.

This points us to the possibilities that all legally plural situations entail, namely that norms inform each other and are in the process often synthesized, blurring seemingly fixed boundaries between different normative orders. Thus, what emerged was a situation of interlegality.[24] Such situations of interlegality are probably more common than might be assumed from academic discussions on these questions, which more often than not focus on legal plurality, conflicts of law and the normative effects of liberal law. These are not hybrids, the mixing of two distinct normative systems. Rather, there is a transformation of all elements, or what Ortiz[25] has called a "transculturation." This transculturation goes beyond the adaptation of one element to another; it is not a matter of mixing two distinct systems or assembling parts in novel combinations. Unlike theories of vernacularization and others that consider processes of normative hybridization, this transformation does not adapt a norm to an existing normative order. Rather, norms are transformed in the process of

---

[22] Judith Butler, *The Psychic Life of Power* (Stanford University Press 1997) 15.

[23] Cf. Julia Eckert, "From Subjects to Citizens: Legalisation from Below and the Homogenisation of the Legal Sphere" (2006) 53–4 *Journal of Legal Pluralism* 45.

[24] Boaventura de Sousa Santos, "Law: A Map of Misreading: Toward a Postmodern Conception of Law" (1987) 14 *Journal of Law and Society* 279.

[25] Fernando Ortiz, *Cuban Counterpoint: Tobacco and Sugar* (first published in English 1947, Duke University Press 1995).

adapting them to a concrete situation. The distinctiveness of situations shapes the transformation of the norms articulated in them.

Law, of course, on the face of it has the opposite propensity: to create or construct comparability, to abstract from context for a particular purpose, to essentialize through categorization.[26] Just as the trajectories of normative orientations are shaped by prevailing normative models, but undetermined in the end, such forms of interlegality and processes of iteration are structured both by the legal models they employ to interpret a situation and by the figurations that make possible that one or the other interpretation gains predominance. Rather than assuming that anything that a group of people treats, perceives or recognizes as law emerges as such,[27] the possibilities of them bringing forth precisely this law need to be examined.

The relations of interdependence that determine such possibilities have been less the focus of legal anthropological perspective. Peter Fitzpatrick, however, once pointed towards such relational processes with his attention to the historical struggles in which institutions were shaped by the interactions between various actors.[28] Fitzpatrick termed the outcome of such interactions "combined law,"[29] a term possibly slightly undermining his valuable insight that at issue were not simply combinations or hybrids, but institutions shaped in particular historical struggles. This insight demands that all analyses of legal pluralism, interlegality or any such model of the relation of different normative orders must in the end analyze the relations of power shaping this relation both in a specific situation and more generally. This analysis regards not merely the positioning of different legal orders towards each other, but rather demands an analysis of each: the power structures implied in each order, the figurations that determine their respective dominance, hegemony or recognition, and the effects of their plurality on social relations.

An empirical exploration of the constitution of the relative power of different normative interpretations can perhaps best be captured with

---

26 Jörg Fisch, "Law as a Means and as an End: Some Remarks on the Function of European and Non-European Law in the Process of European Expansion" in WJ Mommsen and JA de Moor (eds), *European Expansion and Law: The Encounters of European and Indigeneous Law in 19th and 20th Century Africa and Asia* (Berg 1992).

27 Cf. Dupret (n 15).

28 Peter Fitzpatrick, "Law, Plurality, and Underdevelopment" in David Sugarman (ed), *Legality, Ideology and the State* (Academic Press 1983).

29 Fitzpatrick (n 28) 168.

Elias's concept of "figuration,"[30] webs of (local and global) interdependencies. The concept of figuration captures the far-reaching interdependencies and their fluid nature, embedded in wider, and more long-lasting socio-economic transformations that were seen to be decisive for the force of particular normative interpretations in the course of the struggle over maintenance that Tara fought for her daughter.

These figurations are at once highly situational and specific to this one case: the particular alliances, networks, relations shaping this case are specific both to it and to a specific moment and here they were the particular incentives of the various actors involved in the dispute. These figurations are at the same time of a more general nature, these situational incentives being embedded in the said wider relations, here particularly the global currency of women's rights in a context in which both culturalist hostilities and democratic competition decide about the pertinence of particular issues. These determined what in this particular case law could be.

Thus in order to think about the transformations that might be effected by law's travels we need to explore the synchronic and diachronic interactions and their always specific conditions. Eschewing simple causalities in the analysis of the relation between different normative orders as well as their form and content at a specific historical point, histories – sometimes simply case-histories – of processes of their mutual entanglement[31] or amalgamation can elucidate the multifarious normative connotations that actors articulate in their contestations over the meaning of norms, categories or classifications such as marriage, gender, community or others.

8.6. CONCLUSION

Processes of legal transfer are as ubiquitous as they are diverse. They differ in what pathways they take: law travels together with migrating communities, or is imposed by colonial rule, imported by a national elite as a component of the modernization project; it is propagated by activists to claim possibly novel rights or by governments and others to legitimize their rule. Law is communicated via rumors among laypersons who hope it may help them attain justice[32] or via networks of experts trying to

30 Norbert Elias, *What Is Sociology?* (Hutchinson 1978).

31 Merry (n 8); von Benda-Beckmann (n 8).

32 Cf. Eckert (n 16).

achieve international standardization and global "harmonization."[33] These different forms of law's travels rarely come alone. As David Westbrook held, "the imperial, the fashionable, the systemic and the tribal" forms of law's travels "are interrelated."[34] Law's travels are probably almost always at once (but to different degrees) a matter of export and import, of imposition and adoption, of expert knowledge and lay rumor, of imitation, isomorphism or diffusion.

Thus, there is possibly no one model of the resulting forms of transfers, or their effects on norms. I am not pleading for either amalgamation or interlegality as the valid model. Rather, the normative "results" of processes of transfers will differ widely, and the various descriptions might fit one better than another: whether we see bricolage, superimposition, sedimentation, interlegality or conflicts will depend on the specific process of transfer in question, and on the figurations within which contestations over norms are carried out by variously positioned actors who are involved in this process in different roles.

What I tried to show with the story of Tara and Amita is that rather than approaching processes of transfer from perspectives that entail notions of "originals" or of authenticity that are based either on static accounts of normative orientations ("culture" so to say) or static accounts of norms and legal systems, we might better understand them if we approach them from a perspective that takes into account the figurations that shape their trajectories. Then differences and similarities come into view in their contextual histories rather than being presupposed. Since difference as well as similarity or "sameness" are not givens, but result from adaptations, differentiations, learning, imitations and so on, we can then approach these processes of transformation comparatively. This needs a "thick"[35] understanding of context, but context not in the sense of the history of "a system" (as I would read Geertz, as well as many of the debates about the travels of law), but the history and present of the

---

33 Franz von Benda-Beckmann, Keebet von Benda-Beckmann and Julia Eckert, "Introduction: Law and Governance between Past and Future" in Franz von Benda-Beckmann, Keebet von Benda-Beckmann and Julia Eckert (eds), *Rules of Law and Laws of Ruling* (Ashgate 2009).

34 David Westbrook, "Theorising the Diffusion of Law: Conceptual Difficulties, Unstable Imaginations and the Effort to Think Gracefully Nonetheless" (2006) 47 *Harvard International Law Journal* 489.

35 Clifford Geertz, *The Interpretation of Cultures: Selected Essays* (Basic Books 1973).

situation of encounter: the diachronic and synchronic interactions that extend the context of situations into their global and historic entanglements.

PART IV

Ordering the postcolony – constitutional breaks, continuities, and hybrids

9. "Ordering" constitutional transfers: a view from India

Upendra Baxi

9.1. THRESHOLD CONCERNS

The sphere now known as comparative constitutional studies (COCOS, as I prefer to name this) is of recent origin; of even more recent origin is the study of constitutional "origins" or "borrowals". Understandably, these spheres remain heavily influenced by traditions of "doing" comparative law and jurisprudence, and more particularly by the imagery of "legal transplants" and discourses about juristic convergence and differences.[1] Cutting across this, Professor Günter Frankenberg now proposes the notion of legal "transfers".[2] He maintains that no recourse to "grand narratives" is needed to understand the traffic of ideas and constitutional arrangements and models; instead all that is required is some "more modest claim of the 'IKEA theory' of constitutional (and legal) transfer." A "central tenet" of this theory is the idea of "the global constitution" that "functions as a reservoir or, for that matter, a supermarket, where standardized constitutional items – grand designs as well as elementary particles of information – are stored and available, *prêt-à-porter*, for purchase and reassemblage by constitution makers around the world". Frankenberg insists (no matter how one may read the rather easy metaphorical equivalence between a "reservoir" and a "supermarket") that the "global constitution" is in itself constituted by legal transfers: yet, it is neither an analogue of "a national constitution writ large as an

[1] See Günter Frankenberg, "Constitutional Transfer: The IKEA Theory Revisited" (2010) 8 *International Journal of Constitutional Law* 563; this article will be referred to hereafter by the author.

[2] Rather than replicate standard references to the literature, I "transfer" these via references to Frankenberg; see as concerns "transplants" Frankenberg (n 1) 565–70.

'emerging universal' constitutional system" nor does it entail any advocacy of "the desirability of a novel type of trans-, inter-, or supranational constitution as the result of some adaptation of national constitutions to global requirements".[3]

This chapter does not offer an overview of some of the fresh insights that Frankenberg brings to COCOS spheres or comparative law theory generally; nor does it attempt to read his text for example in the critical lens of Eugene Pashukanis, who strove to establish a complex order of relationship (homology) between the "legal form" and the "commodity form",[4] though I believe that such a reading may enhance COCOS-type understanding. Rather, I foreground a few threshold concerns.

A first threshold concern relates to the politics of naming; by this term I do not merely draw attention to critical etymologies of words (such as "reception", "adaptation", "borrowals", "diffusion", "transplantation", "imposition", "migration", and "transfer"), but also indicate the specific formations of epistemic power which underlie and animate this politics of scholarly naming. A second related concern concerns the uses of Edward Said's notion of "travelling theory".[5] Put another way, some types of travelling theory *traverse* rather well; others do not even begin to *travel*; put still differently, and hopefully stridently, the logics and paralogics of "transfer" constitute, at least as regards COCOS, a one-way street: the thoughtways of the non-European others seem to contribute *nothing at all* to the languages, logics, and paralogics of constitutional "transfer", *as if the gains of learning must always follow the discursive pathways from the Global North to Global South.* Speaking for myself at least, what remains important is a quest for understanding the ways in which the non-European others may also have impacted on the idea of constitutionalism for Euro-American constitutional thought and practice.

A third concern relates to what Frankenberg terms constitutional "oddities".[6] This extraordinary descriptive category emerges as a moment of COCOS only because a standard narrative of constitutionalism is said to be already in place via which constitutional choices may be fully adjudged as "deviant". A larger narrative thus stands entailed, one in which the acts of authorship of postcolonial constitutions must remain

---

[3] Ibid 565.

[4] See, as to this, Isaac D Balbus, "Commodity Form and Legal Form: An Essay on the 'Relative Autonomy' of the Law" (1997) 11 *Law & Society Review* 571.

[5] See, for a brilliant COCOS-type adaptation of Said, Frankenberg (n 1) 570–75.

[6] Ibid 573–4.

mimetic and only crystallize their fancied "originality" as no more than "oddities" in search of explanation via a standardized progress narrative. No doubt, Frankenberg writes in a provocative vein; even so, a bigger concern looms large concerning different ways of imagining the very idea of constitutionalisms.

9.2. THE POLITICS OF NAMING

Naming persons, things, places, phenomena, entities, and states of affairs is indeed serious business as students of identity and difference, semiotics, and human rights well know. People who all too often cite the oft-quoted Bard of Avon's aphorism in *Romeo and Juliet*: "What's in a name? / That which we call a rose / By any other name would smell as sweet" ignore the fact that this observation stands prefaced by Juliet's remark: "Tis but thy name that is my enemy". Naming remains all too often associated with normative politics and entails acts of epistemic, even deontic, power.

Without daring to pursue the various practices of epistemic/deontic power of naming, I merely explore Frankenberg's practice of naming. To start with, his contrast between comparativist "grand theory" (the reference here primarily being to the "Watson/Legrand Controversy") and his own modest approach (in particular the adaptation of travelling theory provides an excellent example of the power of naming). If "grand theory" seeks to explain too much via parsimonious categories, the question surely arises whether Frankenberg's own approach constitutes another example of such a theory via the metaphor of "transfer". The IKEA theory in most basic respects is no less grand or modest than the predecessor approaches it seeks to displace. Prescinding this large concern, we at least need to understand what this emergent naming actually achieves.

The "transfer" metaphor clearly intends to displace certain prior approaches. It suggests upfront that constitutional "ideas and norms, institutions and arrangements", or even "opinions" and "doctrines", "arguments and ideologies",[7] may serve a function as commodities in the market precisely when they undergo "reification, formalization, and idealization".[8] An interesting passage clarifies what is entailed: "Any

---

[7] Frankenberg is not fussy about description of categories as the transferred goods checklist in the text illustrates. Almost any form or element seems commodifiable!

[8] Frankenberg (n 1) 571.

constitutional item has to be decontextualized, to wit, isolated from the circumstances of its production and prepared for transfer. It has to be shock-frozen and packaged, so to speak, for the transgressing of time, space, and context – for the 'passage through the pressure of various contexts as the idea moves from an earlier point to another time and place where it will come into a new prominence.'" Further,

> decontextualization amounts to more than a mere taking-out of a given context and subsequent displacement. The flash freezing and packaging is meant to highlight that constitutional transfers usually imply that the items to be transferred are, first, reified as marketable commodities, then formalized, that is, stripped of their contextual meanings, and, finally, idealized as meaning what they are meant to mean and functioning in the way they are meant to function ...[9]

This sort of decontextualization is necessary for the "transfer" process. If "the global reservoir or constitutional IKEA centre" is at all to come into existence and continue to function, forms or elements which belong to the IKEA warehouse and retail centres must undergo "the decontextualization process by distinguishing as marketable those items that have passed a threshold test and excluding those that have not".[10] Certain normative, ideological, and even historical cleansing is what decontextualization entails; even so, for transfers to eventually happen, the processes of eventual re-contextualization must fully occur and recur; putting this my way, this suggests that the buyers of "thin" global constitutional public goods must eventually convert these into "thick" ones depending on the exigencies of national and even global contexts. In passing, it requires mentioning that in this era of hyperglobalization the latter contexts often overwhelm the national ones.

I, however, lose Professor Frankenberg when he insists further that "the third step in the transfer process leads from the local context to which, in a different theoretical register, could be described as *a collective constitutional consciousness memory* or even as *global constitutionalism*".[11] Collective constitutional consciousness is a fine and moving phrase just as *Volksgeist* was for Fredrick von Savigny and this mighty comparison may warrant a moment of digression. In the great Savigny-Thibaut debate concerning the "reception" of law, Savigny speaks to us about the combination of the "technical" and the "political" aspects of the codification of Roman law and its "reception" into

---

9 Ibid 571.
10 Ibid 572.
11 Ibid (emphasis added).

"Germany". The distinctively "political" in Savigny speaks to us about transmissions of cultural inheritance in the life of peoples; the distinctively "technical" invites attention to the juristic capacity to receive (that is, indigenize) alien law formations as already compatible with extant popular legal cultures.[12] Other inaugural figurations include, surely, Henry Maine and Paul Vinogradoff, and above all Max Weber. Surely, these eminent thinkers wrote much before the advent/invention of the fancy term "legal pluralism" and the birthing moments of COCOS. Yet each gifted thinker in his own distinctive mode presents to us imaginaries of continuities/breaks/hybrids within the Euro-American past times of the "reception" of "law" as constitutive of state formative practices.[13] The debates they launched variously – in terms of "reception" (Savigny), evolutionary histories of law and jurisprudence (Maine and Vinogradoff, among significant others) and ideal types of law as domination (Weber) – provide some crucial reminders concerning at least the need for epistemic humility in approaching the contemporary histories of "ordering" constitutional transfers. To sum it up, an enormously large question concerns ways of reading Euro-American constitutional pasts as laying the foundations, as it were, of some contemporary shopping malls and arcades for the non-Euro others. If this be the case at all, we stand invited further to revisit "Western" medieval "constitutional" theory, articulated as "Hegel's Ghost".[14] The ways in which Professor Frankenberg enunciates and operates his category of collective constitutional consciousness entails a certain tendency towards an order of willed juristic amnesia about the hybrid past European times of constitution-making and constitutional development and towards "de-historicization".

This said, we need to resolve some perplexities by articulating anxieties concerning the source of (or our ways of sourcing/outsourcing) collective constitutional consciousness. In this context, at least this much

---

[12] See, as to this, Julius Stone, *The Social Dimensions* of *Law and Justice* (Stevens 1966).

[13] See, as concerns this specific notion, Upendra Baxi, "Constitutionalism as a Site of State Formative Practices" (2000) 21 *Cardozo Law Review* 1183.

[14] See, for an extraordinary rich analysis, Constantin Fasolt, "Hegel's Ghost: Europe, the Reformation and the Middle Ages" (2008) 39 *Viator* 345. See also Brian Tierney, *Religion, Law, and the Growth of Constitutional Thought, 1150–1650* (Cambridge University Press 1982); Brian Tierney, *The Idea of Natural Rights: Studies on Natural Rights, Natural Law, and Church Law, 1150–1625* (Atlanta 1997); Francis Oakley, "Legitimation by Consent: The Question of the Medieval Roots" (1983) 14 *Viator* 303; John Neville Figgis, *Studies of Political Thought from Gerson to Grotius, 1414–1625* (2nd edn, Cambridge University Press 1916).

may be said here. If we were to outsource collective constitutional consciousness to a global marketplace for constitutional borrowings and transfers, Frankenberg would remain an unerring guide to constructing the idea of the market as the "second nature" (after natural nature), as it were, populated by rational choice theory type constitutional actors. If so, what may we say are the forms of collective consciousness that the IKEA-market construction may suggest or stipulate? Many larger concerns lurk here relating to markets for the growth of cultural and civilizational traditions, even to the point of specialists talking about "market civilization": an aspect that this chapter may scarcely address even by way of extended footnote references. In sum, may I invite Professor Frankenberg to at least situate his innovative discourse within a larger normative/historical frame?

Further, assuming the *necessity*, rather than *contingency*, of speaking about global constitution or constitutionalism, we at least need to probe such practices of naming. For example, some serious-minded neo-Gramscian scholarship regards this latter entirely differently in terms of disciplinary and regulatory globalization.[15] Both these, though in different modes, suggest that the markets for constitutional transfer remain pre-eminently sellers', not buyers' markets. A closer textual analysis of Frankenberg's text suggests that this is indeed the case. For example, Frankenberg suggests a kind of Euro-American ancestral intellectual property rights regime over the phrase-regime of "We, the People"! Given this, he bemuses us with a narrative of some quixotic adaptations/misappropriations, largely, of course, in the context of constitutionalisms of the non-European others.[16] However, even conceding that this constitutional formula may have been typical of Euro-American constitutionalisms, it may not be too much to say that the idea of "people's" we-ness as legitimating forms of sovereignty and suzerainty richly antedates histories of the non-Euro others.

---

[15] See Stephen Gill, "The Constitution of Global Capitalism", www.theglobalsite.ac.uk (2000; last visited 28 May 2003); *Power and Resistance in the New World Order* (Palgrave Macmillan 2003). See also David Schneiderman, *Constitutionalizing Economic Globalization: Investment Rules and Democracy's Promise* (Cambridge University Press 2008).

[16] Frankenberg (n 1) 566–77. See also his similar reflections concerning the rule of law, at 577–8. But, for an acute revisitation of Bruce Ackerman's formulation of popular sovereignty in US constitutionalism, see Daniel J Hulsebosch, "Civicus 2000: Process Constitutionalism at Yale" (1999) 97 *Michigan Law Review* 1520.

If so, the very idea of a supermarket of constitutional forms as commodities exchanged in a free global supermarket seems at the first sight to de-emphasize and de-historicize their modes of production. This becomes pertinent when we recall the idea of memory (to which Frankenberg also refers as an alternate descriptor of collective constitutional consciousness). If one were to consult the specialist domain of memory theory, one would find several crucial distinctions between forms of "causal", "episodic", "functional", static or dynamic, "associative", "abstract", "semantic" and "symbolic" memory. The "thin" theory of constitutional transfers, at least on my reading, suggests a construction of abstract or semantic memory, in which consciousness of constitutional forms and elements must further constitute forms of manifold collective "abstract" memories of and about *symbolic goods*. Further, the matter would become infinitely complicated were we to more fully attend to, and import, Pierre Bourdieu-type notions of symbolic goods and symbolic or cultural capital – the relationship then among "*habitus*", "*doxa*," "field", and "capital",[17] or to the different spheres of "collective intentionality" that create deontic institutional social facts to which John Searle more recently re-directs our attention.[18]

Although Frankenberg's analysis remains context-sensitive, his elaboration of the IKEA theory insists on the virtues of the "transfer" metaphor because it avoids heavy terms such as *legal imposition*, *colonization*, *imperialism* infecting constitutionalisms. Granted that the "transfer" metaphor succeeds in avoiding the heavy hand of ideologies, may it also turn out to be the case that it does so do by mystifying its own ideological elements? While I shall have much more to say about this later in the chapter, I here attend by way of textual fidelity to some hidden ideological traces.

Professor Frankenberg, in one of his few difficult passages, tells us that not all decontextualized "items" become "marketable" (or integrated into the "reservoir") but only those that pass the "threshold" test; thus he is able to suggest that

> Constitutional items that have passed or that might pass this test abound, notably, the basic architecture of legislated constitutions; their status as higher

---

17 See, generally, Pierre Bourdieu, *Outline of a Theory of Practice* (Cambridge University Press 1997); *Language and Symbolic Power* (Harvard University Press 1991); *Acts of Resistance: Against the Tyranny of the Market* (The New Press 1998) especially 29–45 and 94–105.

18 See John R Searle, *Making the Social World: The Structure of Human Civilization* (Oxford University Press 2010).

> law; or their content, including rights catalogues, schemes of government, institutions for protecting the constitution (judicial review) as complemented by doctrines of judicial self-restraint and political questions, and so forth. Constitutional elites, legal consultants, and political activists may then shop in the IKEA center for ideas and institutions, norms and doctrines, arguments and ideologies fabricated and tested in other national or regional contexts. They have the choice between finished products and inspirational ideas requiring a higher degree of constructive elaboration.[19]

It may not be unfair to say to Frankenberg that the list of successful transferable "items" comes very close to liberal constitutional orders; indeed, the reference to judicial self-restraint and political questions doctrine invites attention to some thick histories of US constitutionalism. It is not clear why any "threshold" test may exclude constitutional transfers with the Euro-American orbit:[20] nor is the basis for excluding from such a listing the innovative elements of socialist constitutionalism made clear (in the erstwhile actually existing socialist societies and their live residues in some so-called "transitional societies" and Global South constitutionalisms). To take but one example, the doctrine of abstract judicial review lays the very foundation of post-Soviet constitutionalism in "transitional societies"; why this "item" fails the threshold test for inclusion in the reservoir or the IKEA shopping mall is not easy to grasp. I must here rest content with Frankenberg's own bewilderment at reading Article 15 of the Viet Nam Constitution speaking of a "multi-component economy functioning in accordance with market-mechanisms under the management of the State and following a socialist tradition". Putting back into the discourse of constitutional transfers some entire histories of the Cold War may lessen this perplexity; yet the decontextualization stance of Frankenberg does not seem to allow hospitable space for such thick contextual narratives![21] Much the same may be said about the transfer of the device of Directive Principles of Social Policy from the Irish into the Indian, and from then onwards into almost all South Asian and many African constitutions.

---

19 Frankenberg (n 1) 572.

20 See, Alec Stone Sweet, "Why Europe Rejected American Judicial Review and Why It May Not Matter" (2003) 101 *Michigan Law Review* 2744.

21 Frankenberg (n 1) 573.

9.3. MIMESIS AND ORIGINALITY IN CONSTITUTIONAL "TRANSFERS" IN LATE MODERNITY

Eminent constitutional theorists, and even comparativists, use categories of mimesis without much regard for a theoretical grasp of the dialectic of mimesis and originality. The claims of originality concern the 18th century inventions, constitutions and constitutionalism. From this, and unreflexively, follows the claim that all future constitutions are copies, imitations, or repetitions of a standardized feat/form of Euro-American cultural production. Put another way, this sort of collective ancestral intellectual property-type regime contains by implication the foundational mimetic servitude of all other and later constitutional forms and developments. Those that depart radically from this archetypal liberal constitutionalism do not really, it is often said, deserve that ecumenical name; the very expression "socialist constitutionalism" was held in the decades of the "Cold War" to be an oxymoron and that compliment is also today extended to Islamic constitutionalism. This is clearly an ideological operation and results from the operation of the strong "Western" claim, which this chapter may not address at all. Nor may I address, save indirectly, the weak form of mimetic claim offered by Professor Frankenberg, which articulates not so much the exclusive Euro-American authorship of the basic constitutional ideas and arrangements, but rather posits that the extant constitutional models function as a source of normative opportunity as well as being a constraint on future founding constitutional choices.

Making clear the strong and weak Euro-authorship claims remains a hazardous narrative enterprise, if only because one never fully knows whether this is a logically necessary or historically contingent "implication". The former type of implication would mean at least two things: (a) without the "original" one may not speak about the existence of copies, imitations, or repetitions; and (b) copies, imitations, or repetitions must be adjudged as authentic or fake within the postulation of an originary act of creation. Against this, the historically contingent claim suggests a weaker co-relation: the Westphalian constitutional forms were the first "historically given" constitutions (to adapt Hans Kelsen's phrase-regime justifying the juristic postulate of by and large efficacious and therefore valid constitutions). If so, the weaker claim asserts that, though contingent on the possibility of the historically first given constitution (and models of constitutionalism), it still remains foundational for "later" genera of constitution-making. Yet, the question is: "foundational" in what sense?

There are available several responses to this question concerning "foundations". One answer is that "foundational" signifies a normative basis or frame that provides for structures of power and functions of governance as well as limits on political power. In this sense, the idea of constitutions was known to earth's indigenous ancient peoples as much as to the classical civilizations of the non-Euro others and to Euro-American civilizational traditions. Much the same may be said about a second response that locates normativity in the models of government (monarchic/republican, unitary/federal, secular/religious); it would simply be ahistorical to claim that these are the gifts of the "West" to the "Rest". As concerns both these aspects, I refrain here from illustrating, via copious references, this elementary global social fact.

One may well proceed to argue that the strong and the weak claims, variously, speak to us about constellations of specific histories of normativity inaugurated by the Euro-American constitutional format. In this register, I would want to be among the first among equals to acknowledge that certain forms of constitutional rituals indeed support the strong claim – for example, the specific forms of constitutional oath-taking by public officials, the styles and practices announcing a sovereign decision that convert public policies into authoritative legal forms (executive decrees, legislative enunciations, adjudicative enunciations). I may even go so far as to subscribe to the strong claim that certain forms of governance, such as presidential versus cabinet forms, the inchoate doctrines of the "separation of powers", systems of relatively autonomous justicing, are distinctly "Euro-American" in origin.

However, the deeper point of strong or weak foundational claims must lie elsewhere. These when presented as "items" of constitutional transfer remain over-determined, posing the concern: how may these be subjected to copying, imitation, or repetition? Prescinding here a fuller consideration of this dimension, the deeper foundational claim(s) insist on an exclusive authorship of the *rights-based idea of constitutionalism* (RBC, hereafter). This is a coat of many colours, in terms of both the histories of ideas and institutional histories.

The normative foundations of RBC encapsulate divergent articulations about the *nature* (ethical justifications), their *source* (divine, natural or human), and *scope* (human rights oriented or dependent as well independent exercises of sovereign public power). The *cognoscenti*, as well as *subjects* of constitutionalism, know well the indeterminateness (or to here adapt a Derridean phrase-regime, the *undecidability*) of such articulations of normative foundationalism(s).[22]

RBC, for the most part affirmed and celebrated, were the paradigmatic human rights to property (and specifically in the means of production). Of course, there are other normative candidates (or "items" of constitutional transfer) such as the specifically "religious roots" of human rights with and since Max Weber;[23] or the view of Karl Marx that not only emphasized the class character of human rights but also affirmed that constitutions and laws remain necessary as instruments of struggle against inhuman immiseration, impoverishment, and exploitation.[24] RBC, further, yields today in theory at least to debate over "constitutional essentials" to which I turn for a moment. Given all the variants in the lineage of the RBC, to put it mildly, it is not clear what foundational elements, at a descriptive level in fact and affect, are, may be, and at a normative level ought to be, "mimed".

This chapter may scarcely address theories of/about mimesis.[25] Arne Melberg, for example, guides us to two "alternative ways of describing and *analysing* the phenomenon of *mimesis*": first, the "turning of *mimesis* into *repetition*" and second, *mimesis* as "the meeting-place of two opposing but connected ways of thinking, acting and making: similarity and difference".[26] In this view *mimesis* is "*never* a homogeneous term, and if its basic movement is towards similarity it is *always* open to the opposite".[27] One may also recall the gifted corpus of Paul Ricouer – at

---

[22] Cf. Charles Beardsworth, *Derrida and the Political* (Routledge 1996); Pierre Legrand, *Derrida and Law* (Ashgate 2009).

[23] See, for example, Hans Joas, "Max Weber and the Origin of Human Rights: A Study in Cultural Innovation" (May 2006) IIIS Discussion Paper No. 145; Max L Stackhouse, "Some Intellectual and Moral Roots of Modern Human Rights Ideas" (1981) 20(4) *Journal for the Scientific Study of Religion* 301–9; Upendra Baxi, "Towards De-Colonizing Weber", a paper presented at the Bonn Institute of Law as Culture (October 2012, forthcoming 2013).

[24] See Upendra Baxi, *Marx, Law, and Justice* (NM Tripathi 1993).

[25] See, for example, Arne Melburg, *Theories of Mimesis* (Cambridge University Press 1995); Barbra Fuchs, *Nemesis and Empire* (Cambridge University Press 2001); Matthew Potolsky, *Mimesis* (Routledge 2006); Saija Isomaa, Sari Kivistö, Pirjo Lyytikäinen, Sanna Nyqvist, Merja Polvinen and Riikka Rossi (eds), *Rethinking Mimesis: Concepts and Practices of Literary Representation* (Cambridge Scholars Publication 2012).

[26] Arne Melberg (n 25) 2.

[27] Ibid 3.

least his three forms of "mimesis", which he calls respectively mimesis$_1$, mimesis$_2$, and mimesis$_3$; or "prefiguration", "configuration", and "refiguration".[28]

In these ways, we begin to understand why *labels* (practices of politics of naming) may be borrowed but not "effective" histories; what may be repeated (or transferred) may at best be forms, resemblances, models, but not the distinctive temporal and historical contexts of constitutional enunciations. Contrary to the strong claim asserting patrimony over the very idea and forms of constitutionalism, there may be no *repetition* without *difference*.[29] The histories of the so-called originary forms of "Western" constitutionalism remain inherently repetitive and also dissimilar, even in so far as points of origin may articulate without ambiguity certain "constitutional essentials".[30] In their repetition these "essentials" become differentiated – whether in the forms of articulation of basic human rights and freedoms, imageries of the rule of law, and the idea of citizenship. So remain the originary histories of postcolonial, postsocialist (transitional), and postmodern constitutionalisms.[31]

9.4. A BRIEF OVERVIEW OF "ORIGINARY" ELEMENTS IN POSTCOLONIAL CONSTITUTIONALISM

In what follows, I present some vignettes of postcolonial constitutionalism (PCC, hereafter).[32] Regardless of the potential for *reverse constitutional transfer* from the constitutional imagination and experience of

---

[28] See his *Time and Narrative* (volume 1, translated by Kathleen McLaughlin and David Pellauer, University of Chicago Press 1984) 52–87.

[29] I will not here complicate the discussion with any further reference to George Deleuze's classic text, *Difference and Repetition* (Columbia University Press 1994).

[30] Here I evoke the conception of John Rawls, *Political Liberalism* (Columbia University Press 1993).

[31] See, as to this, Daniel J Elazar, *Constitutionalizing Globalization: The Postmodern Revival of Confederal Arrangements* (Rowman and Littlefield 1998); Jack M Balkin, "What Is a Postmodern Constitutionalism?" (1992) available at http://digitalcommons.law.yale.edu/fss_papers/275.

[32] The term "postcolonial" exercises a fascination even to the point of some eminent constitutional law specialists and historians saying to me that their constitution is the historically first given form of PCC. Of course, it is often necessary to bear in mind at least two caveats: (1) the antebellum US constitutionalism did not depart much from the colonial constitutional form in terms of

peoples living under the conditions of the postcolony, I urge that the community of comparativists and the COCOS folks at least accord the dignity of discourse to some new points of origin in PCC.

9.4.1 Movement-Based RBC

One way to grasp the originality of PCC forms is to accentuate a crucial feature: these are forms of *movement-founded* basic human rights constitutionalisms. The movements and the immanent conception of RBC vary: at one end of the continuum, we have PCC (and not only in Asia and Africa) born out of historic mass struggle to overthrow the colonial yoke and on the other the more contemporary and complex narratives of the Czech to the Arab Spring. Against the effective histories of Euro-colonization resting on the claim of a Divine Right to Empire, the historic forms of de-colonization movements and struggle sculpt a new collective human right to self-determination of peoples. The articulation of this movement-based invention of the right to self-determination also transforms the very idea of constitutionalism. Most PCC go beyond the colonial inheritance privileging of constitutions as a sheer *governance machine*; rather PCC forms articulate the idea of constitutions as providing the time-space of four key and conflicted notions: *governance*, *rights*, *development*, and *justice*[33] in ways not always fully manifest in the foundational choices of Euro-American constitutionalism.

Further these PCC forms have varied histories: the Indian constitution was composed at the same time as the Universal Declaration of Human Rights was being drafted; in contrast the post-apartheid South African constitution occurs within the full maturation of international human rights enunciation (and so does the East Timor constitution much later). While the Indian constitution prefigures the distinction later to be drawn in international human rights enunciative spheres demarcating judicially enforceable civil and political rights and social/economic rights, the South African constitution is able to fashion a community of human rights equally subject to judicial refashioning. While I may not here pursue the narrative of different founding choices, it is clear at the very least that more is at stake than many of the theories of, and about, constitutional transfers.

---

being a constitution of oppressive legal subjectivity for the non-Euro-American others and (2) despite further internal human rights-based transformations, formations of constitutionally validated foreign policy during the "Cold War", and much beyond, led to sustainable indictments of "legal imperialism".

[33] See Baxi (n 24).

The more recent movement-based constitutionalisms (from the Czech to the Arab Spring and indeed manifold passages in-between, ranging, for example, to South Asian PCC forms such as Pakistan, Nepal, and Burma) unfold resistance against neocolonial formations described memorably by Kwame Nkrumah as codifying practices/formations of "power without responsibility" and "exploitation without redress". Professor Oketh-Ogendo, a leading Kenyan constitutionalist, was later to describe this feature jurisprudentially as "constitutions without constitutionalism".[34] The current wave of the Arab Spring movement articulates resistance to these forms of massive and near-permanent states of exception, confronting the more limited grasp of the "state of exception" offered by gurus such as Carl Schmitt and Giorgio Agamben and their devout disciples. The post-PCC movement-based imagination addresses the problematic of internal colonization fostered and remaining mired in the play, and war, of strategic geopolitical global power formations. If so, how may any IKEA-type discourse address all this?

In a sense, forms of popular sovereignty present an extraordinary articulation of different forms of RBC, though not as precisely known to the imagination and experience of the Euro-American bicentennial constitutional forms. Tahrir Square and its specific equivalents in Tunis and elsewhere evoke images of "We, the People" as a permanent constituent assembly in constant motion. Further, these movements mobilize even associations of judges and legal professionals to foster alternate RBC conceptions in ways that redefine the everyday notions of public/popular participation in constitution-making. An entirely novel history of popular constitution-making is here on full display;[35] to subsume this recent history and to collapse it into mimetic instances of Westphalian/Euro-American histories ill-serves (to say the least) the imagery of a global

---

[34] See HWO Okoth-Ogendo, "Constitutions without Constitutionalism: Reflections on an African Political Paradox" in Douglas Greenberg, Stanley N Katz, Melanie Beth Oliviero and Steven C Wheatley (eds), *Constitutionalism and Democracy: Transitions in the Contemporary World* (Oxford University Press 1993). See, further, Issa Shivji, *The Concept of Human Rights in Africa* (African Books Collective 1989).

[35] One must here note the extraordinary originality manifested in the making of the post-apartheid South African constitution, though it is unlikely to be repeated: that constitution was made by widespread participation of different publics; the draft constitution was subjected to a regime of basic principles (especially of Ubuntu); the Constitutional Court had already the power to ensure that the interim constitutional text accorded full well with these principles and in fact there exists an unprecedented judicial discourse finally "certifying" the draft constitution.

constitutionalism. Put another way, the collective constitutional consciousness of "We, the People" always carries with it a reservoir of cultural memories of multifarious forms of insurgent, popular, and public reason, always contesting the "reason of the State".[36] Indeed, this very renovation of the moral architecture of the idea of constitutions/constitutionalisms renders constitutional dictatorship, in all its varied PCC forms, inherently problematic and unviable in the long term.

9.4.2 The Fusion of Constitutional Time

We are schooled to think about constitutional *space* rather than adjudicative *time*. To offer only two examples: the federal design and detail and the doctrine of separation of powers (which animates much debate about judicial role and function and the generalized notion of the rule of law) speak to us spatially in terms of distribution of spaces (jurisdiction/competence) *of* and *for* governance. The notion of constitutional time gets spatialized for the most part in the languages of geographies of power and demography of rights.

Constitutional time emerges only in distinctions conventionally made in terms of *constituent* time (CT-1) and *constituted* time (CT-2). CT-1 signifies the time of constitutional founding; CT-2 represents the time of putting a constitution to work or to sleep. Again, this difference gets depicted, for the most part, in spatial terms: thus, one speaks of constituent time as a foundational site of distribution of powers of governance by which the sites and substance of CT-2 decisions must be developed as well as adjudged. Prescinding further elaboration of this thematic here, one may at least address CT-1 and CT-2 in terms of *time-spaces* of constitutionalism. These vary immensely in PCC and (the bicentennial) RBC constitutionalisms.

In normative narratives, CT-1 is a time of insurgent public/popular reason, often posited as "treason". In its inaugural moment CT-1 remains "extraordinary" because it gives birth to a new political and social order. Its "new 'politics' is always extraconstitutional" (as adjudged by extant constitutional orders and regimes); it "aims either at core constitutional matters or at central social imaginary significations, cultural meanings, and economic issues, with the goal of transforming the basic structures of

---

36 See Upendra Baxi, "Public and Insurgent Reason – Adjudicatory Leadership in a Hyper-globalizing World" in S Hill (ed), *The Crisis of Global Leadership* (Cambridge University Press 2011).

society and resignifying social reality".[37] Extraordinary politics characterizes what we today name as transformative constitutionalism.[38] CT-2, however, is the everyday time of constitutional politics which is said to derive its legitimacy from the foundational texts of CT-1 and of the determination of the legality of sovereign public decisions. If CT-1 is the time of the founding text and of the polity, CT-2 is the time of construction of the constitutional conceptions of the good life envisaged by the founding moment (and its text) and it is a time often marked by deep disruptions and fusions. CT-2 cannot but routinize the charismatic CT-1. Put another way, CT-2 is the time of constitutional structures (institutions/arrangements) and their relatively autonomous functioning and thus a differential time of collaboration, complicity, and collisions amongst the wielders of institutionally channelled sovereign power. Whatever terms like "governance", "democracy", "justice", "development", "rule of law" and "human rights" may normatively signify, CT-2 puts this variations in terms of the differentiation of the time of the state, or the time of institutional differentiation of the construction of politics and of the distinctively "political". In many a sense, this is hermeneutic time – the time of interpretation of constituted power and functions belongs to all state institutions; these co-equally wield hermeneutic/deontic powers; it, however, happens that adjudicative time often captures the commanding heights of centralization of the operative (juridical and social) meaning of what constitutional texts may mean by what they say (and do *not* say).

9.4.3 The New Lifetimes of Adjudicative Time

Adjudicative time is an aspect of constituted time – the time of interpretation of public decisions by other branches of governance. Adjudicative time may not, in conventional narratives of judicial role and

---

[37] See Andrea Kalvyas, *Democracy and the Politics of the Extraordinary: Max Weber, Carl Schmitt, and Hannah Arendt* (Cambridge University Press 2008) 7; see, further, Antonio Negri, *Insurgencies: Constituent Power and the Modern State* (translated by Maurizia Boscagli, University of Minnesota Press 1999).

[38] See, as to this notion in the contexts of Brazil, South Africa, and India, Upendra Baxi, "Preliminary Notes on Transformative Constitutionalism", BISA (Brazil, India, South Africa) Conference, Courting Justice 11, 27–9 April 2009 (forthcoming 2013); Baxi, "Modeling Optimal Constitutional Designs for Government Structures: Some Debutant Remarks" in S Khilnani, V Raghavan and A Thiruvengadam (eds), *Comparative Constitutionalism in South Asia* (Oxford University Press 2012).

function, be invested with concerns about the *legitimacy* of such decisions; rather, the constitution is said to "command" that justices and courts should use their time wisely and well only to decide their *legality* and *constitutionality*. Adjudicative time in most PCC forms often acquires a salience disrupting the hegemonic time installed by other state apparatuses. Most PCC then furnish narratives of this salience.

Adjudicative time marks in PCC forms, however, both the forms of fusion and disruption of constitutional temporalities. Disruption rather fully occurs via constitutional dictatorship or authoritarianism, which results in sustained states of emergency that suspend the original constitution in order to serve its ends better in the future – a state of affairs that Carl Schmitt was to describe as "commissariat dictatorship". Disruption also occurs when massive practices of peaceful civil disobedience or armed rebellion cast into deep doubt the legitimacy of constrictions produced by CT-1 (to generalize here the insights of Antonio Negri's notion of constitutional insurgencies).[39] Fusion occurs variously, as for example when the constituted power to amend the constitution is deployed serially or cumulatively as a form of constituent power to transform the nature of the constitution.

I may here only mention, by way of an enormous illustration, the ways in which the Indian Supreme Court invents and fashions the discipline of basic structure doctrine. Initially, this invention addressed the tasks of interpretive/hermeneutic leadership, seeking to discipline the excessive use of amendatory power. The Court, while recognizing the plenary power of the Indian Parliament to amend the constitution, still subjected it to some strict constitutional scrutiny in the name of the preservation of the basic structure and essential features of the constitution. In effect, the Court insists, in the first place, that it singularly possesses the power to grasp the charismatic moment of CT-1 and in its name may superintend the exercise of CT-2 powers. A constitutional amendment may be upheld or invalidated when interlocuted as violating the essential features – variously named as "democracy", "the rule of law", "federalism", "fundamental rights", "republicanism", "secularism" and even "socialism". Over time, the Court extends this judicial surveillance to the function and exercise of other constitutional powers and even fashions this into a canon of construction for the exercise of statutory powers.[40] What is

---

[39] Negri (n 37).

[40] See, for a recent analysis, Sudhir Krishnaswamy, *Democracy and Constitutionalism* (Oxford University Press 2009). See also Z Hasan, E Sridharan and R Sudarshan (eds), *India's Living Constitution: Ideas, Practices, Controversies* (Permanent Black 2002); Upendra Baxi, "'A Known but an Indifferent Judge':

remarkable is the fact that this doctrine (and social technique) now extends to almost all South Asian constitutionalisms.[41] Incidentally, I must leave aside the question why these ways of fashioning adjudicative time may not enter the collective consciousness or memory in the IKEA model of constitutional transfers.

9.4.4 Towards Demosprudence, Not Just "Jurisprudence"

"Demosprudence" is what the Indian Supreme Court has been practising, though the term is of recent origin, engaging the studies of the US Supreme Court, now also extended to the South African Constitutional Court.[42] Of course, had the US constitutional/comparative jurisprudence specialists the time and inclination to study the ways of Indian adjudicatory leadership, they may have readily acknowledged the Indian Supreme Court's originary contribution to this concept-formation.

Indian "demosprudence" emerges with acute and often anguished concern for popular (as distinct from legal) sovereignty. *Kesvananda Bharathi* is an inaugural feat of Indian demosprudence.[43] This hallmark of hermeneutic judicial leadership finds sustained articulation in the post-Emergency moment of "judicial populism"[44] and further in the manifold charismatic founding moment of Social Action Litigation (SAL – misrecognized as "public interest litigation"), which marks a decisive transformation of the Supreme Court of India towards a court for the deprived and disadvantaged *worst-off* Indian citizens.

SAL adjudicatory leadership, I have maintained, articulates and for the most part also sustains the emergence of a *fiduciary* conception of adjudicative leadership, function, and power. Put in a one sentence formulation, this means that courts and justices may not take human rights at all seriously without also taking human/social *suffering coequally seriously*. SAL practices fully suggest (in the immortal words

---

Situating Ronald Dworkin in Contemporary Indian Jurisprudence" (2003) 1(4) *International Journal of Constitutional Law* 557; Baxi, "The Justice of Human Rights in Indian Constitutionalism" in Akash Singh and Silika Mohapatra (eds), *Indian Political Thought: A Reader* (Routledge 2010) ch 17.

41 See Brian Ray, "Demosprudence in Comparative Perspective" (2010) available at: http://works.bepress.com/brian_ray/5, visited 6 November 2010.

42 Lani Guinier, "The Supreme Court 2007: Foreword: Demosprudence Through Dissent" (2007) 22(4) *Harvard Law Review* 138.

43 Especially, in the opinions of Justices MH Beg, SN Dwivedi, KK Mathew and YV Chandrachud.

44 Baxi (n 13) and (n 24).

of Justice Goswami) that the Supreme Court remains the "*last refuge of the oppressed and bewildered* Indian humanity".[45]

The maturation of Indian demosprudence entails further reconstruction and repair of this "last refuge".[46] The Apex Justices (as well as the Indian High Court Justices, whose specific contributions remain even today under-studied) have converted the idea of *jurisdiction* into spaces/sites of civic *conversation* about acts of remaking/transforming *constitutional cultures*. Notably, they have accomplished this conversion via fostering ways of dialogue between social movement and human rights activists, and related learned professions. New techniques of justicing have contributed to the establishment and consolidation of a creative jurisprudence of human rights. All this, and more, has resulted in manifestations of adjudicative leadership hard at work towards re-democratizing India, indeed to the point where the Supreme Court itself assumes the appearance of a new social movement.

Yet, one may never lose sight of the fact that at the end of the day courts and justices remain apparatuses of sovereign state power. This institutional brute fact chastens, in India, and elsewhere, our understandings of the salience of adjudicative time. This time now remains subjected to the imperatives of the structural adjustment of demosprudence in an era conjointly marked by disparate states of affairs such as the wars *of* and *on* "terror", "military humanism" (the law and politics of regime change), making the future world safe from the ravages of global financial markets, and the regimes of "constitutionalizing austerity" now amidst the Eurozone crises. All these features put into question, to say the very least, the templates of "constitutional transfers" governed, as it were, by an IKEA model.

---

[45] *State of Rajasthan v. Union of India* (1977) 3 SCC 634 at 70 (emphasis added).

[46] See, for example, Sandra Fredman, *Human Rights Transformed: Positive Rights and Positive Duties* (Oxford University Press 2008); SP Sathe, *Judicial Activism in India: Transgressing Borders and Enforcing Limits* (Oxford University Press 2002); Upendra Baxi, "The Avatars of Judicial Activism: Explorations in the Geography of (In) Justice" in SK Verma and K Kusum (eds), *Fifty Years of the Supreme Court of India: Its Grasp and Reach* (Oxford University Press and Indian Law Institute 2001) 156.

9.5. A CONCLUDING WORD

My tremulous fascination with Professor Frankenberg's framework has so far addressed the need for a more cosmopolitan reading of collective constitutional unconscious and different evocations of cultural memories of constitutionalisms.

I must now conclude with two additional remarks.

One: as concerns the imagery of transfers, the idea of constitutional time remains astonishingly diverse, constituting the registers – to here adopt the metaphors of a leading anthropologist of time – of "enduring time, trickle-down time, and *deceptive* time, *erratic* time, *cyclical* time, *retarded* time, time in *advance*, *alternating* time, and *explosive* time."[47] It would not advance the tasks of comparison or of the COCOS were we to think only of the Eurocentric (whether progressive or regressive) "enduring" and "cyclical" time, relegating PCC time only to other non-Euro erratic manifestations. In sum, the problematic consists in taking constitutional time *seriously as already invested by these conflicted temporalities.*

Two: as concerns the imageries of "ordering transfers" we need to go much beyond "pseudo-philosophical analyses of popular sovereignty, the rule of law, or the communicative procedures that regulate the formation of public opinion and political will"; we need much more arduous labours to understand "the boundaries of public law, extending up to the fundamental conceptions of the economy and the very idea of reproductive life of human societies".[48]

[47] I adapt here the phrase-regime of Alfred Gell, *The Anthropology of Time*, 62.8 (Berg 2001), emphasis added.

[48] Girgio Agamben, *The Kingdom and the Glory: For a Theological Genealogy of Economy and Government* (Homo Sacer *II*, 2) (translated by Lorzezo Chiesa, Matteo Mandarini, Stanford University Press 2011) xii and 4.

10. Constitutional autochthony and the invention and survival of "absolute presidentialism" in postcolonial Africa

H Kwasi Prempeh

The sheer breadth and reach of presidential power in Africa, as well as its highly personal character, has often caused scholars and analysts of African politics to look beyond the conventional vocabulary and typology in search of an appropriate descriptor. "Big Man rule,"[1] "personal rule,"[2] "presidential monarchy,"[3] "neo-presidentialism"[4] and, borrowing from Arthur Schlesinger Jr,[5] "imperial presidency"[6] are only a few of the many colorful names and epithets by which Africa's one-man-dominated political and constitutional systems – what I refer to in this chapter as "absolute presidentialism" – have been called. The prevalence in postcolonial Africa of this form of rule, in which practically every state institution is subordinated to the dictates of the president, has been largely responsible for the popularity among Africanist scholars of neo-patrimonial and other personalistic theories and accounts of politics and political phenomena in Africa.

---

1 Oda Van Cranenburgh, "'Big Man' Rule: Presidential Power, Regime Type and Democracy in 30 African Countries" (2008) 15 *Democratization* 952.

2 RH Jackson and CG Rosberg, *Personal Rule in Black Africa: Prince, Autocrat, Prophet, Tyrant* (University of California Press 1970).

3 Ali Mazrui, "The Monarchical Tendency in African Political Culture" (1967) 18 *British Journal of Sociology* 231.

4 BH Selassie, *The Executive in African Government* (Heinemann 1974) 19.

5 AJ Schlesinger, Jr, *The Imperial Presidency* (Houghton Mifflin 1973).

6 HWO Okoth-Ogendo, "Constitutions without Constitutionalism: Reflections on an African Political Paradox" in Douglas Greenberg et al (eds), *Constitutionalism and Democracy: Transitions in the Contemporary World* (Oxford University Press 1993) 65–80.

How did absolute presidentialism become a defining and dominant feature of political and constitutional governance in postcolonial Africa? Why does it persist? Is the absolute president an authentically African form of rule, with roots in "African" culture? Or might it be a "foreign" borrowing?

As a regime type, postcolonial Africa's tradition of absolute presidentialism was constitutionally installed in the 1960s – the first decade of African independence. It was the centerpiece of a series of constitutional and legislative changes introduced by postcolonial Africa's new leaders soon after the dust of decolonization had settled. One-party rule, elimination of subnational or quasi-federal structures, curtailment of judicial independence, subjection of the civil service to party control, and suppression of civil and political rights were some of the other legal and political changes that accompanied and, in many ways, propped up absolute presidentialism in the early years after independence. Since the 1990s, however, democratic and constitutional reforms introduced across Africa have transformed the political and constitutional landscape significantly. The *de jure* one-party system, once a fixture in politics in Africa, has now all but disappeared, making way for multiparty competition. Consequently, legislative and presidential elections, once episodic and farcical events, are now routinely and vigorously contested, and frequently result in defeat for incumbents. Traditional legislative and oversight functions have also been restored to Africa's now-representative and multiparty parliaments. And the courts, once passive judicial rubber-stamps for Africa's "Big Men" presidents, are now empowered to adjudicate citizens' complaints and challenges against governmental action and often exercise their power of judicial review in favor of challengers. Africa's political elites also must now contend with critical reporting and scrutiny from a newly invigorated and diverse private media. A growing number of nongovernmental organizations are similarly revitalizing African civil societies and opening new avenues for the mobilization and expression of civic activism.

Arguably the most profound change in Africa's postcolonial constitutional order in recent years is the emergence of presidential term limits. In sharp contrast to the period before 1990, when Africa's absolute presidents, whether civilian or military, held on to power indefinitely and worried mainly about the prospect of a *coup d'état*, constitutional rules in a growing number of African countries now impose a maximum limit, usually no more than two terms, on the duration of presidential office holding. Currently, nearly thirty African constitutions contain presidential term-limit provisions. Importantly, these new constitutional provisions have begun to work, confounding many who once thought it impossible that presidential rule in African states could be terminated by legal rules.[7] Term limits have ended the tenure of nearly twenty presidents in Africa since 1990, including some of the longest-serving Big Men of the nationalist generation. As a result Africa now has, for the first time in its postcolonial history, a club of retired presidents.

Amidst this flurry of democratic and constitutional activity, the one feature of the *ancien régime* that has defied transformation and outlasted other pillars of the old authoritarianism is absolute presidentialism. In many respects, the African presidency has emerged from the recent round of democratic and constitutional reforms with many of its extant powers and prerogatives substantially intact. In general, presidential rule in post-authoritarian Africa has become less openly repressive, and the climate for civil and political liberties has improved perceptibly. Still, effective power in the African state, and with it control of the public purse, patronage, public contracting, local administration, and the instruments of coercion, both military and civilian, continues to reside almost exclusively with the president. Even where legislative decision-making is shared nominally with a parliament, legislative initiative and agenda-setting, as well as bill drafting and amending powers, have remained primarily an executive preserve. The contemporary African president's power of appointment remains similarly vast and often exclusive, extending in many cases even to those nominally independent constitutional and statutory offices that must assure the integrity and professionalism of law enforcement, prosecutions, corruption investigation, public financial management, monetary policy, and the conduct of national elections. As before, the contemporary African president enjoys absolute immunity from civil and criminal liability (or investigation) and judicial process while in office. Rule by presidential *diktat*, often in the form of "directives" or "press releases" issued from the seat of the presidency, survives as a common mode of governing in post-authoritarian Africa. In short, even where the African presidency has been democratized and term-limited, the substantive power of the incumbent African president has not been tamed or diminished in the process.

The persistence in post-authoritarian Africa of essential elements of absolute presidentialism represents a puzzle for a variety of reasons. First, as a regime type or mode of governance its record in Africa has been one of unmitigated disaster. Rampant corruption, official impunity, subversion of the rule of law, decay of state capacity and institutions are

---

[7] DN Posner and DJ Young, "The Institutionalization of Political Power in Africa" (2007) 18 *Journal of Democracy* 126, 131.

only a few of the political costs that decades of absolute presidentialism brought in its trail. Second, the perennial and chronic failures of absolute presidentialism in postcolonial Africa were prominent among the drivers of the social protests and pressure for democratic and constitutional reform that led to the recent political transitions and regime changes in many African countries. Third, the tradition of absolute presidentialism was underwritten, in large part, by the indefinite tenure African presidents enjoyed. Indefinite tenure turned the African presidency into a freehold estate of the incumbent and guaranteed presidential impunity. By reversing these tendencies, it was presumed that presidential term limits would discipline and moderate the grandeur and omnipotence that has historically surrounded presidential office in postcolonial Africa. Lastly, the heroic Big Men of Africa's nationalist generation that pioneered absolute presidentialism and lent it legitimacy for much of its life has now all but disappeared from the political arena, three of the longest-serving among them (Moi of Kenya, Kaunda of Zambia, Banda of Malawi) having been swept aside by the democratic tide of the 1990s. The new breed of leaders that has emerged in their place does not have nearly the same reservoir of organic legitimacy the nationalist generation easily took for granted. Africa's post-authoritarian leaders must now count on democratic elections of uncertain outcome to gain or retain power. Still, once in office, they, too, have remained exceptionally powerful, even if they have not always been willing to exercise the full range of their authority and prerogatives. In short, despite evidence or indications that point to a loss or diminishment of legitimacy for essential elements of the *ancien régime*, including absolute presidentialism, Africa's presidents continue to possess and exercise a huge preponderance of power. What explains this seemingly puzzling persistence of absolute presidentialism in contemporary Africa?

To many the answer to this question is neither hard to find nor particularly complicated: the survival of African imperial presidency, despite recent counter-authoritarian political and constitutional reforms, must be proof that that form of rule is culturally embedded. This is indeed a fairly routine or common explanation for various political and social phenomena or practices in Africa. Even where the experience or practice is widespread or universally shared, as is the case with the phenomenon of imperial presidency,[8] African manifestations of the same

[8] See, e.g., Gary Rosen, "The Time of the Presidents" *New York Times* (New York, 16 July 2006) 21 ("Around the world, the imperial presidency appears to be alive and well.").

tendency tend to be viewed or explained in terms of "African culture." This failure to apply universal categories of explanation to understanding political and social phenomena in Africa fosters and reinforces the notion of African exceptionalism – which often accounts for the marginalization of Africa in comparative discourses.

In the case of postcolonial Africa's tradition of absolute presidentialism, the cultural explanation looks for antecedents in, and draws parallels with, the monarchical institution of chieftaincy (which is assumed to be uniformly indigenous to societies across Africa). Writing about the persistent "strong" presidency in Nigeria's constitutional system, one comparative constitutional scholar invoked the African culture thesis thus:

> The role of the "strong leader" is consistent with the traditional perception of tribal leadership that is familiar to many people throughout this region of Africa. … The traditional political role of the Nigerian president, especially in terms of such matters as patronage, safeguarding the country, and being the focal point for administering and distributing all resources may be based more firmly upon traditional cultural expectations than upon the powers and institutions (which may be extensive but, also, comparable to the experiences of other democratic constitutional systems) that are expressly linked to that office.[9]

Importantly, the view that the "strong" African president, whether authoritarian (old) or democratic (new), is but the African chief *writ large* is not restricted to non-African commentators. Cultural explanations of political practice or observed tendency in Africa have long been a staple of Africa's own political elites. The African culture thesis was particularly popular with Africa's first generation of leaders who were widely regarded, with some justification, as philosopher-kings.[10] Tanzania's Julius Nyerere, for example, strongly defended his socialistic policies as deeply rooted in the communalistic and egalitarian ethos of traditional African society.[11] His Kenyan and Senegalese counterparts, who

---

[9] James Hugh, *Comparative Constitutional Traditions* (Lang 2002).

[10] See Goran Hyden, "The Failure of Africa's First Intellectuals" (1967) 28 *Transition* 14, 17 ("Plato's idea of the philosopher-king has hardly anywhere been more deliberately put into practice than in Africa. As the philosopher-kings, the intellectuals in power have often been considered the 'national conscience'").

[11] Julius Nyerere, *Ujamaa – Essays on Socialism* (Oxford University Press 1968) 12 ("We in Africa have no more need of being 'converted' to socialism than we have being 'taught' democracy. Both are rooted in our past – in the traditional society that produced us."). See also Tom Mboya, *The Challenge of Nationhood* (Praeger Publishers 1970) 83–4 (defending "African socialism" by

advocated a similar course, backed him up on this point.[12] The move toward a one-party state in postcolonial Africa was also defended by its elite originators and practitioners as reflecting the cultural norm in indigenous African political systems, where consensus supposedly reigned and organized opposition was unknown.[13] The leading advocates and practitioners of absolute presidentialism in postcolonial Africa similarly sought cultural legitimacy for their constitutional and political project by evoking comparisons with chieftaincy or rulership in Africa's traditional polities.

With absolute presidentialism re-emerging in post-authoritarian Africa, it is appropriate to interrogate seriously the question whether this political tendency or regime type is indeed culturally embedded and thus inevitable. If, as I shall argue, this question must be answered in the negative, what then explains why Africa's tradition of absolute presidentialism has survived recent democratic and counter-authoritarian reform?

THE POLITICAL SEARCH FOR CONSTITUTIONAL AUTOCHTHONY

Africa's former colonies entered the ranks of sovereign states in the postwar period with constitutions that generally mirrored the metropolitan constitutional systems of their European colonizers. Thus, while the Westminster parliamentary system served as the blueprint for the "independence constitutions" of anglophone Africa, the constitutions of France's former colonies bore the imprint of the Constitution of the French Fifth Republic. Accordingly, there were, from the beginning, important differences between the constitutional systems of anglophone and francophone African states. Following the Gaullist precedent, which had come into effect in France (in 1958) almost contemporaneously with the independence in 1960 of most of France's African colonies, the

---

contrasting African traditions and conceptions of ownership and property rights with Europe's).

[12] See, e.g., Republic of Kenya, *African Socialism and its Application to Planning in Kenya* (Government Printer 1965) ("The sharp class divisions that once existed in Europe have no … parallel in African society. No class problem arose in the traditional African society and none exists today among Africans.").

[13] See, e.g., Julius Nyerere, *Freedom and Unity* (Oxford University Press 1966) 196–7. See also Convention People's Party (CPP), "Program for Work and Happiness," reprinted as Appendix B in David E Apter, *Ghana in Transition* (Atheneum 1963) 394, para. 11 ("a multi-party system is alien to the traditional conception of government in African Society.").

independence constitutions of Africa's francophone states were both republican and president-dominant in character. By contrast, the Westminster-inspired independence constitutions of anglophone Africa, beginning with Ghana's in 1957, installed a constitutional monarchy, with the British monarch as the nominal head of state. As expected, real executive authority in anglophone Africa's parliamentary-style constitutional systems was vested in a cabinet drawn from the majority party in parliament and headed by a prime minister. Following the Westminster constitutional system, the prime minister in anglophone Africa also owed his position as head of government to his leadership or headship of the majority party in parliament. In that respect, the source and duration of the prime minister's constitutional authority was political; it stemmed from and depended on his continued headship of the majority party. Thus, only in an indirect – and somewhat *ex officio* – sense was the power of the prime minister in anglophone Africa based in the constitution. This contrasted with the strong constitutionally rooted position and term of office of the president as chief executive in France's ex-colonies.

Not surprisingly, given their comparatively inferior constitutional status (compared with their francophone counterparts), it was anglophone Africa's leaders, led by Ghana's Kwame Nkrumah, who led the way to replace their independence constitutions with "autochthonous" ones in the immediate aftermath of independence. To mobilize popular support for their push for so-called constitutional autochthony, Nkrumah and his peers highlighted two symbolically (and thus politically) salient and objectionable facts about their Westminster-style constitutions. The first was that these constitutions, following British imperial constitutional practice, were each enacted or authorized by the Parliament of the United Kingdom and came in the form of an "Order in Council" of the Queen. The second was the Queen's nominal constitutional role as head of state. In practice the Queen was represented in the former colony by a governor-general (who did not have to be European), and her constitutional functions as head of state, including the Royal Assent, were to be exercised strictly in accordance with settled Westminster conventions and were thus merely ceremonial. Nonetheless, the fact that the constitution of a sovereign nation should derive its authority from an external source – namely, an Order in Council of the Queen prescribed and authorized by an Act of the British Parliament – or that the assent of an alien (British) monarch should be required for passage of legislation by the parliament of an independent state made it politically easy for anglophone Africa's new leaders to disparage their independence constitutions as alien impositions and derogations from their national sovereignty.

Thus when in 1960 Ghana's Nkrumah decided that anglophone Africa's first independent state must replace its Westminster 1957 constitution, he highlighted the symbolically alien features of the independence constitution: "… it is the height of incongruity for the inhabitants of the Ghanaian town of Tamale, for instance, to find the Head of their State living in Buckingham Palace, London. The Head of the West African State of Ghana should be a Ghanaian having his residence in Ghana."[14] Replacing the Westminster constitution was also about autochthony in a second, procedural, sense: "Three years after independence we cannot still continue to be governed by a Constitution imposed upon us by a foreign power and which we have found to be unsuitable … Accordingly, I ask you in this Constituent Assembly to declare by the support you give to this Motion that Ghanaians have an indisputable right to think for themselves, to decide for themselves and to act for themselves."[15] Framed in such popular nationalistic terms, the proposed constitutional change was one even Nkrumah's political rivals could not help but embrace. The leader of the opposition in Ghana's parliament expressed strong support for the constitutional proposals.[16]

Yet the content of the constitutional changes Ghana pioneered in Africa in 1960 went far beyond mere constitutional nationalism or symbolism. The Republican Constitution, as its architects preferred to call it, unified in a President the aggregate of the executive powers previously bifurcated between the Queen as titular head of state and the prime minister-led cabinet. In fact, the constitution conferred on the president "more powers than were exercised under the independence constitution by the Queen, the Governor-General, and the Prime Minister combined."[17]

Ghana's shift toward presidentialism was itself unexceptional. But this was no ordinary presidentialism. Although the government White Paper introducing the constitutional proposals claimed that the proposed constitution was "not copied from the constitution of any other country," the broad outlines of the presidency under Ghana's new constitution drew

---

[14] K Nkrumah, *Africa Must Unite* (Heinemann 1963) 81.

[15] See K Robinson, "Constitutional Autochthony in Ghana" (1961) 1 *Journal of Commonwealth Political Studies* 41, 44 (quoting Proceedings of Ghana's Constituent Assembly).

[16] Ibid.

[17] Julian C Juergensmeyer, "African Presidentialism: A Comparison of the 'Executive' under the Constitutions of the Federation of Nigeria, the Federal Republics of the Congo and Cameroon, and the Republics of Ghana, Chad, Congo, and the Entente" (1964) 8 *Journal of African Law* 157, 162.

inspiration from comparative models, including the American constitution.[18] Like the US president, the Ghanaian president held all of the executive authority of the state, which he could exercise directly or through ministers and other officials designated by him. Like his American counterpart, the Ghanaian president governed with the benefit of a cabinet. Again, as in the United States, cabinet officers in Ghana were merely the president's advisers; the president was not bound by the advice of his cabinet. Beyond these few parallels, however, the Ghana president possessed extraordinary, somewhat *sui generis*, powers unfamiliar to American-style presidentialism.

Notably, Ghana's 1960 Constitution reserved certain "special powers" for the "First President,"[19] and Nkrumah was specifically named in the constitution as the First President,[20] having been deemed appointed to that office by the referendum held to approve a *draft* of the Constitution.[21] The tenure of the First President was co-terminus with Nkrumah's, which was indefinite, as it was supposed to "continue until some other person assumes office as President."[22] As First President, Nkrumah had power under the 1960 Constitution "whenever he considers it to be in the national interest to do so, [to] give directions by legislative instrument."[23] A "legislative instrument" could alter any law (other than the constitution itself). In effect, Nkrumah could legislate alone or alter unilaterally a pre-existing statute.

The Ghanaian president assumed other powers that confirmed his supremacy over parliament. For example, his veto power was both absolute and partial; he could reject in whole or in part a bill passed by the legislature, and his veto could not be overridden by the legislature.[24] The president also had power to "prorogue" or terminate at any time a session of parliament.[25] Parliament had power to approve (or reject) each head of the executive's annual budget estimates, but it had no power to

---

18 Nkrumah (n 14) 82.

19 See Ghana (1960) Constitution art. 55.

20 Ibid art. 10.

21 The draft of the Constitution submitted to the national referendum did not include the provision relating to the special powers of the First President, and the enacted constitution included other significant post-referendum changes and additions made by Nkrumah's government. L Rubin and P Murray, *The Constitution and Government of Ghana* (2nd edn, Sweet & Maxwell 1964) 15–31.

22 Ghana (1960) Constitution art. 55(5).

23 Ibid art. 55(2).

24 Ibid art. 24(1).

25 Ibid art. 22(2).

amend them as proposed by the president.[26] The president could authorize moneys to be drawn from public funds outside the statutorily approved budget.[27] The president had power to appoint from among members of parliament any number of ministers to constitute his government.[28] No legislative approval was required for these appointments, and the legislature had no power to censure or remove a minister; only the president could do so.[29] The president was also vested with unilateral appointment power over numerous other constitutional offices, including, notably, the appointment of the chief justice and other judges of the superior courts,[30] the auditor general,[31] the attorney general,[32] and members of the civil service.[33] The chief justice and, by subsequent amendment, all judges of the supreme court or high court, held their offices at the pleasure of the president,[34] as, of course, did the attorney general,[35] whose position had been moved in 1959 from the civil service category to that of a political appointee.[36]

Ghana's Republican Constitution did not expressly contain a bill of rights. What it did contain were certain "Fundamental Principles" to which the president, immediately upon assuming office, had to "solemnly declare" his personal "adherence." It included a declaration "That the powers of Government spring from the will of the people and should be exercised in accordance therewith" and "That subject to such restrictions as may be necessary for preserving public order, morality or health, no person should be deprived of freedom of religion or speech, of the right to move and assemble without hindrance or of the right of access to the courts of law."

Ruling in the first case to test the justiciability of the Fundamental Principles, Ghana's supreme court compared the president's "solemn declaration" to the "Coronation Oath of the Queen of England."[37] As

---

26 Ibid art. 31(2).

27 Ibid arts. 32 and 34.

28 Ibid art. 15.

29 Ibid.

30 Ibid arts. 44(1) and 45(1).

31 Ibid art. 38(1).

32 Ibid art. 47(1).

33 Ibid art. 51(2).

34 Ibid art. 45(3).

35 Ibid art. 47(3).

36 H Bretton, *The Rise and Fall of Kwame Nkrumah: A Study in Personal Rule in Africa* (Praeger Publishers 1966) 48.

37 *Re Akoto et al* [1961] GLR [pt. II] 523, 535.

such, it imposed on the president of Ghana only a "moral obligation,"[38] not a legally binding one. The Fundamental Principles, according to the court, provided, at best, "a political yardstick by which the conduct of the Head of State can be measured by the electorate."[39] The remedy for an alleged breach of any of the solemn declaration was therefore "through the use of the ballot box, and not through the courts."[40]

In short, there was no judicial check on the conduct of the president under Ghana's new Republican Constitution. Nor did the ballot box remedy the court had suggested practically exist at the time, as the very same preventive detention law challenged in that case had been used to detain several opposition members, send others into exile, and silenced the rest or forced them to join Nkrumah's party. By an amendment to the constitution in 1964 what had long been true *de facto* was confirmed *de jure*, as Ghana was officially declared a one-party state. Ghana's Republican Constitution thus abolished a constitutional monarchy only to make way for an absolute president – a "presidential monarch,"[41] in effect. Ali Mazrui has called this the "paradox of monarchical republicanism."[42]

Ghana's installation of a regime of absolute presidentialism in the early 1960s served both as a harbinger and as a blueprint for the constitutional remaking of independent Africa. Between the end of 1960 and early 1962 alone, thirteen newly independent African states adopted new constitutions or made significant changes to their independence constitutions.[43] Many more states followed suit as they, too, became independent. In anglophone Africa, the common thread that ran through these post-independence constitutional revisions was "a movement from traditional parliamentarianism to a new form of presidentialism,"[44] characterized by substantially enhanced presidential power.[45] Equally remarkable is the extent to which "almost every step in Ghana's post-independence constitutional development [was] followed, in almost its precise sequence"[46] by governments across Africa. In the countries of francophone Africa, where Gaullist-inspired hybrid constitutions already provided a starting point

---

38 Ibid.

39 Ibid 540.

40 Ibid 541.

41 Apter (n 13) 371.

42 Mazrui (n 3).

43 See BH Selassie, *The Executive in African Governments* (Heinemann 1974) 39.

44 Ibid.

45 Ibid.

46 Ibid.

for a strong presidency, the post-independence constitutional changes were far less revolutionary; they mainly served to reinforce the existing pattern by reallocating powers to the president from the prime minister and parliament.

IS ABSOLUTE PRESIDENTIALISM "AFRICAN"?

The upshot of the constitutional and legislative changes made by Africa's post-independence governments, both anglophone and francophone, was a convergence in regime type across the continent toward absolute presidentialism. How, then, must we interpret this convergence? Does the rapid emergence of absolute presidentialism as the modal regime type across Africa in the immediate aftermath of colonialism point to a cultural explanation, as some would suggest?

The immediate difficulty with a continent-wide notion of culture as the driver of political or constitutional form and practice in Africa is its empirical implausibility. Africa comprises too many diverse cultures and cultural identities – with wide variation in indigenous political structure and organization – for talk of a monolithic African culture to make analytic or empirical sense. Indeed, not all indigenous African political systems were hierarchically structured with a king or "chief" at the head. Many groups, such as the Ibo (Nigeria) and the Kikuyi (Kenya), were acephalous or "chiefless" (or "stateless") societies in precolonial times.[47] Moreover, there is no uniform pattern to the structure or nature of political organization even in those traditional African states or communities that were governed by some form of centralized authority. For example, while the monarchies of Old Benin (modern southwestern Nigeria), Dahomey (modern Republic of Benin), Rwanda, and Buganda (modern Uganda) were famously authoritarian or despotic,[48] other precolonial monarchies, such as the kingdoms of the Yoruba (Nigeria), the

[47] See RL Tignor, "Colonial Chiefs in Chiefless Societies" (1971) 9 *Journal of Modern African Studies* 339, 340. See generally M Fortes and EE Evans-Pritchard (eds), *African Political Systems* (Oxford University Press 1940) (describing the political systems of eight societies widely distributed over the African continent and distinguishing them into those with "centralized authority, administrative machinery, and judicial institutions – in short, a government" and those societies which lack such "government").

[48] See Rene Lemarchand (ed), *African Kingships in Perspective: Political Change and Modernization in Monarchical Settings* (Routledge 1977) (particularly the Introduction and the chapters on Rwanda and Burundi by Rene

Mossi (Burkina Faso), the Mandinka, and the various Akan kingdoms of present-day Ghana, offer notable counterexamples of indigenous African political systems where monarchical rule, despite appearances to the contrary, was contained harmoniously within a tradition and structure of both vertical and horizontal checks and balances.[49]

The difficulty is not resolved by shifting the unit of analysis from the continental to the national. While precolonial indigenous societies – the relevant sites of distinctive cultural practice in Africa – were each ethnically and culturally homogeneous, their postcolonial counterpart (the contemporary African state) is notoriously diverse and pluralistic, thus making assertions of a single indigenous "national culture" or of a cultural consensus over a unitary national form of rule highly contestable. In short, even at the level of the single African state, it is hazardous to generalize about a unitary African cultural form.

Yet cultural autochthony was one of the grounds upon which the proponents of absolute presidentialism defended their constitutional power grab. Indeed the notion of Africa's absolute president as the African chief *writ large* has resonance among rank and file Africans. Ghana's Nkrumah was exceptionally effective in tapping this political resource to underwrite his absolute presidential rule. Nkrumah adopted customary protocol, titles and symbols of traditional Ghanaian kingship as an integral part of his presidential repertoire. Notably, he appropriated as his official title the traditional Akan royal honorific *Ɔsagyefo*, roughly translated as "warrior-savior" or "victorious in war." Customary protocol reserved for traditional kingship ceremonies and occasions, notably the offering of ritual sacrifice and libation, was performed for Nkrumah on his visits across the country, at political rallies, and upon his arrival back in Ghana from foreign travels. Nkrumah's formal opening of the annual session of parliament was similarly attended by royal pomp and ceremony. His arrival was heralded by the beating of the royal *fontomforom* drum, and he was met at the forecourt of parliament by a retinue of *akyeame* (or linguists) representing different ethno-linguistic groups in Ghana. Libation and special customary prayers were offered for Nkrumah before his formal entry into the chamber of parliament, and his entry was announced by the sound of *mmenson* (the traditional "seven horns" of Akan royalty). For this and other formal ceremonies, Nkrumah usually wore the traditional *kente* cloth of Akan kingship. All of these

Lemarchand). See also David Apter, "The Role of Traditionalism in the Political Modernization of Ghana and Uganda" (1960) 13 *World Politics* 45, 51.

[49] See generally Basil Davidson, *The Black Man's Burden: Africa and the Curse of the Nation-State* (James Currey 1992) 52–73.

performances were part of an elaborate "cult of personality" purposefully constructed around Nkrumah, and were designed, in large measure, to secure cultural legitimacy for Nkrumah's authoritarian projects. The assumption of traditional titles and cultural imagery was not unique to Nkrumah; it was a common feature of absolute presidentialism in the early postcolonial period.

In substance, however, absolute presidentialism fails to find firm support in the constitutional norms and traditions of indigenous African kingship. Indeed its leading proponents and architects offered little specific cultural evidence beyond simple assertions such as this one by Tanzania's Nyerere: "the conception of a Head of State who had virtually no power, and a Prime Minister who did have power was alien to our traditions." This, of course, is only a critique of the Westminster-style bifurcated executive reflected in the independence constitutions of Africa's ex-British colonies. Specifically, the cultural critique here is that the idea of a "titular" head of state is foreign to indigenous African conceptions of political authority and, conversely, that the unitary or "executive" presidency – the merger of all of the executive power of the state in a single office – best accords with African traditional government.

Indeed, the idea of an executive presidency has parallels in the traditional kingship rule of *some* of Africa's indigenous political systems, where the king or chief shared "executive" power with no one. But a unitary executive, even a monarchical one, is not the same as an absolute president. The essence of absolute presidentialism is not merely a ruler who possesses all of the executive power, or even embodies, nominally, the sovereign power, of the state; an absolute president, as enshrined in postcolonial Africa's constitutional systems, implies a ruler with powers and prerogatives that are not subject to meaningful or credible institutional checks or restraint within the constitutional system.

Certain traditional African monarchs were indeed despotic or "imperial" in the sense just described. In Buganda, for example, "the pure authority of the Kabaka was not mitigated by any other countervailing principle."[50] However, this does not uniformly or distinctively describe traditional African kingship as a whole. The claim that the African presidential monarch is simply the traditional African chief in modern secular garb is, in fact, based on a stereotype that has long been refuted authoritatively by anthropologists and other social scientists who

[50] Apter (n 13) 52.

have studied traditional African kingship and constitutional systems. Two examples should suffice.

Take, for example, the Yoruba, one of the largest ethno-linguistic groups in Africa's most populous state, Nigeria. The Yoruba in pre-colonial times were organized into many separate states. Each Yoruba state was a sovereign entity with its own *oba* or king at its head. Yoruba kingmakers approached the selection of an *oba* with an eye toward forestalling or minimizing autocratic rule: "[a] guiding principle was to select a ruler who would respect and conform to the constitutional conventions of the kingdom."[51] The kingmakers thus avoided selecting as king a royal who exhibited an autocratic inclination or even one who merely possessed physical characteristics that were believed to suggest such a tendency. In one recorded instance, "a prince was rejected because he was so tall that he would have looked down on his subjects."[52]

The *oba* was considered a sacred or divine king and accorded appropriate reverence by his people. However the sacral aura that surrounded Yoruba kingship made the *oba* not an autocrat, but the reverse. "Not only was he bound by rules and precedents in his personal life but these also required him to submit all business to councils of chiefs and officers, and only after consultation and deliberation by these bodies could a policy be decided and proclaimed in the *oba*'s name."[53] The composition of the king's council infused Yoruba monarchy with an important element of participatory legitimacy. The chiefs who sat on the council, and thus with whom the *oba* was required to exercise his legislative and judicial functions, were themselves hereditary representatives of the various lineage groups that comprised the kingdom.

The Yoruba political system ensured a "delicate balance of power," one in which, to paraphrase James Madison, "ambition" was checked by "ambition." Notably, in Oyo, the most centralized and most powerful of the Yoruba kingdoms, the king's council was headed by the *bashorun*. As chief military commander, chief kingmaker and the king's "first minister," the *bashorun* exerted an exceptional amount of influence within the governmental system and was occasionally known to have been more powerful than the *oba* himself. Significantly, the important war-making power in Oyo was constitutionally divided between the king and his war chiefs: command and control of the military was in the hands of the war chiefs, but only the *oba* could authorize a military campaign. In modern

---

51 RS Smith, *Kingdoms of the Yoruba* (3rd edn, Methuen 1988) 92.

52 Ibid.

53 Ibid 91.

constitutional parlance, executive power in Oyo would be said to be bifurcated between the *oba*, as president and head of state, and the *bashorun* as prime minister. This feature of Oyo constitutional structure is a refutation of a common claim, popularized by African presidents like Nkrumah and Nyerere, that a bifurcation or sharing of executive power is alien to Africa's indigenous political traditions.

The Akan of Ghana, one branch of which (the Nzimas) Nkrumah belonged to by matrilineage, also shared a system of rule much like the Yoruba's. First, despite occupying a sacral role within the traditional political system, indigenous Akan monarchs were not above the law, as postcolonial Africa's presidential monarchs were (and are). In Asante, an Akan kingdom famed for its precolonial imperial exploits and federal-style constitutional system, it was the Golden Stool (symbolizing the "Crown"), not the person of the king (called the Asantehene), that represented "the highest level of political authority in the land."[54] In other words, it was the institution rather than the personality of the incumbent that commanded authority. To put it in Kelsenian terms,[55] the Golden Stool signified the *grudnorm* in Ashanti. All allegiance in the kingdom, though nominally rendered to the Asantehene as occupant of the Golden Stool, was actually owed and sworn to the Golden Stool. Thus the Asantehene himself was liable to be deposed for infidelity to the Golden Stool, as happened to four incumbents in the precolonial history of the kingdom.

Ghanaian social anthropologist Kofi Busia, later to become prime minister of Ghana after Nkrumah, wrote of the Akan chief that he "was bound, by custom, to act only with the concurrence and on the advice of his Council."[56] Willful disregard of this injunction, which was publicly recited to the king on the occasion of his "enstoolment" (coronation), constituted one of the principal grounds for "destoolment" (equivalent to impeachment and removal). Unlike postcolonial Africa's early absolute presidents, who accorded to themselves indefinite or lifetime tenure without the possibility of constitutional removal, chiefs and kings in traditional Africa typically held office "during good behavior." It was not for them to determine the term or duration of their rule. Additionally, unlike Africa's absolute presidents, who routinely outlawed criticism of

---

[54] I Wilks, *One Nation, Many Histories: Ghana Past and Present* (Universities Press 1996) 30.

[55] H Kelsen, *General Theory of Norms* (first published 1979; Michael Hartney trans., Clarendon 1991).

[56] KA Busia, *Africa in Search of Democracy* (Routledge and Kegan Paul 1967) 24.

their rule and jailed their opponents without trial, African chiefs were not free from criticism or censure by their subjects. Chiefly councils in Africa, where these existed, were typically forums for open deliberation, where "all different points of view"[57] were guaranteed a hearing. Outside the halls of the chief's court, criticism of the chief was regulated by customary "time, place, and manner" restrictions; but the core principle – that the people could criticize their ruler – was not denied. Thus, among the Akan, for example, "there were traditional ceremonies at which the people, particularly the women, could lampoon in song and dance against their rulers with impunity."[58]

Africa's indigenous political systems and traditions could not be called liberal or egalitarian by any contemporary measure, and instances of despotic rule were not uncommon. But where these represented departures from constitutional and customary precepts, they were understood as such: as "a violation of the system."[59] While Africa's traditional monarchies differed widely in their systems of rule, enough influential examples exist of African monarchical rule constrained by constitutional rules and by checks and balances. Attempts by Africa's postcolonial rulers to defend or justify presidential imperialism in the name of "African tradition" are therefore insupportable.

THE POSTCOLONIAL PRESIDENT AS SUCCESSOR TO THE COLONIAL GOVERNOR

A primary defect of the "African culture" thesis as an explanation for the rise of absolute presidentialism in postcolonial Africa is its failure or inability to account for the colonial project and what impact and legacy that intervention might have had on the constitution and practice of politics and government in the postcolonial state. Yet the postcolonial African state is a lineal descendant, not of traditional or precolonial African kingdoms or polities, but of the colonial state. Despite the drama that attended the end of colonialism, independence in Africa was not quite the revolutionary moment it might have appeared to be; there was much less of a rupture or break with colonial practice than is commonly assumed. On the contrary, there were remarkable continuities, some literally, including, crucially, in the legal and administrative infrastructure and practices of the state.

---

57 Ibid 28.
58 Ibid 142–3.
59 Ibid 26.

Thus, when on the eve of independence, the departing European powers introduced new constitutions modeled after the metropolitan template, this created a "dual inheritance or legacy" whose two parts were unbalanced and in tension with one another: "an authoritarian one (colonial practice) and one stressing participation and equity (the metropolitan values of the colonial power)."[60] In terms of impact and influence, the former easily dominated, as it had acquired a fair measure of bureaucratic and popular entrenchment, having been implanted during several decades of colonial rule, while the other represented "a last-minute hypocritical legacy."[61] Not only did postcolonial Africa's new elites receive their political and civic socialization in the familiar colonial order, but also the colonial authoritarian apparatus was well established and, thus, readily available to be turned to the service of the new leaders' equally authoritarian postcolonial projects. In contrast, the independence constitutions, while announcing a new democratic and liberal ethos, lacked a complementary tradition in colonial rule. In rejecting their new independence constitutions in favor of absolute presidentialism, then, Africa's postcolonial leaders were essentially returning formally to the familiar and still operative colonial template. In this regard, the prototype for the postcolonial absolute president was none other than "His Excellency the Governor" – as governors in colonial Anglophone Africa were, in fact, addressed; an official form of address postcolonial African presidents happily kept.

The colonial governor constituted a "[o]ne man government":[62] "The governor alone is responsible for the colony's administration. His authority in the colony is practically autocratic."[63] The powers of the governor were not subject to any checks or brakes from below. Not only did the colonial subjects lack a constitutional avenue for removing him, "those who attacked him also risked the displeasure *lese-majesté* incurs."[64] In many African colonies, the governor ruled by decree or proclamation, and where the colonial constitution included an executive or legislative council, these played a deliberative-cum-advisory role only – or else

---

[60] TM Callaghy, *The State-Society Struggle: Zaire in Comparative Perspective* (Columbia University Press 1984) 411.

[61] Ibid.

[62] JM Sarbah, *Fanti National Constitution* (2nd edn, Cass 1968) 229.

[63] Ibid.

[64] Christopher Fyfe, "The Legacy of Colonialism – Old Colony, New State" (1964) 25 *Phylon* 247, 247.

were dominated by officials of the governor's administration.[65] Even during the period of late colonialism, when legislative councils had an "unofficial" or locally elected majority and had thus begun to function like a representative legislature, the governor was in no way responsible to that body. In fact, as Nkrumah would later remind his critics, the governor "had certain 'reserved powers' by which he could invalidate legislation."[66]

The governor was similarly placed above the colonial judiciary. There was no separation of the executive and judiciary; both were part of the colonial administration, at the apex of which stood the governor. In the colonies of anglophone Africa, the colonial chief justice acted as governor during the latter's absence from the colony. Within the colony, the colonial governor had power to pass and enforce "whatever legislation he thought was right in the public interest."[67] Colonial courts could not countermand or set aside decisions or decrees of the colonial governor. In fact, the governor had power, by decree, to deny access to the courts for persons seeking to challenge a legislative or executive act of the colonial administration.[68]

Lastly, many of the repressive laws upon which postcolonial Africa's rulers would come to rely to neutralize and punish unwelcome opposition to their authoritarian projects had their origin in legislation enacted and enforced by the colonial state. Notably, the preventive detention and sedition and press censorship laws that became a routine part of the legal paraphernalia of Africa's postcolonial rulers were first introduced and used during the colonial period. Some of postcolonial Africa's absolute presidents were themselves victims of colonial era preventive detention laws. Their experience of the political uses of colonial law and justice must have impressed on them the belief that "a Court [was] primarily … the institution through which a government, Colonial or otherwise, imposed its policy behind the cloak of magisterial propriety."[69]

In short, the postcolonial state and its practices, including, notably, its tendency toward presidential absolutism, showed remarkable continuity

---

65 Ibid. See also Michael Crowder, "Whose Dream Was It Anyway? Twenty-Five Years of African Independence" (1987) 86 *African Affairs* 7, 15.

66 Nkrumah (n 14) 17.

67 GE Metcalfe, *Great Britain and Ghana: Documents of Ghana History, 1807–1957* (Thomas Nelson 1964) (quoting a 1934 statement of the Secretary of State for the Colonies).

68 Geoffrey Bing, *Reap the Whirlwind: An Account of Kwame Nkrumah's Ghana from 1950 to 1966* (MacGibbon & Kee 1968) 221.

69 Ibid 215.

with the colonial tradition and, in particular, with the extraordinary power of the governor within colonial society. This, however, was no mere coincidence. As American law-and-development scholar Robert Seidman observed at the time:

> In every African state, the constitutional instrument, or else the first legislation after the introduction of a new constitution, provides that the laws in effect immediately preceding the new constitution shall remain in full force unless expressly amended. Independence itself changed nothing, save perhaps to fill with African feet shoes formerly worn by white administrators.[70]

Having thus inherited the colonial state with much of its legal tools of domination intact, Africa's new leaders felt themselves entitled to use "the same tools and methods of government which the colonial authorities had employed."[71] In fact, the notion that *African* managers of a sovereign African state could be limited in their exercise of power, whereas their *European* predecessors of the colonial era were not so constrained, was not one that Africa's postcolonial elites were willing to countenance.[72] As Nkrumah's first attorney general (himself British) would later ask: "If denial of access to the courts was justified in 1948 [when the European colonialists were in charge] why was it wrong in 1957 [when Africans were now in charge of a sovereign state]?"[73] This confirms Mamood Mamdani's thesis that the African nationalist or postcolonial project was more concerned with "deracializing" or Africanizing the state – in terms of political leadership and control of authority – than with "decolonizing" it.[74]

WHY ABSOLUTE PRESIDENTIALISM PERSISTS IN AFRICA

Perhaps rather than investigate or establish the sources of the continuities between the power of the colonial governor and presidential or executive

---

[70] Robert B Seidman, "Constitutions in Independent, Anglophonic, Sub-Saharan Africa: Form and Legitimacy" (1969) *Wisconsin Law Review* 83.

[71] Bing (n 68) 222.

[72] See Dullah Omar, Address at the African Renaissance Conference on Constitutionalism (16 November 1999), available at http://www.polity.org.za/html/govdocs/speeches/1999/sp1116a.html.

[73] Bing (n 68) 222.

[74] Mamood Mamdani, *Citizen and Subject: Contemporary Africa and the Legacy of Late Colonialism* (Princeton 1996).

power in the immediate period after colonialism, the more interesting and perplexing inquiry is why the phenomenon of absolute presidentialism persists to this day. In particular, why has it survived the current or recent counter-authoritarian and democratic regime changes and constitutional reforms in Africa? To answer this query, we must examine, first, the politics of democratic constitutional reform in contemporary Africa.

The movement for political and constitutional change that gathered momentum in many parts of Africa at the start of the 1990s focused primarily on securing new "rules of the game" designed to make the political system open and competitive. Thus the rules of the game that have dominated this push, from the outset, have been the *rules of exit and entry* that ensure access to the political game. Accordingly, the democratic reform agenda has centered on issues such as the right of opposition parties and candidates to contest elections, free and fair conduct of elections, an end to government monopoly and censorship of the media, and new limits on presidential tenure. The unifying theme is a concern with opening up a previously closed political process to allow pluralistic representation and participation in national government. In terms of constitutional reform, these limited ends have entailed little more than a few amendments to existing constitutions, primarily to remove clauses that had hitherto precluded open contestation for political office. A comprehensive overhaul or redesign of the constitutional order, beyond the restoration of democratic politics, has generally been kept off the agenda by besieged incumbents and regime opponents alike. As a result, while we have witnessed important changes in the constitutional rules of exit and entry in contemporary Africa, the *rules of play* – how much power incumbents control and how and for what purposes power may be used – have not undergone significant reform or transformation.

The limited ambition behind contemporary constitutional reform in Africa reflects, in large measure, the narrow, self-interested agendas of rival political elites. Besieged incumbents, weakened by a loss of popular legitimacy because of their perennial failure to make good on promises of development and social improvement, have generally found little incentive to initiate reform beyond those limited rule changes deemed necessary to restore democratic accountability and placate external financiers. In fact, in those instances where the authoritarian regime remained strong enough politically at the time of transition to retain control of the transition agenda and timetable, as was the case in Ghana, Tanzania, and Uganda, the ensuing constitutional changes were made with regime continuity – and for that matter, presidential dominance – in mind. Thus apart from removing existing constitutional obstacles to multiparty politics, the "structure of the national presidency of Tanzania has not changed substantially since 1985 when [President Julius] Nyerere left office." In Ghana, the Jerry Rawlings-led military junta rejected a proposal by a commission of experts for the executive power in the next constitution to be shared between a nationally elected president and a legislature-backed prime minister. The junta feared that the proposal carried the risk of "personality conflicts" between the president and the prime minister – a fear that was predicated, no doubt, on the assumption (which subsequent events proved to be well founded) that Rawlings would continue as civilian president under the new constitution.

For their part, opposition activists pushing for political change in Africa have been motivated not so much by a desire to *reform* the state or government as by the near-term prospect of *forming* the government themselves. Capture of the extant "political kingdom" has dominated transition politics in Africa so far. Although oppositionists commonly promise far-reaching constitutional reforms, including limits on presidential power, enthusiasm for such transformative change tends to wane once yesterday's electoral insurgents become today's officeholders. Thus in Zambia, Chiluba's Movement for Multiparty Democracy (MMD) called for the removal of certain "dictatorial" clauses from the constitution when Kaunda was in power. But once it had defeated Kaunda, the MMD decided that the constitution was "adequate" after all, and defended "presidential democracy" as "the best system of government." In Ghana, the New Patriotic Party (NPP), during its time in opposition (1993–2001), strongly opposed the president's authority to appoint mayors and called for them to be chosen by local popular vote instead. Yet, as the governing party from 2001 to 2009, the NPP not only zealously guarded the president's power to make appointments to all the country's mayoralties, it further backed the creation of more such offices – and the president proceeded to fill the new patronage opportunities thereby created with NPP loyalists. Similar retreats from vows to push counter-authoritarian constitutional reforms have been seen in Malawi and Nigeria. So far, only Kenya's new constitution, adopted in 2010, has made a credible attempt to revisit the constitutional choices made in the early postcolonial period and undo some of the structural and legal devices that have sustained absolute presidentialism.

But quite apart from the limited goals of contemporary constitutional reform in Africa, the common and longstanding practice of retaining all "existing law" during moments of constitutional change and transition has worked to preserve remarkable formal continuity between the present and the past. Constitution writers in contemporary Africa have continued to follow the practice which Robert Seidman observed in the 1960s, whereby every new African constitution, starting with the first (independence) constitution, includes in it (or else in the first piece of significant legislation enacted under it) a provision "that laws in effect immediately preceding the new constitution shall remain in full force unless expressly amended."[75] This, seemingly innocuous provision in African constitutions, has served as the textual vehicle that has carried along from the authoritarian past, especially from the early post-independence period, to the present a large body of laws and associated regulations that embody the full scope of the "executive power" vested in the president but left undefined in every African constitution.

Again, the Ghana case is illustrative. The office of president, as it currently exists under Ghana's Fourth Republic, is the present-day successor to an office that has been existence in one form or another and under varying titles for as long as the Ghanaian state has existed. Contrary to the transformative or "revolutionary" rhetoric that has often accompanied the overthrow of one regime, including by means of a *coup d'etat*, or the transition to another, there has in fact been a remarkable degree of continuity, legally at least, between Ghana's various successive regimes. In particular, while each new constitution or regime change has reconstituted the *form* of the executive, the authoritative legal underpinnings – and thus the *substance* – of executive power in Ghana have survived these regime changes largely undiminished. In fact, every newly constituted republican president of Ghana has inherited and retained from the previous constitutional order, whether military or civilian, the bulk of the cumulative authority vested in the holder of the highest executive office under pre-existing laws, including military decrees and other subsidiary legislation.

In Ghana's current (1992) Constitution, this outcome is accomplished by a combination of two "holdover" provisions, namely article 11(d) of the Constitution and article 33(a) of the First Schedule to the Constitution. Article 11(d) affirms the continuing validity in the Fourth Republic of all "existing law," which necessarily includes all Acts of Parliament, military decrees and subsidiary legislation enacted by past regimes that are still on the statute books. Additionally, article 33(a) of the First Schedule transfers from the erstwhile military junta, the PNDC, to the President of the Fourth Republic the cumulative powers, authority and prerogatives previously vested in the predecessor government under the laws of that regime.

---

75 Seidman (n 70).

This arrangement, whereby the legal order is rolled over in its entirety from one regime to the next following the adoption of a new constitution, is not a novelty of the 1992 Constitution. Ghana's last three republican constitutions (1960, 1969, 1979) had provisions roughly identical to current article 11(d) and article 33(a) of the First Schedule to the 1992 Constitution. In the 1979 Constitution, for example, the respective holdover provisions were article 126(d) and article 12(a) of the First Schedule to that constitution, and roughly identical language is found in article 4(d) of the 1969 Constitution and article 14(a) of the First Schedule to that constitution. Article 40(d) of the 1960 Constitution, which formally installed Ghana's first absolute president, also preserved all "enactments in force immediately before Republic day."

The cumulative legal effect of this routine practice of carrying over the entire corpus of pre-existing statutes and subsidiary legislation from one regime to the next is to create a president the bulk of whose aggregate powers and prerogatives are derived from statutes, executive orders, and conventions pertaining to the office, that date back to Nkrumah and run through the successive military and civilian administrations Ghana has had. The continuity in the substance and content of executive power in Ghana indeed goes all the way back to the initial transition from the colonial governor/governor-general to the installation of the first president in 1960. Notably, the Constitution (Consequential Provisions) Act, 1960, which came into effect contemporaneously with the 1960 Constitution, provided that, in regard to powers conferred by pre-republican enactments, the president of Ghana, upon the coming into being of the First Republic, will be deemed to have stepped into the shoes of the colonial secretary of state, the governor, the governor-general, and the prime minister. Pursuant to that statute, any reference in a then pre-existing enactment to "Her Majesty the Queen" was to be deemed as also referring to the president.

By far, however, it is Ghana's First Republic that has had the greatest and most enduring influence on the conception, character, and content of presidential and executive power in the contemporary Ghanaian state. There are a few reasons for this. First, the office of president of Ghana was first conceived and installed under the 1960 (First Republican) Constitution, and the mark placed on that office by its first occupant has served, consciously or unconsciously, as the referent for much of our present-day conceptions of executive or presidential power.[76] Second, the formation, growth and

---

76 See Y Saaka, "Recurrent Themes in Ghanaian Politics: Nkrumah's Legacy" (1994) 24 *Journal of Black Studies* 263, 263.

development of the office of president and of presidential and executive power in Ghana generally owes much to a number of influential pieces of legislation enacted by the parliament of the First Republic. Many of these early statutes dealt with the organization and structure of the machinery of government. Notable among these "machinery-of-government" statutes were the Presidential Affairs Act, 1960, the Cabinet and Ministers Act, 1960, the Civil Service Act, 1960, and the Consequential Provisions Act, 1960. Many of these early statutes and others of a more departmental or function-specific nature conferred on the president substantial authority over the administration of the country. While some of the most obnoxious laws of that era were repealed following the fall of the Nkrumah government in 1966, a substantial number of current laws and executive and statutory instruments, on the basis of which contemporary presidential and executive power is exercised in Ghana, have a 1960s origin and, often, a colonial antecedent.

What is true of Ghanaian constitutional practice, regarding successive retention of "existing law," pertains to other African countries as well. Although each of these retained "existing laws," like any statute, may be repealed or amended by new legislation, in practice the vast majority of these "old" laws, especially those that are not easily recognizable as authoritarian or politically obnoxious, have endured, deriving much of their contemporary legitimacy from routinized usage, habit, inertia or common acceptance. In general, once a statute or statutory delegation of executive authority has achieved a degree of institutional and bureaucratic entrenchment as a result of longstanding usage, it tends to be treated as almost a part of a country's constitutional custom and thus easily escapes legislative and constitutional reform. This is a common problem across Africa. And it is a problem with immense consequence for the character and scope of presidential power in Africa today.

In short, through the instrumentality of "existing law" clauses that preserve the legal order between regime changes, the statutory and administrative bases of executive power in Africa have remained remarkably stable over time. In many respects, then, the contemporary African president remains very much the lineal descendant of the absolute president of the 1960s and, indeed, of the colonial governor before him. If, then, the power of the contemporary African president is to be contained or curbed, what is needed is not just democratic reform and constitutional tinkering; what is needed, above all, is a purposeful unpacking and undoing of the vast legislative and administrative bequests from the past, many of them dating back to the colonial and immediate postcolonial periods.

PART V

Ordering hegemony – constitutional moments in occupied territories and colonies

11. Constitution-making in occupied countries

Stefan Kadelbach

11.1. INTERNATIONALIZATION OF DOMESTIC (DIS-)ORDER

Constitution-making in occupied states and territories is an international concern for two sets of partly contested normative reasons.

The first category of norms which internationalize municipal order derives from the Charter of the United Nations (UNC). Since the end of the Second World War, the occupation of foreign countries is no longer a domestic affair for the occupying power. Annexation after armed conflict and colonial domination are equally ruled out by the Charter. Thus, foreign domination must be justified, and it must be transitional. Enacting a new constitution for the occupied country is accepted only as the final point of a peace-building process or of decolonization.[1]

The second rationale for the internationalization of constitution-making points to the contents of a constitution and is debatable. The question is how far democracy, human rights and the rule of law have reached the status of international law principles so that they may limit the possible outcomes of constitution-making.[2] If they serve as a justification for influencing the domestic legal order of the occupied country, a conflict between the claim to the universality of certain rules and the aspirations of local elites, groups, or, at worst, the majority of the population may arise and lead to the paradox of a notion of self-determination defined from outside.

---

[1] See Lakhdar Brahimi, "State Building in Crisis and Post-Conflict Countries" *7th Global Forum on Reinventing Government* (Vienna, 26–29 June 2007) 4.

[2] Cf. Anne Peters, "Membership in the Global Constitutional Community" in Jan Klabbers, Anne Peters and Geir Ulfstein (eds), *The Constitutionlization of International Law* (Oxford University Press 2009) 153; Thomas Kleinlein, *Konstitutionalisierung im Völkerrecht* (Springer 2012).

The ensuing problems of self-determination, legitimacy and efficacy inherent in a constitution-making process influenced by non-domestic actors can be illustrated by distinguishing, for the time being, the two groups of cases in which they occur: post-conflict scenarios and decolonization.[3] Both have different roots and are, at first sight, governed by different rules and principles. However, the concepts of post-conflict state-building and of the acquisition of self-rule by former colonies are treated in such a way that it is difficult to see any governing principles at all. What they have in common is the problems they encounter.

11.2. SITUATIONS

11.2.1 Post-conflict State-building

Even though there had been instances of international territorial administration before, the idea of creating societal and legal orders anew is an inheritance of the Second World War. Over time, a series of precedents has developed, ranging from interstate armed conflict ended by surrender, armistice or treaty to unilateral and collective intervention and to third party resolution of civil war and secession.[4]

The first examples are, of course, the constitution-making processes in Germany, Japan and the other axis states after the Second World War. The intent to change constitutional orders was envisaged in the Potsdam Accord,[5] but there was no common practice as to the different states. Whereas the Constitution of Japan of 1947 was based on Japanese drafts revised by US personnel, the German *Grundgesetz* was worked out by a Constitutional Convent, but subject to allied conditions and approval.[6] With Bulgaria, Finland, Hungary, Italy and Romania, peace treaties were

---

[3] For this distinction see Ralph Wilde, *International Territorial Administration – How Trusteeship and the Civilizing Mission Never Went Away* (Oxford University Press 2008) 237, 289.

[4] For a typology see Carsten Stahn, *The Law and Practice of International Territorial Administration – Versailles to Iraq and Beyond* (Cambridge University Press 2008) 115–54; Kirsten Schmalenbach, "Wiederherstellung von Staatlichkeit nach militärischen Konflikten" in Andreas Zimmermann et al (eds), *Moderne Konfliktformen* (CF Müller 2010) 341.

[5] Cf. John D. Montgomery, *Forced to Be Free* (University of Chicago Press 1957) 4.

[6] Kyoko Inoue, *MacArthur's Japanese Constitution* (University of Chicago Press 1991); Shoichi Koseki, *The Birth of Japan's Postwar Constitution* (Westview 1997); Michael Stolleis, "Besatzungsherrschaft und Wiederaufbau

concluded which contained clauses of a constitutional character, in particular with respect to human rights.[7]

The articles on occupied territories in the 1907 Hague Convention on land warfare would not have provided for such far-reaching encroachment on sovereignty, their basic idea being the maintenance of public order, and the 1949 Geneva Convention No. 4 did not change much in that respect. Looking at the situation from today's perspective, one might argue that the justification lay in an international responsibility for occupied countries, as it was occasionally held even at the time.[8] However, it seems more convincing to assume that the legal bases on which this constitutional interventionism rested were surrender and treaty, respectively.[9]

An international responsibility for post-conflict state-building arose only after the end of the Cold War. State-building missions accompanied by the United Nations assume a wide variety of shapes and they are administered with varying degrees of involvement. The same holds true for the drafting of constitutions if they form part of the process. In some instances, as in the cases of Bosnia and Kosovo, observers speak of "imposed constitutionalism".[10] Other efforts have suffered from the self-interestedness of the intervening powers and the non-participation of important groups or factions, as in Iraq and Afghanistan.[11] In the cases of Kosovo, Iraq and Afghanistan, the United Nations were involved only following military intervention at a late point in time, which reduced the

---

deutscher Staatlichkeit 1945–1949" in Josef Isensee and Paul Kirchhof (eds), *Handbuch des Staatsrechts* (vol. I, 2nd edn, CF Müller 1995) 173.

[7] Ellinor von Puttkamer, "Peace Treaties of 1947" in Rudolf Bernhardt (ed), *Encyclopedia of Public International Law* (vol. 3, Elsevier 1997) 953, 956 and 958.

[8] Michel Virally, *L'Administration internationale de l'Allemagne* (Regie autonome des publications officielles 1948) 23.

[9] Eyal Benvenisti, *The International Law of Occupation* (Princeton University Press 1993) 91–106.

[10] Noah Feldman, "Imposed Constitutionalism" (2004/05) 37 *Connecticut Law Review* 857; cf. also David Chandler, "Imposing the 'Rule of Law': The Lessons of BiH for Peacebuilding in Iraq" [2004] *International Peacekeeping* 11; Bernhard Knoll, "From Benchmarking to Final Status? Kosovo and the Problem of an International Administration's Open-Ended Mandate" (2005) 16 *European Journal of International Law* 637.

[11] Philipp Dann and Zaid Al-Ali, "The International Pouvoir Consituant – Constitution-Making Under External Influence in Iraq, Sudan and East-Timor" (2006) 10 *Max Planck Yearbook of United Nations Law* 423; Cesare Pinelli, "State-Building and Constitution-Making – The Cases of Kosovo, Iraq and Afghanistan" (2010) 16 *Diritto Pubblico* 299.

prospects for neutral monitoring. In terms of an accepted procedure, it appears, the UN was more successful when it was involved in the settlement of internal conflict, as constitution-making in Cambodia and Sudan may indicate.[12]

If the legitimacy and efficacy of these cases are in question, one should bear in mind that governance and domestic order are not the primary, or at least not the only, objectives of these processes. These missions try to react to experience that a conflict is not resolved once an armistice is established and that the responsibility of the intervening states continues afterwards. They form part of the peace-keeping powers of the United Nations. As the concept of responsibility to protect affirms, to restore internal structures may even be understood as an obligation.[13]

11.2.2 Postcolonial State-building

The process of decolonialization complied with an obligation under international law, even though this was at times contested by the colonial states. In practice under the UN Charter, the right of peoples to self-determination (Article 1 § 2 UNC) has been interpreted continuously in that sense.[14] For post-colonial constitution-making, as in post-conflict scenarios, a distinction can be made as to whether external influence was exerted unilaterally or collectively. Often, the constitutions of newly independent states encompass elements of the constitutions of the former colonial powers, and sometimes their adoption was secured by treaty.

The responsibility of the UN emerged where the colonial powers had to cede their overseas conquests after war, as was the case with former mandates of the League of Nations like Namibia or with the former Italian colonies of Eritrea and Libya after the Second World War. In other instances, such as East Timor and Western Sahara, the process of decolonialization was not initiated in time and was later impeded by the interests of the neighboring states.

---

[12] See note 11; cf. also Stephen Marks, "The Process of Creating a New Constitution in Cambodia" in Laurel Miller and Louis Aucoin (eds), *Framing the State in Times of Transition – Case Studies in Constitution-Making* (US Institute of Peace Press 2010) 207.

[13] Jutta Brunnée and Stephen J Toope, "Norms, Institutions and UN Reform: The Responsibility to Protect" (2005) 2 *Journal of International Law and International Relations* 121.

[14] Daniel Thürer and Thomas Burri, "Self-Determination" in Rüdiger Wolfrum (ed), *Max Planck Encyclopedia of Public International Law* (vol. IX, 2nd edn, Oxford University Press 2012) 113, 115–16.

Thus, there is a mixed heritage for these post-colonial occupation regimes in that they result from UN responsibility for non-self-governing territories (Articles 73 and 74 UNC), the trusteeship system (Articles 75–85 UNC) and from the principle of self-determination on the one hand and post-conflict resolution on the other.

As to the practice of constitution-making, post-conflict and post-colonial regimes differ in inclusiveness. Since, however, unresolved colonial situations have the potential to disturb peace and security, there is not necessarily much of a difference any more with respect to the modes of territorial administration and constitution-making under external sponsorship. Maintenance of peace is the common denominator for both so that state-building and constitution-making tend to be considered as a means to this end.

11.3. PROBLEMS

The legality of internationalized constitutionalism is not seriously disputed in state practice. It is more difficult to explain how a legitimate constitutional order may arise from such processes. One might argue that respect for human rights, democracy, and the rule of law have become part of international law or are at least emerging principles as such so that legitimacy would derive from international law itself.[15] Other justifications offered are consent by delegation of the population concerned, emergency, participatory democracy, expertise of UN personnel, or the neutrality of international institutions.[16] Probably the most forceful argument of international law is the purpose of restoring and maintaining peace. But also if a justification can be found which would provide for what one could call international legitimacy, the question of "domestic legitimacy"[17] has yet to be addressed. The problems to be dealt with can be understood as matters of constitutional law, comparative law, and legal theory.

The first question is how domestic legitimacy can be measured. Notions of factual legitimacy deriving from power or normative concepts like fairness and participation may deliver explanations, but they still address the international dimension. Already at that level the problem of double standards arises; international constitutional processes are not

---

[15] See note 2.

[16] See the discussion in Stahn (n 4) 518–31.

[17] Bernhard Knoll, "Legitimacy and UN – Administration of Territory" (2007) 8 *German Law Journal* 39, 43.

infrequently accompanied by actors whose record with respect to the norms required as part of the future constitution is doubtful. Furthermore, from a constitutional standpoint, there is no reason why the interests of foreign states should be accommodated, as was the case in the constitution-making in Iraq and Afghanistan. The rationale for such inconsistencies can only be the appeasement of parties to the underlying conflict.

Thus, the price to be paid in the worst of cases consists in the whole range of problems described by theories of legal transfer:[18] misleading projections from outside and misunderstandings of normative contents within the social, legal and political order concerned; a lack of ownership by the people; the abstract normative existence of parts of the constitution without social efficacy; and the paradoxical coexistence of different normative layers as theories of legal pluralism put it.

To avoid such an outcome and to make the people concerned own their constitution,[19] it has become common knowledge that self-restraint is advised and an idea of a "light footprint approach" should be adhered to.[20] The same rationale advocates multilateral rather than unilateral sponsorship, transparency and publicity of the process, and inclusive participation of the relevant societal groups.[21]

The following two contributions will present two different perspectives on the area. The chapter by Philipp Dann analyzes constitution-making from an international law perspective. It describes the conditions under which the process unfolds, addresses the shortcomings of a purely instrumental approach and draws lessons from past experience. Felix Hanschmann takes us to a former colony before it became Namibia.[22] He describes the less than pragmatic dual legal regime of imperial Germany and its so-called protected areas and points to the interesting repercussions of German citizenship law, thus making visible a dark epoch in the past of what is today a constitutional state.

---

18 See Günter Frankenberg, Chapter 14, in this volume.

19 Cf. Simon Chesterman, *You, the People: The United Nations, Transitional Administration, and State-Building* (Oxford University Press 2005) 5.

20 Brahimi (n 1) 4.

21 Dann and Al-Ali (n 11) 460 f.

22 Cf. Edzard Schmidt-Jortzig, "The Constitution of Namibia: An Example of a State Emerging under Close Supervision and World Scrutiny" (1991) 34 *German Yearbook of International Law* 413.

12. International influence on post-conflict constitution-making

Philipp Dann

Conflicts create traumas – and opportunities. They question identities and undermine structures but they also provide openings for the creation of something new. Post-conflict situations are hence as fragile as they are inviting. The international community has increasingly taken up this "invitation". In the attempt to provide order international actors have become especially involved in the processes of post-conflict constitution-making which have become a central element of the post-conflict ordering. Unavoidably, these ordering interventions also involve the transfer of ideas, norms and values. To some extent, the insistence on constitution-making itself might already contain the transfer of an idea of what order should look like.

Such international influence on constitution-making in post-conflict situations is not an entirely new phenomenon.[1] The cases of Germany and Japan, who received major input from the US (to put it mildly) into their post-war constitutions, can serve as prominent examples of previous instances. However, not only has the number of cases grown immensely in recent years, but so too have the (legalized) techniques and agents of influence, suggesting that a general shift has occurred concerning respect

[1] However, academic interest in these cases is more recent, especially among constitutional lawyers and legal theorists. See Ulrich K Preuss, "Perspectives on Post-Conflict Constitutionalism: Reflections on Regime Change through External Constitutionalization" (2006/07) 51 *New York Law School Law Review* 467; Armin von Bogdandy et al, "State-Building, Nation-Building, and Constitutional Politics in Post-Conflict Situations: Conceptual Clarifications and an Appraisal of Different Approaches" (2005) 9 *Max Planck Yearbook of United Nations Law* 579; Daniel Thürer, *Kosmopolitisches Staatsrecht* (Berliner Wissenschafts-Verlag 2005) 3.

for the constituent power of a nation, once believed to be the most fundamental privilege of a nation.[2]

This internationalization and accompanying shift raise fundamental questions of legality and of legitimacy. The present chapter wants to address these questions and ask to what extent such ordering can be regarded as legal and legitimate. To that end, it analyzes three concrete examples of such external influences (Sudan, Iraq and East Timor), and assesses them from the perspective of their legality and their legitimacy. The chapter will start out by briefly sketching the different categories of external influence on constitution-making processes in order to explain the choice of case studies and place them in a broader context (12.1). It will then analyze three specific cases (12.2), before undertaking a general assessment of the legal and political elements (12.3).

12.1. CATEGORIES OF EXTERNAL INFLUENCE

Looking at the broad variety of cases in which external forces have influenced constitution-making processes, the question arises as to how to compare and distinguish between them. The approach taken here is to distinguish by the degree of influence.[3] Even though this is obviously in itself a vague yardstick, one can distinguish three categories.

There is first the category of major or *total* influence: the recent history of Bosnia-Herzegovina provides a distinct example of such total influence.[4] Here, the new constitution was neither drafted nor adopted by national actors. It was instead the result of international negotiations which were conducted between the presidents of the warring parties

---

[2] Martin Loughlin and Neil Walker, *The Paradox of Constitutionalism* (Oxford University Press 2007); Ernst-Wolfgang Böckenförde, *Staat, Verfassung, Demokratie* (Suhrkamp 1991) 91; Bruce A Ackerman, *We the People* (Belknap Press 1991).

[3] Other yardsticks can certainly be applied too, especially the question of what instigated the constitutional process and hence whether it is an endogenous or exogenous process. For the purpose of the current chapter, the question of degree seems more relevant though. On other yardsticks and categories, see Andrew Arato, "Forms of Constitution Making and Theories of Democracy"(1995) 17 *Cardozo Law Review* 191; Daniel Thürer, *Kosmopolitisches Staatsrecht* (Berliner Wissenschafts-Verlag 2005) 8, 23.

[4] Karin Oellers-Frahm, "Restructuring Bosnia Herzegovina: A Model with Pit-Falls" (2005) 9 *Max Planck Yearbook of United Nations Law* 179; Sienho Yee, "The New Constitution of Bosnia and Herzegovina" (1996) 7 *European Journal of International Law* 176.

(Bosnia-Herzegovina, Croatia, Yugoslavia). It came into force not by a referendum, but by the signing of the peace agreement – by these three parties. Hence, we observe an almost entirely exogenous development. Here, one can speak of a totally internationalized constituent power. The nation as a political actor was basically eclipsed.

At the other end of our tripartite scheme is the category of *marginal* influence. Here, the external influence consists only of the advice of external experts, which is sought voluntarily by domestic actors. These domestic actors are clearly in control of the process and substance of constitution-making, but want to get intellectual stimulation from others. South Africa and its constitutional reform in the mid-1990s is an example of such marginal influence.[5] Constitutional reform processes in a number of Eastern European countries could also be included in this category.[6] Here, the constituent power of the nation was not curtailed; rather – it would probably be true to say – it was influenced.

Finally, there is a third category, which falls between the two previous categories and which covers instances of *partial* influence. Here, the external influence is stronger than the voluntarily requested but limited consultation of foreign experts, but it is weaker than the international take-over of the entire constitution-making process. The constitutional process is instead to some extent influenced or even directed by external forces, be it in a procedural or substantial respect, but the ultimate power to draft and adopt the constitution remains in national hands. Instances of such partial influence are plenty, varied and certainly the most challenging to assess in terms of legality and legitimacy.

---

[5] Richard Spitz with Matthew Chaskalson, *Politics of Transition: A Hidden History of South Africa's Negotiated Settlement* (Hart Publishing 2000); Hassen Ebrahim, *The Soul of a Nation: Constitution-Making in South Africa* (Oxford University Press 1999); also Dennis M Davis, "Constitutional Borrowing: The Influence of Legal Culture and Local History in the Reconstitution of Comparative Influence: The South African Experience" (2003) 1 *International Journal of Constitutional Law* 181.

[6] Jon Elster, "Constitution-Making in Eastern Europe: Rebuilding the Boat in the Open Sea" (1993) 71 Public Administration 169, 192–3. This is not to say that such influences are not organized and that constitutional assemblies are not lobbied by external actors (like the Venice Commission). However, it is decisive that the ultimate control over process and substance remains in national hands. On the Venice Commission, see Jeffrey Jowell, "The Venice Commission: Disseminating Democracy through Law" (2001) 24 *Public Law* 675.

12.2. THREE CASES AND TYPES OF PARTIAL EXTERNAL INFLUENCE

External influence on constitution-making processes is most often exerted to a partial degree, producing a blend of national and international control over the process. Such partial influence can again come in different degrees and in different forms. The three cases examined now shall demonstrate three types of such partial influence. In each case, the factual context of the constitution-making process, the legal framework and finally the actual process and its leading actors are examined.

12.2.1 East Timor

Perhaps the most transparent example of how the international community can instigate and conduct a constitution-making process took place in East Timor. The constitutional process was organized by the UN Transitional Administration in East Timor (UNTAET).[7] This had been created by a Security Council Resolution (1272 – of 25 October 1999) in order to fill a political vacuum after a referendum on independence from Indonesia, and hence organize a peaceful transition from occupation to independence. UNTAET's mandate did not explicitly cover the instigation and conduct of a constitution-making process. However, it was soon recognized that a successful transition would require a constitutional basis.[8]

The legal framework for constitution-making in East Timor was established in a regulation issued by UNTAET (Regulation 2001/2 of 16 March 2001). The regulation is remarkable in that it is detailed yet flexible in respect of the procedural regime, but very restrained as to the substance. The *procedural rules* set out the basic structure of the Constitutional Assembly which was elected. It also set out how the Assembly was supposed to go about its business and how and in what timeframe the final constitution was to be adopted. Moreover, the head of UNTAET wanted to make sure that civil society would have a direct voice in the Constitutional Assembly. He therefore issued a directive

[7] For a concise analysis of the historical background as well as the international intervention see Markus Benzing, "Midwifing a New State: The United Nations in East Timor" (2005) 9 *Max Planck Yearbook of United Nations Law* 295, 302–5.

[8] Jonathan Morrow and Rachel White, "The United Nations in Transitional East Timor: International Standards and the Reality of Governance" (2002) 22 *Australian Year Book of International Law* 1.

requiring the authorities to consult the people and establish so-called Constitutional Commissions, on which people could formulate their interests and expectations.[9] The regulation is less explicit as to *substantive content.* It states only that the mandate of the Constitutional Assembly is to "prepare a Constitution for an independent and democratic East Timor".[10] However, independence and democracy were probably not really contested aspects of the future constitution anyway. The general purpose of the Assembly was described as being to contribute to the goal of "protecting the inalienable human rights of the people of East Timor, including freedom of conscience, freedom of expression, freedom of association and from all forms of discrimination".[11]

While the legal framework for the constitution-making process was provided by the international actors, the actual proceedings were in the hands of the Timorese.[12] The UNTAET seems to have exerted very little influence once the process got started. UNTAET experts were consulted, but had little substantive influence. The Timorese instead used the legal framework and reformed it with their own needs in mind, for example by extending the deadline for approval of the constitution.[13] A letter from the UN Special Representative raising some procedural as well as substantive issues was largely ignored. The problem seems to have been rather that the leading political force of the Timorese, the Fretilin, was acting authoritatively and thus perhaps suppressing other political opinions.

In sum, some striking features emerge with regard to the Timorese process: first, there was a clear separation between the instigation and procedural regulation of the process on the one hand, which was done by external forces, and the actual process and its substantive outcome on the other hand, which was entirely in the hands of the Timorese. Hence, the process was characterized by a fairly restrained role for the external actors. Secondly, external involvement was entirely multilateral, carried out by the UN. Even though Australia seems to have played a special

---

[9] UNTAET Directive No. 2001/3 on the Establishment of District Constitutional Commissions [2001] UNTAET/Dir/2001/3.

[10] UNTAET Regulation No. 2001/2 on the Election of a Constituent Assembly [2001] UNTAET/REG/2001/2, art 2.1.

[11] UNTAET Regulation No. 2001/2 on the Election of a Constituent Assembly [2001] UNTAET/REG/2001/2, art 1.1.

[12] Simon Chesterman, *You the People: The United Nations, Transitional Administration, and State-Building* (Oxford University Press 2004) 140–41.

[13] Morrow and White (n 8) 37–8, footnote 155.

role, it was always integrated into the UN approach. Thirdly and following from the point just made, the process had very clear legal yardsticks.

12.2.2 Iraq

In the case of Iraq, the factual context is well-known.[14] Suffice perhaps to say that the constitutional process would certainly not have started without the American military attack and was thus based on a foreign intervention. This was also part of the reason why a large number of the country's elite decided to boycott the new political system and thus the constitutional process.[15]

The central document with regard to the legal framework that governed the constitution-making process is the Law of Administration for the State of Iraq for the Transitional Period, in short TAL.[16] It was drafted by the Iraqi Governing Council, a body appointed by the Coalition Provisional Authority, i.e. the Americans, and composed along sectarian lines. US officials were, however, involved in the drafting process and made sure that certain provisions were included (e.g. a US-style bill of rights).[17]

The TAL covers a wide range of issues, including the basic rights of Iraqi citizens in the transitional period and the structure of the provisional

---

[14] Generally speaking, the Iraqi constitutional process took place in two stages. The first phase began during the period immediately following the invasion of the country in March 2003 by the United States and its allies and ended with the election of a Transitional National Assembly in 30 January 2005. During that time, the framework for the drafting of the permanent constitution was established mostly by the occupation authorities, but also in collaboration with a number of appointed Iraqi actors. The second phase, during which the constitution was actually drafted, began after the elections in 30 January 2005, and ended with the referendum that took place on 15 October 2005. See Rüdiger Wolfrum, "Iraq: From Belligerent Occupation to Iraqi Exercise of Sovereignty" (2005) 9 *Max Planck Yearbook of United Nations Law* 1; Andrew Arato, "Post-Sovereign Constitution-Making and its Pathologies in Iraq" (2006/07) 51 *New York Law School Law Review* 535.

[15] Mona Iman, "Draft Constitution Gained, but an Important Opportunity Was Lost" (United States Institute of Peace, October 2005) <http://www.usip.org/publications/draft-constitution-gained-important-opportunity-was-lost> accessed 27 August 2012.

[16] Law of Administration for the State of Iraq for the Transitional Period 2004 <http://www.mpil.de/shared/data/pdf/tal-_engl.pdf> accessed 27 August 2012.

[17] Wolfrum (n 14) 25.

government. Most importantly for our purpose it set out the mechanism according to which a permanent constitution was supposed to be drafted. In that respect, it mainly prescribed a precise and fairly tight timetable for the process, which included the holding of general elections for a National Assembly that was supposed to draft the constitution (Art. 61 a). It also provided the rules on the required majorities to adopt the constitution (Art. 61 c). These rules caused a serious breakdown of the consensus mechanism otherwise adhered to in the Iraqi Governing Council.[18] The TAL, mostly concerned with the procedural regime for the constitution-making process, hence already had a very substantial meaning, as the question of the necessary majorities showed.

The legal context of the Iraqi process includes another layer however, which raises the question as to the legal grounds on which the TAL was issued. It is important to notice that the TAL was drafted while Iraq was still formally occupied and not a sovereign entity.[19] The legal situation at that time was thus that of a regular occupation and the status of the US and its allies was that of occupying powers, as the UN had recognized in Resolution 1483 of May 2003. After the TAL had been drafted, the UN and the international community did endorse the TAL framework in the Security Council Resolution 1546 of June 2004. It did so, however, in a somewhat ambiguous way, since the Resolution does not mention the TAL itself and assigned the task of promoting consensus-building on the drafting of the constitution to the UN mission for Iraq – and not the occupying powers.

The occupying forces were not formally involved in the actual process of drafting the constitution, but they nevertheless reserved their influence in informal ways. The official body set up to draft the permanent constitution was the Constitutional Committee, which was established by the National Assembly and was a subcommittee thereof.[20] It was first made up of 55 members, but then had to be extended when it became clear that the Sunnis, who had mainly boycotted the election and were thus not directly represented, had to be included. Twenty-five individuals

---

[18] Larry Diamond, *Squandered Victory: The American Occupation and the Bungled Effort to Bring Democracy to Iraq* (Henry Holt and Company 2005) 177.

[19] Wolfrum (n 14) 33.

[20] "Shia Majority for Iraq Parliament" (*BBC News*, 17 February 2005) <http://news.bbc.co.uk/2/hi/middle_east/4273931.stm> accessed 27 August 2012.

were therefore added later. However, that happened only some three weeks before the deadline for the drafting period.[21]

Once the deadline had arrived, on 15 August 2005, and since the US forces would not allow for the period to be extended, control over the still unfinished business of drafting shifted from the Constitutional Committee to the so-called Leadership Council. The Leadership Council's membership and procedures, however, were largely undefined – and this at a time when the US certainly had considerable influence on the substance too. The US ambassador attended the meetings, other officials became involved and at least on one occasion the session was even held at the US embassy. In terms of *substance*, there are several points on which the US would either bias the ongoing negotiations (e.g. towards the Kurds) or impose its own interests (e.g. as to women's rights or the role of Islam).[22]

In sum, the contrast between the cases of Iraq and East Timor is stark: first, in Iraq it was only a small group, if not just one external actor, who wielded influence (the US). External involvement was thus not a truly international undertaking, but more or less a bilateral one. And secondly, the influence extended considerably beyond giving a merely procedural framework.

12.2.3 The Sudan

A third case demonstrates yet another way in which partial external influence can occur – and be rather successful. In the Sudan, the adoption of a new constitution in the summer of 2005 marked the end of a civil war between the central government in Khartoum and various rebel movements in the South, which had ravaged the country for over 20 years.[23] National efforts to end this conflict and to negotiate a peace

---

[21] International Crisis Group, *Unmaking Iraq: A Constitutional Process Gone Awry* (Middle East Briefing No. 19, 26 September 2005) 4 <http://www.crisisgroup.org/~/media/Files/Middle%20East%20North%20Africa/Iraq%20Syria%20Lebanon/Iraq/B019%20Unmaking%20Iraq%20A%20Constitutional%20Process%20Gone% 20Awry> accessed 27 August 2012; also International Crisis Group, *Iraq: Don't Rush the Constitution* (Middle East Report No. 42, 8 June 2005) 7 <http://www.crisisgroup.org/~/media/Files/Middle%20East%20North%20Africa/Iraq%20Syria%20Lebanon/Iraq/Iraq%20Dont%20Rush%20the%20Constitution> accessed 27 August 2012.

[22] Zaid Al-Ali, *The Evolution of the Iraqi Constitution – From the Constitutional Committee to the Leadership Council* (forthcoming).

[23] Douglas H Johnson, *The Root Causes of Sudan's Civil Wars* (Indiana University Press 2002); International Crisis Group, *God, Oil and Country:*

started early (in the late 1980s), but kept collapsing. In the mid-1990s, a regional group of East African states, the so-called Intergovernmental Authority on Development (IGAD),[24] were called in to help find a settlement, but had little success. It was only when the United States in particular stepped in (especially from 2002 onwards) that the peace negotiations gained momentum and led to success.[25]

To understand the process and the role of external forces, one has to distinguish between two phases of the process. First came the peace negotiations themselves, which led to an extensive peace agreement in January 2005, and then, secondly, there was the actual constitution-making which followed in the months after the peace accord. External involvement took place only in the first stage, the peace negotiations, while the constitution-making itself was an entirely endogenous national process. However, the actual constitution-making in the second phase was based on and heavily predetermined by the results of the peace agreement. To some extent, the constitution-making was more of a ratification of the peace agreement than a self-standing process of drafting.

If we therefore have a closer look at the peace negotiations and the role of external forces, we can perhaps grasp the process best if we ask three questions. Who was involved? On what legal basis did the process take place? To what extent and how did this influence relate to the later constitution-making process?

First and with respect to the protagonists of the process, external involvement included three different types of actors: there was first the above-mentioned East African community of states, IGAD. This hosted

---

Changing the Logic of War in Sudan (Africa Report No. 39, 28 January 2002) 3–33 <http://www.crisisgroup.org/~/media/Files/africa/horn-of-africa/sudan/God%20Oil%20and%20Country%20Changing%20the%20Logic%20of%20War%20in%20Sudan> accessed 27 August 2012.

[24] The Intergovernmental Authority on Development (IGAD) was established in 1996 and superseded the Intergovernmental Authority on Drought and Development (IGADD), which had been founded in 1986. Members of IGAD are Djibouti, Ethiopia, Kenya, Somalia, Sudan, Uganda and Eritrea. For further information, see <http://www.igad.org/>.

[25] International Crisis Group, *God, Oil and Country: Changing the Logic of War in Sudan* (Africa Report No. 39, 28 January 2002) 153–177 <http://www.crisisgroup.org/~/media/Files/africa/horn-of-africa/sudan/God%20Oil%20and%20Country%20Changing%20the%20Logic%20of%20War%20in%20Sudan> accessed 27 August 2012; Hatem Elliesie, "Quo vadis bilad as-Sudan? The Contemporary Framework for a National Interim Constitution" (2005) 8 *Recht in Afrika* 63, 64–5.

the talks (mainly in Kenya) and provided the centrally important mediator, a retired general (General Lazaro Sumbeiywo[26]). Sumbeiywo was himself assisted by international experts on constitutional law, especially a Swiss (Julian Hottinger) and a South African (Fink Haysom[27]), two experts, by the way, who are members of a small class of constitutional experts who fly around the world and provide mediation and constitutional expertise.[28] There was, secondly, a group of four non-African states that were directly represented at the talks and contributed human and especially financial resources (a major role being played by the US).

---

[26] See on his role esp. Waithaka Waihenya, *The Mediator: Gen. Lazaro Sumbeiywo and the Southern Sudan Peace Process* (Kenway Publications 2006).

[27] On Haysom's understanding of constitutional mediation, see Nicholas Fink Haysom, "Engaging Armed Groups in Peace Processes: Lessons for Effective Third-party Practice" (Conciliation Resources 2005) <http://www.c-r.org/sites/c-r.org/files/Accord16_20Engagingarmedgroupsinpeaceprocesses_2005_ENG_0.pdf> accessed 27 August 2012.

[28] The role of experts in the Sudanese as well as many other processes is an especially important and curious aspect of such constitution-making processes, which has seldom been analyzed. Constitutional expertise often comes from individuals who have gained the reputation of being particularly qualified for their substantive expertise or mediation skills (a prominent example is the Kenyan Yash Gai, a law professor teaching in Hong Kong, who has been involved in several constitutional advisory missions). In addition to such individuals, two more actors dominate the scene: private, international law firms or consultancy firms have increasingly offered their services. Even though constitutional advice is seldom offered by them, they offer other types of legal and drafting service, for instance regarding municipal laws or economic laws (see David M Trubek, "The 'Rule of Law' in Development Assistance" in David M Trubek and Alvaro Santos (eds), *The New Law and Economic Development: A Critical Appraisal* (Cambridge University Press 2006)). Finally, the UN is involved in many constitutional processes, providing constitutional help. While the idea to establish a permanent "Constitutional Support Group" seems to have failed, the UN usually sets up a specific office for that purpose and tries to appoint very senior constitutional scholars in order to head up those offices. Such offices are usually located in the country in question and typically have significant budgets which they use to implement specific activities to contribute to the constitutional process both from a substantive and procedural point of view. The types of activities that the UN usually implements in the context of a constitutional process include organizing study tours to countries that have relevant experience to share, roundtable discussions with international experts, roundtable discussions that are organized at local level to encourage grassroots participation in the constitutional process, commissioning comparative studies for the constitutional drafters, and ensuring that they have access to international and constitutional materials.

Finally, there was a mixed bag of international actors with very different roles: the UN, for example, was always represented by an observer/ liaison person or the Max Planck Institute for Public International Law in Heidelberg/Germany, which provided constitutional expertise to both parties, but rather from the sidelines.[29]

Secondly, the legal basis for the involvement is of interest. It is important to note that the peace negotiations and the external involvement were not based on any kind of legal mandate at all. The conflicting parties had called upon IGAD in the mid-1990s and signed a fairly basic declaration of principles. But this did not clarify the roles of any actor or any procedural rules.

Finally, on the question of the extent to which external actors shaped the process, one has to acknowledge that the role of the external actors was mainly organizational and procedural. None of the external actors had any decision-making role. Instead, their task was to moderate, mediate and, very concretely, to keep the parties at the table, which required a lot of arm-twisting. Another important task of the international experts was to help create a level playing field in respect of skills and expertise. There was a considerable gap between the highly skilled lawyers of central government – and the comparatively disadvantaged negotiators for the South who had been fighting in the bush for some 20 years. As to substantive inputs, the results are mixed: some efforts by externals to push for certain points (e.g. the US tried to strengthen the Christian community) backfired massively. In other respects, their traces are recognizable.

After the peace agreement was signed, a National Constitutional Review Commission was formed to draft a new constitution. Peace negotiations and constitution-making were hence two different processes as to time, place, and most of the actors. However, the peace agreement had set the procedural and substantial tracks on which the constitution-making process would go forward. The peace agreement had already determined the membership of the constitutional assembly; it had also determined how it would be adopted and was so extensive that it was almost a constitutional text in itself.[30] In fact, one could say that the National Constitutional Review Commission only ratified what the peace

---

[29] For details on the Sudan Peace Project and the Heidelberg Dialogue, see <http://http://www.mpil.de/ww/en/pub/research/details/know_transfer/africa_projects/sudan_peace_project/support_in_the_constitution_ma.cfm >.

[30] On a central means to keep the peace agreement alive, see Noha Ibrahim, "Post CPA: Restructuring and Enhancing the Sudanese Judiciary as a Means to Preserving Peace" (2007) 40 VRÜ 471.

agreement had already decided. It is fair to say that the actual constitution-making in the Sudan occurred in the guise of peace talks.

In sum, the Sudanese case provides an interesting contrast to the experience in East Timor or Iraq. The international actors acted on no legal basis or mandate. Their influence was one of procedural and organizational (and financial) help, but they did not write any rules, either procedural or substantive. The final adoption of the peace agreement as well as the constitution was an entirely domestic affair. In effect, the constituent power of the Sudanese remained autonomous and national. However, one also has to say that without the external expertise, pressure and help it is highly unlikely that the Sudanese would have reached the point of exercising their constituent power.

12.3. ASSESSMENT: LEGALITY AND LEGITIMACY OF EXTERNAL INFLUENCE

As indicated at the beginning, these three cases will now be assessed from two angles: first, from the angle of the legality of external influence and, secondly, from the angle of the legitimacy of such influences.

12.3.1 Legality of External Influence

Looking at the legality of external influences, one has to distinguish between two questions: first, the question of which legal regime is actually applicable in the respective case (12.3.1.1). This question also implies an inquiry into whether one could claim that there is at least a nascent legal regime for external influences on domestic constitution-making processes. The second question is whether these rules (if they exist) have been complied with in reality, i.e. with regard to the cases described above (12.3.1.2).[31]

[31] It should be pointed out that we are concerned here with the question of how far international law determines the *process* of constitution-making, not the final product (i.e. the constitution). On the impact of international and emerging standards of comparative constitutional law on the substance of constitutions, see Daniel Thürer, *Kosmopolitisches Staatsrecht* (Berliner Wissenschafts-Verlag 2005) 25–30; see also the contributions by Brun-Otto Bryde, "Constitutional Law in 'Old' and 'New' Law and Development" (2008) 41 VRÜ 10 and Francois Venter, "Globalization of Constitutional Law through Comparative Constitution-Making" (2008) 41 VRÜ 16.

12.3.1.1 Applicable law

Applicable law governing external influences over constitution-making processes and providing standards for their assessment can be derived mainly from three sources: situational law, i.e. legal rules which have been created just for this situation (e.g. UN Security Council Resolutions); the law of belligerent occupation, if such a case is at hand; and, thirdly, one could inquire whether general principles of international law provide relevant standards for the cases at hand.

With regard to situational law, UN Security Council resolutions provided concrete rules for the mandate of international actors, at least in the cases of East Timor and Iraq, even though to different degrees. To some extent, they even set up certain substantive standards or guidelines for the new constitutional and governmental system. Obviously, though, not all cases are in fact subject to such resolutions, as the case of the Sudan demonstrates. Also, in the case of Iraq, the UN and its resolutions covered only a minor part of what was supposed to happen – and what actually happened.

If the constitution-making follows a war and takes place during occupation, a second set of norms is applicable, the law of belligerent occupation.[32] This is laid down in the Hague Regulations (Arts 42–56), the Fourth Geneva Convention (Arts 27–34, 47–78) and the Additional Protocol I. These rules mainly provide for the treatment of the population and do not make permanent changes to the fundamental institutions of the occupied country. As such, these provisions therefore contain major legal roadblocks for constitutional changes by the occupying forces. However, these rules obviously apply only in a very limited number of cases.

More challenging is a third set of norms and the related question as to whether there are general principles of international law that apply in cases of constitution-making.[33] One could perhaps argue that the *right to self-determination* provides a limitation on foreign influence over the constitution-making process or that it imposes an obligation to act as

---

[32] Eyal Benvenisti, *The International Law of Occupation* (Princeton University Press 1992); also Michael Bothe, "Occupation, Belligerent" in Rudolf Bernhardt (ed), *Encyclopedia of Public International Law* (North Holland 1997) vol III, 763–5.

[33] On the concept of general principles Hermann Mosler, "General Principles of Law" in Rudolf Bernhardt (ed), *Encyclopedia of Public International Law* (North Holland 1995) vol II, 511–27.

unobtrusively as possible.[34] It has also been argued that a *right to democratic governance* and certain *human rights* has evolved, which the constitutional sovereign as well as his external advisors would have to respect.[35] However, to be realistic, these rules hardly command a consensus even among lawyers, are not fixed in any general document and hence do not constitute a distinct set of rules, precise enough to outline effective criteria for the process of drafting a constitution.

In the end, one has to return to situational rules (such as Security Council resolutions), where they exist, or to the law of occupation, if it is applicable. A general legal regime for constitutional interventions as such does not exist.

12.3.1.2 Compliance in practice?

But even if one has a set of legal rules that apply, the equally important question is whether the applicable rules have actually been complied with. Here, we have to proceed on a case-to-case basis.

With respect to the *Sudan*, the case is pretty straightforward. There were no concrete rules applicable and general rules, as just argued, are too vague to provide concrete standards. Hence, the Sudanese case is legally not tangible. In the case of *East Timor*, we do have concretely applicable law in the form of the UN Security Council Resolution 1272 and, indeed, it has been asked whether Regulation 2001/2, which organized the constitutional process, was covered by and in accordance with this resolution. However, there is no real indication that this was not the case. Also, the actual process which took place on the basis of the UN regulation seems to have been in accordance with the law. Hence, the Timorese case was in fact, even though on a very low level, legally regulated, and these laws have been complied with.

Finally, the *Iraqi* case is more complex and different. First, we have to distinguish between the time before sovereignty was handed back to the

---

[34] Antonio Cassese, *Self-Determination of Peoples: A Legal Reappraisal* (Cambridge University Press 1995); on the interplay of self-determination and the law of occupation, see Jean L Cohen, "The Role of International Law in Post-Conflict Constitution-Making: Towards a Jus Post Bellum for 'Interim Occupations'" (2006/07) 51 *New York Law School Law Review* 498.

[35] Thomas Franck, "The Emerging Right to Democratic Governance" (1992) 86 *American Journal of International Law* 46; James Crawford, "Democracy and the Body of International Law" in Gregory H Fox and Brad R Roth (eds), *Democratic Governance and International Law* (Cambridge University Press 2000); for a concrete examination see Julia Leininger, "Democracy and UN Peace-Keeping – Conflict Resolution through State Building and Democracy Promotion in Haiti" (2006) 10 *Max Planck Yearbook of United Nations Law* 465.

Iraqis and after. In the time *before*, i.e. until the end of June 2004, the law of belligerent occupation as well as Security Council Resolutions 1483 and 1511 applied.[36] If one considers that the law of belligerent occupation prohibits tinkering with the governmental system, then the TAL (the law that provided the legal framework for the constitutional process) was certainly in violation of these rules (e.g. by introducing a new federal structure for the new Iraq and by starting the constitutional process as such). Also, the Security Council resolutions do not specifically allow for these constitutional changes and the drafting of a new constitution. In fact, the resolutions do not acknowledge the TAL's existence. Hence, here we can see a clear breach of international law in pursuing such wide-ranging constitutional changes.

In the time *after* sovereignty was handed over, Security Council Resolution 1546 is the only legal source of international law available. However, the resolution is rather unspecific when it comes to the constitutional process. It certainly does not mandate the roles later played by the occupying powers, especially not their rather wide influence over process and even substance. But it also does not prohibit them. In a sense, one has to acknowledge that there was simply no legal regime to judge. Hence, no violation.

This is a somewhat astonishing result. But it could support an argument that this area would actually benefit from more international rules. Especially it could be helpful to have rules that set limits upon the capacity of single foreign countries to influence constitutional processes.

12.3.2 Legitimacy of External Influence

The legitimacy of external influence is even harder to assess than its legality.[37] I would like to approach the question by highlighting five aspects, which have the potential to contribute to the legitimacy of external influences, without – of course – being a guarantee thereof. I will use examples from the case studies to demonstrate these points. At the same time, it should be stressed that these remarks concern the

---

36 The American occupation has triggered an intense debate about the justification for and limits of external influences there; see Conor McCarthy, "The Paradox of the International Law of Military Occupation: Sovereignty and the Reformation of Iraq" (2005) 10 *Journal of Conflict and Security Law* 43; Cohen (n 34); Nehal Bhuta, "The Antinomies of Transformative Occupation" (2005) 16 *European Journal of International Law* 721.

37 See Preuss (n 1) 469–74.

legitimacy of external influence, *not* the legitimacy of the constitution itself. It is however assumed that any external influence which is considered to be legitimate will at least not diminish the standing of the new constitutional order.

The first aspect is perhaps obvious or repetitive, but nevertheless valid: *legality* contributes to legitimacy.[38] If you think of US involvement in Iraq, it is not only the widely assumed illegality of the original attack, but also the disrespect which the Coalition forces have repeatedly shown towards other UN rules, which has undercut their claim to a legitimate role there.

The second possible source of legitimacy lies in the potential for an international force to act as the *enabler and guardian of a constitutional process*.[39] In East Timor, as well as the Sudan, the constitutional process and thus settlement of major rifts in the respective societies would not have been possible without external intervention. Such intervention provides a neutral actor, which might be needed given internal conflicts, provides external pressure to not let go and, not least, external actors provide human and financial resources to see through a constitutional process. Of course, this aspect can also entail dangers: the US in Iraq exercised major pressure to have the Constitution finished by a prearranged date, even though it became very clear that there were fundamental reasons in favor of a (moderate) extension, as had occurred in the Timorese case. Nevertheless, the US did not cede and thereby undercut the final outcome. On the other side, one also has to acknowledge that in the Sudan a settlement would not have been possible without the US pressure.

A third aspect that follows from the second, but deepens it, is the attempt by external actors to make constitutional processes *more inclusive*. This attempt can point in two directions. On the one hand, it can mean that mechanisms are encouraged whereby the broader population and *civil society* is brought into the process. For example, the UN in East Timor installed so-called Constitutional Commissions which would be open to civil society groups to voice their interests in the constitutional process (similar attempts were made in Sudan). However, this is difficult to achieve and can be fruitless, as was in fact the case in East Timor. But inclusion can also reach in another direction – that of *local elites*. Especially with respect to Iraq it has been debated whether it was

---

38 Max Weber, *Economy and Society: An Outline of Interpretive Sociology* (first published 1968, Guenther Roth and Claus Wittich eds, University of California Press 1978).

39 Cf. the examples, given above (12.2.1–3); see Chesterman (n 12).

counter-productive to first shun broader parts of the entrenched Sunni elites.[40] It is often argued that external help in constitutional processes can only work if local elites are on board and can actually be convinced to pursue their own interest in and through the constitution-making process. The interests of these elites can, however, also stand in contrast to those interests that the external actors have – or that can be considered as in the enlightened interest of the country concerned.

These aspects are complemented by a fourth consideration: the question of who the external actors are. Put more directly, it can be of major importance whether the influence is exerted by a *broad group of states* or a *multilateral institution* – or whether by *only one state*. The most compelling case in point is, of course, the United States in Iraq, which has quite rigorously pursued its own self-interest at the obvious expense of the country concerned. On the other side, the UN involvement in East Timor seems to have avoided pursuing any country's particular interests. If this indicates that multilateral interventions are more legitimate than unilateral, this is perhaps not the end of the story: it is also possible for a group of states (for example the OECD states) or a multilateral institution (the IMF for example) to pursue pretty particular and specific interests. However, overall one would assume that a multilateral institution or diverse group of states would be less prone to disregard the interests of the country whose constitution is at stake.

Finally, there is a fifth aspect which has less to do with the procedure and actor of external influence, but more with the substance – even though in an abstract way. External actors can be of highest value, if they contribute to the *technical improvement* of the constitutional text while restraining themselves from meddling with the substance. In all the case studies, especially in the cases of Iraq and Sudan, the quality of constitutional advice given by external actors was appreciated and very welcome. However, wherever substantial influence was attempted, it majorly backfired. In the case of Sudan and East Timor, the parties were independent enough to disregard such attempts. In the case of Iraq they were not – with grave consequences for the constitution itself, but also for the reputation of the US as external actor and thus the legitimacy of the whole process.

---

[40] Noah Feldman, "Imposed Constitutionalism" (2004/05) 37 *Connecticut Law Review* 857; Madhavi Sunder, "Enlightened Constitutionalism" (2004/05) 37 *Connecticut Law Review* 891.

12.4. CONCLUSION

External influences on constitution-making processes and the internationalization of the constituent power of nations have risen sharply since the end of the Cold War. To get a better understanding of these cases and their implications, it makes sense to distinguish between different categories according to the degree of influence. South Africa's constituent power was not internationalized but rather internationally inspired. The constituent power of the Bosnian people was not internationalized, but was simply eliminated. However, there is a group of cases, in which external forces have partially influenced the process. These cases stood at the center of this contribution.

From a legal as well as a factual perspective the cases of East Timor, Iraq and Sudan represent three different types. In East Timor, the process and the organizational framework of the constitutional process were determined by the UN as mandated in a Security Council resolution. In substance, however, the external influence was minimal and choices were left to the indigenous actors. In Iraq, the process could have been regulated by UN Security Council resolution and the law of belligerent occupation, but was in fact driven by the US and its minor allies. The US set the relevant procedural benchmarks. It also influenced certain substantial aspects of the new constitution. External influence in the Sudan manifested itself in the form of international mediation. The constitution-making process took place mostly under the guise of peace talks. Here a group of regionally affected and of interested states exerted influence, at the invitation of the warring parties but without any legal mandate. The Sudanese constituent power remained autonomous in a procedural as well as in a substantial way.

Do these observations add up to something like an (evolving) legal concept of an internationalized *pouvoir constituant*? Probably not. By and large there is not a clearly describable legal regime for constitutional intervention or an internationalized constituent power. Instead, there is a certain vacuum and the need for clearer rules – and their observance.

13. German citizenship and its colonial heritage

Felix Hanschmann

13.1. POST-COLONIAL THEORIES AND GERMAN JURISPRUDENCE

Post-colonial theories have their disciplinary roots mostly in the cultural studies of Anglo-Saxon countries, from which they have only recently and somewhat slowly permeated German science as a transdisciplinary field of literature, cultural studies, social sciences and history. Although they have also found their way into the work of some non-German legal scholars,[1] they have received to date little attention in German jurisprudence. This is doubtless due in part to the marginal role ascribed to German colonialism in Germany's collective consciousness. Germany's colonialism may indeed have been, as not only Edward Said believed, of "negligible quantity"[2] in terms of duration and dimension, compared with other and more visible and established colonial powers, such as Portugal,

[1] The jurisprudence in other countries seems to be more receptive to post-colonial theories. See for example Martti Koskenniemi, *The Gentle Civilizer of Nations* (Cambridge University Press 2004); Antony Anghie, *Imperialism, Sovereignty and the Making of International Law* (Cambridge University Press 2008); id, "Francisco de Vitoria and the Colonial Origins of International Law" (1999) 40 *Harvard International Law Journal* 1; id, "Time Present and Time Past" (2000) 32 *NYU Journal of International Law* 243; BS Chimni, "Third World Approaches to International Law" (2006) 8 *International Community Law Review* 3; id, "International Institutions Today" (2004) 15 *European Journal of International Law* 1; Makau Mutua, "Critical Race Theory and International Law" (2000) 45 *Villanova Law Review* 841; Lauren Benton, *Law and Colonial Cultures* (Cambridge University Press 2002); Upendra Baxi, "The Colonial Heritage" in Pierre Legrand and Roderick Munday (eds), *Comparative Legal Studies* (Cambridge University Press 2003) 46.

[2] Edward Said, *Orientalism* (Vintage Books 1978) 16. For a convincing critique see Lewis H Gann, "Marginal Colonialism: The German Case" in Arthur

Spain, Great Britain, France, and even the Netherlands. On the eve of the First World War the German empire had acquired a comparatively small number of colonies that altogether encompassed an area of nearly 3 million square kilometers and a population of about 13.63 million persons.[3] However, that it does not seem wholly convincing to judge the significance of colonialism in political, social and scientific life solely on the basis of quantitative criteria, becomes obvious, as I will show in the following, when taking a look at the public, scientific as well as the parliamentary discourse on citizenship in Germany from the beginning of the 20th century.

13.1.1 Post-colonial Theories I: The Discourses of Colonialism

Firstly, one of the most important elements of post-colonial theory is the analysis of the discourses which have accompanied, structured, and legitimized colonial expansion. These epistemologies are not seen as a mere narrative accompaniment to economic, political, military or legal structures, but as independent, constitutive elements of colonial rule. It appears therefore foreshortened to draw a distinction between "colonization as a system of rule, of power and exploitation, and colonization as a system of knowledge and representation".[4] Within the colonial project, physical expropriation, military force and legal submission are unavoidably linked to the production of a certain kind of knowledge implying what may be called a type of cognitive exploitation. Colonialism is always an inextricable amalgam of fantasies, political strategies and practices that constituted an insoluble mélange of epistemic structures and real activities.[5] While it is therefore important to stress the political and economic background of colonial ventures, it is, on the other hand, indispensable to outline the interrelated ways in which the colonial discourse has steadily produced representations of an "other" in order to

---

J Knoll and Lewis H Gann (eds), *Germans in the Tropics* (Greenwood Press 1987) 1–17.

[3] Winfried Speitkamp, *Deutsche Kolonialgeschichte* (Philipp Reclam 2005) 39.

[4] Stuart Hall, "When Was the 'Postcolonial'?" in Iain Chambers and Lidia Curti (eds), *The Postcolonial Question* (Routledge 1995) 242, 254.

[5] See the contributions in Susanne Zantop, *Colonial Fantasies* (Duke University Press 1997); Birthe Kundrus (ed), *Phantasiereiche* (Campus 2003).

claim and maintain the distinction and superiority of the colonizers.[6] Of course, negative or exotic attributes have been ascribed by the colonizers to the colonized. However, particularly in colonial constellations, which by definition assume there are those who govern and those who are governed, attributions are always binary in structure. Thus, the colonizers always simultaneously define their own identity as the reverse characteristic when labeling the "others" as foreign (hard-working/lazy, developed/undeveloped, feminine/masculine, civilized/barbaric, rational/emotional, cultivated/savage, progressive/primitive etc.). Although this has happened tacitly, unnoticed by contemporaries, in this way the colonial experience became a powerful element in the self-perception of the colonial center. And when it comes to the law, there is hardly any other institute like citizenship where one could trace the self-perception of a particular community and its members.

13.1.2 Post-Colonial Theories II: Repercussions on the Colonial Center

Though generalizations inevitably give cause for concern considering the multiple disciplinary roots, the diversity of authors and the heterogeneous theoretical approaches, post-colonial theories have been shaped by a few central research questions. Firstly and in contrast to earlier approaches which focussed almost exclusively on the dominating influence of colonizers over colonized people, the primary focus of post-colonial theories has rightly been the repercussions of colonialism on the colonial center. They have shown that any conceptualization of colonialism as a "one-way street"[7] is inadequate and that colonialism should be understood instead as a process of interdependent relationships and mutual transformations which take place not only in the colonies as the periphery but also in the colonial center.[8] Repercussions on the colonial

---

[6] Ann Laura Stoler and Frederick Cooper, "Between Metropole and Colony" in Ann Laura Stoler and Frederick Cooper (eds), *Tensions of Empire* (University of California Press 1997) 1, 4 and 18.

[7] Sebastian Conrad, *Deutsche Kolonialgeschichte* (2nd edn, Beck 2012) 10.

[8] Shalini Randeria, "Entangled Histories of Uneven Modernities" in Yehuda Elkana et al (eds), *Unraveling Ties* (Campus 2002) 284; Sebastian Conrad, "Double Marginalization" in Heinz-Gerhard Haupt and Jürgen Kocka (eds), *Comparative and Transnational History* (Berghahn Books 2009) 52, 53 and 58.

center have been detected within economic relationships,[9] with regard to the origin of ecological ideas and practices,[10] in centralized city planning, including sanitary and traffic-related requirements, as well as the segregation of different population groups,[11] and also in relation to medical experiments, such as large-scale active immunization.[12] The case of the German empire rather testifies to the fact that despite relatively limited colonial efforts, colonial ideas and enterprises became crucial elements of the empire's constitutional discourse and influenced the configuration of the legal relationship between the center and the periphery in a way that can hardly be overestimated. Colonialism was not only inextricably linked to the concepts of race, gender, civilization and hygiene, whose understanding – shaped by the colonial situation – is in turn reflected in jurisprudence. The colonial constellation also had a direct impact on legal terms such as sovereignty, legal personality, property, state, people, and citizenship.

13.1.3 Post-colonial Theories III: The Lasting Effects of Colonialism

Finally, the prefix "post" indicates that post-colonial theories are interested not only or even not primarily in the past, but rather in analyzing the lasting effects of colonialism. They pay particular attention to the – seemingly innocuous – guise in which elements of colonial discourse and structures have outlived the formal end of colonial rule and continue to exert a strong influence today in politics, culture, economics, art, science

---

[9] For this see Sidney Wilfred Mintz, *Sweetness and Power* (Penguin Books 1985); Albert Wirz, *Sklaverei und kapitalistisches Weltsystem* (Suhrkamp 1984) 198 et seq.

[10] Richard H Grove, *Green Imperialism* (Cambridge University Press 1995). For the retroactive effect of colonialism on the creation of an ecological consciousness in the metropolis: Joachim Radkau, *Nature and Power* (Cambridge University Press 2008) 184 et seq.

[11] Anthony Sutcliffe, *Towards the Planned City* (Blackwell 1981); Gwendolyn Wright, *The Politics of Design in French Colonial Urbanism* (University of Chicago Press 1991); id, "Tradition in the Service of Modernity" in Stoler and Cooper (eds) (n 6) 322.

[12] Marion Wallace, *Health, Power and Politics in Windhoek, Namibia, 1915–1945* (Schlettwein 2002); Warwick Anderson, "Excremental Colonialism" (1995) 21 *Critical Inquiry* 640; Timothy Burke, "'Sunlight Soap Has Changed my Life'" in Hildi Hendrickson (ed), *Clothing and Difference* (Duke University Press 1996) 189; Wolfgang U Eckart, "Medizin und kolonialer Krieg" in Peter Heine and Ulrich van der Heyden (eds), *Studien zur Geschichte des deutschen Kolonialismus in Afrika* (Centaurus-Verlagsgesellschaft 1995) 220; Wolfgang U Eckart, *Medizin und Kolonialimperialismus* (Schöningh 1997).

and, last but not least, law. This concerns not only human rights, which can be described as the "Trojan horse of recolonization,"[13] both because of their potential for being instrumentalized in political, economic and military interventions and their facilitation of individualized structural and systematic injustice. It is also relevant for those legal provisions which define and limit the polity membership of a certain state, i.e. the rules of citizenship. It seems precisely here that the emancipating potential of post-colonial theories lies in practice, as they provide a means of identifying and scandalizing forms of rule, influence, control, exploitation, exclusion, inequality or violence which obscure colonial structures, all the while enabling their continuing propagation and consolidation.

13.2. IMAGININGS OF "OTHERS"

Scientific, literary or artistic imaginings of the "others" as foreign did not only become a crucial element in the constitutional debate in the German empire in general. As they were negative (or, less frequently, exotic) reflections of one's own self, they particularly influenced the definition of citizenship. Once the German empire actively began to pursue a colonial policy in the last third of the 19th century, German lawyers were already preoccupied with and influenced by academic perceptions of the oriental, African or Asian "other", accompanied by an authoritative claim.[14] Karl May's books on the oriental and African adventures of Kara ben Nemsi and his Muslim companion Hadji Halef Omar found an impressively large readership. Travel reports (Heinrich Barth and Gustav Nachtigal, Georg Schweinfurth and Samuel Graf Teleky) and Hegel's remarks on Mohammedanism in his *Lectures on the History of Philosophy* had left their imprint on academic thinking. And academics were intrigued by Friedrich Schlegel's treatise "On the Language and Wisdom of the Indians" (published in 1808), Goethe's *West-Eastern Divan,* Friedrich Rückert's poetic translation of the Koran and Mozart's *Abduction from the Seraglio.* Those literary and musical excursions to the Orient or

---

[13] Gustavo Esteva and Madhu Suri Prakash, *Grassroots Post-Modernism* (Palgrave 1997) 110 et seq.

[14] For German orientalism see Baber Johansen, "Politics and Scholarship" in Tareq Y Ismael (ed), *Middle East Studies* (Praeger 1990) 71; Sarah Roche-Mahdi, "The Cultural and Intellectual Background of German Orientalism" in Azim Nanji (ed), *Mapping Islamic Studies* (Mouton de Gruyter 1997) 108.

Africa were complemented in the European environment by representations of a different, particularly an oriental "other" in architecture or painting.[15] The imaginings created in those reports, lyrics, fantasies, and novels were introduced into both constitutional statements and legislative procedures as a natural element of one's own gaze on the world and this gaze became relevant both in the colonies and in the colonial center.

13.2.1 The Distinction between "Natives" and "Citizens"

Because the German *Reich* and its colonial authorities established a dual legal order depending on the distinction between "natives" and citizens in the colonies, one would expect a clarification of the term "native". Nevertheless, neither legal provisions nor orders by the German emperor defined who was considered a native. As a consequence of the lack of a legal specification, authorities in the colonies could arbitrarily classify persons as "natives". Furthermore, depending on what an administrative official or judge decided, a person could be considered a native one day and a non-native (*Nichteingeborener*) the next.[16] Far from being a negligible legal sophistry, the concrete classification was crucial for the legal status of a person and legal decisions opened or closed the possibilities for marriage, education, the acquisition of property or a pension. The definition could ultimately determine whether a person "could be killed or raped with impunity".[17] Since the term "native" was neither an inherent attribute nor a stable essentiality but rather something that had to be constantly redefined with respect to the particular colonial situation, definitions led to permanently shifting social boundaries.

13.2.2 "Mixed Marriages"

The almost unlimited flexibility and arbitrariness of the classification of the colonies' inhabitants is mirrored in the legal treatment of so-called "mixed marriages", i.e. marriages between the indigenous population and

---

[15] For this, see the impressive illustrated book by Kristian Davies, *The Orientalists* (Laynfaroh 2005).

[16] Lora Wildenthal, "Race, Gender, and Citizenship in the German Colonial Empire" in Stoler and Cooper (eds) (n 6) 263, 266. This arbitrariness has already been criticized in the contemporary literature. Cf. Friedrich Gentz, "Die rechtliche Stellung der Bastards in Deutsch-Südwestafrika" (1902/03) 4 *Zeitschrift für Kolonialrecht* 90, 91.

[17] Stoler and Cooper, "Between Metropole and Colony" (n 6) 1, 6.

German nationals, and the related discussion in legal as well as parliamentary debate. According to the German law in the colonies, German citizens were, at least theoretically, legally enabled to celebrate marriage with natives. However, local colonial offices in German South-West Africa instructed register offices in 1905 not to conclude marriages between whites and natives and so-called half-castes respectively. In the year 1906 a similar administrative decree was adopted for German East Africa. When in 1912 Colonial State Secretary Wilhelm Solf prohibited intermarriage and thereby inserted race as a legal category into the citizenship law of the empire, this was the first time that the empire's government itself rather than the administration in the colonies had banned intermarriage. In consequence, it was debated in parliament and in judicial discourse whether or not such marriages could be validly concluded.[18] While the Social Democrats and the Zentrum Party introduced a bill aimed at ensuring both the validity of these marriages and the rights of mixed-blood children in all German colonies,[19] the majority of German legal scholars vehemently denied the validity of mixed marriages. They supplied a variety of reasons.[20] It was argued that the progeny of conjugal relationships could form a new class threatening social dissimilation not only in the colonies but also within the empire, the "biological quality" of the white race, the assumed superiority of the colonizers and thus the legitimacy of colonial rule. In particular, after the insurgency of the *Herero* and the *Nama* in German South-West Africa, these worries were increasingly vocalized and the fear became prevalent

---

[18] For the legal discussion see Lora Wildenthal, *German Woman for Empire* (Duke University Press 2001) 79 et seq; Birthe Kundrus, *Moderne Imperialisten* (Böhlau 2003) 219 et seq. For the debates in the *Reichstag* see Cornelia Essner, "Zwischen Vernunft und Gefühl" (1997) 45 *Zeitschrift für Geschichtswissenschaft* 503.

[19] Due to the resistance of the government this draft never became law.

[20] Georg Braun, *Zur Frage der Rechtsgültigkeit der Mischehen in den deutschen Schutzgebieten* (Abel 1912) 26 et seq; Julius Friedrich, "Die rechtliche Beurteilung der Mischehen nach deutschem Kolonialrecht" (1909) *Koloniale Rundschau* 361; Johannes Gerstmeyer, *Das Schutzgebietsgesetz* (Guttentag 1910) § 7 Rn. 7; Kurt Hedrich, *Der Rassegedanke im deutschen Kolonialrecht* (Gatzer & Hahn 1941) 48 et seq; Hermann Edler von Hoffmann, *Einführung in das Deutsche Kolonialrecht* (Göschen 1911) 117; Joachim H Lücke, *Bevölkerung und Aufenthaltsrecht in den deutschen Schutzgebieten Afrikas* (Friederichsen 1913) 24 et seq; Karl Neumeyer, "Privatrechtliche Mischbeziehungen nach deutschem Kolonialrecht"(1913) 6 *Zeitschrift für Völkerrecht und Bundesstaatsrecht* 125, 193 et seq.

that mixed-bloods could become leaders of native rebellions.[21] But it was by no means only violent conflict that led to mixed-marriage bans and to related sophisticated redefinitions of the term "native" along racial, cultural, and gender lines. Rather, this was dependent on numerous conditions of the particular colonial situation such as the abolition of slavery that curtailed symbolically and, in some senses, actually, the claim to domination by the colonizers through their status as slave-holders,[22] the pauperization of white settlers that undermined the prestige of the colonizers, the rising presence of white women in the colonies who had to be "protected" against the rampant libido of black men and moral disgrace.[23] Against this background the ban on intermarriages safe-guarded the colonizers' sense of a common identity against internal dissension among whites themselves, clarified the social segregation between colonizers and colonized through a judicial dividing line, and, ultimately, secured the antagonism indispensable for colonial domination at a time when supposedly stable classifications of the population were collapsing.

13.2.3 German Jurisprudence and "Mixed Marriages"

However, for German lawyers another argument, always connected with the motives mentioned above, was decisive for banning "mixed marriages". Since, under the law valid at the time, the wife of a German citizen and her progeny received German nationality, they would have gained the status of a legal person, including all corresponding rights and duties. The importance of avoiding these legal consequences for German lawyers becomes obvious when it is taken into account that nearly 99 percent of mixed-blood children in the colonies did not originate from

---

[21] For the contemporary legal literature see Karl von Stengel, "Die Eingeborenenfrage und die Regelung der Rechtsverhältnisse der Eingeborenen in den deutschen Schutzgebieten" (1910) 12 *Zeitschrift für Kolonialrecht* 183, 193 et seq; id, "Zur Frage der Mischehen in den deutschen Schutzgebieten" (1912) 14 *Zeitschrift für Kolonialrecht* 738, 773 et seq.

[22] Pamela Scully, "Rape, Race, and Colonial Culture" (1995) 100 *American Historical Review* 335, 340 and 356 et seq.

[23] Ann Laura Stoler, "Making Empire Respectable" (1989) 16 *American Ethnologist* 634, 640 et seq. See also Margaret Strobel, "Gender and Race in the 19th and 20th Century British Empire" in Renate Bridenthal et al (eds), *Becoming Visible* (2nd edn, Houghton Mifflin 1987) 375, 378 et seq.

conjugal relationships, but rather from concubinage.[24] So the mixed-marriage bans were not aimed at preventing sexual relationships between whites and natives.[25] Rather, the deprivation of rights was embedded in an effort to legally perpetuate the colonial system with its racial implications.[26] Legal principles, considered sacrosanct within the empire, were subordinated to racial purity as a necessary constituent of colonial rule.[27] In comparison with other colonial states, these bans on intermarriage were unique. Though it was never left to chance "who bedded and wedded whom in the colonies of France, England, Holland, and Iberia",[28] and while discussion on which adults and children could be acknowledged as citizens rather than just subjects of colonial rule, designating who were legitimate progeny and who were not, was a transnational element of colonialism,[29] the regulations of other colonial states were strikingly different and less uncompromising. Although other colonial powers prohibited sexual relationships between white men and native women, as well as in principle denying access to the colonies for married men or the celebration of marriage for Europeans while in the service of a colonial company, in practice interracial unions were systematically tolerated, sometimes condoned or even endorsed in order to put comparatively little financial burden on western low-salaried employees and to motivate them to acquire native language and customs.[30] And even if the

---

[24] It is hard to find reliable numbers. The percentage mentioned here refers to a debate in the German *Reichstag*. See Verhandlungen des Reichstages. Stenographische Berichte, XIII. Legislaturperiode, 56. Sitzung, 8. Mai 1912, P. 1740.

[25] This has been seen already in the contemporary literature: "The prohibition of racial intermarriages in the German colonies is ineffective against the crossbreed, because the concubinage remains." See Theodor Grentrup, "Die Rassenmischehen in den deutschen Kolonien und das kanonische Recht" (1914) 94 *Archiv für katholisches Kirchenrecht* 3, 9. A similar argument was made in the parliament by a Social-Democrat representative. For this see Verhandlungen des Reichstages. Stenographische Berichte, XIII. Legislaturperiode, 53. Sitzung, 2. Mai 1912, P. 1649.

[26] Ann Laura Stoler, "Rethinking Colonial Categories" (1989) 31 *Comparative Studies in Society and History* 134, 146.

[27] Dieter Gosewinkel, "Rückwirkungen des kolonialen Rasserechts?" in Sebastian Conrad and Jürgen Osterhammel (eds), *Das Kaiserreich transnational* (Vandenhoeck & Ruprecht 2004) 236, 249.

[28] Stoler (n 23) 634, 636 et seq.

[29] Stoler and Cooper, "Between Metropole and Colony" (n 6) 1, 24 et seq; Ann Laura Stoler, *Carnal Knowledge and Imperial Power* (University of California Press 2002) 53.

[30] For Great Britain see Helen Callaway, *Gender, Culture and Empire* (Macmillan Press 1987) 48; Elizabeth B van Heyningen, "The Social Evil in the

underlying motivations and goals of intermarriage bans pursued by other colonial countries might have been to a large extent similar to those that motivated the implementation of the German bans, they were far more pragmatic and the definition of the "native" could be constantly readjusted in a more flexible way. They could more or less easily be adapted to the changing conditions of the particular colonial situation. Therefore, outside Germany, the legal category of citizenship was only loosely, if at all, tied to an ethnic origin framed by a discourse of racial purity. As a result and in contrast to the German legal regime, spouses as well as mixed-blood children could become citizens of the colonial power, with all the rights and duties this entailed. To acquire the status of a citizen natives of the Dutch colonies had, in 1884, to be Christian, to speak and write Dutch, to have a European upbringing and education, and, finally, to demonstrate a suitability for "European behavior".[31] Though there were widespread fears that half-castes might claim political rights and express resistance to the colonizers' rule on behalf of the native inhabitants, the methods used by other colonial powers to cope with these fears were more inclusive or even assimilatory. Though the assimilationist rhetoric in French colonial policy had long been compromised by the need to maintain a distinction from the colonized population,[32] it was nevertheless based on the idea of an obligation to "civilize" the world, including the widely shared assumption that the upbringing and protection of children from bi-racial relationships "was a cause célèbre of European woman (…) at home and abroad. European colonial woman were urged to oversee their 'moral protection,' to develop their 'natural' inclination toward French society, to turn them into 'partisans of French ideas and influence' instead of revolutionaries".[33] Likewise the provision of orphanages run by the state, the church or private associations, and aimed at imparting education and adaptation to European morality, was customary for the increasing number of illegitimate children of mixed

---

Cape Colony 1868-1902" (1984) 10 *Journal of Southern Africa Studies* 170; Pamela Scully, "Rape, Race, and Colonial Culture" (1995) 100 *American Historical Review* 335, 342. For France see Alice L Conklin, *A Mission to Civilize* (Stanford University Press 1998) 168 et seq.

[31] Stoler (n 26) 134, 153 et seq.

[32] For these discussions in France see Raoul Girardet, *L'Idée coloniale en France de 1871 à 1962* (La Table ronde 1972); Herman Lebovics, *True France* (Cornell University Press 1994).

[33] Stoler (n 23) 634, 648. For the French Indochine: Henri M Sambuc, "Les Métis Franco-Annamites en Indochine" (1931) 5 *Revue du Pacifique* 256.

parentage in British colonies.[34] Furthermore, since at least the 17th century, British nationality had been extended to the whole of the British Empire. Everyone who was born within its territory "was a British subject of the Crown and shared British nationality and identical rights. All British subjects had the right to enter the United Kingdom, to reside and to hold property, to take up employment, to vote (if suitably qualified), and were equal before the law."[35] British nationality was therefore a rather inclusive concept, symbolizing the unity of the empire, instead of being, as was the case in German colonialism, a means to reinforce racial segregation and to disenfranchise the colonies' native inhabitants. So even if instruments like orphanages were often implemented in order to create "perfected natives, not imitation Europeans"[36] and could still be considered an expression of the efforts to constantly redefine and uphold the social boundaries between "colonized" and "colonizers", such politics, and the citizenship law in particular, feature an underlying impetus of inclusion rather than exclusion. While in the case of other colonial powers "citizens" and "natives", though sharply segregated, can hardly be taken as synonymous with the categories "rulers" and "the ruled," the German intermarriage bans were adopted exactly to make these categories virtually congruent.

13.3. LASTING REPERCUSSIONS: THE RECONCEPTUALIZATION OF CITIZENSHIP LAW

The discussions about the legal treatment of German settlers in the colonies, the classification of native inhabitants, and the handling of intermarriage as part of the colonial ventures of the empire did not only affect the legal regimes in the German colonies. In fact, they had, in turn, tremendous repercussions on the colonial center and can only be adequately understood in a perspective that moves beyond the geographical borders of the German nation state. During the two decades of reform processes concerning German citizenship law, colonial expansion

[34] For India see also David Arnold, "European Orphans and Vagrants in India in the Nineteenth Century" (1979) 7 *The Journal of Imperial and Commonwealth History* 104.

[35] Pat Thane, "The British Imperial State and the Construction of National Identities" in Billie Melman (ed), *Borderlines* (Routledge 1998) 29, 41. See also Bernard Porter, *The Lion's Share* (Longman 1975) 336.

[36] Stoler and Cooper, "Between Metropole and Colony" (n 6) 1, 7.

constantly influenced the debates in the *Reichstag* on the reconceptionalization of German citizenship. In particular, the issue of mixed marriage and the possibility of half-castes receiving German citizenship led to an intense judicial and public debate and "tested the limits of citizenship law and forced Germans to clarify their terms".[37] While in 1871 German citizenship law was neither nationally nor racially determined, the question of whether German nationality should be oriented towards racial homogeneity came to the fore and dominated parliamentary debates almost obsessively. Yet demands to racialize citizenship, based on an abhorrence of mixed marriages and children descending from mixed parentage in the colonies, threatened the essential principles of the colonial center because they challenged the patrilinear model of citizenship valid at the time, according to which the husband and father passed on his citizenship automatically to his wife and his children. By contrast with French law, for example, German citizenship law was based solely on the principle of *ius sanguinis*, i.e. on a "community of descent from German men" both within and beyond the boundaries of Germany.[38] This concept was, indeed, ideologically charged with ethnic and cultural content, but was by no means congruent with the term "race" in a biological sense.[39] It was exactly this legal framework in which citizenship was based on paternal descent and not on race that troubled those who took race seriously and was held to trigger the threat of a "racial amalgamation" of German nationality.[40] Above all colonial activist groups like the "*Alldeutsche Verband*" or the "*Deutsche Kolonialgesellschaft*" argued in favor of a clearly racially oriented redefinition of the citizenship law and a statutory ban on mixed marriages, while the parliamentary majority, mainly consisting of the Social Democrats and the Christian parties, were opposed.[41]

These issues not only occupied the German *Reichstag* but also preoccupied the wider public and led in particular to an extraordinary

---

37 Wildenthal (n 16) 263, 264. See also Conrad (n 8) 52, 66 et seq.

38 Rogers Brubaker, *Citizenship and Nationhood in France and Germany* (Harvard University Press 1992) 122 et seq.

39 That does not mean that colonial racism did not contain cultural elements and that cultural racism is no racism. For this see Etienne Balibar, "Is There a 'Neo-Racism'?" in Etienne Balibar and Immanuel Wallerstein (eds), *Race, Nation, Class* (Verso 1991) 17.

40 Gosewinkel (n 27) 236, 243.

41 For the debates in the parliament see Cornelia Essner, "Zwischen Vernunft und Gefühl" (1997) 45 *Zeitschrift für Geschichtswissenschaft* 503.

number of judicial statements, articles and opinions.[42] It is no exaggeration to say that, with all this diversity of perspectives, the question of the legality and of the consequences of intermarriage received the largest amount of scientific attention of all colonial phenomena.[43] Yet, in the end, no explicit prohibition of intermarriages was adopted through the new citizenship law of 1913. As a result of the majority's resistance in parliament, no legal category of race was inserted. Instead, the patrilinear model of citizenship remained untouched until the Nuremberg laws of the National Socialist regime in 1935.[44] It might very well be, as Hannah

---

[42] Amandus Acker, "Zur Frage der Rassenmischehe" (1912) 4 *Koloniale Rundschau* 462; id, "Zur Frage Mischrasseehe in den deutschen Schutzgebieten" (1913) 30 *Deutsche Kolonialzeitung* 90; Christian von Bornhaupt, "Zur Frage der Mischehen zwischen Reichsangehörigen und Eingeborenen in Deutsch-Südwestafrika vom Rechtsstandpunkte" (1909) *Deutsche Kolonialzeitung* 2; Max Fleischmann, "Die Mischehen in den deutschen Schutzgebieten vom Rechtsstandpunkte" (1911) *Verhandlungen des Deutschen Kolonialkongresses* 548; id, "Die Mischehenfrage" (1910) 12 *Zeitschrift für Kolonialpolitik* 83; Julius Friedrich, "Die rechtliche Beurteilung der Mischehen nach deutschem Kolonialrecht" (1909) *Koloniale Rundschau* 361; Viktor Fuchs, "Zur Frage der Mischehen zwischen Reichsangehörigen und Eingeborenen in Deutsch-Südwestafrika" (1909) 1 *Deutsche Kolonialzeitung* 38; id, "Nochmals zur Frage der Mischehen in den deutschen Schutzgebieten" (1909) 1 *Koloniale Rundschau* 493; Friedrich Gentz, "Die rechtliche Stellung der Bastards in Deutsch-Südwestafrika" (1902/03) 4 *Zeitschrift für Kolonialrecht* 90; Theodor Grentrup, "Die Rassenmischehen in den deutschen Kolonien und das kanonische Recht" (1914) 94 *Archiv für katholisches Kirchenrecht* 3; Hans Hasenkamp, "Rassenmischehe und Kirche" (1914) 16 *Zeitschrift für Kolonialrecht* 21; Hermann Edler von Hoffmann, "Die Mischehenfrage" (1909) *Deutsche Kolonialzeitung* 793; Franz-Josef Sassen, "Das Personenstandsrecht in den deutschen Kolonien" (1910) 12 *Zeitschrift für Kolonialpolitik, Kolonialrecht und Kolonialwirtschaft* 297; Wilhelm Schreiber, "Zur Frage der Mischehen zwischen Weißen und Eingeborenen im deutschen Schutzgebiete Deutsch-Südwestafrika" (1909) 11 *Zeitschrift für Kolonialpolitik, Kolonialrecht und Kolonialwirtschaft* 88; Karl von Stengel, "Die Eingeborenenfrage und die Regelung der Rechtsverhältnisse der Eingeborenen in den deutschen Schutzgebieten" (1910) 12 *Zeitschrift für Kolonialrecht* 183, 193 et seq; id, "Zur Frage der Mischehen in den deutschen Schutzgebieten" (1912) 14 *Zeitschrift für Kolonialrecht* 738, 773 et seq. Even dissertations were written on the issue; see for example Georg Braun, *Zur Frage der Rechtsgültigkeit der Mischehen in den deutschen Schutzgebieten* (Abel 1912).

[43] Kundrus (n 18) 220.

[44] Birthe Kundrus, "Von Windhoek nach Nürnberg?" in id (n 5) 110, 115; Wildenthal (n 16) 263, 266 et seq. For contemporary judicial discourse see Max Fleischmann, "Die Mischehen in den deutschen Schutzgebieten vom Rechtsstandpunkte" (1911) *Verhandlungen des Deutschen Kolonialkongresses* 548.

Arendt suggested, that the practices of genocide and the construction of concentration camps during the wars against the *Herero* and the *Nama* anticipated the National Socialist politics of annihilation,[45] and that the colonies thus functioned as a "laboratory of modernity". At least as far as the citizenship law is concerned, however, this thesis can hardly be verified. It was only the National Socialist regime that turned to a strictly racially oriented citizenship law, not least by shedding the legal ties of the 1913 citizenship law of the German empire.[46] Despite the agitation of colonial associations who feared that the predominant principle of *ius sanguinis* was failing to protect the integrity of the German nation as a "community of race", the patriarchal rights of German men were not limited in the interests of the racialization of the citizenship law. However, intermarriages were not explicitly declared to be lawful, implying that the arbitrary and haphazard practice of the administration and the courts in the colonies could continue to operate with the tacit backing of the government.[47] Thus one might say that citizenship law does not provide any evidence for the direct transfer of the racial politics within the colonies into the law of the colonial center.[48] But even if the division between the two legal spheres did not dissolve, the experience in the colonies was certainly not without impact on the law of the German empire. The 1913 citizenship law did appease one essential demand of the colonialist associations and racially oriented nationalists, for example,

---

[45] Hannah Arendt, *Elemente und Ursprünge totaler Herrschaft* (Piper 1984) 307 et seq. For the ongoing discussion see Jürgen Zimmerer, "Colonialism and the Holocaust" in A Dirk Moses (ed), *Genocide and Settler Society* (Berghahn Books 2005) 49; Isabel V Hull, "Military Culture and the Production of 'Final Solutions' in the Colonies" in Robert Gellately and Ben Kiernan (eds), *The Specter of Genocide* (Cambridge University Press 2003) 141; Benjamin Madley, "From Africa to Auschwitz" (2005) 35 *European History Quarterly* 429. More critical: Russel A Berman, "German Colonialism: Another Sonderweg?" (1999) 16 *The European Studies Journal* 25; Kundrus (n 18) 277 et seq; id, "Von Windhoek nach Nürnberg?" in id (n 5) 110, 122 et seq; Dirk van Laak, "Kolonien als 'Laboratorien der Moderne'?" in Conrad and Osterhammel (n 27) 257, 270 et seq.

[46] Gosewinkel (n 27) 236, 254 et seq.

[47] Despite the lack of a ban on intermarriages and although the new citizenship law provided in section 33 a provision under which a native could receive German citizenship, the ministry of the interior, shortly after the entry into force of the new citizenship law in 1913, announced that "purebred natives" would not be naturalized and mixed-bloods only in very exceptional cases. See the Statement of the director in the ministry of the interior, Dr Lewald, RT-Prot., 13. Legislaturperiode, 155. Sitzung, 30. Mai 1913, P. 5334.

[48] Gosewinkel (n 27) 236, 254.

by introducing a provision under which Germans abroad would not lose their citizenship after a certain period of time as long as they fulfilled their compulsory military service. Moreover, and in contrast to its predecessor, according to the new law, citizenship could even be passed on to one's descendants.[49] These provisions, originally adopted with regard to the situation of German settlers in the colonies and the strengthening of their ties to the German state, legally institutionalized the conception of an ethnic and cultural sense of solidarity across borders and gained special relevance after 1945 in the post-colonial environment. The provisions enabled so-called "resettlers," in particular from the Soviet Union, to enter German territory without legal impediments.[50] In addition, the new citizenship law included an "imperial citizenship," the so-called *Reichsangehörigkeit*, unmediated by citizenship in one of Germany's federal states. This was not only part of a legal nationalization, but, far more importantly, had a tremendous influence on the self-understanding of the people in the colonial center as well as the genuine idea of a German nation as a direct result of the empire's colonial experiences.

---

[49] For this see Dieter Gosewinkel, *Einbürgern und ausschließen* (Vandenhoeck & Ruprecht 2001) 310 et seq.

[50] Gosewinkel (n 27) 236, 256; Conrad (n 8) 52, 67.

PART VI

Ordering Europe – Europe ordering. Constitutional transfers to Latin America in the nineteenth and twentieth centuries

14. Constitutional transfers and experiments in the nineteenth century

Günter Frankenberg

14.1. CONSTITUTIONAL EXPERIMENTALISM IN NINETEENTH CENTURY EUROPE

Contrary to its reputation as the "dark age of constitutionalism," nineteenth century Europe was an era of intense, at times feverish, constitution-making – in particular at the beginning, then again around the middle in 1848/9 and also throughout the last decades[1] – witnessing an impressive array of constitutional projects in Europe (and abroad). In 1848/9 alone, forty new constitutions sealed successful or unsuccessful revolutionary upheavals all over Europe.[2] Like their predecessors and successors they oscillated uneasily between the poles of revolution and restoration, constitutional monarchy and parliamentary democracy, monarchic and popular sovereignty as well as rule-of-law principles and royal prerogatives.

Rather than recognizing the nineteenth century as a constitutional laboratory and tracing the pathways of constitutional projects, treatises on constitutional history and comparative constitutional law[3] have until

[1] Later threshold phases of constitution-making were: the post-World War I period and the era of decolonization, the aftermath of the "velvet revolution" in Central and East Europe in the 1990s and more recently during and after the "Arabellion" since 2011 in the Arab world.

[2] Peter Brandt et al (eds), *Handbuch der europäischen Verfassungsgeschichte im 19. Jahrhundert* (Dietz 2006).

[3] John A Hawgood, *Modern Constitutions since 1787* (Macmillan 1939); Kurt Breysig, *Kulturgeschichte der Neuzeit*, (2 vols, first published 1900/01, BiblioBazaar 2010); Karl HL Pölitz, *Die Constitutionen der europäischen Staaten seit den letzten 25 Jahren* (Leipzig-Altenburg 1817); Conrad Bornhak, *Genealogie der Verfassungen* (M & H Marcus 1935); Fritz Hartung, *Deutsche*

fairly recently[4] tended to indulge in surveys of a universal or European constitutional history, often providing only a cursory treatment of this century,[5] or operatingwith a focus that was either too broad, covering cultural history, or too narrow, such as histories of the state and of nation-building or of fundamental rights.[6]

The dominant historical reading of this century's "constitutional moments" assumes a close nexus between constitutionalism, on the one hand, and revolution/liberation or restoration/reaction, on the other.[7] Quite commonly, constitutional activity in the founding era and thereafter is regarded as translating ideas of the Enlightenment and the ideology of liberalism into normative orders, preferably republic, democracy, and rule

---

Verfassungsgeschichte vom 15. Jahrhundert bis zur Gegenwart (7th edn, Köhler 1959); Hans Fenske, *Der moderne Verfassungsstaat. Eine vergleichende Geschichte von der Entstehung bis zum 20. Jahrhundert* (Schöningh 2001).

4 See, for example, Martin Kirsch and Pierangelo Schiera (eds), *Verfassungswandel um 1848 im europäischen Vergleich* (Duncker & Humblot 2001) with further references; Martin Kirsch, *Monarch und Parlament: Der monarchische Konstitutionalismus als europäischer Verfassungstyp* (Vandenhoeck & Ruprecht 1999); Otto Büsch and Arthur Schlegelmilch (eds), *Wege europäischen Ordnungswandels: Gesellschaft, Politik und Verfassung in der zweiten Hälfte des 19. Jahrhunderts* (Kovač 1995); Arthur Schlegelmilch, *Die Alternative des monarchischen Konstitutionalismus* (Dietz 2009); notably Brandt et al (n 2); and Hartwig Brandt, *Der lange Weg in die demokratische Moderne. Deutsche Verfassungsgeschichte von 1800 bis 1945* (Wissenschaftliche Buchgesellschaft 1998).

5 Raoul van Caenegem, *An Historical Introduction to Western Constitutional Law* (3rd edn, Cambridge University Press 1995) 1–6, considers constitutional law in general as a "delayed" area of research and study. Some of the notable exceptions are listed under the previous footnote.

6 See, for example, Otto Hintze, *Staat und Verfassung* (2nd edn, Vandenhoeck & Ruprecht 1962); Wilhelm Roscher, *Politik: Geschichtliche Naturlehre der Monarchie, Aristokratie und Demokratie* (1897); Georg Jellinek, *Allgemeine Staatslehre* (Verlag O Häring 1900); Georg Jellinek, "Die Erklärung der Menschen- und Bürgerrechte: Antwort an Emile Boutmy" in Roman Schnur (ed), *Zur Geschichte der Erklärung der Menschenrechte* (Wissenschaftliche Buchgesellschaft 1964); Carl J Friedrich, *Constitutional Government and Democracy* (4th edn, Blaisdell Publishers 1968); Martin van Creveld, *Aufstieg und Untergang des Staates* (Gerling Akademie-Verlag 1999); Wolfgang Reinhard, *Geschichte der Staatsgewalt* (CH Beck 1999); Dietmar Willoweit and Ulrike Seif (eds), *Europäische Verfassungsgeschichte* (CH Beck 2003).

7 Van Caenegem (n 5) 174–243 with further references; Reinhard (n 6) 406–40; Bill Brugger and Kate Hannan, *Modernization and Revolution in East and West* (Croom Helm Ltd 1983).

of law,[8] and following, however flexibly and with deviations, the teleology of gradual democratization. Guided by implicit or explicit modernization theories[9] and mesmerized by the glamour of a philosophical enlightenment agenda encapsulated in the triad "liberté, égalité, fraternité," constitutional historians and theoreticians looked at nineteenth century Europe and beyond and interpreted what they perceived as the constant unfolding of both the liberating and liberal inheritance of the French and American Revolutions.[10] Thus, they bypassed what will be addressed here: the correspondences, tensions and contradictions between constitutional projects, and between violent nation-building and imperial-colonial expansion, as framers – elites, protest movements, scholars – experimented with ideas and institutions, norms and ideologies and agonized over the conflicting imperatives of revolutionary and restorative politics and the antagonistic projects of the Enlightenment and *Realpolitik* to accommodate competing claims to sovereignty, power and recognition.

Neither by definition nor by necessity were constitutions then and are today only national phenomena. They were not strictly bound to the territory of nation-states. While it is true that at the beginning of modern constitutionalism and throughout the era under review here, constitutional documents defined polities as nation, state or people and stayed within "an epistemic horizon and political imaginary that pre-supposes and refers to the particular form of the state,"[11] some were related to a supranational context of federalist or confederate unions of states – the

[8] JJ Chevallier, *Histoire des institutions et des régimes politiques de la France de 1789 à nos jours* (4th edn, Gallimard 1972).

[9] See Robert Inglehart, *Modernization and Postmodernization: Cultural, Economic, and Political Change in 43 Societies* (Princeton University Press 1997); Reinhard (n 6) 406–40; Arthur Schlegelmilch, "Das Projekt der konservativ-liberalen Modernisierung" in Kirsch and Schiera (n 4).

[10] Van Caenegem refers to the German *Vormärz* as the unfulfilled liberal dream, van Caenegem (n 5) 219; George L Scherger, *The Evolution of Modern Liberty* (Longmans 1904); Otto Vossler, "Studien zur Erklärung der Menschenrechte" in Schnur (n 6); Gerhard Ritter, "Ursprung und Wesen der Menschenrechte" in Schnur (n 6) 202; See also Dieter Grimm, *Deutsche Verfassungsgeschichte, 1776–1866* (Suhrkamp Verlag 1988). A critique of the teleological understanding of European history informs a research project designed by Martti Koskenniemi and Bo Stråth, "The Research Project Europe 1815–1914: Between Restoration and Revolution, National Constitutions and Global Law: An Alternative View on the European Century 1815–1914."

I am indebted to the members of this research group for critical comments on an earlier version of this chapter.

[11] Neil Walker, "Taking Constitutionalism beyond the State" (2008) 56 *Political Studies* 519.

German *Bund* (1815–66) and the 1871 Imperial Constitution of Germany. Moreover, information concerning the vocabulary, grammar, style and design, i.e. the idiom of modern constitutions, referred to questions of membership (nationality) but also transgressed national borders and, once included in the developing global reservoir, became available for the framing of constitutions virtually everywhere. From Norway to Sicily, from the Netherlands to Greece, numerous minor and major independent territories were re-invented as constitutional states after the breakthrough of this concept between 1791 and 1815.[12] Aside from the network of intra-European transfers, constitutional projects and information traveled from Europe, in particular from France (the constitutions of 1791, 1814 and 1830), Spain (Cádiz 1812), and Belgium (1831), to other continents.[13]

How and to what effect the actors of constitution-making operated with transferred and therefore different[14] information will be shown by looking at "sets of initial circumstances" that call into question the notion of "origin" (14.2) and by highlighting the short tenure of many constitutions that underscores their experimental character (14.3). The actual analysis of transfers will focus on the pathways of three lead constitutions and their encounters with new environments and political constellations within "host" countries (14.4). The focus on nineteenth century constitutional development in Europe is not to imply that elsewhere there were neither constitutional experiments nor constitutions of short tenure, let alone constitutional transfers. As constitutional reforms or revisions are generally related to political-social struggles and constellations of power, none of these aspects – constitutionalism, experiment, tenure or transfer – was or is a specifically European phenomenon.[15]

---

12 Reinhard (n 6) 406–26.

13 Mario Rodriguez, *The Cádiz Experiment in Central America* (University of California Press 1978); Victor C Folsom, "Constitutional Development in the Countries of the Americas" (1977) 9 *Lawyer of the Americas* 495.

14 Concerning the relationship between transfer and difference: Rudolf Stichweh, "Transfer in Sozialsystemen: Theoretische Überlegungen" in Vanessa Duss et al (eds), *Rechtstransfer in der Geschichte: Jahrbuch junge Rechtsgeschichte 1* (Meidenbauer 2006).

15 That socialist constitutions were generally revamped several times, albeit according to a developmental logic quite different from experimentalism, has been noted above (see "Constitutions as commodities: notes on a theory of transfer," section 5). To name a few other examples dating from the nineteenth century: Costa Rica was reconstituted seven times between 1821 and 1871; due to the redesigning of the territory and to changing power constellations, Colombia underwent several constitutional revisions (Folsom (n 13) 501–3).

14.2. ORIGIN AND ORIGINALITY: THREE SETS OF INITIAL CIRCUMSTANCES FOR CONSTITUTIONAL MONARCHY

During the first decades of the nineteenth century and later, three constitutions began to get a reputation as highly original documents and developed a remarkable degree of marketability, albeit for a long time outside the Russo-Austro-German sphere. Interestingly enough, these constitutions were internally related as varieties of constitutional monarchy, lending themselves to neither revolutionary nor restorative agendas, but nevertheless each came with the aura of originalism.

1791 – Civilizing the Revolution

France opened the dance with its 1791 September Constitution. Though promulgated four months after Poland's May Constitution,[16] it may nevertheless be credited, due to its revolutionary genesis and philosophical pedigree, with having initiated the transformation of absolutism into a regime of constitutional monarchy. Incidentally, both documented a founding moment of rather *courte durée*[17] and integrated ideas of the French Enlightenment. The authors adopted Rousseau's concept of people's sovereignty and the separation of powers from Montesquieu's *Spirit of the Laws* and thus ended "fourteen centuries of despotism" in France. Despite deficiencies in the construction and political divisions many contemporaries[18] celebrated what the National Assembly had achieved, such as for instance the Jacobin club of Loches, but overestimated its lasting effect within France:

> Two and one-half years of work have redressed the unhappiness of fourteen centuries; in fourteen centuries the gratitude that we express to you today for

---

[16] Jan Kusber, "Vom Projekt zum Mythos – Die polnische Maiverfassung 1791" (2004) 52(8) *Zeitschrift für Geschichtswissenschaft* 685.

[17] For all intents and purposes the September Constitution was repealed when in August 1792 the monarchy was suspended. The May Constitution was annulled during the 1793 Second Partition of Poland.

[18] Unlike historians today, for example François Furet, "A Commentary" (1990) 16 *French Historical Studies* 795.

> the completion of so sublime a work will not yet have weakened in the hearts of the French.[19]

The 1791 Constitution included the rights declaration but in its own text toned down the radical rhetoric of 1789 and established a constitutional monarchy, much later re-labeled somewhat too enthusiastically as a "republican monarchy".[20]

If one tries to identify what Edward Said called a "set of initial circumstances," the 1789 *Déclaration* gave the Revolution constitutional definition and was of crucial importance not only because it survived as the preamble of the 1791 Constitution and its republican successors in France but, more importantly, because of the contemporary revolutionary events and the debates that led to its adoption and the debates and projects that ensued. The "work of six days of heated debate in August 1789" focused with a certain "prefigurative innocence" on the new ideal of political legitimacy,[21] replacing the "King of France" by the "King of the French," who embodied and executed the will of the nation, and on a new normative vision based on freedom and equality, ending privilege and recognizing and "nationalizing" the Third Estate.

Though the 1789 *Déclaration* had all the trappings of originality as the first continental rights declaration, it was indebted to earlier ideas, ideals and ideologies: the French constitutional elites had consulted other documents of anti-despotism, notably the Declaration of Independence and the rights catalogues of the New England states, most prominently the 1776 Virginia Bill of Rights, as sources of inspiration, and re-contextualized them not as "slavish imitations" but with a modicum of *bricolage*:

> The French declaration is, of course no slavish imitation of the American [the Virginia Bill of Rights – GF], … because the political conditions of France in the year of 1789 were quite different from those in America in the year of 1776. A people which adopts strange institutions and laws, never does so without changing the strange ideas according to the national character.[22]

---

19 Quoted by Michael P Fitzsimmons, *The Remaking of France: The National Assembly and the Constitution of 1791* (Cambridge University Press 1994) 248.

20 François Furet and Ran Halévi, *La monarchie républicaine* (Fayard 1996).

21 Marcel Gauchet, *La Révolution des droits de l'homme* (Gallimard 1989) 145. See also Skadi Krause, *Die souveräne Nation: Zur Delegitimierung monarchischer Herrschaft in Frankreich 1788–1789* (Duncker & Humblot 2008) 11.

22 Georg Jellinek, *Die Erklärung der Menschen- und Bürgerrechte: Ein Beitrag zur modernen Verfassungsgeschichte* (Duncker & Humblot 1904) 60.

During the two years following the adoption of the *Déclaration*, the members of the National Constituent Assembly debated about the regime and institutions that might be compatible with their revolutionary ideal and their social-political interests.[23] These debates from 1789 to 1791[24] were impressive because of the discipline, relatively speaking, and the almost democratic spirit with which the factions of the Third Estate handled their different political agendas and visions.[25] They disproved the thesis that to make a good constitution quiet deliberation is needed most when, because of political turmoil or social unrest, it is least available. However, the deliberations in the *Assemblée national constituante* were somehow out of tune with and disconnected from the revolutionary dynamics and the proliferation of anti-monarchic, anti-constitutional, democratic, and egalitarian convictions and movements, the manifold resistance against the replacement of feudal by capitalist structures and the dramatic growth of social and economic problems.[26] "For as soon as the constitutional agenda neared completion, a social agenda stood ready to take its place."[27]

In the end, the *Assemblée* followed the majority of moderates on the path toward constitutional monarchy although the monarch, Louis XVI, had made it quite clear that in spite of the oath he had taken he was not likely to support the constitution and, thus, would undermine its mission to stop the revolution "from below" from proliferating further. Therefore the 1791 Constitution – with its pragmatic, prudent and naïve adherence to an unreliable king and a scheme of separated powers – comes across as an ambivalent project. It failed in so far as it hoped to retain the monarchy by giving the king a suspensive veto, which he exercised excessively and forestalled legislation for years. However, it succeeded in

---

[23] CJ Mitchell, *The French Legislative Assembly of 1791* (EJ Brill 1988); Keith M Baker (ed), *The Political Culture of the French Revolution* (Pergamon 1988); Keith M Baker, *Inventing the French Revolution: Essays on the French Political Culture in the Eighteenth Century* (Cambridge University Press 1990).

[24] Fitzsimmons (n 19); Martin Kirsch et al, "Frankreich", in Brandt et al (n 2).

[25] CJ Mitchell, "Political Divisions within the Legislative Assembly of 1791" (1984) 13 *French Historical Studies* 356.

[26] Arthur Schlegelmilch, *Europäische Verfassungsgeschichte 1780–1830, Kurseinheit 1: Ideal und Wirklichkeit des bürgerlichen Verfassungsstaates* (Fernuniversität 1999) 24.

[27] Peter M Jones, *Reform and Revolution in France. The Politics of Transition, 1774–1791* (Cambridge University Press 1995) 243.

elegantly transforming "the unrelenting condemnation of privilege" on 4 August 1789 into both the myth and the institutions of the nation.[28]

Nevertheless and much to the chagrin of many members of the Second Estate of the still dominant feudal aristocracy,[29] the *Assemblée national constituante* introduced a new normative order – the constitutional state and the *société corporative* – which accommodated the demands of the rising capitalist bourgeoisie. By issuing two constitutional documents and several laws between 1789 and 1791, challenging the executive authority of the king and introducing something like "cabinet responsibility," the *Assemblée* prepared the way for the republic.[30] Abolishing feudal privileges and instituting a new political regime, the 1789 *Déclaration* and 1791 Constitution symbolized the birth of a new political imaginary which crystallized around the bourgeois state, the *volonté générale* expressed by law, more importantly a parliamentary constituent power, and a modern constitutional idiom.

Cádiz – A Historical Compromise

The Cádiz Constitution of 1812 was drafted and decided by the Cortes during a dynastic crisis in the absence of the exiled king. It was widely reputed as a document of resistance against Napoleonic occupation, even though it became fully operational only after the return of the Spanish king in 1820. The Cortes gleaned ideological aspects and institutional models for their *monarchía moderada* from Montesquieu's *The Spirit of the Laws*, the Anglo-American constitutional experience, and from the French Constitution of 1791, notably the moderation of state power by an institutional design of separated competencies, and the people's influence through political representation. To appease the conservative camp, they borrowed, from the pre-absolutist Spanish tradition, among others, the concept of moderation as a political virtue, the idea of the Cortes as a medieval institution, and the concept of the Spanish nation. The different and quite heterogeneous strands of (pre-)constitutional history tapped by the Cortes shifted their overall project from philosophical constitutionalism to political pragmatism. As genuine, albeit cautious, *bricoleurs*, they operated with an eye toward history and *Realpolitik.*

---

[28] Michael P Fitzsimmons, "Privilege and Policy in France, 1786–1791" (1987) *American Historical Review* 269.

[29] See Alison Patrick, "The Second Estate in the Constituent Assembly, 1789–1791" (1990) *Journal of Modern History* 223.

[30] Kirsch et al (n 24) 220–21; Gwynne Lewis, "Review" (1992) *The English History Review* 489–90.

The Cortes introduced a new vocabulary – including "national sovereignty," "individual rights," "equality," and "constitution" – a new grammar of power by shifting sovereignty from the king to the Cortes as representatives of the people and the division of powers, and thus forged a hybrid form of liberal constitutionalism. Moreover, they established the normative basis of the nation-state, its territorial boundaries and principles of citizenship.[31] The Cortes used in particular the pre-modern notion of "nation" and the thirteenth century law book "Siete Partidas" as a unifying myth and to facilitate acceptance of their concept of constitutional monarchy, gleaned from the 1791 Constitution conjoined with English bicameralism. While Cádiz also shared the 1791 spirit of anti-privilege, it still and prudently granted the church, Roman Catholicism, and the military a privileged status:

> The Constitution of 1812 abolished seigniorial institutions, Indian tribute, and forced labor, such as the *mita* in South America and personal services in Spain; ended the Inquisition, and established firm control over the Church. [...] The new charter created a unitary state with equal laws for all parts of the Spanish world. It substantially restricted the king and entrusted the Cortes with decisive power.[32]

The Cádiz Constitution can be read as a declaration of independence from France and a cautious and significant step from absolutism toward constitutionalism. It therefore met with strong disapproval on the part of the unholy alliance of the absolutist regimes of Austria, Prussia and Russia, relying on France as their stooge. Following its adoption, the concerns of the defenders of monarchy in Europe focused on three questions related to the Cádiz Constitution. First, for the Indians, "the forgotten Americans", the Cortes had planned a scheme of legal protection and a reform of the tribute system. Despite its silence over the slave trade, there was reason enough for colonial powers to worry about the Spanish and their own colonies. Second, revolutionary movements, notably in Italy, adopted or copied Cádiz ideas and institutions. Therefore

---

[31] Matthew C Mirow, "Visions of Cádiz: The Constitution of 1812 in Historical and Constitutional Thought" in Austin Sarat (ed), *Studies in Law and Policy* (vol 53, Emerald Group Publ 2010); Miguel Artola, "Estudio preliminar" in Miguel Artola and Rafael Flaquer Montequi (eds), *La Constitución de 1812* (vol II, Iustel 2008).

[32] Jaime E Rodriguez, *The Independence of Spanish America* (Cambridge University Press 1998) 91; see also Mirow (n 31) 70.

absolutist rulers felt threatened by the "codex of anarchy"[33] and the revolutionary spirit it inspired. They decided to intervene in Naples for the protection of monarchy. By the same token, the members of the Holy Alliance were determined to curb the dangers of the Spanish revolution, notably the prohibition on royal power in Spain impeding the convocation of the general Cortes and obstructing their work. This the protagonists of monarchy unanimously condemned as too democratic and evil. Therefore they charged France with intervening again and restoring both Ferdinand VII to the throne and his absolutist regime.

Even after the assault by French troops in 1823 and while under siege, the Cortes did not accept the restoration of the absolutist monarchy. They retreated to Seville and then to Cádiz again where they had taken King Ferdinand VII. Rather than mediating between the Cortes and the French invaders, Ferdinand VII, once in the camp of the French occupants, broke his oath, defected and again declared the Cádiz Constitution null and void.

1831 – Deconstructing Originalism in Belgium

After a series of occupations and divisions, revolutions and restorations, the Belgian provinces were reintegrated into France as departments in 1795. At the end of Napoleonic rule they were united, according to the decision of the victorious allies, with the Northern Netherlands in 1815. Encouraged by the July Revolution in Paris, surprisingly large protests were launched against this forcible union and the government, calling for independence and constitutional reforms. Belgium successfully seceded from the United Kingdom of the Netherlands, was then declared independent and finally established as a constitutional monarchy on 7 February 1831, again with the blessing of the major powers, France and Great Britain.[34]

The 1831 Constitution of Belgium lends itself to an ironic deconstruction of the term "origin." It also illustrates the transformation of a single document into a "moisaïque constitutionelle."[35] John Gilissen estimated that 40 percent of its text was taken from the Basic Law of the

---

[33] Quoted by Juan Ferrando Badía, "Die spanische Verfassung von 1812 und Europa" (1963) *Der Staat* 153, 173.

[34] Hans Fenske, *Der moderne Verfassungsstaat* (Ferdinand Schöningh 2001) 322–7; John Gilissen, "La Constitution belge de 1831: Ses sources et son influence" (1968) *Res Publica* 107.

[35] E Descamps, *La mosaïque constitutionnelle: Essai sur les sources du texte de la Constitution Belge* (Charles Peeters 1891).

Netherlands (1815), 35 percent from the 1830 version of the French *Charte constitutionnelle*, 10 percent from the 1791 Constitution and 10 percent from English public law.[36] These imports leave only a marginal 5 percent for original provisions, an estimate that meets with broad scholarly approval.

As was mentioned before, the new Belgian framers drew a great deal of inspiration from British constitutionalism and French *Charte* constitutionalism – with the 1814 *Charte* Constitution and its 1830 revision serving more than indirectly as points of reference.[37] The *Charte* provided the dualist model that confronted the monarch and his council of ministers with a bicameral structure of senate and chamber of deputies. Along the lines of the *Charte*, the Belgian framers also shifted the accent from the separation of powers to a more cooperative scheme of checks and balances, in particular by providing for the joint execution of legislative power and also placing the right to initiate laws into the hands of the Crown and the two chambers.[38]

The Belgian document deviated from the *Charte*, though, and from most European constitutions of the time by stating in Art. 25 (today: Art. 33): "All powers emanate from the nation." With this formula the Belgian framers turned to the principle of popular sovereignty and arguably returned to the radical core of the reformist conception of the French 1791 Constitution:

> Sovereignty is one, indivisible, inalienable, and imprescriptible: it belongs to the nation: no section of the people nor any individual can attribute to himself the exercise thereof. (Title III 1)

In retrospect one can trace the concept of popular sovereignty to the 1789 *Déclaration* – "The principle of all sovereignty resides essentially in the nation" (Art. 3) – or to the Greek constitution of 1827: "Sovereignty resides in the nation." Hence, looking for its origin appears to be quite futile. One should rather assume that this concept had already been commodified and become part of the global constitution at the end of the second decade of the nineteenth century.

Underscoring popular sovereignty with a catalogue of rights, the Belgian constitutional elite distanced themselves from early constitutionalist leanings toward traditional or monarchic conceptions of the prerogatives of the Crown. With the formula "le roi est le chef suprême de

---

[36] Gilissen (n 34).

[37] Ibid; Schlegelmilch (n 26) 70f.

[38] Schlegelmilch (n 26) 79.

l'État" and the joint exercise of the legislative power by the king and the two chambers of parliament, they appear to have followed – while also stressing local autonomy – the *Charte* Constitution of 1814 and the example of the Cortes in Cádiz.

The peculiar appeal of the document may have been the triangle of people's sovereignty, rights (including the rights of minorities), and strong legislature. This triangle lent itself to mystifying the constitution as inaugurating a parliamentary monarchy:

> La Constitution est d'inspiration libérale. Elle instaure un État de droit, favorise les libertés locales (autonomie des communes) et protège les droits de l'homme. … Elle institute un régime de monarchie parlementaire fondé sur la separation des pouvoirs. En effet, le Parlement est appelé à contrôler le Pouvoir exécutive, caractéristique tirée de la Charte française, elle-même inspire du régime politique britannique. À ce tire, la Constitution belge a servi de modèle pour bon nombre de Constituants du XIXe siècle.[39]

The power of the king to dismiss ministers, his other executive and legislative powers, and in particular the extremely restricted franchise, which allowed for merely a little over 1 percent of the population to be represented in the two chambers, do not really argue, however, for a genuine parliamentary monarchy but a constitutional monarchy inspired by the 1791 Constitution. Moreover, the franchise concerning the Senate was based on an even more limited suffrage and eligibility. All these regulations point toward the ideological content of the concept of "nation".

These brief profiles of constitutional documents suggest that, no matter their "set of initial circumstances" and degree of originality, they have to be read as being always already part of something else – continental constitutionalism, a restorative or revolutionary agenda, national pride, a strategic concept of the major powers, fear of military intervention by neighbors or other hegemonic forces, etc. Therefore the best way to deal with the question of origin and originality may be to look not for first instances but rather for transfers, duplication, parody, ironic repetition or hybrids by *bricolage* elsewhere.

---

[39] Yves Lejeune, *Droit constitutionnel belge: Fondements et institutions* (Larcier 2010) 69; see also B Mirkine-Guetzevitch, "1830 dans l'histoire constitutionnelle de l'Europe" (1931) *Revue d'histoire moderne* 248; John Gilissen, *Le régime representative Belgique depuis 1790* (La Renaissance du Livre 1958).

14.3. EXPERIMENT AND TENURE

The experimental nature and short tenure of constitutions is illustrated by the frequent reconstituting of states throughout the nineteenth century in Europe and abroad. Whereas Belgium's 1831 Constitution, revised several times but still in force today, has the status of a solitaire, France became the model for both constitutional experimentalism[40] and short-lived constitutions in Europe.[41]

On the way to the constitutional state, France took the lead in Europe, translating, in the manifesto of 1789, the spirit and rhetoric of Rousseau's *Contrat Social* and declared the *nation* as the holder of popular sovereignty and the *law* as the expression of the general will (*volonté générale*).[42] Despite the *courte durée* of only ten months, the 1791 Constitution was to provide some of the frequently imitated patterns for European constitutionalism: popular sovereignty, separation of powers, strong parliamentary assembly, and *monarchie limitée*. Following the brief interlude of the popular 1793 Constitution – the Constitution of the Year I – which rekindled the spirit of 1789 but never went into force, the radical Jacobins introduced their "Revolutionary Government," a decree-based terror regime. *La Terreur* was soon and from then on to overshadow not only the French Revolution but also the development of constitutionalism in France.

After the downfall of Robespierre, the moderate Thermidor, instead of returning to the constitutional monarchy of 1791, passed the more liberal, albeit somewhat complicated, Constitution of the First Republic in 1795, which reveals the ambivalences of the liberal paradigm: the introduction of a bicameral legislature was combined with the establishment of the

---

40 Reinhard refers to France as "the constitutional laboratory", Reinhard (n 6) 413.

41 The constitutional history testifies to an impressive sequence of revisions and reconstitutions throughout the nineteenth century, beginning with the Temporary Constitution in 1822, leading via three constitutions to the 1844 return to monarchic sovereignty and the establishment of a "Crowned Democracy" in 1864. Regarding the equally rich twentieth century: Dimitis Tsatsos and Xenophon Contiades (eds), *The Constitutions of Greece 1975/1986/2001* (Sakkoulas 2001); Eleftheriadis Pavlos, "Constitutional Reform and the rule of Law in Greece" (2005) 28 *West European Politics* 317.

42 See Brandt et al (n 2) 214–335; Fenske (n 34) 147–85, 212–34; Kirsch (n 4) ch II.

five-man Directory and strong emergency powers reserved for the executive.[43]

Finally, the "short and obscure" 1799 Consular Constitution (Constitution of the Year VIII), a mourning gift of the French aristocratic and bourgeois elite for Napoleon, replaced the Directory with the Consulate, and sealed the closure of the revolutionary process. It was the first post-1789 document that did not contain a rights catalogue but only a few, rather indeterminate rights guarantees dispersed throughout the text.[44] Furthermore, the Consular Constitution was not debated by a constitutional assembly but drafted by members of the *nobilité constitutionnelle* – actually imposed by Napoleon upon the two legislative commissions. After its enactment it was submitted to the people and adopted in a plebiscite by a wide margin,[45] thus introducing the Bonapartist pattern of legitimation to be replicated by the organizational statutes of 1802 and 1804 as well as later by Louis-Napoléon III. Napoleonic constitutionalism helped increase Napoleon's power as First Consul and later as Emperor over a domesticated, soon very docile and dysfunctional parliament. It camouflaged Napoleon's autocracy under the guise of a constitutional state.

After this series of what might be called interim constitutions, French constitutional history took an archetypical turn away from the grammar of (imposed) legislated constitutions to the contracted constitution. In 1814, after the military defeat of France, a *charte octroyée* sought to accommodate the interests of Great Britain and Austria[46] by integrating France in the balance of European powers as well as to secure the Bourbon Restoration against a return to the Napoleonic regime.

The *Charte constitutionnelle* became almost universally applicable or rather transferable because of its political pragmatism and despite its openness to change being limited to the range of monarchic or autocratic regimes. It was quite successful as a constitutional model for the royalist clientele.

The document resulted formally from royal authority, but was, in fact, negotiated and agreed upon between King Louis XVIII, who promised a

---

43 George Lefebvre and Albert Soboul, *The Directory* (Routledge 1962). Regarding the ambivalences of the liberal paradigm see Günter Frankenberg, *Staatstechnik – Perspektiven auf Rechtsstaat und Ausnahmezustand* (Suhrkamp Verlag 2010).

44 See Title I (citizenship) and Title VII (general provisions).

45 G Lowes Dickinson, *Revolution and Reaction in Modern France* (Allen & Unwin 1892) 36–41.

46 Kirsch (n 4) 303–4.

revival of constitutional monarchy, and eighteen deputies representing the two chambers of the legislature. On the one hand, the *Charte* turned back the wheel of history and bestowed upon the monarch considerable powers as head of state and sovereign. He dominated the executive, not least because of his emergency powers. And the king also towered over the legislative process because of his exclusive right to initiate legislation, his absolute veto, his right to convoke and dissolve the chamber of parliament, and his right of budgeting.[47] On the other hand, the *Charte* tried, albeit without restricting the royal prerogatives, to balance the conflicting claims to power.[48] It guaranteed parliamentary representation, still based on extremely limited suffrage, with eligibility restricted to a mere fraction of the property-owning male population, accorded (fairly weak) rights to the bourgeoisie and appeased the aristocratic opposition with indemnity.[49] Upon Napoleon's return from Elba, the *Charte* rendered proof of its limited flexibility and was amended by the Additional Act of June 1814 with scant "popular" participation in the ensuing plebiscite. In 1830, the marginally revised and slightly more liberal *Charte* was re-instituted after the failed July Revolution.[50]

Following a period of political discontent and political upheaval, mainly in Paris, against the *juste milieu* plutocracy, which culminated in the February Revolution, yet another constitution came into existence in November 1848 – the Constitution of the Second Republic. It introduced the directly elected president and a national assembly that could no longer be dissolved at will by the monarch. It failed, however, to install a mechanism for the resolution of conflicts between the president and the parliament. This structural deficit, as well as the limited and non-renewable term of the president, prompted the first office-holder, Louis-Napoléon Bonaparte, to initiate a *coup d'état* on the model of the 18 Brumaire. He appealed to the people to "end the era of revolutions," and then introduced the Constitution of 1852, which established a dictatorial regime under the guise of a restored monarchy (making him Napoléon

---

47 Ibid.

48 Schlegelmilch (n 4) 25.

49 Fenske (n 34) 212–14.

50 Markus Prutsch, "The Revision of the *Charte constitutionnelle* in the Crisis of 1830" in Szabolcs Hornyák et al (eds), *Turning Points and Breaklines* (Meidenhauer 2009).

III)[51] – inspiring Karl Marx's famous dictum that history repeats itself "first as tragedy, then as farce."[52]

In comparison with previous documents, Bonaparte's constitution experienced a remarkable durability of more than two decades. After the Emperor had begun to liberalize with moderation his dictatorial regime and had restored constitutional monarchy, in particular, by strengthening the role of the national assembly (since 1869), and, after a series of political crises, the *Constituante* opted in 1875, with a majority of only one vote, for the republic and passed three constitutional statutes that laid down – under the title of the Constitution of the Third Republic – the design of the new governmental structure.

In short, constitutional development in France reveals a pattern of cyclical change from monarchic/authoritarian to parliamentary regimes and then back to autocracy. Discontinuity – not affecting the infrastructural continuity of administrative centralism – rather than continuity or the unfolding of a teleological project, characterizes French constitutional history. By the same token, transfers, for instance, from Rousseau's *Contrat social* to the *Déclaration*, or from English constitutionalism to the Constitution of 1791, were either short-lived, like this constitution and the social rights of the revolutionary Constitution of 1793, or were subject to considerable *bricolage* and re-designing under the various dramatically different power constellations, such as the institutional set-up of the legislature. The early French experience suggests that, in the context of political regimes which lack a modicum of ideological stability and institutional consolidation, constitutional transfers *may* occur, but are likely to have neither lasting nor predictable effects.

Other European states followed the French example and experimented with the modern constitutional idiom throughout the nineteenth century. Two aspects of constitutional experimentalism are particularly striking: first, patterns of constitutional instability – notably in Spain, the Netherlands, Italy, and some of the German territories – mirror-changing power constellations, competing claims to sovereignty, economic crises, collapsing social realities, and also the fragile and changing territorial boundaries. Second, as European states were forced to re-order themselves

---

[51] TAB Corley, *Democratic Despot: A Life of Napoleon III* (Barrie & Rockliff 1961); Roger Price, *The French Second Empire: An Anatomy of Political Power* (Cambridge University Press 2001); Theodore Zeldin, *The Political System of Napoleon III* (Oxford University Press 1958).

[52] Karl Marx, *The Eighteenth Brumaire of Louis Napoleon* (Progress Publishers 1937).

under the pressure of revolutionary, anti-monarchical or nationalist movements, elites supported by academics and consultants transferred constitutional items across the continent – at the delivering and the receiving end, thus establishing the IKEA market.

Spain is an interesting case in point, as it experienced a highly fickle constitutional development and still produced one of the century's lead constitutions. Its political elite, led by the Cortes, translated the modern idiom of constitutionalism into two competing constitutional designs drafted and passed under extraordinary circumstances: the Napoleonic occupation, states of siege, and regimes of martial law. The monarchic Constitution of Bayonne (1808), a French *octroi*, was hardly effective but at least documented a temporary and institutionally cautious turn from absolutism to the constitutional state, and offered a platform for later constitutional movements. It was soon superseded, however, by the 1812 Cádiz Constitution, with which the Cortes instituted a constitutional monarchy with a fairly strong, yet overly complex, parliamentary legislature.

When the king returned from exile, his followers, who constituted only a minority in the Cortes, urged that all acts of the Cortes including the Constitution contravened Spain's traditions, law, and history and therefore should be abolished. When Fernando realized that he had the support of the military, the bureaucracy and many traditionalists, he abolished the Cortes and its acts. And "[t]he constitutional structure collapsed like a house of cards. The regular army pursued the *liberales*, and the people did not defend them. On the contrary, in many places the masses eagerly destroyed the symbols of the Constitution."[53]

In the decades that followed, the Cádiz Constitution was intermittently suspended and re-animated several times, while the country was constantly driven from constitutionalism and reform to absolutism and restoration – and back.

14.4. PATHWAYS AND TRANSFERS

Transferring Constitutional Monarchy

The reformist design and radical, anti-privilege rhetoric of the 1791 Constitution traveled long distances and, despite its short life in France, became a rather attractive choice for constitution-makers all over Europe

---

[53] Rodríguez (n 32) 103–6.

and abroad, such as in Haiti. Combining a declaration of war on privilege with a pragmatic constitution of politics apparently rather appealed to constitutional elites and architects outside royalist circles. Framers with a liberal penchant would borrow from the 1791 Constitution, as is illustrated by the Belgian 1831 Constitution, which, together with the French document, served as a source of inspiration in many countries and accommodated itself to different political constellations.

In Spain a rebellion forced the regent to install a constitutional assembly which later revised the 1834 imposed constitution by integrating elements from Cádiz and Belgium. After its independence in 1830, Greece saw many constitutions, none of which was implemented. Since 1832 King Otto had ruled without a constitution, but was forced by a military coup to convoke a constitutional convention in 1843. The 1830 version of the French *Charte* and the Belgian Constitution served as models for the Greek document of 1844 and, more importantly, the 1864 Constitution, prompting a return to popular sovereignty and a more elaborate rights catalogue.

The Belgian text was reproduced as a modified copy in Romania (1866), ironically conjoining religious freedom with the pre-eminence of the Greek Orthodox religion.[54] That the re-contextualized "rights of the Belgians" and popular sovereignty would be attractive items for transfer for the 1848 revolutionary movements in Italy and Germany does not come as a surprise. However, only the basic statute of the Kingdom of Piedmont-Sardinia survived the time of political reaction and was later synthesized with the 1830 *Charte* and the Belgian Constitution to become the Constitution of the Kingdom of Italy.

Even the Prussian 1850 Constitution was indebted to the Belgian document, although Prussia tried to stay aloof from liberal constitutionalism.[55] Its mélange of heterogeneous constitutional ideas betrays a variable genesis. The king rejected the first draft as too liberal and imposed another instead. The following attempts by a constitutional committee, handpicked by the king to create a document to his majesty's liking, transferred the design and forty articles verbatim from the Belgian model, but failed to import the liberal reputation it enjoyed in Belgium.

---

[54] Alexandre Tilman-Timon, *Les Influences étrangères sur le droit constitutionnel roumain* (Sirey 1946).

[55] Rudolf Smend, *Die preußische Verfassungsurkunde im Vergleich mit der belgischen* (Vandenhoeck & Ruprecht 1904) 79ff.

Constitutionalism à la *Charte*

The 1814 *Charte* Constitution and its modified 1830 version turned out to be at least as successful on the European market as the 1791 Constitution, if not more so, albeit for a different clientele. The royalist grammar of the original *Charte* regarding its making (*octroi*) and content accounted for its amazing marketability during the European restoration period and even thereafter. Monarchic constitutionalism à la *Charte*, establishing the political prerogative of the monarch and the dualism of parliament and monarchic government, was transferred and re-contextualized notably in the monarchic states of Southern Germany (1818/19), in Spain (1834), Greece (1844), Prussia (1850), Austria (1861), Imperial Germany (1871), and Russia (1906).

Interestingly enough, the liberal documents of the early German constitutionalist period in Bavaria and Baden 1818 and Württemberg 1819 subscribed to the dominant position of the monarch in legislature, whereas the statist constitutions of Prussia (1850) and Imperial Germany (1871) had to accommodate the interests of the bourgeoisie and leaned toward the modified *Charte* and the Belgian Constitution. Both strengthened the role and rights of the representative body somewhat within the dualist interplay between monarch and parliament by granting each the right to initiate laws and by improving parliamentary control of the budget.[56]

The Cádiz Compromise in Transfer

The hybrid created by the Cortes in Cádiz did not win widespread popular support in Spain where "people awaited the return of their desired king"[57] and attributed what had been achieved in the previous six years – including liberation from French occupation and the turn to constitutional monarchy – to the monarch. Nevertheless, the Cádiz Constitution was both adopted and adapted by constitutional movements and elites in Southern Europe and Hispano-America.[58] The initial reception in some countries of the Americas was particularly splendid:

---

56 See Kirsch (n 4) 322–9; Schlegelmilch (n 26) 67.

57 Rodríguez (n 32) 104.

58 Andreas Timmermann, *Die "gemäßigte Monarchie" in der Verfassung von Cadíz (1812) und das frühe liberale Verfassungsdenken in Spanien* (Aschendorf 2007) 355–72; Manfred Kossok, "Revolution – Reform – Gegenrevolution" in id, *Studien zur vergleichenden Revolutionsgeschichte* (Akademie-Verlag 1974) 143.

> Every ten minutes a cannon shot reverberated throughout the city reminding Guatemalans that at eight o'clock that morning Captain General José Bustamante y Guerra would present his copy of the Constitution to the crowd assembled in the Plaza Mayor. The day was Thursday, September 24, 1812, exactly two years since the Spanish Cortes had begun its memorable task. When Bustamante raised the charter in a gesture of presentation, the troops fired into the air. From the Plaza Vieja a detachment of artillery replied with a cannonade of its own – the signal to launch the parade along a select route through Guatemala City. It was remarkable sight: "The presence of such a brilliant entourage, the stately air of the marchers, the happiness that beamed in their faces, the gaiety of the large crowd, the adornments on the houses, the general pealing of bells, the din of the artillery, and the pleasant harmony of the military bands, produced a grandiose effect, a sublime picture, that charmed spirits and brought tender tears to all eyes."[59]

Thus, representatives from all the leading corporations and military bodies of the capital and its environs participated in the procession to celebrate the constitution: The colors of the Muy Noble y Real Ayuntamiento de Guatemala led the parade; the Royal Audiencia of Guatemala surrounded José Bustamante, its president; the religious and military units filed solemnly by; and a group of Indian justices, bearing the insignias of their respective villages, played simple tunes in honor of the constitution. After returning to the main square, three secretaries took it in turns to read the Constitution of Cádiz to the people of Guatemala City. Everyone was quiet, listening attentively to the articles of the long-awaited charter. One reporter observed: "It seemed more like a religious act than a civil ceremony."[60] San Salvador, Mexico and other countries of the Americas likewise celebrated the occasion with dignity and pageantry, evoking the acknowledgment of a grateful Spanish Cortes.[61] The constitutions of Puerto Rico, Cuba, Peru, Columbia and Venezuela followed the Cádiz model.

While the migration of the Cádiz Constitution[62] to the Americas was certainly facilitated by the pathways and structures of Spanish colonialism, its success was also due to the American representatives at the Cortes who had presented many issues and had participated in shaping the ultimate document. Constitutional transfer was further facilitated by successful revolutions in the United States and Haiti and by independence movements in other American countries which welcomed Cádiz as

---

59 *Gazeta del Gobierno de Guatemala*, Guatemala City, 2 October 1812.
60 Ibid.
61 Quoted from Rodriguez (n 32) 101–2.
62 Badía (n 33); Rodriguez (n 32).

proof of the revolution within the Spanish world and the dissolution of the Spanish monarchy.[63] "This dissolution provided some Americans the opportunity to press for local control and autonomy, often in the name of the Spanish king."[64] In some countries, like Mexico, it served as a reference point for independence and a document around which a constitutional culture could crystallize.[65] In the long run the positive impact of Cádiz constitutionalism should not be overrated, though:

> The Constitution of Cádiz failed to take root in any meaningful way because of its immediate repeal by Fernando VII in 1814 and because by 1820, Latin American countries were already well on the road to independence.[66]

Likewise, one should not overrate its lasting negative impact.

> The Constitution of Cádiz and its subsequent history can be seen as the origin of many of the constitutional challenges facing the region today. In abolishing the Constitution of Cádiz and the work of the Cortes, Fernando VII sent a message that had lasting constitutional implications. His actions demonstrated that there was nothing special about the constitution of Cádiz, constitutions, or constitutional laws. It was, unfortunately, a lesson learned.[67]

That, in the Americas, it left behind a pattern of constitutional instability for lack of entrenchment and therefore can be held accountable for what might be characterized as "failed constitutionalism"[68] gives too much credit to the ideas and ideology of Cádiz, respectively their monarchic enemies, and underestimates the specific local conditions of governance, political struggles and socio-economic problems[69] which informed the cycle of constitutionalism, anarchy, and militarism.[70]

The spirit and the document of Cádiz also transgressed the borders of the Spanish sphere of economic interest and political domination. Colonialism can hardly be held accountable for its career as a source of

---

63 Rodriguez (n 32).

64 Mirow (n 31) 71.

65 Ibid 79–81.

66 Ibid 84–5.

67 Ibid 86.

68 See Jorge Esquirol, "The Failed Law of Latin America" (2008) 56 *American Journal of Comparative Law* 75.

69 Cádiz or rather Fernando VII can hardly be held accountable for Bolivia experiencing 200 coups in 155 years by 1980 with the concomitant constitutional flux.

70 Bernardino Bravo Lira, *El estato constitucional en hispanoamerica 1811–1991* (Escuela Libre de Derecho 1992) 167.

inspiration for constitution-framers, among others, in Naples, Portugal, Sicily, Sardinia, and Piedmont (1820–21) and, more generally, for German liberalism and constitutionalism.[71]

The resilience of the Cádiz Constitution and its success, if not in Spain then in Europe and, ultimately, the global IKEA market of the nineteenth century, may be explained with regard to the normative and political appeal of the underlying ideology of compromise that the text expressed and the institutions embodied. *Moderación* appears to have been the mantra of the Cortes; it was the guiding formula for their political survival as well as the accommodation of both liberal and conservative ideas. In the absence of the king, they introduced the *monarchía moderada*, a scheme of government the intransigent camps of liberals and conservatives were likely to find acceptable.[72] The general spirit of moderation did not prevent royalists in other countries from regarding the Cádiz Constitution as a threat and intervening to prevent its transfer.

14.5. PLURALITY, AGENDA, AND SOURCES OF NINETEENTH CENTURY CONSTITUTIONALISM

Constitutionalizing the "Great Transformation"

The nineteenth century witnessed from beginning to end a hectic drafting and re-drafting, suspension and re-animation, as well as flagrant violations of constitutions in France, Spain, and almost all other areas of Europe. Thus, one would expect constitutional history and theory to discuss, and the actors – primarily the élites but also social movements – to address the question of *why* constitutions *mattered.*

Despite their rather short "half-life period," constitutions appear to have been considered important. A number of different reasons come to mind. One may infer from the pattern of constitution-making and amending that constitutional documents were regarded as useful to record historical developments and events, seal agreements, sanctify borders, and legitimize political authority. As written (supreme) law, they came in handy for revolutionaries and reformers alike who intended to destroy the

---

[71] Badía (n 33) 165; Horst Dippel, "Die Bedeutung der spanischen Verfassung von 1812 für den deutschen Frühliberalismus und Frühkonstitutionalismus", in Martin Kirsch and Pierangelo Schiera (eds), *Denken und Umsetzung des Konstitutionalismus in Deutschland und anderen europäischen Ländern in der ersten Hälfte des 19. Jahrhunderts* (Duncker & Humblot 1999).

[72] For a thorough and thoughtful analysis see Timmermann (n 58).

absolutist logic of symbolic incorporation or to replace it with the constitutional logic of representation, because constitutions magically de-personalize political power and manifest the abstraction of the modern idea of the state as pure script.[73] By the same token, supporters of parliamentary democracy, however moderate, clearly cherished, one might even say fetishized, constitutions as a useful instrument to tame the sovereignty claims of monarchs, estates, and the people, by striking a constitutional compromise, such as the symbolically powerful formula of "King/Queen-in-Parliament". Conservatives – in particular, the old estates and the *grand bourgeoisie* – resorted to constitutions to restore the *status quo ante* or to de-legitimize protest agendas, and to prevent or curb revolutions. Finally, the "learned public" and reform-minded elites, and later even the people, although excluded from any meaningful political participation almost all over Europe, submitted constitutional projects and surrendered to constitutional rituals[74] that seemed to offer a platform for their hopes and visions within a secular society.[75]

Nineteenth century constitutionalism came into existence and developed under extremely adverse and complex, historical circumstances. First and foremost, constitutional projects had to cope with the legacy of the French Revolution – its ideas, ideals, and ideology as well as the trauma caused by the Jacobin *Terreur*. They had to accommodate the sharply conflicting demands and interests of the supporters of *ancien régimes*, the emerging propertied class, and the industrial and agricultural proletariat. Nineteenth century constitutionalism had to process Napoleonic and other wars and military occupations, struggles for national unity and the re-designing of territorial boundaries that they entailed. While eighteenth century constitutionalism focused on emancipation and liberation, the following century was preoccupied with preventing revolution, and establishing unity and order. Furthermore, constitution-makers were confronted with countless political upheavals, a

[73] Albrecht Koschorke et al, *Der fiktive Staat: Konstruktionen des politischen Körpers in der Geschichte Europas* (Fischer 2007) 248.

[74] Even the indigenous population of Mexico joined in the official ceremonies where the Cádiz Constitution was proclaimed; see Silke Hensel, "Zur Bedeutung von Ritualen für die politische Ordnung. Die Verkündung der Verfassung von Cádiz in Oaxaca" (2009) 36 *Zeitschrift für Historische Forschung* 597.

[75] Kirsch mentions a sweeping change of mentality accompanying secularization, Kirsch (n 4) 97.

great deal of social dislocation, poverty (the "Social Question") and other side-effects of "The Great Transformation."[76]

As a consequence, the collapsing and rapidly changing reality highlights a practical paradox of constitutionalism: constitutions are least available or efficient when they are needed most. Moreover constitutions mirror the troubled spirit and unstable reality of the times. To cope with unpredictability and complexity, the framers either resorted to too much detail,[77] or abstained from laying down the necessary ground rules for the resolution of conflicts,[78] which means that the texture of the "constitution of politics" turned out to be either overly complex or deficient in crucial respects. With regard to their architecture and themes, many nineteenth century constitutions part company with the late eighteenth century's rights euphoria,[79] and reveal their architects' preoccupation with questions of organization.[80] The various brands of constitutionalism focused on the constitutional state which republican reformers introduced and defended, and which royalists and conservatives opposed or tried to turn into a constitutional monarchy. Most constitutional documents unpack the dimensions of the constitutional state, in so far as they address questions of (a) *authority*, in terms of sovereignty and separation of powers, (b) *territory*, by demarcating borders, (c) *nationality*, by defining citizenship, the rights of citizens and those of minorities, and (d) securing the state's *financial resources* with provisions concerning the budget and taxes.

---

[76] Karl Polanyi, *The Great Transformation: The Political and Economic Origins of our Time* (first published 1944, Beacon Press 1957).

[77] For example, Directorial Constitution (1795); Cádiz Constitution (1812); Swiss Constitution (1874).

[78] Such as the legislative competences of the monarch (initiative, veto power); the parliamentary responsibility of ministers; the separation of legislative and judiciary or the relationship of the two chambers of parliament. For example, *Charte constitutionelle* (1814/30).

[79] Notably the French constitutions after 1795 and the German Imperial Constitution (1871).

[80] For example, the French Consular Constitution (1799), Bonapartist Constitution (1852), and constitutional statutes of 1875; *Bundesakte* (1815); the republican and monarchic constitutions of the Netherlands (1798, 1801, 1805, 1806); the bureaucratic-absolutist constitutions of Germany (1848/49; 1850, 1866); the Imperial Constitution of Germany (1871) and Austria (1867); the Cádiz Constitution (1812); the French *Charte constitutionelle* (1814/30); the constitutions of Greece (1831/64); the "Turkish Constitution" of Serbia (1838); and the constitutional documents of Sweden.

Ideological Strands and Projects of Constitutionalism

Nineteenth century constitutionalism was anything but a unified intellectual and political movement or archive. In fact, it consisted of a plurality of quite different ideological strands and offered different institutional arrangements, which endowed it with its diversity, tensions, and idiosyncratic charm: These strands covered liberal-parliamentary, absolutist-bureaucratic, monarchic, and conservative-statist agendas, to name only the most prominent.[81] With regard to societal integration, the different agendas were centered on either the preservation or the transformation of traditional corporative society (*altständische Gesellschaft*) and, with regard to political authority, the competing sovereignty claims within the constitutional state, calling for a monarchic or republican form, centralist or federal organization, and national and/or transnational (imperialist) extension and scope of action.

The different constitutionalisms would tap any ideological source if it promised support for the respective revolutionary, reformist or restorative project. Not only conservatives and royalists, but also the more cautious reformers,[82] invoked one or the other ancient constitution, a pre-absolutist concept of legitimacy, or the tradition of the medieval *leges fundamentales* for their concept of legitimate authority based upon corporative (*ständische*) representation.

Framers with a modernist-reformist, parliamentary mind-set sought to adopt or to adapt the republican constitutionalism of the pre-Jacobin era of the French Revolution, which accounts for the relative success of the 1791 document in the European theater.

English constitutionalism, apparently, had a lot to offer, even before the de facto establishment of parliamentarism in the middle of the nineteenth century,[83] for both the anti-modernist and the modernist camp. Both the role of tradition and the idea of a "grown" constitution favored conservative (royal, aristocratic, etc.) visions of a stable constitutional state protecting the status quo and were introduced as antidotes to the revolutionary mind-set. In contrast, reformers were fascinated by the moderation of both royal and popular sovereignty claims within the

---

[81] See Büsch and Schlegelmilch (n 4) and Brandt et al (n 2) 119–64.

[82] The Cortes referred to the ancient, pre-absolutist constitution of Spain so as to legitimize their reformist move from monarchic absolutism to a constitutional monarchy with a fairly powerful legislature.

[83] See Eric J Evans, *Parliamentary Reform in Britain, c.1770–1915* (Longman 1999), and Eric J Evans, *Britain before the Reform Act 1815-1832* (Longman 2008).

compromise formula of the "King-in-Parliament," characterizing what was generally seen as a flexible, mixed government.[84]

It is therefore virtually impossible to distinguish between different constitutional paths clearly and to trace with accuracy the influence of what are generally considered the dominant models of nineteenth century constitutionalism. However, if one continues to focus only on competing sovereignty claims and the relationship between the monarch and the parliament, one may perceive different lines of constitutional development and transfer: (1) *Charte* constitutionalism (1814/30), modified by the Belgian Constitution (1830), with its dominant monarchic vocabulary; (2) Cádiz constitutionalism (1812), characterized, despite its arguably strategic, pre-absolutist connotations, by the idea of a constitutional monarchy with a strong parliament; (3) Austro-Prussian (fake) constitutionalism, still adhering to the absolutist grammar; and (4) parliamentary constitutionalism, based upon (almost) general elections and stripped of monarchic vocabulary or reducing it to a symbolic *décor* of the state.

From a comparative study of nineteenth century experimentalism, one may learn that constitutions, regardless of their socio-political and cultural context, share many of the archetypical features and structural properties. Such similarity on the surface may, however, only point to the limited imagination of constitution-makers, their strategic preferences, and the manner in which polities began to dress for their appearance on the global theater's stage as secular and abiding by the rule of law.

Aside from the coincidence of birth, none of what has been mentioned above supports the claim that constitutions are "national" and nothing else. Beyond their description and normative definition of societies as national polities, the epistemic horizon and political imaginary which refer to the particular form of the state,[85] constitutions have always referred to federalist or confederate states. More importantly, the pathways of transfer illustrate that the semantics and rhetoric of the constitutional enterprises appear always to have been transnational and open-textured.

Territorial aspects tended to play a greater role in the constitution as contract, due to its preoccupation with defining borders and laying down rules of citizenship (nationality). However, they do not render an exhaustive account even of constitutional contractualism in the nineteenth century and may very well be considered as contingent on the formative

---

84 See Gottfried Niedhart, "Großbritannien" in Brandt et al (n 2).

85 Walker (n 11) 280; as to the "political imaginary" see Ulrich Rödel, Günter Frankenberg and Helmut Dubiel, *Die demokratische Frage* (Suhrkamp Verlag 1989) ch IV.

period of modern constitutions and nation-states when constitutional movements opposed Napoleonic occupation (Spain), fought for national unity (the German territories/Prussia; and Italy) or challenged the borders of multi-people empires (Austria).[86] Generally speaking, only the territorially consolidated states of England and France – with the notable exception of Russia – advanced vigorously on the path towards parliamentarism and democracy and participated in constitutional transfer. States with an unstable or unsettled territorial identity, like Austria and Prussia, either rejected constitutionalism and remained in constitutional paralysis or were preoccupied with nation-building and with defusing emancipatory agendas within the overall scheme of constitutional monarchy.[87]

In the end, the question of why transfer happened – which "factors" determined the transition from absolutist *ancien régimes* to constitutional orders, and which considerations motivated concessions on the part of the privileged classes and rulers – will have to be left unanswered. The reasons and motivations mentioned above cover only part of the political-legal aspects. For a more complete picture, constitutional transfers and reforms would have to be related to socio-economic transformations, fiscal problems (caused, in particular, by military expenditures and poverty), and debt crises of states motivating the "powers that be" to seek broader social support by establishing constitutional schemes of controlled participation and entitlements.[88]

---

[86] Constitutional movements in the late eighteenth century struggling against tyrannical or arbitrary *ancien régimes* were primarily concerned with independence, liberation, emancipation, and empowering the male property owners of the *tiers état* by securing them fundamental rights within schemes of limited government.

[87] See Dieter Langewiesche, *Europa zwischen Restauration und Revolution 1815–1849* (Oldenbourg 1985) 37–112; Kerstin Singer, *Konstitutionalismus auf Italienisch* (Niemeyer 2009).

[88] See, for example, Kirsch (n 4) 306–8; Paul Nolte, *Staatsbildung als Gesellschaftreform* (Campus 1990) 165–82.

15. Leon Duguit's influence in Colombia: the lost opportunity of a potentially progressive reform

Helena Alviar García

15.1. INTRODUCTION

Since the early 1900s, constitutions in Latin America have included the social function of property, a limitation on property as a natural, fundamental, individual right, which in turn demands a more active role for the state in order to promote social policy. The need for this rethinking of the absolute content of property was triggered both in Europe and Latin America by the starkly unequal distribution of land that characterized the late 19th and early 20th centuries. In one of the best articles about land reform and the social function of property, Thomas T Ankersen and Thomas Ruppert describe this shift in the following terms:

> Once the individualist notion of private property was enshrined in multiple civil codes, this liberal conception of property held the upper hand for almost 100 years. During the late nineteenth and early twentieth century, however, increasing inequality in property began to foment a reaction against the absolutist nature of property inherited from the French Declaration of the Rights of Man and of the Citizen as well as the 1804 Napoleonic Code. The reaction to this disparity and other manifestations of unbridled capitalism presented itself as the "socialization" of law.[1]

In this chapter I propose to analyze the social function of property as an element of what Günter Frankenberg calls the global constitution. In

[1] Thomas T Ankersen and Thomas Rupert, "Tierra y Libertad: The Social Function Doctrine and Land Reform in Latin America" (2006) *Tulane Environmental Law Journal* 69, 94, available at <http://www.nationalaglawcenter.org/assets/bibarticles/ankersenruppert_tierra.pdf> accessed 5 May 2011.

his work on constitutional transfer, he proposes a way of understanding the way constitutional theories and ideas travel. In his words:

> Rather than joining the recent competition between grand narratives, I start from the more modest claim of the IKEA theory of constitutional and legal transfer. According to its central tenet, the global constitution is created by or rather emanates from processes of transfer and functions as a reservoir, or for that matter, a supermarket, where standardized constitutional items – grand designs as well as elementary particles of information – are stored and available, prêt à porter, for purchase and reassemblage by constitution makers around the world.[2]

Professor Frankenberg is inspired by Edward Said's "travelling theory." He quotes Said:

> Like people and schools of criticism, ideas and theories travel – from person to person, from situation to situation, from one period to another. Cultural and intellectual life are usually nourished and often sustained by this circulation of ideas, and whether it takes the form of acknowledged or unconscious influence, creative borrowing, or wholesale appropriation, the movement of ideas and theories from one place to another is both a fact of life and a usefully enabling condition of intellectual activity.[3]

In order to contribute to the unpacking of how constitutional ideas and theories travel, this chapter will describe the evolution of the social function of property in Colombia. In the early 20th century, the Colombian Constitution – a conservative, authoritarian document – was transformed in order to incorporate ideas about solidarity and social responsibility. The 1936 reform covered a range of subjects which included: the partial elimination of privileges for the Catholic Church; the setting in place of religious freedom; the promise of public education; the right to protest; universal voting rights for all men (before this reform, only property owners could vote)[4] and, most importantly, it established that both the state and individuals had social responsibilities. This

---

[2] Günter Frankenberg, "Constitutional Transfer: The IKEA Theory Revisited" (2010) *International Journal of Constitutional Law* 563, 565, available at <http://icon.oxfordjournals.org/content/8/3/563.full.pdf+html> accessed 9 August 2012.

[3] Edward Said, *The World, the Text, and the Critic* (Library of Congress 1993) 226.

[4] Álvaro Tirado Mejía, "La Reforma Constitucional de 1936" (Editorial Oveja Negra 1982) 36.

entailed greater state intervention and a justification for the inclusion of the social function of property clause.

This limitation on property was reinstated and broadened (to include the ecological function) in the 1991 Constitution. Even though Duguit was not directly quoted as an influence during the discussions in 1991, the social function remained almost intact. Thus, in 1936 article 10 of the Constitution stated: “Property is a social function that entails obligations”[5] and the 1991 Constitution established: “Property is a social function that entails obligations. As such it inherently includes an ecological function.”[6]

Notwithstanding the progressive impulse of these reforms, more than ten years into the 21st century most distributive promises of social transformation continue to be elusive. In addition to describing how transformations have traveled, this chapter’s objective is to provide an interpretation of why this constitutional reform did not significantly change the distribution of power and resources within Colombian society. This is part of a broader project I have been working on for the last few years, which is to understand why, even though there have been constitutional and legal reforms aimed at correcting striking inequalities across class, gender and race, they have been so ineffective in radically transforming the distribution of power and resources in the region.[7]

---

[5] Tirado (n 4) 137.

[6] Article 58: “La propiedad es una Función Social que implica obligaciones. Como tal, le es inherente un función ecológica.” Colombia, Legis. Constitución Política de Colombia. Bogotá: 2010.

[7] See Helena Alviar García, “Legal Reform Social Policy, and Gendered Redistribution in Colombia: The Role of the Family” (2011) 19(2) *American University Journal of Gender Social Policy and Law* 577, available at <http://digitalcommons.wcl.american.edu/cgi/viewcontent.cgi?article=1516&context=jgspl&sei-redir=1&referer=http%3A%2F%2Fwww.google.com%2Furl%3Fsa%3Dt%26rct%3Dj%26q%3Dlegal%2520reform%2520social%2520policy%252C%2520and%2520gendered%2520redistribution%2520in%2520colombia%253A%2520the%2520role%2520of%2520the%2520family%26source%3Dweb%26cd%3D1%26ved%3D0CDUQFjAA%26url%3Dhttp%253A%252F%252Fdigitalcommons.wcl.american.edu%252Fcgi%252Fviewcontent.cgi%253Farticle%253D1516%2526context%253Djgspl%26ei%3DgqhJUcCMOImc8gT61oD4CA%26usg%3DAFQjCNFdLHE584vonVEEa_VCfpzHn4-IhQ%26bvm%3Dbv.44011176%2Cd.eWU#search=%22legal%20reform%20social%20policy%2C%20gendered%20redistribution%20colombia%3A%20role%20family%22> accessed 20 March 2013; Helena Alviar García, “The Unending Quest For Land: The Tale of Broken Constitutional Promises” (2011) 89 *Texas Law Review* 1895, available at <http://www.texaslrev.com/sites/default/files/issues/vol89/pdf/AlviarGarcia.pdf> accessed 10 August 2012; Helena Alviar García, “Searching for Women and

One of the most prevalent explanations of why constitutional and legal reforms are so ineffective comes from comparative law discussions. This is why this piece starts with a broad description of comparative legal scholars' explanations of transplant success or failure. In section 15.3 I propose a different interpretation of this inefficacy. Finally, I present some conclusions.

15.2. LOCAL COMPARATIVE LAW EXPLANATIONS OF LEGAL TRANSFORMATION'S INEFFECTIVENESS

Both liberal and conservative academics in Colombia have tried to approach the question of ineffective legal reforms by critiquing the way these reforms have traveled from developed to developing countries.

One of the most frequent critiques is that they are artificial transplants which don't take into account national conditions. This argument has a right- and left-wing version. From a conservative perspective these legal reforms are set forth when a society is not ready for them, as in the case of the female vote in the 1950s or giving same-sex couples equal rights with heterosexual ones. The left-wing version of this argument is that certain reforms are set in place in a fragile way because they are an imposition by the North. When analyzing economic reforms, both of these versions argue that context matters. From a leftist point of view, for example, in a country with very high levels of land concentration, writing that property should have a social function is ludicrous. For classical liberals, economic conditions on the ground create structural path dependence, which in turn makes legal reforms useless.

All of these explanations assume a straightforward instrumental understanding of law, and underestimate the diverse ways in which law contributes to the structural rigidity of progressive reforms. My objective, therefore, is to bring a more complex concept of law into play.

In order to introduce more complexity, I will use the steps proposed by Günter Frankenberg in his IKEA theory. The four steps include

---

Sustainable Development in Colombia: Restructuring the Limits" (2012) 23 *Fordham Environmental Law Review*; Helena Alviar García, "Social Policy and the New Development of State: The Case of Colombia" (University of Wisconsin Law School, 2012), available at <http://www.law.wisc.edu/gls/documents/social_policy_and_the_new_development_state_helena_garcia.pdf> accessed 20 March 2013.

diffusing the single origin assumption;[8] the decontextualization of the constitutional item that travels;[9] the transfer process from the local to the global constitution and finally, the globalized item has to be recontextualized into the new environment. Even though this chapter concentrates on the third and fourth steps, I will briefly discuss some thoughts on steps one and two.

15.3. SOCIAL FUNCTION OF PROPERTY TRAVELLING IN SPACE AND TIME

15.3.1 Preliminary Remarks

In the literature, the idea of de-individualizing constitutions in order to include ideas about social duties and responsibilities[10] has many different origins. Without denying Duguit's influence, the relevance of other

---

[8] In his own words: "I propose to handle the 'point of origin' with caution as it may be fictitious and always already preceded by some 'before' – at least after the last three decades of the eighteenth century when modern constitutions came into existence and the constitutional state experienced its historical breakthrough". Frankenberg (n 2) 571.

[9] Decontextualization is explained in the following terms: "Decontextualization amounts to more than a mere taking-out of a given context and subsequent displacement. The flash freezing and packaging is meant to highlight that constitutional transfers usually imply that the items to be transferred are, first, relied on as marketable commodities, then formalized, that is, stripped of their contextual meanings, and, finally, idealized as meaning what they are meant to mean and functioning in the way they are meant to function." Frankenberg (n 2) 571.

[10] Duncan Kennedy describes this incorporation of the social in the following terms: "Their basic idea was that the conditions of late nineteenth-century life represented a social transformation, consisting of urbanization, industrialization, organizational society, globalization of markets, all summarized in the idea of interdependence. Because the will theory was individualist, it ignored interdependence, and endorsed particular legal rules that permitted antisocial behavior of many kinds. The crises of the modern factory (industrial accidents pauperization) and the urban slum, and later the crisis of the financial markets, and the Great Depression, all derived from the failure of coherently individualist law to respond to the coherently social needs of modern conditions of independence. After 1919, they extended this analysis to the problem of war, understood as the product of failures of an international order based on the logic of sovereignty, highly analogous to the problems of the markets based on the logic of property." Duncan Kennedy, "Three Globalizations of Law and Legal Thought" (2003) *Suffolk University Law Review*, available at <http://heinonline.org/HOL/Landing

authors and constitutions can also be traced. For Latin Americans, the Mexican revolution has played a fundamental role in incorporating ideas about solidarity and the social.[11] Nevertheless, the Mexican revolution wasn't the only influence; the Weimar and Spanish Constitutions were also referred to as inspirational.[12]

Speaking specifically about the social function of property, this idea was first decontextualized in order for it to travel. According to Duncan Kennedy, the social was equally hostile to classical liberalism and Marxist-style socialism. It saw itself as a compromise between both ruthless individualism and communism.[13]

This decontextualization operated in the 1936 Colombian reform and is evident in two ways. First, critics of the constitutional reform (as I will describe later) stated at every possible opportunity that the social function of property was a socialist or Marxist transplant. The decontextualization operated in order to hide the compromise that "the social" represented and in this way to be read as a communist reform. On the other hand, liberals who promoted the reform saw it as a compromise but failed to get any additional political leverage in order to develop the provision through legislation and administrative regulation.

15.3.2 Local Historical Context

In Colombian history, the 1920s have been described as a time of social turmoil, a period during which there was an extensive increase in the

---

Page?collection=journals&handle=hein.journals/sufflr36&div=42&id=&page=> accessed 10 August 2012.

11 Ankersen (n 1) 96: "In Latin America, the Mexican Revolution coincided with this era and its 1917 constitution, discussed below, represents the world's first example of what has been called 'social constitutionalism'. Following Mexico, other states in Europe and Latin America explicitly incorporated the Duguitian idea of social function in their constitutions."

12 Tirado (n 4) 21: "The opposition between the old individualistic conception and this new one that renewed Colombian institutions is well stated, using Duguit solidarist thinking and converging thesis, which were reflected in the Mexican Constitution, Weimar's and the Spanish Constitution in 1931."

13 Kennedy (n 10): "They had in common with the Marxists (the other significant early twentieth-century school critical of CLT) that they interpreted the actual regime of the will theory as an epiphenomenon in relation to a 'base' in the case of the Marxists, the capitalist economy and in the case of the social, 'society' conceived as an organism. The idea of both was that the will theory in some sense 'suited' the socioeconomic conditions of the first half of the nineteenth century. But the social people were anti-Marxists, just as much as they were antilaissez-faire. The goal was to save liberalism from itself."

amount and forcefulness of the demands of the small, but growing, urban working force as well as the landless peasants.[14]

During this decade, union organizing began and fierce demonstrations against state policy were staged.[15] Diverse associations of workers, tailors, shoemakers, railroad, port and public works employees, as well as women workers whose slogan was "equal pay for equal work," led illegal strikes or violent public demonstrations.[16] At the center of their demands were calls for a minimum salary, a social security system, compensation for job-related health problems, legal protection for women and children's labor and minimum hygiene standards.[17]

Disputes over land ownership were also at the heart of the struggles.[18] At the time, many peasants, "colonos" who had tenant-type arrangements – agreements by which they were allowed to use a piece of land at a price which could be either money, work or part of the harvest – were expelled from the land. This expulsion occurred for two reasons, first, because landowners found it more efficient and in some cases cheaper to hire them as workers[19] and second, because as land was

---

[14] Tirado (n 4) 62: "In 1928, the military had produced a massacre of the workers who were on a strike demanding better working conditions and more humane treatment from the United Fruit Company."

[15] Gerardo Molina, *Las Ideas Liberales en Colombia: 1914–1934* (Tercer Mundo 1974) 113–14 " (…) The presidential guard shot the demonstrators, who exalted even more, generating looting in stores, military attacks and riots in different parts of the city. The results were seven dead, none of which were military, several injured, and a greater distancing between government and labor and opposition forces, which were unanimous in condemning the massacre."

[16] Molina (n 15) 115: "The principle of 'equal pay for equal work' was far from having effect, so entrepreneurs preferred women's labor to reduce the price of production."

[17] Molina (n 15) 117: "On social issues we were behind Chile, Peru and Argentina, which in 1923 converted in legal realities the request for a minimum wage, compulsory insurance, compensation for occupational diseases, labor protection for women and minors, hygiene in factories, etc."

[18] Tirado (n 4) 65: "The peasants, organized into leagues, demanded changes in the agrarian structure and a different treatment of conflicts. The government acted differently from the traditional sense, since in the agrarian conflicts it did not systematically break in favor of the landlord, as was usual in the country, but acted with a spirit of conciliation".

[19] Molina (n 15) 112–29: "In sum, the dislodging of the most experienced independent workers, in areas of highest potential landowner as Cundinamarca, Boyacá, Bolívar, Tolima y Cauca, not only implied a marked tendency to proletarianization of peasants but also led to the accumulation of capital in the hands of some owners".

becoming more and more valuable, landowners saw a risk that the tenants would claim ownership of it (after 20 years of possession). The eviction of independent laborers in the regions of highest land quality increased property concentration and at the same time fired social unrest.[20]

The solution to this combination of demands[21] was provided by the incorporation of Leon Duguit's ideas of property rights limited by a social purpose.[22] Among members of the liberal party, it was understood that the party needed to transform its political objectives in order to try to put an end to the escalating social conflicts, get the votes of the workers and landless peasants, while modernizing the agricultural sector. The basis of this modernization was protecting landless peasants who worked the land and giving them titles over small plots of land, after the style of Hernando de Soto's formalization project in the 20th century.

Duguit's theory provided the liberal party with a middle ground solution. On the one hand, it replaced a natural, individualistic, absolute understanding of property, and through this is tilted the balance toward peasants who had worked the land but were not owners. In one of the most complete studies of the social function theory in Latin America, an article by Thomas T Ankersen and Thomas Ruppert, the authors explain the incorporation of Duguit's ideas in the region in the following terms:

> Most commentators ascribe the modern articulation of the Social Function Doctrine to the French jurist, Leon Duguit. Writing in 1919, Duguit reasoned that the state's real authority emanates from the functions it performs; key among these functions is for the state to provide for certain social needs. In this context, state protection of private property remains justified only insofar

---

[20] Catalina Villegas del Castillo and Helena Alviar García, *La Función Social de la Propiedad en las Constituciones Colombianas* (Ediciones Uniandes 2012) 4: "The tensions in Colombia's agriculture were not a new situation then; to the contrary (…) peasant revolts go back to the end of the XIX century, when the settlers and tenants began to organize to defend themselves against big land owners".

[21] David Bushnell, *Ensayos de Historia Política de Colombia. Siglos XIX y XX* (La Carreta Editores EU 2006) 147: "'La Revolución en Marcha' (The Ongoing Revolution) was an ambitious plan, both in its declared objective which consisted in fully incorporating the masses and the middle class sector into political and economic life, and in some of the concrete innovations such as the official support to the unionization of workers, a first agricultural reform law, and even some measures which negatively affected the position of the Catholic Church."

[22] Ankersen (n 1) 95: "[…] state protection of private property remains justified only insofar as its protection by the state furthers the state obligation to ensure that property provides 'social function.'".

as its protection by the state furthers the state obligation to ensure that property provides a "social function". This view, and the fact that it gives the state the right to seize property for failure to effectively utilize the property for the benefit of society, fits comfortably within the historical context of the times, when socialism was on the march and the concept of "economic and social rights" gained currency. In Latin America, the Mexican Revolution coincided with this era and its 1917 constitution, discussed below, represents the world's first example of what has been called "social constitutionalism". Following Mexico, other states in Europe and Latin America explicitly incorporated the Duguitian idea of social function in their constitutions.[23]

Once the progressive wing of the liberal party was in power, they needed to institutionalize this ideological shift by providing the constitutional and legal instruments they considered necessary.

Duguit was chosen for three reasons: first, because at the time modernization was generally linked to the British and French. Particularly in terms of public law, the French were an important influence. On the other hand, the social, solidaristic component represented a negotiation and de-radicalization of worker and peasant demands. In sum, even though detractors both of Duguit in France and of the liberal party in Colombia accused this transformation in the understanding of property as being communist, the truth is that it was a way of appeasing both conservatives (by including the prevalence of individual property) and progressives (by including its social function).[24]

The interior secretary, in response to accusations about the communist content of the reform, described this middle ground in the following terms:

> No, Senator, because the Russian Constitution has another article that shifts from private ownership of capital to collective proletariat ownership. For me the difference (between the reform definition of private property and the one established in revolutionary Russia) is perfectly clear. And I am not the only one to say this, it is also said by those who have the scientific authority to do

---

[23] Ankersen (n 1) 95–6.

[24] Eliecer Batista Pereira and James Ivan Coral Lucero, "La función social de la propiedad: la recepción de León Duguit en Colombia" (2010) 10(1) *Criterio Juridico* 63, available at <http://criteriojuridico.puj.edu.co/archivos/59_Batista_Coral.pdf> accessed 9 August 2012: "We must make it clear that the social function does not have a 'socialist' inspiration. In the case of property, the intention is to incorporate its social value, which includes labor and human life. Property could then be defined as a legal institution that has been formed to meet a social need whose objective is guaranteeing certain individual and collective needs".

so, such as the leading academic of Private Law, Josserand, who is not a socialist but a practicing and convinced Catholic, as are almost all of his colleagues at the University of Paris.[25]

Finally there is the importance of academic networks developed at the time. From the mid 19th century a few Colombian intellectuals travelled to France and brought back literature that was later translated and taught at Universidad Externado, a university intimately linked (then and now) to the liberal party. In addition, the interior secretary (who promoted the reform in Congress) had read the work of a constitutional law professor who had just published his lectures on the Colombian Constitution. In these he used Leon Duguit's ideas extensively to critique the Constitution for being excessively individualistic.[26]

15.3.3 Recontextualizing Locally the Social Function of Property in the Early 20th Century or How to Water Down Redistribution

The reform discussion

On 10 September 1934, Dario Echandia, the Colombian Interior Secretary, presented a constitutional reform project whose objective was to "de-individualize" the concept of rights and to transform the role of the state according, in his words, to a "modern" idea.

Echandia explained this in a speech in which he presented the reform:

> As you can see, honorable representatives, the project substitutes an excessively individualistic conception of private rights that characterizes the current Constitution, for another that defines the exercise of individual rights as a social duty whose limits must be provided by public usefulness. Individual private rights understood within their social purpose as opposed to absolute

[25] Darío Echandía, *Obras Selectas: El Gobernante, El Parlamentario* (Editorial Banco de la Republica 1981) 170.

[26] Batista and Coral (n 24) 74: "Tascon's influence on the early reception of Duguit and Echandía (first as a government minister and then as Minister of Education), allowed the entry of the 'social' into Colombia. These two thinkers, scholars of Duguit's ideas, contributed from two different perspectives: while Tascón created doctrine criticizing the 1886 Constitution and influencing with his theories the thinkers of the time, Echandía propelled the project within Congress which would lead to the reform of 1936 and with it, a change in the role of the State".

> individual private rights; that is the ultimate objective of the constitutional reform that the government places for your consideration.[27]

During the debates, the influence of Duguit is quite striking, mostly in terms of the way in which the dichotomy between absolute individual rights versus social purpose is presented.[28] Furthermore, liberal members of Congress who defended the reform[29] based their support on Duguit's ideas by referring to his theories about solidarity, social interdependence[30] and a different role for the state. This new role of the state shifted from regulator to promoter of social responsibility.

Nevertheless, discussion of the proposed reform was far from peaceful. Conservatives and the Church opposed it vehemently. Miguel Ángel Builes, a prominent bishop, summarized the feelings of conservatives and many Catholics in the following terms:

> This private property definition with a communist flavor, copied from other extreme left constitutions … the reformers of 1936 gave a mortal blow to the right of property because according to this constitutional doctrine, private property can be arbitrarily ignored by authorities and by everybody in the name of its social function. And we ask ourselves: don't you think that thieves and all type of criminals that violate the seventh commandment and the

---

[27] Darío Echandía, "Exposición de Motivos" in Alvaro Tirado Mejía and Magdalena Velásquez (eds), *La Reforma Constitucional de 1936* (Editorial Oveja Negra 1982) 162.

[28] Echandía (n 29) 64: "With the constitutional reform of 1936, the concept of property generated new disputes. The main debate in Congress would be to try to redefine the concept of a purely individual property and change it to one that protects its social function, based on the theories of Duguit."

[29] Echandía (n 29) 66: "The most important part of the arguments presented by the liberal majority is greatly influenced by the reading of Duguit's ideas, specifically the concept of social interdependence, which places it as a purpose for the state. Therefore, the State had obligations towards society, not as a simple regulator of private interactions, but as a true agent that promotes social policies."

[30] Jaime Vidal Perdomo, "La Reforma Liberal de 1936, un Programa Liberal" in Álvaro Tirado Mejía and Magdalena Velásquez (eds), *La Reforma Constitucional de 1936* (Editorial Oveja Negra 1982) 9: "The majority and minority reports of Congress committees that examined the project exemplified ideological differences between liberals and conservatives. Liberals start with a comparison between the previous and proposed precepts – and they invoke Duguit: his idea of social interdependence, social law, social function, limitations on acquired rights thesis to support the project. The conservative party, on the other hand, is not in favor of the constitutional amendment concerning expropriation and compensation and much less to leave these definitions to the Law."

natural right to property, will support their deeds in this constitutional amendment?[31]

Even though the constitutional transformation was translated into a land reform law in 1936,[32] strengthened in 1961[33] and reinstated in the 1991 Constitution, the results have been a disappointment to say the least.[34] Each of the laws had different problems. In the case of the 1936 law, the distributive impulse of the constitutional reform – the reassignment of big extensions that were unproductive, unused or that were harvested by tenants – was watered down and the law concentrated on adjudicating unused publicly owned land.[35] This weakening of a potentially progressive law was brilliantly described in the following words by the only self-proclaimed socialist in Congress at the time:

---

[31] Miguel Ángel Builes, *Colombia en el caos por la masonería y el comunismo* (Santa Rosa de Osos, Granamérica, 1965) in Villegas and Alviar (n 20).

[32] By the enactment of law 200 of 1936 "Concerning the Land Regime".

[33] By the enactment of law 135 of 1961 "Concerning the Social Land Reform".

[34] There are many articles which in different periods describe frustrating results. Among them: Kenneth L Karst, "The Colombian Land Reform Law: The Contribution of an independent Judiciary" (1965) 14(1) *American Journal of Comparative Law* 118; Roger W Findley, "Ten Years of Land Reform" (1972) *Wisconsin Law Review* 880; Peter Dorner and Herman Felstehausen, "Agrarian Reform and Employment: The Columbian Case" (1970) 102 *International Law Review* 221; Roger W Findley, "Presidential Intervention in the Economy" (1980) 28(3) *American Journal of Comparative Law* 423; Thomas T Ankersen and Thomas Ruppert, "Tierra y Libertad: The Social Function Doctrine" (2006) 19 *Tulane Environmnetal Law Journal* 69; Joseph R Thome, "Limitaciones de la Legislación Colombiana para Expropiar o Comprar Fincas con Destino de Parcelación" (1966) 8 *International Law Review* 281; Marco Palacios, *De quién es la tierra? Propiedad, politización y protesta campesina en a década de 1930* (Fondo de Cultura Económica, Universidad de los Andes 2011); Absalón Machado, "Cambios en las políticas públicas y el sector rural: Desafíos y retos para los campesinos" in E Prada, C Salgado and C Castellanos (eds), *Volver los ojos al campo* (CINEP, ALOP, ILSA 1999) 109.

[35] Palacios (n 34) 26: "Despite the fact that Law 200 of 1936 contributed to extract the vacant lands from the context of public goods and transfer them to a social legislation oriented to solve the economic problems of the peasantry, and more recently, the environmental, indigenous and afro-descendant causes, it was not enough to transform the mentality around the concept of property dominated by a Civil Code reading in its most 'formalist' interpretation which, in judicial Colombian practice, has sided with landlords and predatory capitalism.".

> Some speakers have said that this Project is liberal and not Marxist; that is evident. The project is liberal and less than liberal, as in other places liberalism has gone further. In Europe, for example, because of the war, the agrarian reform was made by directly expropriating large estates to distribute them; and it was a liberal reform. Here, we have not dared to follow that path, and that is why we have taken an indirect road, one based on property termination due to lack of use … I want to ease the nervous elements of the Senate, telling them that in the process of this legal initiative there is no inkling of socialism.[36]

Law 200 was reformed partly because of its lack of results, partly out of fear of the Cuban revolution, partly because inequality was seen as an obstacle to modernization. Therefore, in 1961, liberal president Alberto Lleras Camargo proposed a social agrarian reform whose objectives were: to transform high property concentration in rural areas, to increase productivity in rural areas and to harmonize this increase with other economic sectors, to guarantee access to land and credit for small property owners, to improve the welfare of peasants and to promote the conservation and adequate use of agricultural resources.[37] This law faced important obstacles, among them administrative inefficiency, clashes with an economic development model which concentrated resources on urban-industrial projects and the fact that judges interpreted property rights in their most classical formalist way.[38]

---

[36] Gerardo Molina, "Congress Intervention" in Palacios (n 34) 193.

[37] Law 135 de 1961, art. 1.

[38] In another article about the social function, I describe these obstacles in the following terms: "(…) my objective in this Article was to flesh out how law and legal institutions have prevented the constitutional promise of the social function of property. New notions of property rights – such as environmentally-protected areas, collective property for indigenous and Afro-Colombian groups, and informal possession arrangements – have met resistance from formalistic, rigid definitions of property that have remained mostly unchanged since 1887. In both the historical evolution and recent history, the constitutional distributive impulse has been weakened by establishing rigid, time-consuming, and elaborate administrative and judicial procedures. In addition, the institutional arrangement set in place in order to develop land adjudication policies has struggled with financial constraints and personnel problems, and it has concentrated its efforts on assigning public domain plots and raising productivity. All of these facts – combined with clear biases toward urban industrial development, agro-industries, and mining – have created a system in which land distribution is marginal or nonexistent." Helena Alviar García, "The Unending Quest for Land: The Tale of Broken Constitutional Promises" (2011) 89 *Texas Law Review* 1895, 1912, available at <http://www.texaslrev.com/sites/default/files/issues/vol89/pdf/Alviar Garcia.pdf> accessed 10 August 2012.

15.3.4 Recontextualizing It Once Again: from Duguit to the Catholic Church

In the discussions on the 1991 Constitution, the inclusion of the social function of property did not pass without conservatives opposing its insertion in the text. The fear of it being a communist transplant and a tool for criminals was expressed in the same fashion as in the 1930s:

> We have seen an alarming and insane proliferation of the widest range of offenses against the owners and their property. In the fields, fences are torn down, farmers are victims of threats, invasions, extortion, assault, destruction, theft, muggings, kidnappings, assassinations, with no value to life has led to moral insanity expressed in all sorts of horrible murders and all kinds of atrocities [...] it is necessary to restore respectability in the law of private property, which is the legal, social and psychological symbol of economic development purposes, and is also a guarantee of the democratic freedom which should be enjoyed by Colombians. Without such a right they would be inevitably slaves of the State.[39]

Those who defended it, and ultimately were able to include it, argued that the social function of property was not communist, but Catholic, tapping into the social/solidaristic sensibility of Catholic members of Congress. In their words:

> The social function and the socialization of property are not as communist as the statements of some writers. There is no need to panic, The Catholic Church is the one who promotes such a position. Indeed, according to the encyclical Rerum Novarum, Pope Leo XIII develops the theory as a middle ground between liberal individualism and Marxism, both of which are critiqued in the document. This concept is reinforced 40 years later in the fortieth annual encyclical of Pius XI.[40]

In addition, with a rural law set in place after the 1991 Constitution, the institutional setting and the role of judges weakened the distributive impulse in ways that were similar to what happened after 1961. First, the 1990s marked the setting in place of neoliberal reforms. In terms of land distribution, this meant that the state would no longer lead distributive

---

[39] Raimundo Emiliani and Cornelio Reyes, "Intervention in the Congress" in Villegas del Castillo (n 31) 40.

[40] Iván Marulanda Gómez and Jaime Arias López, "Informe – Ponencia Primer Debate en plenaria. Propiedad" (Asamblea Nacional Constituyente, Proyecto de acto reformativo de la Constitución Política de Colombia. Gaceta Constitucional, num 82, 25 de Mayo de 1991) 5.

agendas. Instead, subsidies and credits would be given to peasants in order for them to acquire land directly through the market. In addition, the institutional setting put in place in 1961 was dismantled and transformed in an impulse to reduce the size of the state.[41] Finally, even though since 1936 and in the 1991 Constitution there were a range of definitions for property rights, judges continued to center their analysis on the single classical interpretation of it.[42]

15.4. CONCLUSIONS

My objective in this chapter was to propose a different reading of the incorporation of an element of the global constitution – the social function of property – in the Colombian context.

This different reading moves away from both left- and right-wing explanations aimed at interpreting why the incorporation of this clause taken from the global constitution failed. In my opinion, most of these explanations assume a direct, univocal understanding of legal transplants, how they travel, how they are decontextualized and recontextualized. At the same time, classical interpretations underestimate the diverse ways in which institutional arrangements and background norms contribute to the structural rigidity of progressive reforms.

---

[41] Alviar (n 7) 1903: "The distributive thrust of the 1991 constitutional provision was further toned down through a combination of legal, administrative, and judicial acts. The first land reform law set in place after the constitutional reform, Law 160 of 1994, reduced the state's scope of action by setting the grant of credits as the main mechanism for peasants to acquire land. Thus, distribution was left to market forces, as opposed to previously enacted systems where the state had some power in distributing land. At the same time, the procedures set in place in order to expropriate and redistribute land were far from being expeditious or flexible."

[42] Alviar (n 7) 1906: property is defined by the civil code as "the right over a corporal thing to dispose of it arbitrarily, in accordance with the law and the rights of others." This involves, according to Colombian civil law, an absolute, exclusive, and perpetual right of property. Three distinct problems for land distribution have emerged from this view of property: (1) the way in which property is in fact transferred is not reflected by the categories contained in the civil code, which leads to informality or lack of legal stability; (2) access to credit turns on whether one is a property owner or not, which in turn depends on the formal categories of "property" – categories that do not reflect the de facto relationships of property in rural Colombia; and (3) the state uses these civil law categories in the design of public policy, thereby creating severe hurdles for national land policy.

I brought a denser understanding of law and how it moves from one place to another by using the steps proposed by Günter Frankenberg in his IKEA theory: debunking the single origin myth; decontextualization of the global concept that travels; a shift from the local to the global and finally, the process of recontextualization.

From this analysis, one can draw several conclusions. First, many issues are determined in the decontextualization process: forcefully progressive ideas are watered down, distributive concepts are appropriated by centrist politicians more interested in compromise than in transformation. At the same time, conservatives exaggerate the radical tilt of reforms in order to prevent their incorporation into the local arena.

Second, once an idea like the social function of property is brought from the global constitutional market and incorporated in a local setting, the institutions and institutional arrangements put in place determine its thrust. For example, administrative regulation is essential. In Colombia, the rule which established what it means to violate the social function – namely large extensions of unused land – came almost 40 years after the constitutional reform. In addition, the public agency in charge of expropriating land has historically been politically weak and understaffed. Therefore it didn't expropriate, but rather concentrated its attention on the distribution of land that was in the public domain.

Finally, we must pay attention to background norms which include private law and economic development regulation. In relation to private law this means that land reform laws that developed the social function concept had to interact with rigid and formal rules to sell and acquire property. Up to this date, the classical individualistic definition of property in the civil code has not been transformed. In addition, economic development ideas determine where the state is concentrating its efforts and resources. As a matter of fact, import substitution industrialization, the major economic development definition from the 1960s to the late 1980s, had a bias against rural development and redistribution. In the 1990s, the shift from the state to the market meant that the social function was left in the hands of the market.

16. Constitutional grafts and social rights in Latin America

Roberto Gargarella

INTRODUCTION

The 1917 Mexican Constitution, which was adopted after a revolutionary period, decisively changed the history of Latin American constitutionalism. Gradually, following its adoption, most countries in the region began to change their basic constitutional structure. In fact, and following the early Mexican pioneering example, most countries began to include a long list of social rights in their constitutions, which was a complete legal novelty in the western world.[1]

This substantive constitutional change represented a remarkable achievement. Latin American societies were able to translate into constitutional language part of the profound social changes that they had gone through since the end of the 19th century. In particular, the new, 20th century constitutions managed to express in legal language the incorporation of the working class as active political citizens at this time. However, this fact came together with another remarkable circumstance, namely the enormous difficulty experienced by these Latin American societies in setting those new rights in motion. In fact, and for almost half a century, the entire region experienced unusual problems in enforcing the newly adopted social rights. The resulting picture was surprising. On the one hand, the region had constitutions that seemed to be unique in the world, given their extremely robust commitment to the resolution of the "social question." Most Latin American countries (with certain rare exceptions, such as that of Chile) seemed to reject the US constitutional model of a Spartan constitution – a thin, negative, merely procedural constitution, void of social clauses. Latin Americans wanted to be more

[1] Through the notion of "social rights" I will be making reference to the social, political, cultural and participatory rights incorporated in Latin American constitutions during the 20th century.

in line with the novel constitutional model, finding inspiration in the 1917 Mexican Constitution or the German Constitution of Weimar. On the other hand, however, these bold, socially ambitious constitutions ran into systematic difficulties when it came to being enforced: social rights appeared to be a failure in actual practice. This assertion is supported by a long-standing consensus that pointed to the many decades during which social rights fell into a constitutional slumber, cast aside on the desks of judges throughout Latin America who considered such rights as not directly operative. Within modern legal thinking, the problem is well-known: time and again, and for decades, judges opted to consider the new social rights as non-enforceable or mere programmatic rights, in contrast to traditional first-generation rights, which were normally subject to judicial enforcement. Social rights were seen as political objectives to be promoted through law, by the political branch, rather than as traditional rights under the jurisdiction of tribunals.[2] Unfortunately, in the end, neither judges nor the political branch seemed to take social rights seriously.

Finally, the vast majority of Latin American countries had chosen to write challenging, somehow radical, socially thick constitutions, which encountered extremely serious enforceability problems. How to explain that result? How to explain the decision to assume, on the one hand, such a strong commitment to social rights, and on the other hand to accept such a poor record on the enforceability of those rights? How could Latin Americans allow such a contradictory result? Why did they reconcile themselves to living with such an explosive situation (a thick constitution and a thin constitutional practice) for so many decades (and, in part, still today)?

In this chapter I want to offer a partial explanation of this significant phenomenon. My main hypothesis is, in essence, that constitutional reforms confront a serious problem that threatens their success when they

---

[2] The discussion in this respect has been very intense. See, for example, Víctor Abramovich and Christian Courtis, *Los derechos sociales como derechos exigibles* (Trotta 2002); Upendra Baxi, *The Indian Supreme Court and Politics* (Eastern Book Company 1980); Prafullachandra Bhagwati, "Judicial Activism and Public Interest Litigation" (1985) 23 *Columbia Journal of Transnational Law* 561; William Forbath, "Constitutional Welfare Rights: A History, Critique and Reconstruction" (2001) 69 *Fordham Law Review* 1821; Rodrigo Uprimny, "Legitimidad y conveniencia del control constitucional a la economía" in R Uprimny, C Rodríguez and M García (eds), *Justicia para todos? Sistema judicial, derechos sociales y democracia en Colombia* (Grupo Editorial Norma 2006).

try to incorporate provisions that are foreign to the institutional "body" through which they are organized. Saying this, however, does not mean that I will try to support two other ideas (which, by the way, I reject): (i) that, in principle, the "importation" of foreign or dominant institutions is normatively objectionable; and (ii) that, in cases where "importation" does occur, it tends to fail ("imported" institutions tend to not work). My argument, in this regard, is more limited: I argue that, under specific circumstances, certain "importations" or "transplants" which might be desirable have the tendency to fail, and to the extent that we have good reason to implement these new institutions, we would be advised to rethink the manner in which we traditionally attempt the "transplant" of new mechanisms into our institutional system.

More specifically, in this chapter, I will argue that certain constitutional texts ("bodies") with a liberal/conservative profile (a "genetic profile"), like those that gained force in the Americas starting at the end of the 19th century, confront very unique difficulties in "importing" reforms (completing the "transplants") of institutions from the radical political tradition (of a different "genetic profile").

In some of their variations, "transplants" have recently been the subject of serious theoretical deliberation.[3] However, the discussion has mainly concentrated on two aspects: the importation of foreign institutions or the reception of foreign judicial decisions and the value of such operations. In this chapter, I will concentrate on other aspects of the discussion related to the adoption of institutional mechanisms originating from different traditions (but not necessarily originating from foreign sources) and, especially, on the possibilities of and difficulties in bringing about such adoption. Finally, I am interested in reflecting on the naivety with which we think about the question of "transplants," and the little attention we dedicate to certain obvious difficulties arising from these types of transplants. In my chapter, I will try to offer some tools that will help us in our project of reflection. Fundamentally, I will present a history which I hope will be useful in thinking about this topic. I will also offer some first intuitions that arise from this history and try to shed

[3] See, for example, Lane Scheppele, "Aspirational and Aversive Constitutionalism: The Case for Studying Cross-Constitutional Influence through Negative Models" (2003) 1 *International Journal of Constitutional Law* 296; Wiktor Osiatynski, "Paradoxes of Constitutional Borrowing" (2003) 1 *International Journal of Constitutional Law* 244; Carlos Rosenkrantz, "Against Borrowing and other Non-authoritative Uses of Foreign Law" (2003) 1 *International Journal of Constitutional Law* 259.

light on it to help us recognize the problems that usually occur in "transplant" situations and that we normally neglect.

"TRANSPLANTS" AND "REJECTIONS"

At the outset, I would like to make several small clarifications about the main concepts that I am going to cover: the concepts of "transplants" and "grafts"; transplant "rejections" or failures; and constitutional "bodies." First, I will clarify the way in which I am using the metaphor of "transplants" and "failures" and then I will make reference to the distinct "bodies" or prevailing constitutional traditions in the Americas.

Obviously, I take the metaphor of transplants, grafts, and rejections from the definition of such terms within the medical sciences. I think about this metaphor of transplants and rejections in medical terms: that, as I suggest, "when a foreign object is introduced into an organism that is not genetically identical, the organism defends itself and tries to reject the intruder or tries to diminish the pathological effects of its presence." Applying this idea to the constitutional field, this idea raises, first of all, an intuitively plausible possibility (although one not explored in this chapter): that constitutional transplants have a greater chance of succeeding (which does not mean that they are going to be successful) when the graft in question finds itself genetically related to the "receiving" organism of the graft. This situation arises, for example, when institutions associated with liberalism are "grafted" onto constitutional models that are also liberal in nature. Second (and this is the case that I am going to explore in the course of this chapter), the metaphor suggests that the grafts of those institutions characteristic of the radical institutional scheme onto the "bodies" affected by liberal conservatism are going to tend to fail, given that the organism that receives them will "defend itself" and work to "reject the intruder or diminish the pathological effects of its presence."

The idea of success or failure/rejection in the transplant, in any case, is more difficult to recognize in the constitutional context than in medical practice. For now, I am going to measure success based on its opposite. In what follows, a reform will be considered successful when it has not failed or been "rejected," and the idea of constitutional failure or "rejection" will depend on our judgments, developed after observations about the "operation" of the reforms. The operation will depend on the level of obstacles that the new institution encounters in the process of trying to establish itself inside the "body" on which it is "grafted," a task for which certain definitions and examples can be helpful. So, in principle, we could say that, in relation to American constitutionalism, changes to electoral systems, in the form of a package of measures directed towards reducing, limiting, or expanding an electoral mandate (i.e. the exclusion or inclusion of a re-election clause, term limit changes, and the inclusion of new accountability mechanisms), have not encountered major obstacles to acceptance as part of the constitutional "body." Other measures, on the other hand, such as those related to the constitutional incorporation of social rights, have been viewed by the discipline (and for now, I will consider these views as valid) more or less unanimously as unsuccessful reforms, given that they try to incorporate rights that the legislators haven't taken seriously, and that judges have not regarded as judicially enforceable by the courts.

I should clarify that I don't believe that *every* institution that is adopted or eliminated should be viewed as exclusively associated with a certain tradition: numerous institutions seem, in principle, compatible with most constitutions (for example, most constitutional texts turn out to be perfectly compatible with the abolition of slave labor). Another issue that complicates the analysis (and where the parallel holds with the medical transplant) is that many grafts require a long period of adaptation before they can be considered to have been successfully transplanted. At the constitutional level, transplants are not necessarily an "all or nothing" as a general rule: what often happens is that they tend to be rejected or accepted.

THREE "BODIES" OR CONSTITUTIONAL TRADITIONS IN THE AMERICAS

Elsewhere, I have tried to demonstrate the important role that three constitutional traditions have played in the foundational period of constitutionalism in the Americas.[4] I refer to three very distinct views on the foundations of the new constitutional project: liberalism, conservatism, and radicalism. Of course, things are always more complex than one would like. First of all, different events occurred in different countries, even though they occurred in the same region and during the same era, which complicates enormously any attempt to speak about events at a regional level. Second, in almost no case can we speak of constitutional models as paradigms without preventing ourselves from adding numerous

[4] Roberto Gargarella, *The Legal Foundations of Inequality* (Cambridge University Press 2010).

additional caveats and nuances. It is clear that, in each particular context, the constitutional trends in dispute were much more "impure" or "mixed" than my argument suggests. Regardless, I pose a much more modest hypothesis. On the one hand, I believe that it is unquestionable that, in spite of the undeniable and important differences that exist, many of the countries to which I will refer appear united by a similar history, struggles, theoretical influences, economic crises, and disputes. On the other hand, I would like to point out that constitutional disputes (disputes that culminate, normally, in the ratification of a new constitution) do not solely represent the product of confrontation between opposing factions, motivated exclusively by the ambition of the current leader or general. Such conflicts also contain more abstract theoretical disputes that include more or less visible references to the principles of justice, political ideologies, and religious beliefs that regularly conflict with each other. I am concerned, in any event, to stress the presence of such commitments to fundamental values, even in struggles that many have wanted to describe as merely self-centered and parsimonious.

I introduce here, in a stylized manner and in the form of "legal types," the three trends I referred to above that manifest themselves in different contexts in more or less "impure" forms. I will summarize the content of these views, focusing, in particular, on the way in which each of these conceptions conceived of the constitution in its two principal parts: (i) the organization/division of power, and (ii) the list of rights.

Conservatism is the ideology most closely associated with the colonial era, and it can be regarded as the philosophy endorsed at that time by the British or Spanish Crown. In this last version, the combined force of the military and the church – the mark of conservatism in the Americas – reached the peak of its power. In any case, this way of conceptualizing power was dominant for around four centuries and, after independence, continued to influence the philosophy of many elites in the newly independent nations, who were confronted with the threat of the revolutionary spirit that thought of constitutionalism in terms of the model inherited from the French Revolution. The constitutional translation of such commitments was very clear. In short, what the conservatives wanted was a constitution capable of establishing order, an order charged with securing the dominance of religion. In other words, they wanted a system organized around a hyper-powerful executive, while at the same time defending a system of individual rights conditioned on respect for the dominant religion (i.e. a right to freedom of expression or association on condition that the expressions or associations in question did not affect the teachings of the Catholic Church). Latin America's constitutionalism offers numerous examples of such conservative constitutions, including those of Chile 1823 and 1833, Colombia 1843, Ecuador 1869, and Peru 1860. The authoritarian president Garcia Moreno of Ecuador, soon after he began his second term as president, had a clear commitment to both objectives. The new president insisted that his government would be directly bound by a certain conception of the good – connected with the Catholic Church – and would seek to restrain by force all who opposed it: his principal guide was Catholicism – the "correct" belief – so all of his detractors were turned into enemies of the state. Thus, Garcia Moreno maintained that "the first [of the objectives of the government, will be to put] our political institutions in harmony with our religious beliefs; and second to invest the government with enough power to resist the threat of anarchy."[5]

The project of *radicalism* took its name from extreme opposition to the remaining forces of the past – which were identified, precisely, with conservative thought. To a certain extent, its members advocated a vision of the constitution that was directly opposed to the one the conservatives proposed. Thus, while the latter asked for the centralization of power, the former asked for maximum decentralization; while the latter advocated a strong president, the former pushed for a president that was weak and subordinated to the legislature; and while the latter disdained the enumeration of traditional rights, the former – with reservations – put the focus on affirming and extending political rights (which were extremely weak and restricted during this era), and were concerned with social problems (similar to what today we would call social rights) that tried to address these in the constitution as well. One does not find many radical constitutions in the early history of Latin America (perhaps one example might be the 1814 Apatzingán Constitution, in Mexico), but there are many significant examples of radical constitutional thinkers and radical constitutional projects (such as that advanced by José Artigas, in the *Banda Oriental*, or the one proposed by the Chilean Francisco Bilbao, in 1848), inspired by Rousseauian ideas and French Revolutionary Constitutions (the 1793 Constitution, in particular, which Bilbao considered to be the only constitution worth considering in the 18th century).

Finally, *liberalism* appeared to react against the other two forces, conservatism and radicalism. James Madison's saying, "Against tyranny and against anarchy," which was regularly cited all over the Americas, summarizes perfectly what political objective the liberals took as their

[5] José L Romero, *El pensamiento político de la derecha latinoamericana* (Paidós 1970) 115.

own. They rejected the tyranny of the "one" that the conservatives supported, and at the same time rejected the anarchy of the "many" – anarchy, which, according to them, was the natural product of the influence of radical thought. Liberals found themselves equally far away from both options, which they painted as unacceptable alternatives.

When one examines the main constitutional proposals of liberalism, the differences that separated this model from its two rival proposals become even clearer. Thus, the central proposal of liberals concerning the organization of power was that of "checks and balances," which were designed to exercise as much control over the executive (which had tyrannical tendencies) as over the legislature (the favored body of the radicals, which liberals considered prone to abuses and excesses). Meanwhile, they proposed a limited list of rights designed to protect certain fundamental individual interests against abrogation by the state. The metaphor of a "wall of separation" between church and state, utilized in the North American context, is a good example of this idea: rights such as freedom of expression, freedom of association, freedom of religion, or property rights appeared as designated institutional forms rendering impossible some of the principal demands of their opponents. The United States Constitution of 1789 probably comes closest to representing the "ideal" liberal type, but many other constitutions in the region and many other authors were known to be clearly in tune with this mode of thought. In Latin America, one find significant constitutional initiatives, of a liberal character, in Argentina's early years of independence (particularly, perhaps in the so-called *Asamblea del año 13*); in the 1828 Chilean Constitution; in Colombian constitutionalism (1853–86); in the legal writings of the Mexican José María Mora, and so on.

A PACT BETWEEN LIBERALS AND CONSERVATIVES. THE EXCLUSION OF RADICALISM

Towards the end of the 19th century, and after almost a century of dramatic constitutional instability, several of the principal countries of the region succeeded in reaching a kind of social peace that was accompanied by economic and political stability. Economically, these countries were successfully incorporated into the international economy through their export of raw materials. Politically, the main political factions seem to have reached a truce, which was normally reflected in more or less explicit pacts between liberals and conservatives – a truce, it should be recalled, which followed decades of violent confrontations between the two factions. We find significant expressions of this compact in Argentina's Constitutional Assembly of 1853 and also in the Mexican Assembly of 1857. In other countries, the constitutional convergence of these two models involved a longer process: in the case of Chile, for example, convergence emerged through the gradual *liberalization* of the extreme conservatism of the 1833 Constitution; and in the case of Colombia, through the increasingly conservative extreme liberalism of its constitutional life (which had acquired a radical liberal character in the second half of the 19th century). At the constitutional level, these pacts were especially evident, which I will explore in more depth below.

All these constitutions, with variations, succeeded in resolving the difficulties in bringing these two opposing visions together. The federalism-centralism tension that separated the two factions tended to be resolved in favor of central-federalist agreements, or very moderate versions of federalism. The dispute between the proposal of the all-powerful executive (supported by the conservatives) and the strongly controlled executive (supported by the liberals) was settled through the design of executives subject to controls but also given special powers (such as, typically, the power to declare martial law; to declare federal interventions and for a president to remove his ministers at his own discretion). The most hotly contested topic between the two factions was the place of religion within the constitutional framework, and it forced a search for different strategies of compromise.

The "fit" between the objectives of the two factions was obviously significant. Politically, they guarded against mutual aggression, and against mutual threats of destabilization. Legally, which is what interests us here, they succeeded in creating a mutually beneficial constitutional framework, which demonstrated a number of assumptions and objectives that the factions shared. It is important to note, moreover, that the convergence between the liberals and conservatives had a strong and wide base of support. Many of the factors that influenced this partnership are obvious: undoubtedly, part of the explanation is due to weariness, past failures, the passage of time, and the tolerance that comes with maturity. Interestingly, however, this partnership was influenced by other factors as well. In particular, it is interesting to note that while both visions were diametrically opposed in the way in which they thought about certain rights (freedom of religion and, from there, such basic liberties as freedom of expression and association), they were, on the whole, very close together on other rights and, above all, in how they thought about some relatively fundamental questions relating to the organization of the government.

In fact, the theoretical structure of conservatism almost seems to have been superimposed on the structure of liberalism in several areas of great importance. Above all, both theoretical structures were united in their hostility towards radicalism. One could say that liberalism and conservatism were united by a tendency towards counter-majoritarian politics. In other words, both factions were united by a common distrust of the capacity of citizens to participate in politics, which translated into a shared preference for the design of institutions that allowed limited majoritarian involvement. Both views rejected the centrality of the legislature that radicals advocated; they were predisposed against the idea that the legislature would have the last institutional word; they renounced the participation of Latin American town councils, or North American town meetings; and in general were very hostile to the involvement of the people in politics. This resulted in the design of less open institutions or direct opposition to this type of participation. This political consensus was prominently reflected in the manner in which both factions decided to enumerate constitutional rights. Principally, this liberal/conservative consensus translated into a common fixation on the establishment of limits on the political rights of the majority.

The other major point of consensus between the liberals and conservatives on the subject of rights (which was, perhaps, the agreement that allowed them to overcome the great disputes that separated them) was the one that concerned property rights. Perhaps, the ultimate theoretical reasons that, in each case, explained this coincidence were diverse. For conservatives, the protection of property implied, in general terms, the preservation of a state of affairs that they regarded as appropriate and to which they were directly committed. More specifically, the protection of property implied, at the time, the protection of the church's property, which was threatened by new governments that were more anti-clerical by nature. For liberals, meanwhile, the protection of property (together with contractual rights) was viewed, at least in theory, as essential to the promotion and protection of individual liberties. In the minds of many liberals, the state should be limited to protecting property, contracts, and individual security: such protections, they believed, provided the fundamental requirements for both social development and individual liberties.

Now, the constitutional compact celebrated between liberals and conservatives, in the second half of the 19th century, was not only relevant in terms of the legal changes that it suggested for the new constitutions, but also for the legal changes that it rejected. In particular – and this point is particularly important for the purposes of this chapter – the new liberal/conservative constitutions became notable for what they excluded. In fact, the new constitutions left the "social question" completely outside their texts: they did not include initiatives for popular participation; they did not incorporate references to basic social needs; they did not embrace social rights of any kind; they did not refer to the problems of land, social inequality, poverty or the like.

In sum, the claims and proposals of radical constitutionalism were left decisively outside the liberal-conservative consensus, and were effectively excluded from the constitutional deliberations at the end of the century. The core proposals of radicalism – proposals designed, with more or less success, to make possible the ideal of collective self-government – ended up being rejected. This fact is remarkable, among other reasons, given the support that the radical proposals had garnered in the final moments of the fight for independence, and the momentum behind implementing a system that assured democratic participation.

A question arises, then, as to what happens when radicalism, as a force capable of uniting similar demands, is completely displaced in the political sphere. To what extent was the liberal-conservative pact, which tended to exist at the center of the political scene in the Americas, capable of resisting the pressures of an electorate that grew more numerous and vociferous in their demands? As we shall see, the passage of time seemed to prove that the main requirements of radicalism could not remain outside the public domain and, therefore, the main representatives of that pact from the turn of the century called (in the middle and at the end of the 19th century) for the very ideal against which they had fought so strongly at the time.

THE RE-EMERGENCE OF RADICALISM: NEW WAVES OF CONSTITUTIONAL REFORMS IN THE AMERICAS

Up until now, we have examined the foundations of the constitutions of the Americas that were largely put in place in the 20th century, many of which still remain, essentially, in force. Now that we have arrived at this point, I would like to call attention to the two main waves of reforms that have swept the continent during recent decades, and to reflect on the significance, strength, and limits of these reforms. In what follows, I will make two assertions. First, I will argue that the main constitutional reforms that were carried out in the 20th century in the Americas were intended, at least in part, to reclaim some of the institutional characteristics associated with radical constitutionalism that were fought for and eventually displaced in previous centuries. As usual, these reforms were proposed in response to situations of growing conflict and social unrest and – consciously or not – they tried to pacify those critiques by resorting to similar solutions to the ones that radical constitutionalists had advocated in previous centuries. Second, I will show that these reforms have had a very limited impact on the life of the people in the region, which might lead us to believe that this has been a case of a failed attempt at "constitutional graft."

Even though the constitutional reforms that occurred in the region were numerous and varied, there were essentially two main waves of reform: the first, in the middle of the 20th century, and the second, in the last decades of the 20th century. The first wave of reform materialized during the societal crisis of the 1930s and could be regarded as the political-legal response in the face of a new tide of social radicalization – a way of avoiding what had happened in Europe as a result of the expansion of the ideology and demands of socialism. Brazil modified its constitution in 1937; Bolivia in 1938; Cuba in 1940; Uruguay in 1942; Ecuador and Guatemala in 1945; Argentina and Costa Rica in 1949. Those texts included, on some occasions, labor rights and working conditions, social security, and provisions that referred to governmental commitments to housing, health, and education; references to the protection of the family and the right to paid vacations; provisions regarding the rights of children and the elderly; provisions securing the rights of unions, the right to strike, and collective labor agreements; protection against arbitrary firing, references to unemployment insurance, and so on.

The second wave of important reforms arrived at the end of the 20th century and involved, once again, many of the main constitutions of the region: among others, Brazil 1988, Colombia 1991, Argentina 2004, Venezuela 2007, Ecuador 2008, Bolivia 2009. Such reforms were motivated by diverse intentions, among which I would give two particular emphasis: one of them intended to revisit some of the causes that radicalism had taken up in the past (related, for example, to the promotion of political participation), and the other one aimed at recovering the more liberal character of the constitution (such as the establishment of a system of "checks and balances"). Here, I will concentrate exclusively on reforms related to the old radical project, that is, to reforms dedicated to the return of participatory politics motivated by theories of radicalism in previous centuries. Appearing in the context of a crisis of representation, distrust in the political class, distrust in the government, corruption surrounding the welfare state, manipulation of justice, and rising levels of economic disparity, the new reforms were addressed to various sides. The majority of the reforms included provisions that created new participatory opportunities, such as plebiscites and referenda; several established or reinforced the social obligations of previous constitutions (in particular, those of Colombia, Brazil, and Argentina); many created "Magistracy Councils" or similar positions to end once and for all the reality of judiciaries dependent on the executive branch (in Peru, Bolivia, Mexico, Argentina, Paraguay). They also addressed the dearth of representation in parliament, with a diversity of measures (changes to the electoral system; additions to the number of representatives of the opposition; specially reserved seats for representatives of indigenous or minority groups). At the time they tended to reduce the exaggerated power of the executive, limiting the (hyper) presidentialism of the region (such as in constitutions like those of Argentina, Chile, Bolivia, Paraguay and Peru).

To a large extent, all these reforms came to restore – at least in their articulation and promises – many of the old aspirations of radical constitutionalism: to reduce the powers of the president, to increase the political participation of the people, to reinforce the connection between the represented and the representatives; to strengthen the social commitments of the constitution. And yet, it is difficult to think that radicalism would have been satisfied with the scope of these reforms and the ways in which they were designed.

Taking this panorama into account, it is possible to recognize the existence of areas of partial convergence and conflict among the different models. We have known of such agreements and disagreements throughout our study of history, but we are able to anticipate and explain them by paying attention to the areas of conflict and existing tensions between these various schemes. The intersections range from the common anti-majoritarianism of liberals and conservatives, to the shared rejection of liberal neutrality on the part of conservatives and radicals; they include the habitual resistance that liberals and radicals jointly presented when faced with the religious authoritarianism so common in Latin America.

In short, the possibility of a successful transplant is increased when the institutions being introduced are part of the constitutional model in force (i.e. institutions with a liberal character with a constitutional scheme in force that is also liberal). For example, one might introduce a new comptroller's office within the existing system of checks and balances – say, "Auditor General of the Nation" or "Tribunal of Accounting" – without expecting strong resistance ("rejection") from the established legal body. The likelihood of success is also increased when the institutions that are introduced form a part of a distinct constitutional model, but in areas where both models are compatible. This could occur, for example, with the introduction of liberal reforms that tend to limit the power of controlling authorities within a conservative institutional scheme, when the reforms are seen as clearly hostile to a radical political majoritarianism. To illustrate this by example, one might examine a case where the judiciary is given the power to conduct constitutional review and to invalidate laws deemed unconstitutional, an option typically considered counter-majoritarian. Such a constitutional change could be well received by both liberal and conservative constitutionalism, if both are suspicious of legislative power and especially if the conservative suspects the government may have a particular influence in the nomination of members of the highest court.

Meanwhile, the most difficult grafts would occur in connection with efforts to merge institutions belonging to different constitutional models in areas where they tend to conflict. We would talk, in this case, about *mixed constitutions*, this is to say, constitutions that combine institutions coming from different constitutional models and, more specifically here, about peculiar mixed constitutions, which combine institutions that are in direct tension. This is the situation which was reported, for example, by Lucas Alamán about the Mexican Constitution of 1824, which was seen as an imperfect attempt to amalgamate the constitutions of the United States, Cadiz, and revolutionary France.[6] This is also the situation that, according to some, characterized the pioneering Mexican Constitution of 1917 – the first to explicitly make a compromise between conservative liberalism and social rights. The jurist Emilio Rabasa described it, justly, as "a document with two well defined parts: the liberal and the social, or more precisely that of political juridical liberalism and that of economic social liberalism."[7] This was the case because the constitutional project adopted the tone of the domineering general Carranza, who tried to combine the "political philosophy of the 1857 [Constitution]," which was liberal in style, with new elements of social content, demanded by the growing influence of marginal sectors, participants in the social revolution that was taking place.

Introducing social rights into a liberal-conservative scheme – the most relevant case for our present study – would be a crucial contemporary example of the phenomenon described above. This "graft" seems to face significant problems, if one, first, takes into account that social constitutionalism was expressly rejected by both liberals and conservatives during constitutional conventions in the 19th century. Moreover, one might add, social constitutionalism requires an institutional framework

---

6 José Aguilar Rivera, "Alamán en el período de Bustamante" in JA Rivera (ed), *Lucas Alamán, Examen Imparcial de la Administración de Bustamante* (Conaculta 2008) 21.

7 Emilio Rabasa, *El pensamiento político y social del Constituyente de 1916–1917* (IIJ-UNAM 1986) 97.

that directly challenges the current order, and is characterized by institutions more responsive to popular demand. An institution of this sort is a far cry from the models that either liberals or conservatives would be willing to support.

Something similar happens with mechanisms for direct democracy such as those introduced by Latin America's constitutions in recent years – a "graft" that was promoted without introducing additional changes in constitutions that tended to remain hostile to civic participation. Once again, we can anticipate that tensions will run high as a result of attempting to combine institutions whose aspirations are contradictory in principle. Moreover, we might predict, for such cases, that the president in power will boycott or undermine those attempting to implement reforms that would affect the president's authority (we will soon examine some examples in this respect). This is why, for example, the Bolivian intellectual Raúl Prada pointed to the strong contradictions that seem to affect the new Bolivian Constitution. For him, the new document works "against colonization," but at the same time preserves colonial features, for example in the organization of the state. It declares that the state is plurinational, communitarian and autonomic, but it maintains a political geography that resembles that of colonial times, and preserves institutions and powers that are eminently liberal in character. It incorporates institutions for popular participation and social control, looking for a new relationship between the state and society, but at the same time maintains institutional forms and a representative system that is clearly liberal. It combines, in the end, institutions of a communitarian and participatory democracy, with others that come from the old representative democracy.[8]

---

[8] Interview in Maristella Svampa et al (eds), *Debatir Bolivia: Perspectivas de un proyecto de descolonización* (Taurus 2010) 186. In any case, it must be said that the final profile of the constitution was not only the result of the government's initiatives (say, its decision to keep the concentration of powers), but also (in good measure) the consequence of the negotiations that took place between the government and the ("*Media Luna*") opposition (that is to say, the opposition groups coming from the richest areas of the country, which threatened to force the country's secession). Thanks to Salvador Schavelzon for a conversation upon this point.

TWO EXAMPLES: ECUADOR AND MEXICO

There are numerous examples that illustrate, in actual practice, the difficulties that beset constitutions that want to expand social rights and promote popular participation, while, at the same time, keeping power organized in a centralized and vertical way (following the model of the old 18th or 19th century constitutions in this latter respect). In what follows, we shall examine these tensions through examples from Ecuador and Mexico.

The case of Ecuador is particularly interesting in this regard. Although its last reforms were incorporated during a period dominated by a surge in anti-presidentialism, the constitution did not direct its principal efforts toward limiting or tempering presidential powers – rather the reverse. Regarding presidential faculties, it has been said with good reason, in one of the most interesting works written to analyze the new constitution, that the 2008 text fails not only by "not reducing the excessive presidential power consecrated by the constitution of 1998, but rather increases it, and correspondingly diminishes the faculties of the legislature" (above all in the naming of functionaries).[9] At present, the president exerts special functions over judicial issues (granting pardons for common crimes). Independent institutions, such as the central bank, have lost their capacity to set exchange, credit, or monetary policy. Moreover, the president has gained legislative faculties that no longer derive from delegation by the legislature or that formerly belonged jointly to both powers. The president, in effect, issues implementing regulations, both delegated and autonomous (article 147), can propose legislation, and constitutional amendments and reforms (articles 134 and 442), can qualify projects of law about economic issues as "urgent," and in the face of legislative omission, can implement these projects as a decree-law (article 140). Further, the president can object to laws approved by the national assembly either for reasons of opportuneness or on the grounds of unconstitutionality (articles 138, 139, 438).

According to some, these additional faculties conceded to the president can be seen as compensated, ultimately, by a series of controls and alternative institutions. On one hand, the legislative assembly can demand the fall of the executive by calling early elections for both powers – the assembly and the executive (this right emerges from *the*

---

[9] Raúl Oyarte Martínez, "Relaciones Ejecutivo-Legislativo" in S Andrade et al (eds), *La nueva Constitución del Ecuador* (Universidad Andina Simón Bolívar 2009) 45.

sudden death clause, and is parallel to the executive's same right, with equal consequences; articles 130, 148). On the other hand, we find a number of participatory mechanisms. Also notably, the Ecuadorian Constitution tries to defy the traditional "tri-partite" organization of powers by including a "fourth" state function: that of "transparency and social control." By means of this entity, all the organisms of control are coordinated and various forms of popular participation are promoted (including the people's faculty to revoke a mandate or binding instructions – even the constitution itself, and can revoke the mandates of those who fail to comply with its will).[10]

In any case, the evolving constitutional practice showed the limits of some of the expectations created by the letter of the Constitution. This was so not only because the strengthened presidential system ended up blocking the evolution of other reforms favorable to political participation, but also because of the way in which the hyper-presidentialist dynamic also contributed to an expansion of presidential powers. This expansion in presidential powers was thus produced, for example, through the dismissal of deputies from the opposition; or the removal of all the members of the Constitutional Court by pro-governmental legislators.[11]

According to what was anticipated, in addition, the new participatory clauses added to the constitution were soon undermined by the practice of a centralized executive. In effect, and according to what we maintained above, it was not at all clear that the strengthening of the presidential powers could in fact be compensated or counterbalanced through the emergence of more controls or more participatory institutions. We have here claimed that the two different parts of the constitution were in tension, and that the section related to the organization of powers exercised a powerful influence upon the other. Not surprisingly, in this as in other parallel cases, we find that the new participatory clauses have performed weakly.

The immediate practice that followed the ratification of the constitution reaffirmed every one of the aforementioned suspicions. In a wholly unsurprising manner, it was the very president of the Republic who limited popular participation by discouraging the civic organization

[10] Nevertheless, regarding these possibilities, it bears saying in the first place that the *sudden-death* escape clause can only be used once; it is a dramatic extreme, requiring an enormous percentage of votes (two-thirds of the assembly members), and it involves the "death" of the posts of its own promoters.

[11] Luis Torres, "El presidencialismo constituyente y el Estado Constitucional de Montecristi" in Andrade et al (n 9) 432.

fomented by the constitution or by directly vetoing legislative initiatives designed to implement the institutions created during the Montecristi debates.[12] The testimony of key personages at the convention, such as Alberto Acosta, who was president and principal ideologist of the new constitution, simply confirmed what was already known: presidential practice that followed the prescriptions of the constitution did not help to strengthen and activate its participative clauses, but rather limited them.[13]

Similarly, the "fourth state function" can and has been subjected to resounding criticism for limiting or directly diluting, rather than ensuring and promoting, citizens' participation (which was constrained by a series of bureaucratic state mechanisms). With regard to this it is said that, in this sense, "the attempted participation, the supposed power of the people, are not designed to be exercised by the society, but rather to be assumed as a function of the State; the society does not control public activity, but is substituted by State's institutionalism."[14]

Another Ecuadorian professor, Julio Echeverría, arrives at a similar conclusion, which is also consistent with the main point that we present here. For him, the new constitution has to be seen as one "advanced from the perspective of the rights it includes, but at the same time retarded with regard to its organic part."[15] For him, "the constitutional improvements" that the text presents come hand in hand with different problems and disfunctions included in connection with the organization of powers. These problems, he claims, affect in the end the institutional structure in

---

[12] See, for example, in particular, the presidential veto of the Organic Law of Citizen Participation, http://www.asambleanacional.gov.ec/201003252802/noticias/boletines/pleno-se-allano-al-veto-presidencial-a-seis-articulos-y-la-disposicion-transitoria-de-la-ley-de-participacion-ciudadana.html.

[13] For Acosta, the most worrisome conflict of the post-constitutional phase occurs, exactly as he warns, between "what was written in the new Constitution of Montecristi, with great popular participation, and what Correa's government is doing, which was also supported by the constitution." In this sense, no issue appears more serious to him than the fact that "the conditions for a broad and active participation by the social movements" were not created. (http://crucesinbarreras.blogspot.com/2011/01/entrevista-ecuatoriano-alberto-acosta.html; see also http://www.rebelion.org/noticia.php?id=91644).

[14] Juan Aguilar Andrade, "La cuarta función del Estado. Análisis de una ficción" in Andrade et al (n 9) 97; Ramiro Ávila, *El neoconstitucionalismo transformador: El estado y el derecho en la Constitución de 2008* (Universidad Andina Simón Bolívar 2011).

[15] Julio Echeverría, "El Estado en la Nueva Constitución" in Andrade et al (n 9) 33.

charge of putting in motion the "public policies required" for the implementation of the new rights.

The next collection of examples that we shall examine relates to the case of Mexico. This example differs, at least in part, from the previous one. In effect, the example does not derive from a constitution that is actually in place, and which is then impaired by its internal organization (usually, problems connected with the concentration of powers in the hands of the executive). What we find in Mexico is a group of para-constitutional agreements, derived from the so-called *Acuerdos de San Andrés*, which came about to introduce more inclusive constitutional reforms, but which were finally not implemented because of restrictions deriving from the existing concentrated powers. The *Acuerdos* were mainly directed at incorporating new indigenous rights. However, as in the other two cases, the agreements were resisted and undermined from the very first moment by an institutional system that seemed to be well prepared to reject them. In the end, the demands and promises of democratic participation and inclusion suffered from the presence of a concentrated and vertical political organization.

The *Acuerdos de San Andrés Larraínzar* (Chiapas) were signed in 1996, between the Mexican government and the Zapatista Army for National Liberation (EZLN), some years after the unexpected Zapatista uprising of 1994. The agreements followed a long and arduous process of negotiations between the two parties – a process that combined armed confrontations and democratic dialogue – and had constitutional reform as their primary object. The reform's main objective was the satisfaction of traditional claims coming from indigenous groups. The Zapatistas then received advice from different representatives from the civil society, and initiated a process of debates on the constitutional reforms with representatives of the community. The most important demand that appeared was one in favor of indigenous autonomy. Other demands included claims for a "profound reform of the State;" a "re-orientation of the political economy;" and a "re-invigoration of the social expenditures".[16] Representatives of Zapatism then maintained that "without a profound and consensual reform of the political and constitutional framework," the claim for autonomy would become senseless.[17]

One of the main products of these difficult negotiations was the creation of the Commission for the Pacification and Concord of the

---

[16] Héctor Díaz-Polanco, *La rebelión zapatista y la autonomía* (Siglo XXI 1997) 198.

[17] Ibid.

Congress of the Union (COCOPA). The Commission was formed by representatives of the two chambers of the National Congress, and representatives of the local Congress. After some time, the COCOPA presented a project for constitutional reform directed at guaranteeing basic social and political rights for the indigenous population, thus ensuring them a place within the national political structure. However, the conflicts that emerged in the relationship between the indigenous community and the state were so significant that they ended up frustrating the whole bargaining process.

The problems at stake were diverse, and began at a very early stage. From the very beginning, it seemed clear that the national government wanted to challenge the main indigenous demands, as expressed in the original *Acuerdos*. The same COCOPA initiative appeared as a downgraded version of what the Zapatistas had demanded in the first stage. The project was accepted by the Zapatistas as showing goodwill towards the government. However, as the expert Díaz-Polanco maintained, "in each of the following phases of the negotiation" the government appeared to be "pressing towards the bottom," trying to nullify the Zapatistas' demands.[18] (In this respect, the process seemed to reproduce the same dynamic that had taken place at the beginning of the 20th century, after the revolutionary movement – the process that has been described as the road from Ayala to Aguascalientes).

Attacks against the indigenous demands – particularly those directed against their claims for more autonomy – grew after some time, when the three branches began to act in concert against the agreements. The legislative branch, for example, defied the reformist proposal by challenging the representative character of their authors. More significantly, the Supreme Court rejected more than 300 constitutional controversies, which had been presented by different indigenous municipalities (the municipalities were questioning the process for constitutional reform, which seemed to contradict some of the most basic indigenous demands). Against those claims, the Court maintained that it had no faculty to judge the constitutionality of the reforms of the constitution proposed by the legislative power.[19] In the end, the Zapatistas decided that, after years of showing goodwill towards the state, they were only receiving disrespect

[18] Ibid 228.

[19] See, for example, http://www.cedoz.org/site/content.php?doc=414&cat=6.

in response, and consequently decided to abandon the negotiation. The bargaining process was considered a failure and a mistake.[20]

In the end, the Mexican case seems to ratify what we had already explored in the previous case, that is to say that the dominant institutional matrix has enough capacity to block reformist initiatives directed at expanding the political and social rights of disadvantaged groups.

CONSTITUTIONAL "GRAFTS," "TRANSPLANTS" AND "REJECTIONS"

If we accept that the suggestions that were presented in the previous section (suggestions that I find difficult to prove in a convincing way in this context) are true, what do they tell us in relation to the constitutional reforms implemented in the 20th century? Above all, in my view, they inform us about the excessive ambitions of constitutionalism, and about an unjustified confidence in the potential of the law to change reality (not to mention what all this means about the cynical and hypocritical uses of the law and legal rhetoric).

What interests me most is emphasizing the capacity to successfully implement a constitutional "transplant." My impression, as a result of the preceding discussion, is that such "transplants" encounter special difficulties when the "graft" in question is not genetically linked to the "receptor" organism. In this chapter, we don't explore the opposite possibility of successful transplants. In any event, I suggest that transplants have a higher likelihood of success if, for example, institutions from the liberal tradition are inserted into liberal "bodies." Of course, this is not to say that new institutions are going to function exactly as we want them to, but rather that they face better prospects in such cases – where the existing institutions do not tend to react to "reject the intruder" or "diminish the pathological effects of its presence."

---

[20] According to an expert in indigenous law, Silvina Ramírez, lack of respect towards the *Acuerdos de San Andrés* has subsequently marked the relationship between the state and the indigenous peoples, creating more resistance and lack of confidence towards each measure of government (Ramírez, doctoral dissertation, 2012. Manuscript on file with the author). See also Miguel Ángel Sámano, Carlos Durand Alcántara and Gerardo Gómez González, "Los Acuerdos de San Andrés Larraínzar en el contexto de la declaración de los derechos de los pueblos Americanos" (paper presented at Jornadas Lascasianas, Antigua, Guatemala, March 2000), available at <http://biblio.juridicas.unam.mx/libros/1/1/12.pdf>.

For example, towards the end of the 20th century, a multiplicity of judicial reform initiatives swept through Latin America, financed by important international agencies, and basically intended to serve the interests of foreign investors.[21] These reforms – intended to ensure the independence of the judiciary, for example – were more or less successful, but in no case could it be said that they threatened to produce a crisis in the legal structure currently in force. The introduction of the already mentioned Magistracy Council, for example, occasionally provided substantial benefits – such as in Argentina – by making judicial appointments more transparent. And even though multiple critiques deserve to be made about the institution, multiple obstacles were encountered in implementing the institution, and multiple "disfunctionalities" can still be recognized in the actions of this new "body," it seems evident that the institution could function without great inconvenience, and still comply with the various limited objectives that had been put forth before the transplant. This example, I believe, is particularly interesting because it challenges the unjustified critiques that enemies of importations may make in the name of local "identity," native practices, and national traditions; the "mistake" of wanting to bring institutions (of either Spanish or Italian origin) to the country that "had nothing to do" with the local law. The truth is that all of these critiques that have invoked the national identity and the peculiarities of the local have proven to be of little use: the new institution was able to be incorporated and assimilated by the political scheme without major inconvenience and was able to accomplish the goals of the institution relatively well, namely, to provide more transparency in the appointment of judges, and to secure their political independence. The "transplants" that fail tend to be of another type, because the problem lies not in the importation of institutions, but rather in the importation of *certain* institutions, and in the extent to which certain precautions are not taken.

In this sense, the history that we reviewed above speaks of the failure of one type of "transplant" such as the one that was attempted in the 20th century in the Americas. I talk about a "graft" of institutions associated with the radical tradition on "bodies" genetically associated with liberal-conservatism. That observation can help us to better understand the history of social rights in the region, as well as the history that is developing with the new introduction of "participatory" institutions. As I understand it, we are confronted with cases of unsuccessful transplants,

---

[21] Pilar Domingo and Rachel Sieder, *Rule of Law in Latin America* (Institute of Latin American Studies 2001).

which was predictable beforehand. In these cases, in my opinion, we can speak of "transplant" failures even discounting the fact that there will always be inefficiencies in the adoption of any institution (even more in a new institution, even more in countries that are institutionally fragile), because in the face of new institutions certain resistance is always going to be generated on the part of those who are most likely to lose power in the new institutional scenario – those who hold positions in institutions that appear to lose power vis-à-vis the new ones.

At this point, I would like to say a bit more about what occurred with social rights during the 20th century (which is similar to what is occurring with the new "participatory" rights today) to reaffirm what has been said. The legislators, clearly, demonstrate that they have not taken these constitutional mandates seriously. It is otherwise difficult to explain the level of inequality that has remained more or less constant throughout the 20th century and throughout a diversity of indicators (housing, health, and education). However, the question is: could it be hoped that legislators would develop a special sensibility towards the interests of the most disadvantaged in society given the distance – geographic, economic, social – that separates them from the most disadvantaged, and the strong links that they develop with the most powerful sectors of society? Judges and legal scholars, for their part, have created special categories in order to purposefully disable and knock the life out of these reforms until they are discarded in the trashcan. But are these results surprising? Can one hope for another reaction from the judiciary – with members elected as they are elected, provided with the privilege with which they are provided, and characterized by the homogeneity of origin with which they are characterized? It is worth insisting on this: obviously, it is not argued here that, occasionally, some judges or groups of judges just like members of any legislature in particular cannot identify themselves with the most disadvantaged in society or work to turn the rights of those who are in worse conditions into a reality. Rather, what it is contended is that an effective implementation of those rights requires a social and institutional network that no one has sought to recreate or favor. Thus, the absence of such a network helps explain the commonly accepted fact that, during the 20th century, social rights did not tend to be implemented in practice in the vast majority of countries, in spite of the very explicit social commitments that these countries had undertaken in their constitutional rhetoric.

It should be noted that what has been examined so far does not pretend to constitute an argument against constitutional or social reforms. Rather, what is contended is that we should stop the superficiality with which we usually approach these reforms. The introduction of significant changes in the functioning or orientation of the constitutional model cannot be realized through cosmetic changes or weak reforms.

In the same way, the common observation that social rights are manipulated and bastardized by the political and judicial branches does not give us an argument against the constitutionalization of such rights, as if there were something intrinsic in such rights that produced such lamentable effects.

Such reflections bring us back to the memory of the Madisonian teaching in the Federalist Papers no. 51, according to which a good constitutional design requires that we worry about assuring the presence of "constitutional means and personal motives"[22] designed to obtain the results we want (thus, it is hypothetically possible, but not to be expected, that a conservative power is converted into the most cutting edge radical constitutional objectives). It is in this sense that one can say that the implementation and support of reforms like those the radicals demanded required the presence of certain motivational grounds as well as a reassurance of a certain constitutional structure, in order to succeed. Such preconditions were not, however, assured.

These suggestions, like the metaphor of the rejected transplants, only come to reaffirm our common-sense intuitions (despite the fact that these intuitions seem to be hardly common within the legal academia). They tell us, on the one hand, what should be obvious: that it is not enough to include a few provisions in the constitutional text to change the political orientation of the institutional system. It is not enough for a constitutional reform to guarantee a more just, a more participatory, or a more inclusive society. No significant change of the institutional legal system makes sense – nor should we expect it to work – if it is not accompanied by reflection and by changes that transcend those particular institutions. In this sense, it is usually crucial that we think about the social, economic, political, and institutional conditions within which we are going to insert new institutions. We need to determine if the social framework (in the broadest sense of the term) within which they are going to be inserted is going to tend to accept or reject such innovations. We need to determine if they are compatible with the existing institutions and practices, or if it is possible to expect that these institutions and practices will end up "rejecting," hindering, or undermining new ones.

---

[22] "But the great security against a gradual concentration of the several powers in the same department, consists in giving to those who administer each department the necessary constitutional means and personal motives to resist encroachments of the others."

In political and institutional terms, we have to ask ourselves if the existing framework will tend to support or work against the new proposed institutions. The compatibility between the political aspirations of radicalism and this framework can be seen at various levels. First and most obviously, institutions that invite participation, such as those proposed by the radicals, do not tend to get along well with (or cannot even be activated inside of) a framework that seems to require very low levels of popular involvement. If it were true, for instance, that the institutional framework in force in many modern democracies actively discouraged political participation, then, it could be predicted that the project of radicalism is going to be deprived of the support that it indispensably needs. It makes little sense to invoke political participation within an institutional framework that does not prohibit it but discourages it. Moreover, the project of radicalism does not only require an institutional system that does not undermine political participation: it needs one that encourages and nurtures it. Thus, for example, the cause of radicalism cannot succeed as long as the most disadvantaged groups of society – the subjects of social rights – cannot effectively access the courts, present their legal claims, make the rest of the society know about their points of view, appeal to their representatives, criticize them publicly, reproach them institutionally for their inactions, force them to change their course of action, and so on. The institutions, anyway, are full of people who are going to secure the preservation of the status quo that favors them. Normally, but not always, this status quo is threatened or put in crisis by reforms designed to provide society with greater powers of civic involvement. For this reason, it is predictable that the current political actors will work against these reforms. This obvious observation, however, often seems disregarded by those who propose reforms associated with radicalism, who act as if mere declarations were enough to create these reforms, and as if such reforms will not pass through the "sieve" of a group of government officials that can be hostile to such changes.

What we have discussed so far helps us realize to what extent the political and institutional framework relies on certain social/relational/personal conditions, and it suggests the way in which these aspects are closely interrelated and mutually influenced by each other. Intuitively, it suggests that political apathy is not merely a factor exogenous to politics – as if there existed societies with individuals who are "naturally" more apathetic or more participatory – but rather, it is to a large extent an endogenous factor produced by the institutional system. The rise and, especially, the stabilization of radical politics require the presence of certain moral conditions that the institutional system can help create or preserve. Thus, for example, someone could say that the advance of the radical project is undoubtedly going to be affected in a context in which "state neutrality" is demanded or in which the values of consumerism and individualism are imposed directly or indirectly (despite that rhetoric of neutrality). In contexts where these values are constantly praised, associating personal and professional success with money, surely it will be more difficult to recreate the spirit of social solidarity that the radical project seems to require. The same occurs if charitable activities are converted, as a matter of fact, into highly "expensive" activities, not only because they are not prize-winning or praised by the media, but also because they imply taking time away from activities that are economically compensated and, furthermore, necessary to secure the subsistence of the family (in other words, in contexts where solidarity with others ends up entering into conflict with family and private life).

Finally, in order to be transformed into a successful project, the radical constitutional project needs to extend its influence beyond the scope of political institutions. We need to give regular attention as well to the existing distribution of resources. Thus, we could say that it is evident that the reforms that radicalism sought to advance were reforms that required a distribution of economic resources very different from the one created and protected by liberal-conservative constitutionalism. Within the framework of economically unequal societies, it is plausible to expect that those that regard themselves as economically harmed by the promised radical reforms (because they are no longer going to have some of the resources that they enjoy today) will do anything possible to turn these reforms into ineffective ones. Moreover, this is usually facilitated by the existing connection between economic power and political influence. The concentration of economic power often comes hand in hand with the concentration of political power. If this is true, then decentralized, democratized, open institutions that are defended by radicalism might encounter difficulties that predictably threaten them with becoming unviable. It is definitely difficult to imagine the success of the political project of radicalism in the context of its failure as an economic project.

Is this to say that it does not make sense to propose an institutional reform inspired by radicalism if it is not possible to assure, at the same time, a radical change in the existing institutional framework (understanding this framework in the broad sense I explain above)? In part yes, but what interests me more is to make a more limited point, which is that constitutional reforms like the ones that have been carried out in the last century in many western countries, appear defined by unnecessary features of naivety or hypocrisy that we need to confront. On one side, the reforms usually require reflection that is much more profound than we are used to, in terms of how to adjust the rest of the institutional structure to the changes that we want to introduce. On the other side, it is usually necessary to go beyond the limits of the constitution when thinking about such constitutional changes: the introduction of certain institutional changes can demand the re-evaluation of the way in which we organize the rest of the "basic structure" of society (for example the way in which we distribute resources). No one has an obligation to deliver this type of radical reform, but the idea is that no one should tell us that he or she pretends to carry out such reforms if at the same time he or she is not willing to implement indispensable changes to support the success of the proposed reforms (for example, readjusting the rest of the constitutional structure accordingly).

Is this to say that the incorporation of social or participatory rights in the constitution with the hope – at least – of setting goals that can be accomplished slowly and gradually over time does not make any sense? I am not interested in affirming this idea, but in pointing out the risks – of manipulation, of generating unnecessary expectations, of discrediting the law – that have characterized the reforms introduced in the last few years. Personally, I prefer that provisions invoking social change and political participation be present in a constitution, but I believe that their creators have not taken seriously the commitments they have publicly undertaken, and I think that this irresponsible act is harmful for the law. My suggestion, however – and contrary to what many would suggest when faced with a similar dilemma – is not to eliminate these provisions, but rather to change the rest of the law, given the political philosophy on which these provisions are based, and to which I personally subscribe. It is thus that the assertion about the futility of certain constitutional transplants makes sense: what is demanded is, finally, to comply responsibly with the public commitments undertaken, regaining the common sense of constitutionalism, and abandoning, finally, the false and non-committed rhetoric of reformism.

Index